WORKSHOPS IN COMPUTING
Series edited by C. J. van Rijsbergen

Also in this series

continued on back page...

Yakup Paker and Sylvia Wilbur (Eds)

Image Processing for Broadcast and Video Production

Proceedings of the European Workshop
on Combined Real and Synthetic
Image Processing for Broadcast and
Video Production,
Hamburg, 23–24 November 1994

Published in collaboration with the
British Computer Society

 Springer

London Berlin Heidelberg New York
Paris Tokyo Hong Kong
Barcelona Budapest

Yakup Paker, PhD, MBCS, CEng

Sylvia Wilbur, BA, MSc

Department of Computer Science, Queen Mary and Westfield College,
Mile End Road, London, E1 4NS, UK

ISBN-13:978-3-540-19947-2   e- ISBN-13:978-1-4471-3035-2
DOI: 10.1007/978-1-4471-3035-2

British Library Cataloguing in Publication Data
Image Processing for Broadcast and Video Production: Proceedings of the European
Workshop on Combined Real and Synthetic Image Processing for Broadcast and Video
Production, Hamburg, 23–24 November 1994.
– (Workshops in Computing Series)
I. Paker, Yakup II. Wilbur, Sylvia III. Series
   006.37
ISBN-13:978-3-540-19947-2

Library of Congress Cataloging-in-Publication Data
European Workshop on Combined Real and Synthetic Image Processing for Broadcast and
Video Production (1994 : Hamburg, Germany)
    Image processing for broadcast and video production : proceedings of the European
Workshop on Combined Real and Synthetic Image Processing for Broadcast and Video
Production, Hamburg, 23–24 November 1994 / Yakup Paker and Sylvia Wilbur, eds.
       p. cm. – (Workshops in computing)
    "Published in collaboration with the British Computer Society."
    Includes bibliographical references and index.
    ISBN-13:978-3-540-19947-2 (Berlin : acid-free paper)
    1. Computer animation–Congresses.   2.   Image processing–Congresses.
I. Paker, Yakup.   II.   Wilbur, Sylvia, 1938–
III.   British Computer Society.   IV.   Title.   V.   Series.
TR897.7.E87 1994   94-49416
778.59– dc20   CIP

Typesetting: Camera ready by contributors

34/3830-543210 Printed on acid-free paper

Preface

The papers comprising this volume were presented at the European
Workshop on Combined Real and Synthetic Image Processing for
Broadcast and Video Production held at the VAP Media Centre, Hamburg,
23–24 November, 1994. The papers cover three major areas of research:
hardware, image analysis, and image synthesis, and include the key
contributions to these areas from the MONA LISA project (MOdelling
NAturaL Images for Synthesis and Animation). MONA LISA is a
collaborative venture funded by the European Union (EU) RACE II
programme. The consortium partners are the British Broadcasting
Company (BBC), Daimler-Benz, Digitale VideoSysteme (DVS), Queen
Mary and Westfield College, Siemens AG, Thomson Broadband Systems,
University of Balearic Islands – Mallorca, University of Hannover, and
Video Art Productions (VAP).

The workshop, sponsored jointly by RACE II and MONA LISA,
attracted over one hundred delegates from European industrial, research
and academic institutes engaged in TV and video production. This level
of participation is a tribute to the achievements of MONA LISA, and
emphasises the significance of the area to the future of the European
broadcast industry. What has been achieved is technology to create
electronic film-sets or "virtual studios" by combining live video with
computer-generated 3D animated images. It was appropriate, therefore,
that the workshop at Hamburg should itself be presented in a virtual 3D
scenario using live video, created for the occasion to demonstrate the
capabilities of the technology. Many opportunities for novel presentations
were created by showing live video of speakers combined with synthetic
backgrounds created from electronic images.

The importance of broadcast TV and video for entertainment and
information in our daily lives hardly needs emphasising. It is becoming
increasingly significant also for professional and business life, with
advances in digital transmission and the trend to merging of computing,
telecommunications and broadcast technologies. These developments
will result in high bandwidth, two-way digital transmission of images,
sound and data to the office and the home, enabling TV and broadcast
video to become interactive media. The move towards more interactive

broadcasting is already underway, with members of the public increasingly taking part by expressing their views and experiences.

With continuing rapid increases in computing power and high-bandwidth networking, real-time processing and transmission of video images, audio and data increasingly becomes a practical reality. Applications of these techniques to video-on-demand, teleworking, telemedicine, and remote education, have been widely discussed and piloted. However, the hardware, software tools and algorithms required for the generation of electronic film sets have presented greater challenges. The successes in this area described in the following papers are due to extensive collaboration between European experts in broadcasting and computer science, who have led the way in developing appropriate solutions to the technical issues involved. The results of this collaborative work will be vitally important to the future of European industry.

The consortium was formed to consider the question of how computer-generated 3D images could be used to form the background to TV production using live actors. A crucial aspect of this problem is camera-tracking, that is, synchronisation of the motion of a real camera with that of an electronic or "virtual" camera panning an electronic background. This problem has been solved using an advanced camera-tracking algorithm and real-time combination of real images with computer-generated 3D images capable of modelling natural scenes for broadcast-quality production. The main deliverable of MONA LISA is a demonstrator system, called ELSET™, which can be used for TV production with electronic sets. This system provides an integrated software/hardware environment for generating "virtual studios". ELSET was demonstrated initially at the IBC exhibition in Amsterdam, September 1994, and later at the Hamburg workshop. The presentation of papers in a virtual studio added a new dimension to the workshop and provided a spectacular launch of the new VAP Media Centre.

The implications of the developments for the broadcast industry are immense, since electronic film-sets would replace traditional studios, leading to reduced production costs and faster turn-round times (making set shifters and storers redundant). New artistic opportunities are also opened up by the possibility of designing virtual sets with features not possible in the real world . Mixing of real and synthetic images will also have wider application potential to areas such as virtual reality, multimedia applications, industrial vision, medical image processing, and collaborative tasks involving the manipulation of remote images.

The purpose of the Hamburg workshop was to provide a public forum for researchers and professionals in this exciting new area to exchange knowledge and experience, and to raise issues for future research. Papers have been grouped under the headings of hardware, image analysis, and image synthesis. The hardware session includes papers describing the specialised parallel hardware accelerator and Z-mixer, as well as the systems software and user interfaces developed within MONA LISA. It also includes the P^3I video engine from Thomson Broadband Systems.

The papers on image analysis cover tracking, stereoscopic imaging, and 3D automatic modelling. The topic of tracking covers estimation of camera motion as developed in MONA LISA and its implementation on a DSP processor. A paper on head-tracking is also included. Papers on stereoscopic imaging cover algorithms for accurate depth-estimation from image pairs, and application to 3D model derivation. Here, the MONA LISA contribution is the handling of concavities in object modelling, using the methodology of multiple view silhouettes. The papers on 3D automatic modelling deal with the generation of models from image sequences. MONA LISA undertook work in this area for three different scenarios: external shots, indoor shots and distinct objects. Other papers cover the use of penta-ocular image sequences and the C3D data acquisition system. The final paper in this section is on knowledge-based modelling of natural scenes.

Image synthesis papers cover a variety of issues arising from the MONA LISA work, such as collision detection, image composition for multimedia, posture optimisation, real-time walkthrough, depth of field calculations, realistic image-generation of clouds, and volume metamorphosis.

We wish to thank the EU RACE II programme and the MONA LISA project for sponsoring the workshop, and the VAP Media Centre for making their superb facilities available for the occasion. We would like also to acknowledge the work of the Workshop Programme Committee, and all the contributors to this volume. Finally, we would like to thank the entire MONA LISA team for making the ELSET™ demonstration such a success.

ELSET™ is a trade mark of VAP.   The Editors
                                                               December 1994
                                                                     London

Programme Committee:

Yakup Paker (QMW, University of London), Chairman
Eric Badique (European Commission)
Laurent Blonde (Thomson Broadband Systems)
Mathias Buck (Daimler-Benz)
Ralf Buschmann (University of Hannover)
Josep Blat (University of Balearic Islands)
Thomas Riegel (Siemens)
Richard Storey (BBC)
Sylvia Wilbur (QMW, University of London)
Richard Kunicki (VAP)

Local Organisers:

Ralf Buschmann (University of Hannover)
Jens Bley (VAP)
Wolfgang Schmidt (DVS)

Contents

Session 4: Analysis 3 – 3D Automatic Modelling

Session 5: Analysis 3 (Continued)

Synthesis 1

Session 6: Synthesis 2

Session 7: Synthesis 3

Overview

The MONA LISA Project, General Presentation

Laurent BLONDÉ
THOMSON BROADBAND SYSTEMS, Centre de Rennes
Cesson-Sévigné, FRANCE

1. MONA LISA Project

MONA LISA (short name for **MO**delling **NA**tura**L** Images for Synthesis and Animation), is a European Union supported project contributing to the RACE[*] II programme and involving nine institutions:

BBC	UK
THOMSON	F
SIEMENS AG	D
DAIMLER BENZ AG	D
UNIVERSITY OF HANNOVER	D
DVS DIGITALE VIDEOSYSTEME	D
VAP VIDEO ART PRODUCTION GmbH	D
QUEEN MARY & WESTFIELD COLLEGE	UK
UIB UNIVERSITY OF BALEARIC ISLANDS	E

The prime objective of the project is of developing and integrating technologies (algorithms, software and Hardware) required for the construction, handling and fast synthesis of 3D models for creating image sequences. The project produced a demonstrator, called ELSET™ , for TV production with electronic sets.

2. Highlight: Combining real and synthetic image processing

Following the continuous expansion of the computer world, the combination of real and synthetic image processing becomes a key technology in a number of new application areas. Addressing the most powerful human sense, this technology can be considered as a new tool to put someone 'in the picture', communicating to the observer, ambiances, ideas or concepts corresponding to the programme design.
As a Virtual Reality technique the mixing of real and virtual images gives an access to a parallel reality with on one side the *Actual World* including its complexity and its variety of interpersonal interaction, and on the other side the *Virtual World* with its free design, its easy creation and its flexible modification capabilities.

---

[*]   : RACE = R&D for Advanced Communication in Europe
TM   : ELSET™ is a trade mark of VAP

On this basis of the combination of real and synthetic image processing MONA LISA built an Electronic-Set demonstrator, named ELSET, which will offer tools for TV producers to generate their programmes in a new form: natural live action of actors or presenters mixed with creativity and easy manipulation of virtual backgrounds.

Integrating image analysis, synthesis and parallel hardware technologies in ELSET, MONA LISA can expand the concept of **Parallel Reality** defining it by:

- Automatic creation of a virtual **Parallel World** using 3D analysis:
  MONA LISA developed techniques for the automatic creation of 3D models and for the building texturing and lighting of 3D virtual scenes.
- Actual world / virtual world **Parallel Shooting** and 3D mixing:
  MONA LISA developed techniques for linking coherently an actual camera and a virtual camera and for the 3D mixing of the real and virtual image signals.
- 3D graphics and multisource video **Parallel Processing**:
  MONA LISA developed parallel processing hardware, video processing boards and integrated its application connecting this processing power with high end graphics workstations.

Beside its technical and creative functions, the ELSET operation model may also be an important cost reduction tool for production houses. The flexibility offered to switch easily from one set to another will suppress the current heavy constraint to immobilise studio space and equipment (cameras, lighting, control room...) for recurrent productions. Several programmes (like news or talk shows) could be realised sharing the same tools and studio setting up and this would increase the studio turn over.

Enabling technology for image production, ELSET System will offer a cheaper production process and a greater creativity to broadcasters and production houses.

3. Market needs

The electronic set demonstrator developed by the MONA LISA Project aims primarily at reducing the costs of the day to day production and post-production of video images and thus to permit cheaper creation of TV programmes.

Current practice requires the construction of sets (scenery) before shooting and the dismantling of these after the production is completed. This is an expensive process requiring large studios, costly materials, many production crew hours, and so on. For example, the daily production of news programmes, the requirement of having a specific visual identity requires the use of dedicated studios for each of the morning, noon and evening news productions. Considering that each studio requires cameras, lighting, and all necessary equipment and services, the availability of an ELSET studio, capable of switching easily between different backgrounds, would have a significant impact on the whole TV production industry. For other categories of programmes, the ability to handle synthetic backgrounds should provide more creativity in programme design and promote novel production techniques in television studios.

Several broadcasters' experiments announced in the press prove the soundness of the approach and the interest of TV production staff for the concept. The involvement of some of them in daily production using such tools also confirm the economical gain hypothesis already formulated by MONA LISA project in 1992.

Multiplying the number of channels, new digital television technologies promise an important increase of the TV transmission capacities. Content producers will need more powerful production techniques preserving production quality and with reasonable daily operation costs.

In answer to this, the ELSET system will offer the easier and cheaper generation of image material in volume as well as creative functionalities to design attractive sets. As a new production tool for content providers, ELSET will generate video data traffic for programme exchange between studios and for final distribution to the customers. In that sense, as an enabling technology for digital video transmission, the MONA LISA product range will have a significant impact on the transnational broadband network developed by the RACE community.

Another major challenge in image communication, is the reduction of image data in order to make the handling (transmission, storage/retrieval and manipulation) of video scenes more efficient and less expensive. Currently, image data reduction is achieved by taking advantage of the redundancy contained in the signal statistics in the spatial as well as in the temporal domain. The introduction of concepts such as models of higher complexity (including information relating to behaviour and 3D structure, for example) promises a better description of real world images and therefore better means of data reduction. Specific MONA LISA activities, by applying these techniques to the improvement of image coding schemes, addresses the key domain of image coding and is therefore contributing to the shaping of the future broadband communication systems.

4. Technical approach

As introduced above, the prime objective of the MONA LISA project is to develop and integrate technologies (algorithms, software and hardware) required for the construction, handling and fast synthesis of 3D models for the creation of image sequences. Its demonstrator (the ELSET System) will aim particularly at TV production and post-production with Electronic-Sets by combining real foreground action shot in the studio with computer-generated backgrounds. Generic analysis-synthesis basic functions are developed, driven by this application.

The technical approach of the MONA LISA Project has been the following:

- To develop algorithms and software capable of delivering symbolic object descriptions from natural image sequences. These descriptions consist of 3D shape, 3D motion and reflectance information that are evaluated using estimation of segmentation, motion and disparity derived from image sequences.
- To develop innovative algorithms and software for the realistic synthesis of images by mixing synthetically created objects, objects selected from a

database or generated by an interactive 3D modeller, with natural ones. Mixing techniques will take into account parameters of foreground cameras in studio environment (such as position, zoom, and focus).

- To develop a hardware accelerator and associated systems software, in particular using parallel technology, for fast image analysis and synthesis, aiming at real-time background scenario generation in studio environment.
- To integrate the algorithms, software, and hardware accelerator into a workable demonstrator for implementing and evaluating the image analysis and synthesis techniques developed by the project. This analysis-synthesis system is interfaced to available subsystems in studio environments for TV production and post-production.

To achieve the performance required, especially for the application mentioned above, the project has developed and assembled a hardware platform offering the necessary functionality. A frame buffer interfaced to a host graphic workstation and to studio systems, is used as a central unit for image data communication in the system. This is tightly connected to a high level accelerator consisting of scalable parallel processors running under the systems software developed in the project. The parallel accelerator is designed to meet the real-time requirements of the studio tool (such as camera tracking) as well as the critical parts of the analysis and synthesis preprocessing functions (such as 3D model construction and illumination preprocessing). In addition, a new board has been developed dedicated to real-time mixing of foreground and background, taking the distance (Z) information into account.

5. Project achievements

5.1. Technical developments

The ELSET system is designed, for TV production, to place actors, acting in front of a blue background for separation, into any synthetic scene where set components might cover actors partly or fully. This requires the accurate measurement of real camera parameters and based on this information rendering of the corresponding view of the synthetic image to be mixed for the formation of the eventual image.

To realise this combination of real and synthetic images, a number of steps are to be implemented by the TV production crew according to the following ELSET operation model:

Data acquisition
→ **Virtual scene construction**
→ **Scene preprocessing**
→ **Sequence generation**

This model, guideline for MONA LISA development framework, is described in the following paragraphs where the Project's technical activities are introduced.

Data acquisition in the ELSET system is decomposed into image acquisition and camera parameter acquisition. Image acquisition is performed by studio equipment (cameras, keyers,...) interfaced to the ELSET accelerator frame buffer via high performance I/O interfaces developed in the Project.
Camera tracking is performed by the real-time analysis of the video signal. An innovative algorithm has been designed and tested and a new process for camera position acquisition has been developed. The image analysis algorithm has been optimised, ported to the ELSET parallel accelerator pool and, now, drives in real-time the background scene generation module.

For the **Virtual scene construction** step, image analysis algorithms for the 3D reconstruction of single objects, indoor backgrounds and buildings are being developed. The algorithm development, which involves complex image processing and 3D techniques, are of three kinds, exploiting complementary features of natural sequences: image disparity, optical flow and perspective deformation.
The Virtual Scene Construction step also involves the *scene generation* and *interactive animation control* activities which deal with the computer graphics model assembly and animation. Efforts were put on the Scene Generation module which via a Motif based top level user interface offers to the user 3D object manipulation functionalities for the creation of virtual scenes. Complex scenes can be created mixing automatically generated 3D models with computer generated models under several formats. Collision checking algorithms have been developed to assist the user in this process and various texturing and light specification functions are available to the set designer.

In **Scene preprocessing**, a preparatory step for rendering, software is being developed for 3D frame coherence and illumination preprocessing.
The *3D frame coherence* activity is implementing a Dynamic Object Based Method with the aim of reducing the computational cost of synthesis by detecting moving objects in the scene, allowing temporal coherence to be exploited.
Radiosity based techniques have been developed and optimised in the *illumination preprocessing* activity for the creation of quality images whilst allowing the computational load of real-time rendering to be reduced. Realistic lighting phenomena like surface light sources, diffuse directional light sources (spotlights), soft shadows and penumbra effects have been modelled. Innovative visibility determination and scene cut-out techniques have been developed to optimise the quality/cost ratio.

The **Sequence generation** step begins with the *automatic animation control* module which performs the real-time conversion of camera parameters from the real world to the virtual world. Driven by the real camera motion, this module transmits frame by frame scene information to the rendering module. The rendering module exploits the scene preprocessing results to create in real-time the synthetic scene background. A complementary distance extraction feature has been developed to be exploited by the mixing module.

Implemented on powerful graphics workstations, these functions provide high quality images of the virtual background, matching the foreground camera position and motion.

The Z-mixing (distance mixing) system then combines the foreground action (shot by the real camera) and the rendered background.

In order to run real-time code (for example, for camera tracking) or to accelerate off-line pre-processing, the ELSET hardware platform combines a frame buffer with a DSP-based parallel processor pool. Application software (camera tracking, volume from silhouettes, illumination pre-processing) is being ported to it under the Remote Procedure Call based system software which has been developed.

Studio I/Os and real-time video processing boards for foreground signal keying and for foreground / background Z-mixing have also been developed and integrated in the ELSET hardware platform.

Complementarily, analysis of the specificities of the Electronic-Set sequences has been done with the aim to define new video coding schemes for the transmission of heterogeneous image data including real and synthetic signals.

5.2. System integration

MONA LISA integration actions consisted in two different streams converging to the final system integration and demonstration building: the first stream is the *Model world construction* consisting in the assembly of software modules while the second stream is the *ELSET parallel shooting* system consisting of hardware and software modules running in real-time to create the ELSET sequences.

The *Model world construction*, presented in the figure below, includes first three 3D reconstruction modules for the modelling of respectively single objects, indoor backgrounds and outdoor buildings. These three modules have as input natural image sequences and provide reconstructed 3D models, possibly via an object edition and adjustment tool.

The scene generation module has the aim to combine together scenes and objects coming from various modelling sources, either the automatic modelling modules developed in the Project or external modellers. Concerning the later, mainly two channels were tested in practice: importing TDI format objects and scenes created with the TDI-Wavefront software and importing DXF format objects and scenes designed using the Form-Z CAD software running on an APPLE Macintosh personal computer. Light creation and placement functionalities were used to provide input data to the illumination pre-processing software.

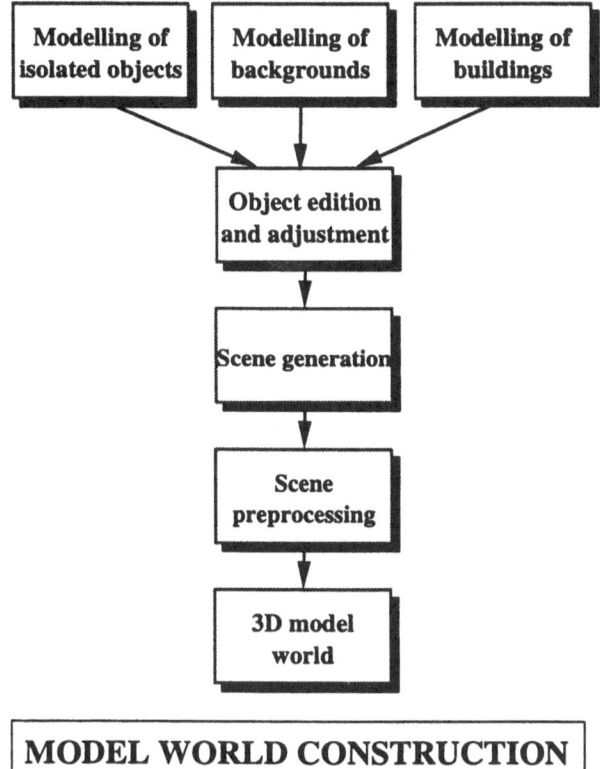

| Modelling of isolated objects | Modelling of backgrounds | Modelling of buildings |

Object edition and adjustment

Scene generation

Scene preprocessing

3D model world

MODEL WORLD CONSTRUCTION

The illumination pre-processing integration consisted in the definition and implementation of data exchanges with the scene generation module: light type, light position and intensity in one direction; pre-processed illumination in return.

For the creation of the parallel shooting system, a studio lab was created permitting to film the foreground action (hereunder named 3D real world) in front of a blue background. The first integrated module was the camera tracking This module is connected to the rendering software on the graphics host, driving a model camera (the renderer) observing the 3D model world. A calibration procedure has been defined and implemented and the rendering software has been adapted to give an easy access to the calibration tools. Also in the rendering software, specific functions were developed to generate and output the depth information and provide it in real time to the Z-mixer system. The Z-mixer system was installed and gave a very interesting result of 3D integration of an actor in a virtual scene.

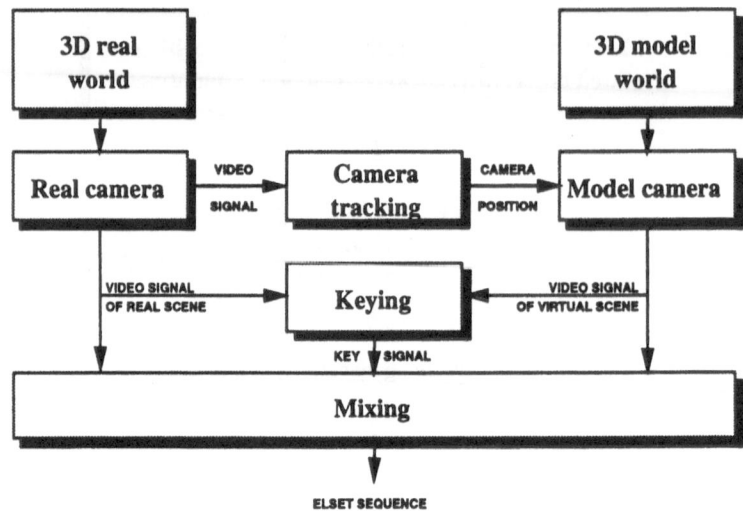

3D real world				3D model world

ELSET : PARALLEL SHOOTING

6. Conclusion

The objectives of the MONA LISA project are to integrate technologies for the construction, handling and synthesis of 3D models to create image sequences. Specifically, the project aims to build an electronic set demonstrator (ELSET) operating in a studio environment. The development work will generate analysis-synthesis expertise that can be used in other application fields.

The main strength of the MONA LISA Project lies in the partnership of major industrial companies, expert academic partners and highly competent end-users all involved significantly in the image communication domain.

This strength is reinforced by the complementary nature of the partners' expertise which cover all relevant aspects in the project: user requirements, image analysis, image synthesis, and hardware acceleration.

Pushed by a market demand - partially generated by itself - MONA LISA Project is currently specifying an exploitation of results phase in which the project achievements and the experience gained will be key points to face the future international competition in the domain.

Session 1: Hardware

A Parallel Accelerator for Using Synthetic Images in TV and Video Production

A V Sahiner, P Lefloch, Y Paker
Dept. of Computer Science,
Queen Mary and Westfield College, London

1. Introduction

With the recent developments in digital media computers are used increasingly in TV production. Computer generated logos, animated objects and characters, and video wizardry generated with complex image processing operations are now part of programs we see daily on our television screens. A large proportion of the techniques employed for this purpose, for example, computer graphics techniques to achieve photo-realism, like ray tracing [1] and radiosity [2], and image transformation applications such as non-linear mapping [3] are computationally expensive and they require high performance computation engines. Multiprocessors provide a possible solution to this problem. Hardware platforms built using high-performance processors such as MIPS R4400, Intel i860, Transputers, and DSPs are already being used for this purpose [4,5].

The multiprocessor accelerator that has been built for the MONALISA project [6] demonstrator has capabilities developed specifically to meet the requirements of a system that will enable the use of computer generated sets in TV studio production and post-production. The market research has shown that the use of virtual sets would dramatically reduce the day to day production and post production costs of a TV studio. The following are the main functionalities provided by the accelerator:

a]   A camera tracking capability for driving a virtual camera in order to arrange the synthesized 3-D background to move in sympathy with the motion of the real camera. This is achieved by image analysis of the live video in real-time [7].

b]   Real-time Z-mixing of computer generated images and live video [8].

c]   Multiprocessing support for automatic 3-D model building [9], illumination pre-processing for radiosity calculations [10], and for various image processing applications such as matching of stereo image pairs [11].

The accelerator incorporates a pool of high-performance processors coupled with an intelligent frame buffer system that has video I/O capabilities, and a dedicated Z-mixing subsystem. It is hosted by a Unix graphics workstation; this allows the accelerator to be used as a shared resource connected to a network.

The development of the system software was based on the SAPS (*Self-Adapting Parallel Servers*) model [12]. This model specifically addresses the issue of accelerating pre-selected and "computationally heavy procedures" in a "target application area" by building a "server-box" (physically a pool of processors). Such a server-box, which is transparent to its users, has the potential of accelerating a library of procedures (each by a server) when requested from workstations networked with it.

The service provided by a server has two aspects: firstly, each server carries out a well defined computational task provided a set of input data (similar to the use of a library call within an application), and secondly this task is achieved in a parallel fashion and therefore is accelerated. The application programmers involvement with parallelism is limited to the utilisation of these servers for the individual application requirements.

The SAPS model separates the utilisation of parallelism within individual applications from the programming of parallelism, i.e. the development of servers. This allows the applications to be programmed with conventional techniques, independent of the concerns for parallelism. The model also provides a template-based mechanism which enables the construction of servers using existing sequential software without major modifications.

The paper is organised into 6 sections. Section 2 gives a description of the accelerator hardware. SPMD Parallelism and the SAPS model are discussed in section 3. A description of the system software follows this. Section 5 presents benchmarks and evaluation. The final section gives our conclusions.

2. The Accelerator

The accelerator hardware comprises of three subsystems namely the processor pool, the frame buffer, the mixing device, and of the interfaces between these (Fig. 1). The processor pool consists of four Motorola DSP96002-based processor boards sitting on a VMEBus back-plane. Each processor board has two DSP processors (operating at 40 MHz with a peak performance of 60 MFlops) each with 4MB local SRAM. These processors also share two global on-board memory banks; a 4MB bank of SRAM and a 16MB bank of DRAM both of which are mapped in the VME address space. Each board also has 2 DbeX (peripheral expansion bus) interfaces which are used for data transfer to/from the frame buffer.

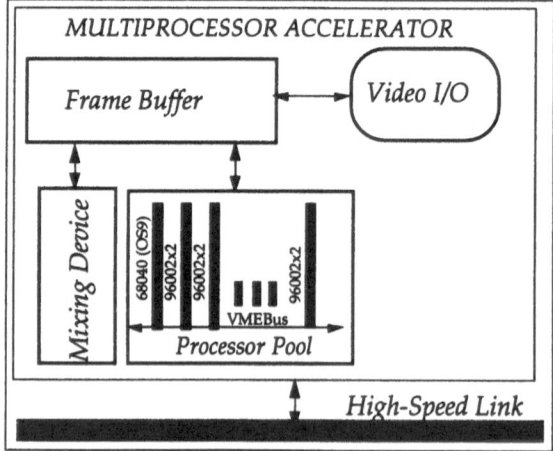

Figure 1. The Accelerator Hardware

The frame buffer subsystem is made up of an address generator, a set of RAM memory boards, and a number of FIFO buffered I/O processor boards which share a high-speed synchronous back-plane bus. A Motorola 68040-based single board processor running the real-time operating system OS9 [13] controls all operations within the frame buffer subsystem as well as the communications to host computers via Ethernet. This processor shares the VMEBus with the processor pool. In terms of the access to the frame buffer the processor pool is organised as a set of clusters: each cluster shares an interface board which is connected to one of the I/O processors. Currently there are two such clusters in the system. CCIR codecs connected to the I/O processors enable simultaneous recording and displaying of video signals. The frame buffer subsystem can handle several independent data streams (in and/or out) in real-time up to a data rate of 400 Mbytes/sec.

The mixing device is a single board hardware with a mixing unit and a number of I/O modules [8].

3. SPMD Parallelism and the SAPS Model

The SAPS model is based on Single Program Multiple Data (SPMD) parallelism [14] . In this mode, a parallel application is composed of a number of copies of the same sequential program each running on a separate processor node. This form of parallelism is widely used on message passing multiprocessor systems because it has a relatively simple and well defined structure, and it facilitates a uniform and easy-to-understand usage of communication primitives. SPMD style also provides a framework for developing parallel application software using sequential programming techniques, and therefore enables application software already developed for sequential machines to be used for parallel architectures, without undergoing major changes. Figure 2 formally illustrates the usage of the SPMD concept in the SAPS model as a means of executing a *compute task* as a set of autonomous *unit tasks*. A compute task $F(D) \Rightarrow R$ is a sequential procedure F (will be referred to as the *task proper* in the rest of the paper) with a list of input arguments $D=(d_1, d_2, ..., d_u)$, and a list of output arguments $R=(r_1, r_2, ..., r_v)$. SPMD parallelism enables the execution of such a task as a set of autonomous *unit tasks*, $\{F(D_i) \Rightarrow [R|D_i]\}$, where D_i denote the data grains and $[R|D_i]$ denote the partial results. X and Σ denote the decomposition and recomposition of data respectively.

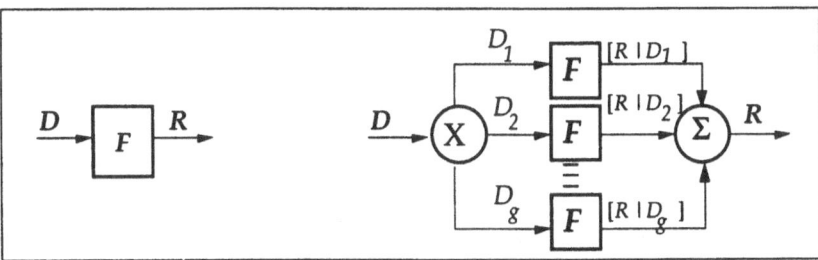

Figure 2. Compute Task & Its Execution as Unit Tasks

Under the SAPS model, the mechanisms for SPMD parallelism are encapsulated within servers. A server when requested executes multiple copies of an associated sequential procedure in parallel in SPMD mode. The data is provided by the client within the service request. The interface between the application programs, as clients, and the parallel servers is conveniently hidden in the procedure call mechanism which is a well-understood facility to develop modular programs. Servers have built-in capabilities for:

a] the replication of the program code on available processor nodes,

b] the decomposition of data into data grains,

c] the distribution of data grains to the running copies of the program, and finally

d] the collection of the partial results and recomposition of the final result.

The scheme utilised in the model is illustrated in Figure 3. The client application program running on an "external" processor (it is assumed that the pool processors are populated exclusively by server processes) invokes SPMD parallelism by calling the sequential procedure $F(I,O)$, with input arguments D and output arguments R. On the processor pool this procedure call is executed by a SAPS, as a service, in parallel.

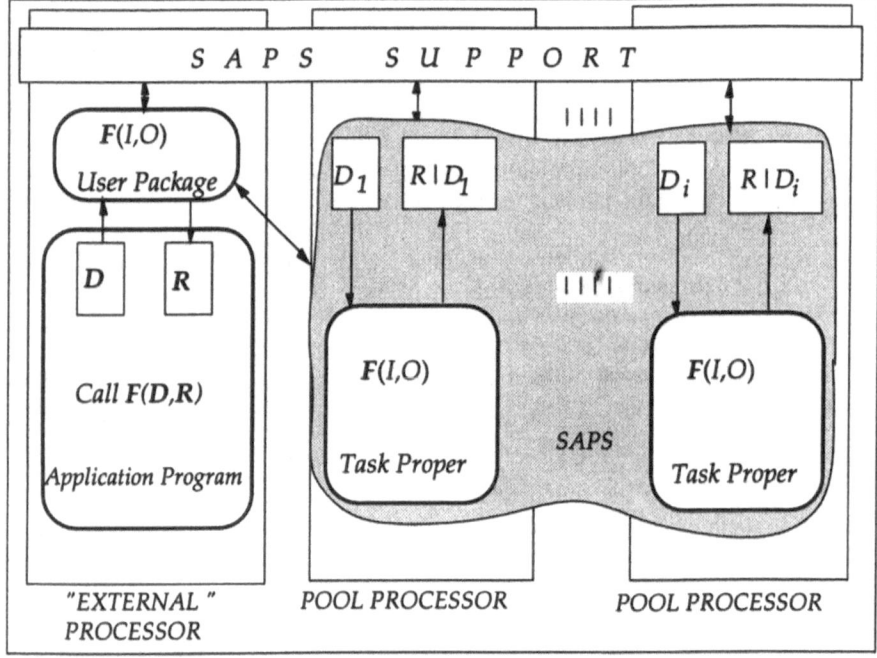

Figure 3. SAPS Model for SPMD Parallelism

The interaction between the client and the SAPS is implemented within the *user package* which is a library procedure linked-in to replace F. The user package locates the required server (a Name Server is supported by the SAPS environment) and passes the service request parameters, i.e., the data arguments to the respective server process. The interaction between a SAPS and an application as its client, for the actual provision of the service, is based on standard remote procedure call [15]. This interaction which is structured as a service-request and a service-reply is also supported by a data objects scheme which enables data decomposition. Servers fetch application data via operation invocations on data objects.

The server-application (client) duality provides the means for the separation of concerns and therefore the separation of the building of servers and their utilisation by the applications. Applications are conventional sequential programs developed independent of the concerns for parallelism. The main building block of a server is also a sequential procedure; a parallel SPMD structure is obtained when this procedure is interfaced to a standard template. This scheme allows building servers using existing sequential software without major modifications.

3.1. SAPS Structure

A SAPS has a multi-process structure (Fig 4). This structure contains the mechanisms for the reception of service requests, their processing, and the transmission of the results back. A *dispatcher process* and a pool of *workers* form a process farm where the dispatcher farms out work to workers and each worker when becomes idle, requests for more work from the dispatcher process. It is the multiplicity of the workers that provide parallelism within the server. Workers run on the pool processors in a one node per worker fashion. The number of nodes used by the workers of a particular server is not statically decided, it depends on run time availability of nodes. A server can start operating with a single worker and dynamically increase its worker population at run time as more nodes become available.

Within the SAPS structure it is the *scheduler* process which is responsible for the resource management activities. It manages the configuration (it creates the dispatcher and worker processes), and it reconfigures the SAPS structure by adding or deleting workers. The scheduler coordinates its activities with other SAPS schedulers through the *pool manager*.

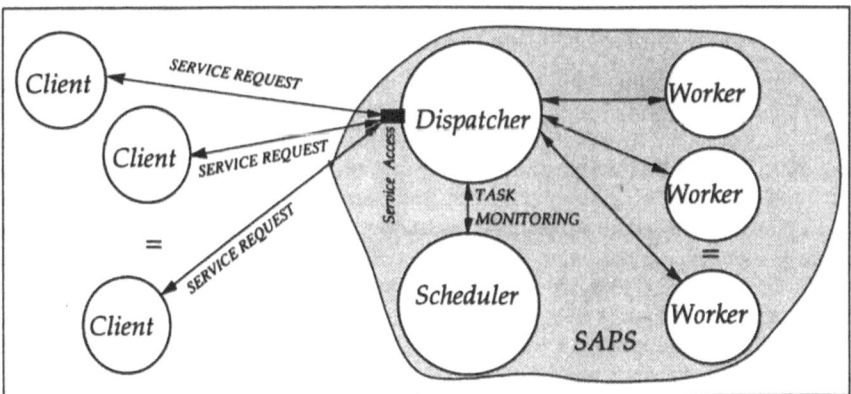

Figure 4. The SAPS Structure

The structure of a server is completely transparent to its clients. Each server has two message communication access points: one for handling service requests (service access point), and the other for monitoring the processor resources and coordinating its resource usage with other computing agents (resource management access point).

The SAPS structure as a whole is supported by a standard software template. The complete functionality of a SAPS as a generic server object is programmed within this template. To create a SAPS blueprint for a particular service all that is required is the interfacing of a conventional sequential procedure (the task proper) to a copy of the template. This is achieved via a local procedure call interface.

3.2. Shared Data Objects

Under the SAPS model, data objects are introduced as a means of making the decomposition details transparent to servers, and for meeting communication protocol requirements between a server and its clients. It is one of the important properties of a server, that it can be built using a standard software template. Decomposition transparency is one of the preconditions for this. Otherwise different decomposition strategies would require different templates.

To request a service each client passes a set of object identifiers (one per data argument) to the SAPS in a service request message. Every identifier is associated with a data object that resides in the frame buffer. Data objects are created either by using data files from the networked workstations or by using input devices such as a video camera or a video tape recorder directly connected to the frame buffer subsystem. Once the SAPS dispatcher receives a service request with the object identifiers in it, it contacts the *object manager* for decomposition. It is the object manager that registers the required decomposition rules with the respective objects and creates the list of unit tasks with the respective data handles encapsulated in them. The decomposition specification files used by the object manager for this purpose are created as part of the server construction process. The SAPS workers use these data handles in accessing the data grains when a particular unit task is assigned to them by the dispatcher. Figure 5 shows a possible usage of data handles in image processing applications. Different workers of a SAPS read individual images from a sequence as input data, and after carrying out the processing, they write the processed images to form the output sequence. To the worker process which possesses a data handle, the way data is partitioned is transparent, e.g, an image sequence partition may correspond to a strip, or an image quadrant, or a full frame.

Two primitives, *GetData*() and *PutData*() are used to program the distribution of the data in the worker template. GetData operation allows a SAPS process to copy a partition data associated with a particular input data handle into the specified local buffer. With the PutData operation a worker can invoke the copying of the data provided in a local buffer into the frame buffer associated with a particular output data handle. These primitives have been implemented using message passing protocols between the object manager and the workers. The object manager when receives a operation request message from the workers it initialise the respective I/O processor for a fast transfer of data between the frame buffer and the DRAM of the respective processor. The decomposition facilities were programmed as part of the Object Manager implementation using the device level capabilities of the frame buffer system.

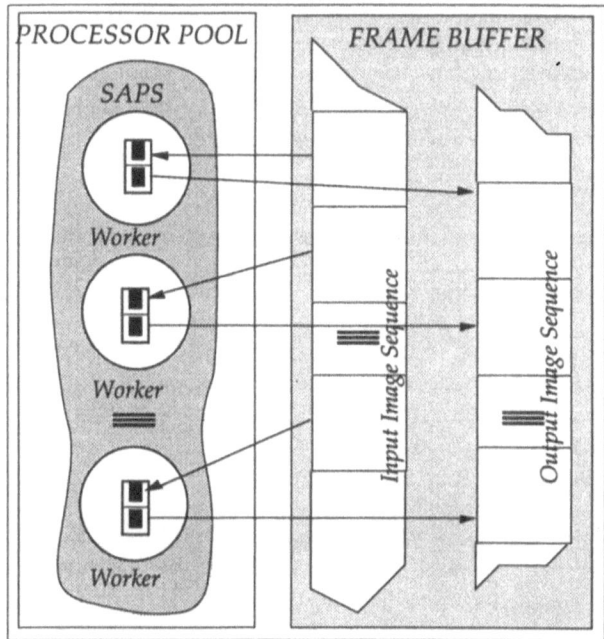

Figure 5. Data Distribution via Invocations on Data Handles

3.3. SAPS Utilisation and Applications

The dynamic nature of a SAPS, in terms of the number of processors it is running on, allows the target processor pool to be shared by a varying number of SAPSs. This means that new services can be introduced and unused services can be withdrawn from the server-box dynamically keeping some of the services running on. This provides a flexible solution in an application environment, for example, all the processors can be assigned to a particular SAPS when it is heavily needed, then others can be introduced according to the requirements of the applications. Figure 6. illustrates a scenario where the processor pool runs three servers each with a different functionality. These services provided by the servers are shared by two client programs running on separate workstations connected to the system via a network (a high-speed link connection is also possible). It must be noted that the number of processors used by each server is completely transparent to the client programs running on the workstations.

Three applications within the project context have been identified to be built as servers due to their compute intensive nature. These are: camera tracking, 3-D volume modelling, and illumination pre-processing for image synthesis. All of the three servers have been built using existing C language sequential code with very little modification in the code.

Camera Tracking

The camera tracking server is a single worker SAPS which operates in real-time. In the implementation, the software template for the workers has been modified to include the primitives for handling real-time requirements. The algorithm used measures the translation and scale change by computing the spatial and temporal luminance gradients at many points in successive images. A set linear simultaneous equations is formed (one equation per point) relating the measured gradients to the motion parameters. The least-squares solution of these equations is then calculated, giving estimates of the motion parameters. See [7] for a detailed description of this application.

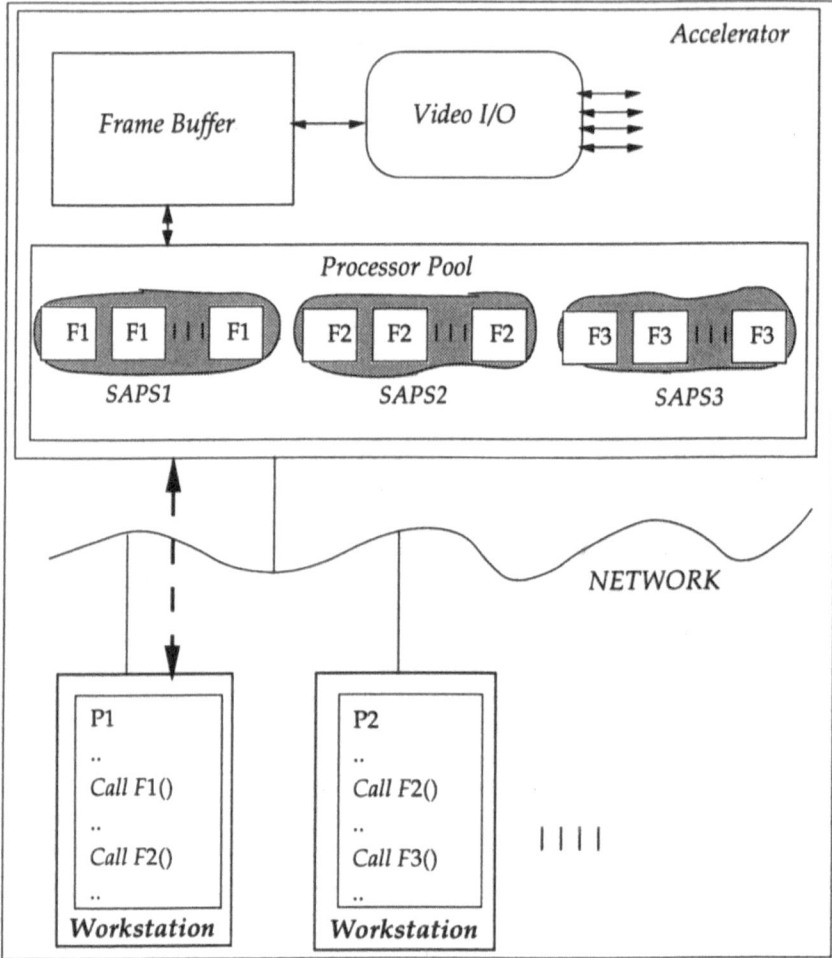

Figure 6. The Server-Box Scenario

3-D Modelling

The algorithm used for the automatic 3-D modelling of isolated objects utilises object silhouettes extracted from images of the respective object rotating on a turn table in front of a stationary camera [9]. In this algorithm a volume model consists of an array of pillar like volume elements, and modelling is carried out by projecting these pillars on to the object silhouettes. The volume modelling algorithm has an inherently data-parallel structure: i.e.; each pillar can be processed independently of the others. As a result the data decomposition was based on the decomposition of the volume model i.e., the array of pillars into subarrays. Since the algorithm. works on the whole image sequence (36 images for 36 different views of the object) in an iterative fashion by successively refining the 3-D model, the primitives for handling locally redistributable iterations have been used.

Illumination Preprocessing

The third server which we are currently working on is used for pre-processing a given 3-D scene description for the purpose of later using the results in real-time visualisation of the scene. The algorithm [10] starts with a selected set of light source facets in the scene description and calculates how much energy every other facet in the scene receives from this source. The selection of the light sources and the propagation of the energy is calculated iteratively until a convergence criteria is reached. In the server implementation this procedure is carried out by the workers in parallel for each separate light source facet in the scene. This requires the scene data base to be replicated at each worker node; however since the frame buffer is used to store the data base, replication is a fast process. The iteration mentioned above however is not locally redistributable; therefore a special operation invocation primitive (*Combine*()) has been used to redistribute the individual workers results to all the others.

4. System Software

The system software for the accelerator consists of a distributed operating environment specifically developed to meet the requirements of the SAPS model. Due to the hybrid nature of the hardware configuration the implementation has been carried out under three separate operating systems (Fig. 7). The user interface runs under Unix on the host graphics workstation. It is made up of two OSF/Motif based tools: the administration tool is used for the initialisation of the accelerator, and for starting and terminating servers; the command tool provides the means to build applications in a module based fashion [16].

The rest of the SAPS support environment runs under OS9 on the frame buffer control processor, and under *WKernel* on the processor pool. WKernel is an operating system kernel purpose built to run on the DSP96002-based pool processors. It provides process creation, management, and communication capabilities for parallel server execution and control. Under WKernel each process runs in a statically mapped memory environment called a slot. A program that will run in a particular slot is compiled and linked to be run explicitly in that slot.

The system servers that support the model, namely the name server, the pool manager, and the object manager were all implemented as OS9 processes. The ISP server is a process that is integrated to the system software for video device control. The SAPS structure itself is also supported by processes running under OS9. A single dispatcher and a single scheduler were implemented as OS9 server processes to be shared by all SAPSs. Only the SAPS workers run exclusively under WKernel.

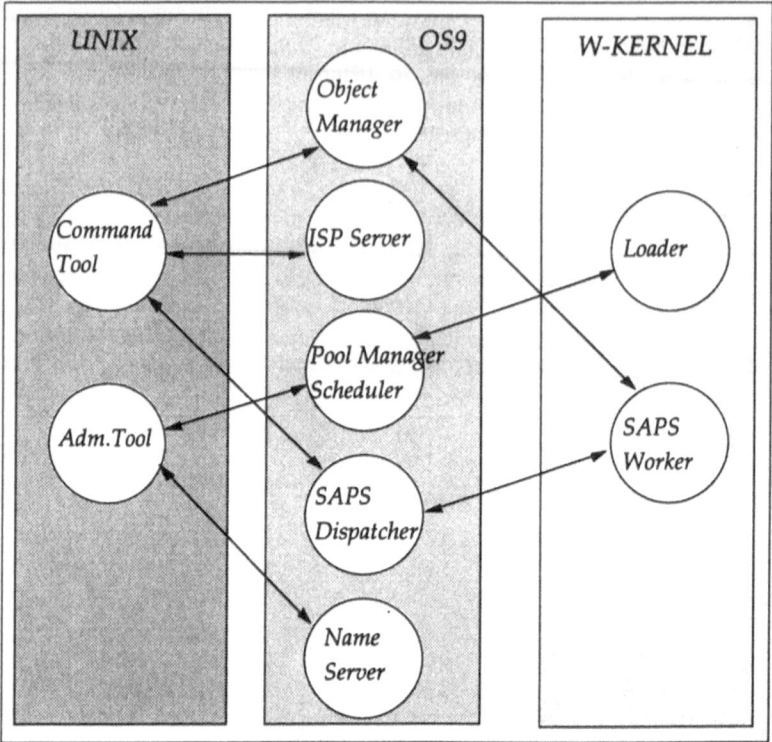

Figure 7. System Software Components

5. Benchmarks and Evaluation

A number of experiments have been carried out to evaluate the performance of the accelerator. The main objective was to investigate:

a]   the effectiveness of the compilation tools currently used, i.e., how much percentage of the peak floating point power can actually be utilised with the existing DSP96002 compiler,

b]   the effects of shared DRAM usage by the twin on-board processors,

c]   the speed of access to the frame buffer by the individual processors,

d]   the overhead caused by simultaneous use of the frame buffer by the pool processors, and

e]   the performance improvements by storing the application data in the local SRAM banks.

For this purpose we have devised a benchmark setup which has enabled us to map out the floating point and memory access performance signatures of the system and compare it to RISC processor based workstations. The algorithm we have used in the benchmarks was based on a local-neighborhood filter which is common to a large number of image processing operations. The algorithm uses a linear combination of the local neighbours of every pixel in an image to calculate a new value for that pixel. By changing the number of neighbourhood cells in a systematic fashion we were able to observe the effects of memory access speed.

The results are shown in figure 8. The two dashed lines show the results obtained by running the benchmarks on MIPS R3000 and MIPS R4000 based workstations. These have floating point specifications of 4.2 MFops and 15 MFlops respectively. The data for the benchmarks consisted of a PAL resolution (576x720 pixels) image sequence of 24 frames, and the experiments have been repeated using 0, 3, 6, and 9 neighbourhood cells in the computations respectively.

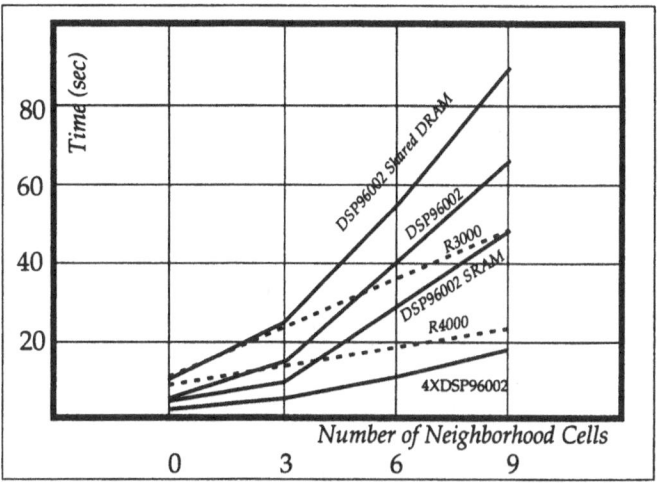

Figure 8. Benchmarks for Local Neighborhood Operations

As it can be observed in the figure, the increase in the rate of access to the memory caused by the increase in the number of neighbours used in the filter causes a degradation of performance; this degradation is especially very high when both on-board DSPs are sharing the DRAM. We have also run the benchmarks using the local SRAM banks for storing application data; this has provided significant improvement.

We have used the same benchmark algorithm to evaluate the multiprocessor utilisation (4 processors had been used and the timings were extrapolated to 8 processors). The results are shown in figure 9.

In these experiments we have also timed the frame buffer I/O access by the pool processors. The transfer rates between the frame buffer and the DRAM banks on the processor boards vary between 3 to 6 MBytes/sec. The figure shows that after 4 processors the speed-up is significantly diminishing; this is due to the shared DRAM usage. Up to 4 processors we could utilise a single DSP per board and avoid the shared DRAM usage. It is also noticeable from the figure that heavier computational tasks (large neighbourhood sizes) have yielded better speed up values.

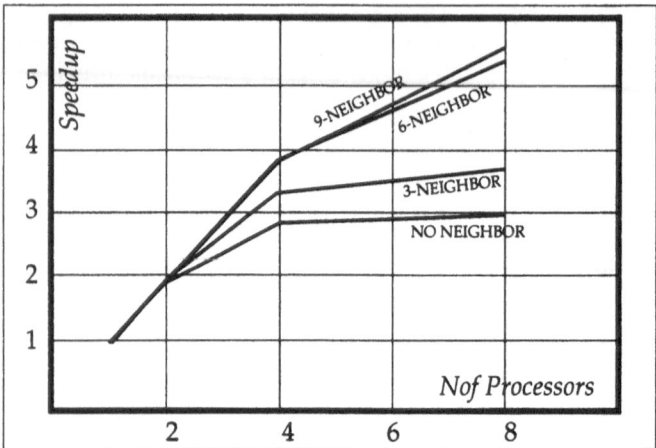

Figure 9. Parallel Processing Benchmarks

6. Conclusions

An accelerator has been built to meet the computational requirements of compute intensive graphics and image processing tasks of a computer graphics based set generation system for TV production. The accelerator is based on a pool of DSP processors tightly-coupled with an intelligent frame buffer system. It has a OSF/Motif windows based user interface running on a host graphics workstation which makes the application acceleration completely transparent to the end-user.

A client-server based computational model for parallelism (the SAPS Model) have been used to achieve parallelism on the processor pool in a modular fashion using sequential code. Utilisation of servers is similar to the concept of parallel software libraries in the sense that customised software which incorporate parallelism is shared or re-used by different application programs. However, here shared software is not linked in to individual application programs but its functionality is provided as an active service by a run-time computing agent.

The application development work has shown that the SAPS model enables the building of servers from existing sequential code with minimum modifications. For all the applications, the distribution of data to the server processes has been easily programmed using object oriented SAPS primitives. The data decomposition and distribution model has particularly fitted well to the utilisation of the intelligent frame buffer for video I/O. Additional primitives have been provided for the implementation of servers with real-time requirements such as the camera tracking server.

The camera tracking server has been successfully tested in a TV studio environment meeting the real-time requirements. The initial evaluations for the more generic usage of the processor pool has shown that the system can be used as a cost effective TV/Video post-processing box. These evaluations have also proved that there is considerable scope for improvement. Especially the memory access rates for individual processors are very low. We have established that the performance of the 3-D modelling server which is based on dense linked-list walking have suffered due to the low memory access rate. The current DSP96002 compilers are also far from producing optimised code. Our future work will involve improvements in these respects.

References

1. Cook, R.L., Porter, T., Carpenter, L., Distributed Ray Tracing, Computer Graphics (SIGGRAPH 84 Proceedings), Vol 18, No 3, July 1984, pp. 213-222

2. Cohen, M.F., Greenberg, D.P., A Radiosity Solution for Complex Environments, Computer Graphics (SIGGRAPH 85 Proceedings), Vol 19, No 3, July 1985, pp. 31-40

3. Wolberg, G., Digital Image Warping, IEEE Computer Society Press, Los Alamitos, 1990

4. Pitot, P., The Voxar Project, IEEE Computer Graphics & Applications, Jan 1993, Vol 13 No 1, pp 27-33

5. Singh, P.J., Gupta, A., Levoy, M., Parallel Visualisation Algorithms: Performance and Architectural Applications, IEEE Computer, July 1994, Vol 27, No.7, pp. 45-55

6. Bley, J., Schmidt, W., Thomas, G., Short Market Report, RACE Internal Deliverable No.7 Report, Sept. 1992

7. Routsis, D., LeFloch, P., Sahiner, A.V., Thomas, G., Real-Time Camera Tracking Server on the ELSET Accelerator, Monalisa Workshop Proceedings

8. Schmidt, W., Real-Time Mixing of Live Action and Synthetic Backgrounds based on Depth Values, Monalisa Workshop Proceedings

9. Niem, W., Buschmann, R., Automatic Modelling of 3D Natural Objects from Multiple Views, Monalisa Workshop Proceedings

10. Dusseux, J-C., Graslin, C., Luo, Y., Mas-Sanso, R., Image Synthesis for Rendering, RACE Internal Deliverable No.14 Report, Sept. 1993

11. Riegel, T., Buschmann, R., Thomas, G., Image Analysis Methods for 2-D Motion, Disparity and Segmentation, RACE Internal Deliverable No.9, Report, Sept. 1993

12. Sahiner, A.V., A Computation Model for Parallelism: Self-Adapting Parallel Servers, Ph.D. Thesis, The Polytechnic of Central London, 1991

13. Dibble, P., OS-9 Insights, An Advanced Programmers Guide to OS-9/68000, Microware Systems Corporation, 1988

14. Karp, A.H., Programming for Parallelism, IEEE Computer, May 1987, Vol.20, No.5, pp. 43-57

15. Coulouris, G.F., Dollimore, J., Distributed Systems: Concepts and Design, Addison Wesley, Wokingham, 1988

16. Le Floch, P., Sahiner, A.V., Paker, Y., Visual Tools for Parallel Server Handling, Monalisa Workshop Proceedings

Real-time Mixing of Live Action and Synthetic Backgrounds based on Depth Values

Wolfgang Schmidt
DVS GmbH, Digital Video Systems
Hannover, Germany

Abstract

This paper describes a new technique for depth sensitive real-time composition of live-action shot in a chroma-key studio and computer generated background images. A dedicated mixing device has been build for that purpose and has been tested in a real-time studio environment.

1 Introduction

Since many years chroma-key is a well-known technique in television production for insertion of foreground action into a selected background scene shot by a different camera at a different place. In the beginning the main reason for using this technique has been the request of artistic directors to film people at places where this is hard to achieve. Later also the economical advantages encouraged film people to use chroma-key. Next step was the usage of synthetically generated backgrounds, firstly painted then generated by computers, to put actors to places which don't really exist.

By consequently following this way, using the possibilities of today's graphics computers, finally standard television production could be done in a chroma-key studio with nothing in than just the actors performing in front of blue or green walls for the matting and all backgrounds generated by a graphics computer in real-time based on a 3D scene description. One key requirement for the acceptance of this production method is the possibility to place actors into the synthetic set, where set components may cover actors partly or fully.

This paper describes a new mixing technique developed for the purpose of depth sensitive composition of live action and synthetic backgrounds, which evaluates additionally to the matting signal from the chroma-key generator also the depth information (Z-values) of both inputs and is therefore called Z-mixing. This technique enables the insertion of an actor into a virtual background, where parts of the set are located in front of the actor, by mixing each foreground image with just one background image which contains set components behind and in front of the actor simultaneously.

2 Existing Video Combining Techniques

2.1 Chroma-Key

The technique known as chroma-key is frequently used in today's television production. It's equivalent in the film industry is the 'travelling matte'. There have always been situations, where separate shots of the desired foreground and background with subsequent combining could solve severe problems for the producers. In television production luminance-keying has been the first approach to mix two different images for such purposes. The principle behind luminance-keying is to operate a switch between two video sources by a key signal derived from the luminance.

The next step was to use the B-Y signal instead of the luminance, since this gives much more freedom in performing the foreground shots. The B-Y signal is at its highest value for highly saturated blues and so chroma-keying with shots against blue backclothes started [1]. There has been a lot of further development, today it's possible to select any colour as background colour, soft transitions and even the extraction of shadows from the foreground image are possible. But the principle keeps the same, chroma-keying involves specifying a desired colour in a foreground image, areas containing this colour are replaced with a background image. For good results this colour must be highly saturated and must not appear on objects or actors of the foreground scene [2].

2.2 Layering

Another technique for composition of a final image out of multiple sources is layering, which is mainly used in post-production to achieve 3D-looking images out of painted or computer generated 2D source images. The principle of layering is to compose an image out of several images (layers), each having a specific distance to the camera, also called priority. Except for the background layer, which has the highest distance to the camera, all layers consist of the image containing the objects to be inserted and a mask which defines the parts of the image covered by objects to be inserted. Composition starts with the background layer and step by step in the order of decreasing distance to the camera new layers are added. In each step the masked parts of the current layer replace the corresponding parts of the composed image.

Since many tapes with the different layers have to be created and to be handled layering is very costly. Since the layers have to be pre-produced, they can normally only used in post-production. When used for live production only predefined movement of the camera (and the actors) is possible. An additional disadvantage is the number of generations necessary to produce the final image, which introduces noise especially using analog devices.

3 Z-Mixing

Contrary to the layering technique, where 2D images are used, the new mixing method described here is based on 3D images. In this context 3D image means an computer generated image from a 3D scene description with additional information about the distance between the virtual camera and each pixel of the generated image. With the knowledge of the distance between the camera and each pixel (this distance is called depth or Z-value respectively) of two input images to be mixed, a decision which pixel to be used for the final image can be made for each video pixel independently by comparison of the corresponding Z-values.

The usage of a hardware Z-buffer for performing real-time 3D rendering is a standard feature of all high-end graphics workstations. Z-values for each pixel are therefore available for the synthetic backgrounds. For the foreground live action shot by a normal studio camera there is unfortunately no information about the depth of individual pixels. Since there is no tool available to provide Z-values in real-time, the first approach is to estimate the distance between the actor and the camera and to use this value as a constant depth value for a whole foreground image. If the actor moves this value can be updated from frame to frame. Of coarse only those foreground pixels belonging to the actor should be inserted into the synthetic background image, whereas all other pixels of the foreground image should be discarded. Therefore a separation is necessary for the foreground image, which can be achieved by standard chroma-key technique.

This means for depth sensitive insertion of an actor into a synthetic background, the foreground images to be inserted have to been shot against a backcloth of a highly saturated colour as in any chroma-key setup. A chroma-key generator provides the matting signal to distinguish between the actor and the backcloth and a unit named Z-key generator evaluates the chroma-key signal as well as the depth values for both inputs, generating a final key signal for a normal mixing unit to combine the two inputs appropriately. Z-key generator and mixing unit together perform the novel mixing technique which we call Z-mixing. Figure 1 shows basically the components necessary to perform Z-mixing.

Supposed the chroma-key generator provides a binary signal which is 0 for the backcloth and 1 for the actor, the Z-key generator performs the following calculation for each pixel of the final image :

$$
\begin{aligned}
&\text{If (chroma-key=0)} \quad \text{then} \quad \text{Z-key} = 0 \\
&\text{else if } (Z1 > Z2) \quad \text{then} \quad \text{Z-key} = 0 \\
&\text{else} \qquad\qquad\qquad\qquad \text{Z-key} = 1
\end{aligned}
$$

where $Z1$ and $Z2$ are the depth values for foreground and background respectively. For Z-values it's assumed that the value is proportional to the camera distance. If the Z-key is 0, the mixing unit forwards the background pixel, otherwise the foreground pixel.

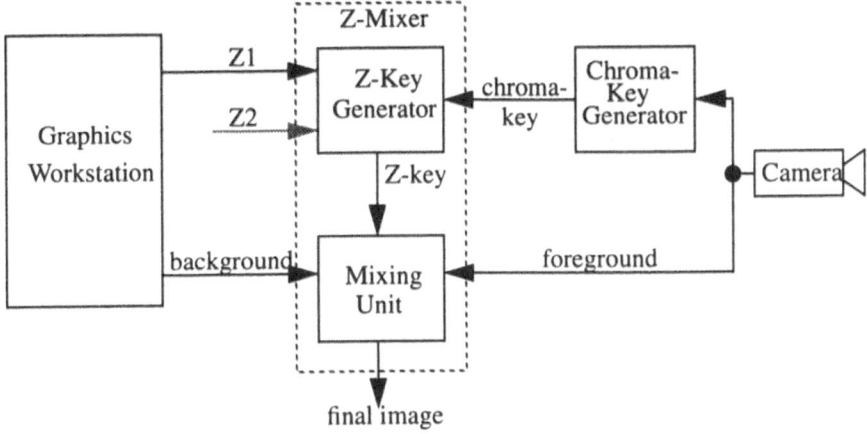

Figure 1 : Block Diagram of Z-Mixing Components

4 Antialiasing Aspects

Just switching between foreground and background based on a binary key signal would result in some aliasing-like artefacts in the final image due to the hard transition. Therefore the generation of a soft Z-key signal is necessary. Performing Z-mixing four different types of transitions between foreground and background have to be distinguished:

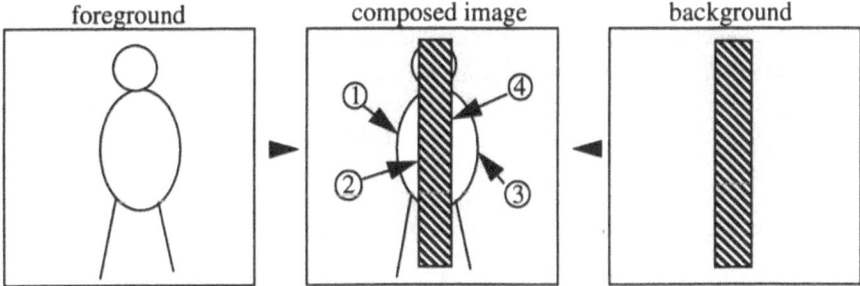

Figure 2 : PossibleTransitions between Foreground and Background

1. From a background object to an actor in front of it

2. From an actor to a background object covering the actor

3. From an actor to a background object behind the actor

4. From a background object to an actor behind it.

Modern chroma-key generators provide already a soft key signal. This softness can be used in case one and three for providing a soft Z-key signal. For case two and four this does not help since the transition is caused by a distance change between foreground and background. To get soft edges for these transitions as well it's necessary to detect transitions of that type and to perform a local 'filtering' in some way.

5 Current Real-time Environment

5.1 Z-Mixer Hardware

VMIX (Video MIXer), a mixing device capable of performing Z-mixing has been designed, manufactured and tested. It consists of a 9U x 400 mm baseboard, which may be plugged into any 9U VMEBus (e.g. SGI Onyx), and several I/O and option modules. Besides the unique Z-key mode it incorporates all standard mixer functions like cut, dissolve, fade, key and downstream key, additional option slots can be used to expand the device by a chroma-keyer, a wipe generator and a text buffer.

Figure 3 show a block diagram of the VMIX baseboard. All data I/O is done via I/O modules, which are used as interfaces between any external video signal, either analog or digital, and the internal video buses. The VMIX device is not dedicated to any specific video raster and can process either RGB or YUV data with sampling frequencies of up to 80 MHz per channel and data width of 8 or 10 bit. In the present demonstrator the VMIX baseboard is equipped with I/O modules for digita¹ video data according to CCIR 601/656.

The cross bar switch connects the I/O modules with the internal modules of the mixing device, the routing can be controlled by software. The mixing unit mixes two input signals based on an key signal coming from the alpha selection unit. The generation of this key signal is based on one or two alpha signals and a distance key coming from the Z-comparison unit in the Z-key mode. One option slot is available for a chroma keyer to generate an alpha signal based on the colour of one video input. Two further option slots may be equipped with a text buffer and a wipe generator. The optional   I/O module may be used to generate an overlay signal for superimposing the mixer output onto the monitor of a graphics workstation.

The Z-comparison unit reads in Z-values from the input modules and generates the distance key signal for the consecutive alpha selection unit. The principal item is a comparator unit, which can be configured by software for 8, 16, 24 or 32 Bits per input. One input is always connected to I/O module 1, the other one can either be connected to I/O module 2 or to a constant value which can be set by software. The distance values are interpreted as unsigned integer values, whereby small values represent pixels having a short distance to the camera and great values pixels having a long distance to the camera. The distance key dk is a 1-bit per pixel value and becomes 1 if the Z-value from I/O module 1 is greater than the one from the second I/O module. A constant Z-value can be used instead of dynamic Z-values from I/O module 2.

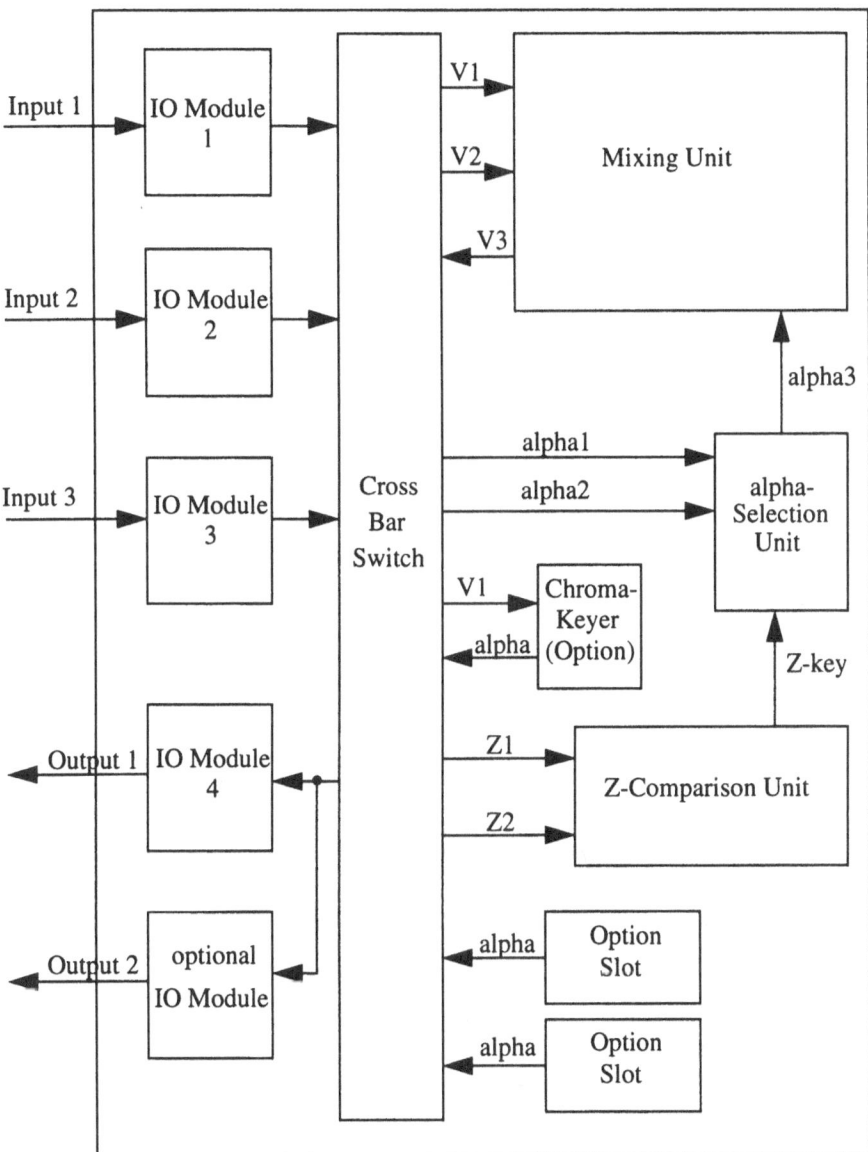

Figure 3 : Block Diagram of the VMIX Baseboard

5.2 Overall System

Figure 4 shows the integration of the VMIX device into the demonstrator of the MONA LISA project [3]. The camera signal and the key signal derived from it are delayed in an ISP500 sequence storage system [4] for approximately 4 frames, which is the delay of the camera tracking and the rendering. The VMIX board gets these delayed signals together with the rendered background and the Z-values for the background both provided by the Onyx graphics computer [5]. The SMPTE 656 dual link interface of the Sirius board [6] is used to get the background video signal and the Z-values for the background in parallel from the Onyx. The Z-values are limited to 8-bit and copied into the alpha plane of the graphics buffer for that purpose. A simple user interface is used to set and adjust the estimated Z-value for the foreground.

In a studio with a maximum distance of 10 m between the camera and the synthetic set component most far away the resolution for the depth is around 4 cm using 8-bit Z-values, which is the maximum what can come out of the Onyx in real-time. For the current system this is fine enough, since there is only one Z-value for all pixels belonging to the actor.

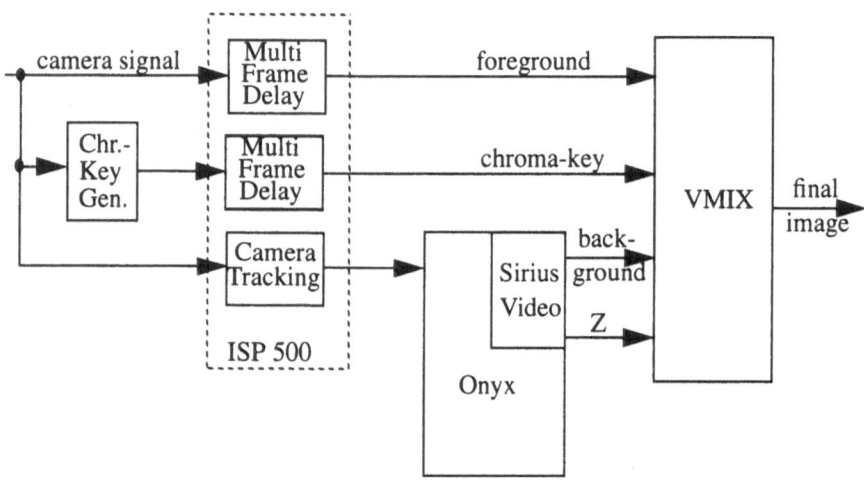

Figure 4 : Block Diagram of the MONA LISA Demonstrator

6 Future Work

Currently a chroma-key generator for the VMIX device is under development, which will replace the external chroma-key generator. It could also be used for live video insertion into the composed image via a second mixing layer. Figure 5 shows the principle. A DVE driven by the camera parameters transforms the live video signal to match the display area in the synthetic background. The area, where the live video should be inserted, will be rendered in a particular colour. The second VMIX layer will replace this area by the signal from the DVE.

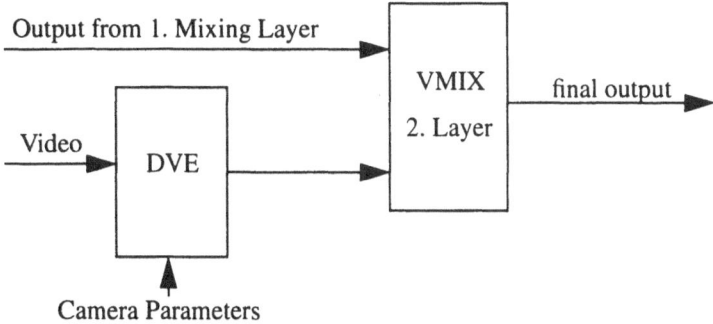

Figure 5 : Realisation of 2nd Mixing Layer

The usage of just one Z-value per foreground frame, estimated and adjusted by hand is the weakest point of the current system. First improvement will be the usage of an automatic actor tracking system based on an ultrasonic sender carried by the actor and corresponding receivers placed in the corners of the studio. This will provide more accurate Z-values, thus enabling the usage of Z-mixing for many applications in television production. But there are still some remaining restrictions :

- There could be only one actor in the foreground normally. If there are more actors, they all must have around the same distance to the camera.

- There could be no direct interaction between actors and synthetic set components. Even for showing the actors feet walking on the synthetic floor, it´s necessary to provide a foreground Z-value slightly smaller than the real value to avoid effects like feet disappearing in the floor due to imperfect calibration of the virtual camera.

To overcome these restrictions it will be necessary to get a Z-value for each pixel of the foreground image. The generation of these values in real-time could be a challenge for the image analysis in the future, provided there's enough computing power available in the next computer generation

7 Acknowledgements

This work has been supported by the RACE II project R2052 "MONA LISA", which has the prime objective of developing and integrating technologies in the fields of image analysis, image synthesis and hardware design. Specifically, the project aims to build an electronic set demonstrator for usage in a studio environment.

References

1. Hughes D 'Ultimatte' Video travelling Matte, Int. Brodcast Engineer 11 (1980) 173:22-25
2. Jack K. Video Demystified: A Handbook for the Digital Engineer, Brooktree Corporation, 1993
3. Blonde L. The MONA LISA Project, these proceedings
4. DVS GmbH ISP500 - User Manual, 1993
5. Silicon Graphics Onyx - Technical Report, 1994
6. Silicon Graphics Sirius Video - Technical Report, 1994

Visual Tools for Parallel Server Handling

P. Le Floch, A. V. Sahiner, Y. Paker
Depart. of Computer Science - Queen Mary and Westfield College
London - United Kingdom

1 Introduction

The notorious complexity of utilising parallel computers has long motivated researchers to use graphics software tools [1]. Graphics user interfaces play a critical role in current methods for controlling parallel architectures: modelling, programming [2], debugging [3], benchmarking, displaying results of parallelized computations, etc...

Under the European project RACE 2052 MONALISA [4] (MOdelling of NAturaL Images for Synthesis & Animation), a hardware accelerator (ELSET-A [5]) has been built. MONALISA's prime objective is to develop and integrate the technologies (algorithms, software & hardware) required for the construction, handling and fast synthesis of 3D models for the creation of image sequences. Its hardware accelerator, based on Motorola DSP96002 boards combined with an intelligent multi-access frame buffer, aims at reducing the time spent during image analysis and synthesis.

In the early phase of the ELSET-A software development, it has rapidly appeared that tools were required to be able to use the accelerator, mainly to initialize the system and run parallel applications.

As the ELSET-A is networked and thus accessible from graphics workstations, graphic user interfaces have been chosen as the basis for the tools and have been designed with the widely used X Window and OSF/Motif windowing system [6]. The Administration Tool was then implemented to initialize the system and manage the processor pool, whereas the application side for parallel execution (applications and data definitions) was attributed to the Command Tool.

After presenting briefly the ELSET™ system, this paper introduces the two visual tools implemented for the system: the Administration Tool and the Command Tool. It first highlights their functionalities, then presents their interface and finally describes how these user interfaces communicate with the ELSET-A machine.

This paper aims at proving once again that user interfaces make certainly life easier for end-users in complex environments with parallel hardware.

2 ELSET™ System

2.1 Hardware overview

ELSET™ system basically consists of two components (figure 1): a commercially available graphics workstation and an especially developed hardware accelerator

(ELSET-A). User interfaces run on the graphics workstation, whereas the hardware accelerator is used to speed up specific algorithms.

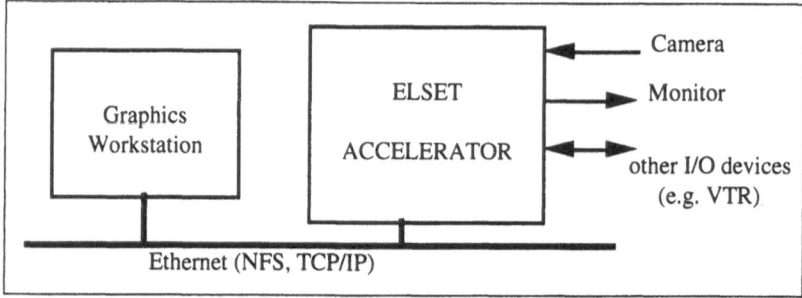

Figure 1. ELSET-A & Host workstation

The ELSET™ system includes a number of capabilities that enable the use of computer generated sets in TV production and post-production. One of the important properties of this system is its hardware acceleration capability which is based on a pool of high performance processors (Motorola DSP96002) closely-coupled with an intelligent frame buffer (figure 2). The accelerator also incorporates a real-time mixing system (Z-mixer) which permits to mix input live actions and generated scenes taking the distance information (Z) into account [7]. This allows an actor to move freely in a synthetic background with objects in front and behind him.

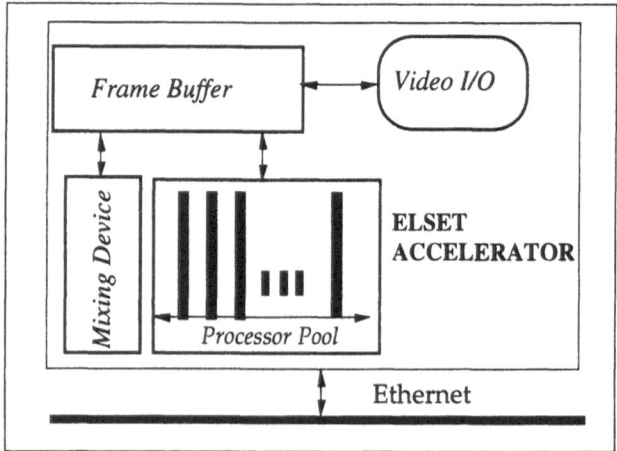

Figure 2. ELSET-A

The frame buffer subsystem is a key component which handles all tasks related to input/output and buffering of video signals. It is connected via I/O channels to the processor pool to provide parallel processing capability directly on video streams.

The accelerator has been built as an extension of the image storage and processing system ISP400 (Image Sequence Processor) [8]. This system is widely used for simulations in digital TV and high definition TV (HDTV) research. Due to its unique multitasking I/O capabilities, the ISP system can handle several independent data streams in real-time, thus obtaining a total data rate of up to 400 MBytes/s. The Control Processor for the ISP system is a 68040 (running OS9 [9]) which shares the VME bus with the pool of processors.

The system provides all the basic functionalities required for effective and efficient control and manipulation of video devices and video data. It allows operations such as simultaneous displaying of image sequences, simultaneous recording and displaying, efficient storage and access to image data, digitizing and recording via CCIR/HDTV codecs.

2.2 Software overview

Due to the hybrid nature of the ELSET™ hardware, software modules run under three separate operating environments (figure 3). User interfaces run on host Unix graphics workstations, whereas processor pool management runs under OS9 and Self Adaptating Parallel Servers (SAPS) under WKernel on the processor pool [10].

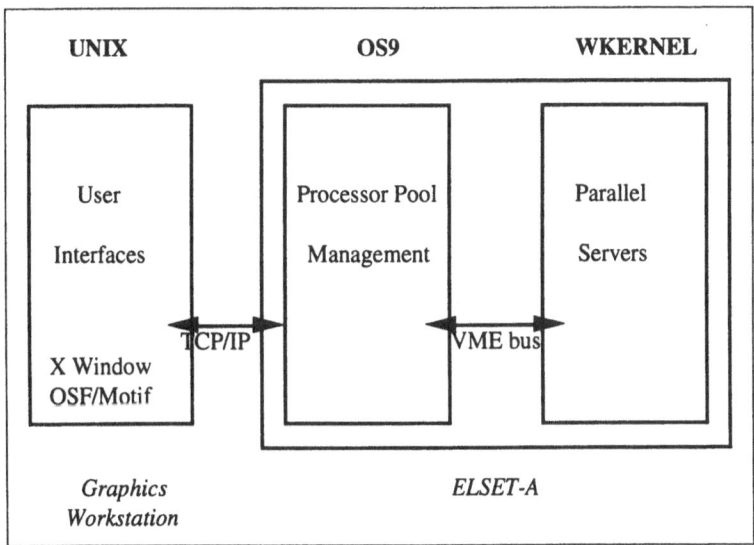

Figure 3. Separate environments

Communications amongst the three environments have been implemented with remote procedure calls (RPCs): at TCP/IP layer between the host Unix workstation and OS9 and with VMEbus and OS9 signals between OS9 and the processor pool.

3 User Interfaces

User interfaces have been designed with X Window/OSF Motif. This widely used environment aims at increasing user effectiveness and satisfaction. It provides different kinds of pre-built objects (widgets) such as buttons, scrolling lists, pulldown menus,·drawing areas, dialog windows, which, arranged and combined together in a shell window, ensure a consistent and attractive appearance. The X Window/OSF Motif system also allows to reduce mouse movements to simplify the actions of the user who does not need to focus on the mechanics of an application.

The ELSET-A user interfaces have the objectives of providing simple means to remotely initialize, monitor, run and debug parallel applications on ELSET-A by hiding the underlying software from users.

3.1 Administration Tool functionalities

The Administration Tool (or ELSET-A System Administration Tool) has been implemented for the system administrator. It provides facilities to initialize the accelerator, starting system management servers under OS9 such as the Pool Manager and the Object Manager.

This tool is used for:

a] Initializing/terminating the ELSET-A system

b] Booting the kernel (which provides the process creation and process management functionalities for parallel server execution on the processor pool),

c] Resetting the processors,

d] Assigning processors to servers,

e] Browsing the SAPS Library

f] Starting servers,

g] Terminating servers,

h] Debugging servers.

3.2 Command Tool functionalities

The Command Tool provides an interface to the ELSET-A system for end-users, and, unlike the Administration Tool, it deals with parallel applications and data. The Administration Tool starts parallel servers (SAPS [10]), but does not provide any data, that is the task of the Command Tool.

Building an application with the Command Tool consists in creating a map of the task to be executed. Maps are created in the Command Tool's work area. A map is a list of modules of different kinds, connected in sequence, which define a particular task. A module is a processing unit in a map. It accepts input data, computes them and send its results to the next module downstreams.

Thus, the main functionalities of the Command Tool are:

a] Building applications using module-based flow diagrams,

b] Providing a module browser to select and popup different kinds of modules and connect them,

c] Assigning tasks to servers,

d] Assigning data to servers,

e] Transferring data into/from the frame buffer,

f] Hiding data decomposition,

g] Hiding data distribution,

h] Viewing data from the frame buffer and disks,

i] Converting data into a format suitable for the frame buffer.

The Command Tool's work area provides facilities for managing modules: adding (selection from the module browser), moving (selection in the work area and dragging), connecting modules together as well as disconnecting modules from each other and removing them from the work area (via the menu after selection of the module).

Connecting modules is made via on-module connectors. Each module has a defined number of input and output connectors (figure 4). Connecting a Data Object module's output connector to a SAPS' input connector means that the data object defined within the Data Object module will be used as input data of the SAPS (whose name has been defined within the SAPS module).

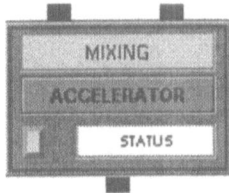

Figure 4. Mixing module accepting 2 inputs and 1 output

Modules obey to their data policy: as well as possibly having several inputs and outputs, they may accept only input(s) or output(s). For example, for a module representing a video tape recorder (VTR), only input or output data is permitted. A VTR indeed cannot read data from a tape and write onto it at the same time. Types of data are also important: modules accept specific types of data (e.g. image, scene description, etc...).

The Command Tool runs concurrently with the Administration Tool. It may run on the same or on a different X Window/OSF Motif-based workstation. Several Command Tools are allowed to share the processor pool. Their requests, therefore, are ordered before executed on the processor pool.

4 Administration Tool

4.1 Description

The Administration Tool (figure 5) consists of several entities: an array of processor buttons, a processor status window, three selection lists (administration commands, parallel servers (SAPS library), and active servers (actually running on the parallel machine)), a message area and a set of operation buttons.

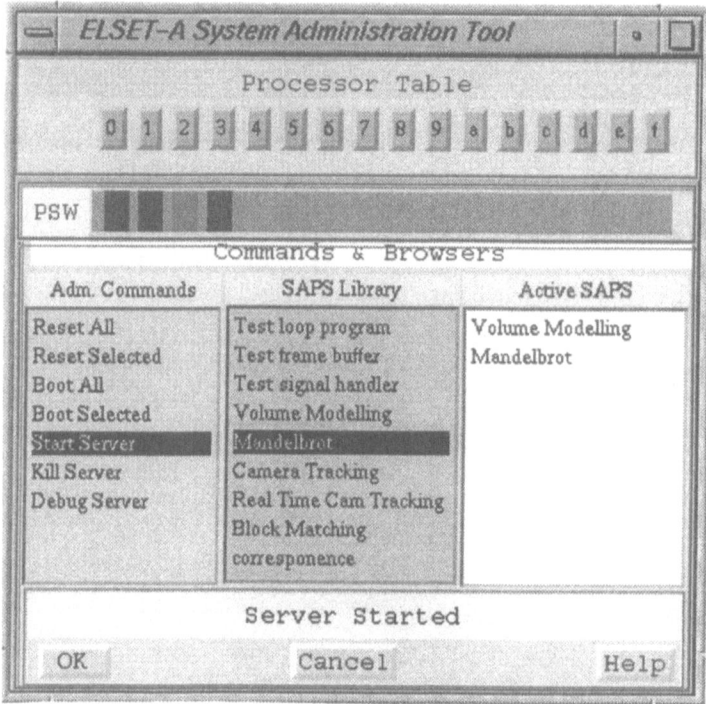

Figure 5. Administration Tool

4.1.1 Processor Table

This table contains buttons, numbered from 0 to 16, that refer to individual processors selected by clicking.

4.1.2 Processor Status Word (PSW) Window

This area shows the colour-coded status of each processor. There are three possible states: Reset, Booted (WKernel running) and Started (SAPS running).

4.1.3 Administration Commands

Administration commands are used for system initialization and server management. The system level consists in selecting processors, resetting them and booting the kernel on them, whereas server management provides commands to start, terminate and debug servers.

System commands (reset, boot) may be executed on a list of nodes or on the whole processor pool for complete initialization/booting of the machine.

Debugging facilities are also included, users may halt server execution, dump registers and memory and eventually resume server execution.

4.1.4 SAPS Library

The SAPS library contains the servers available on the parallel machine. New servers must be registered into that list before to be executed. When a SAPS in this library is selected and started, it becomes active. It can be used then in the Command Tool.

4.1.5 Active SAPS

The Active SAPS list indicates the servers currently running on the accelerator. Starting a server adds its name into this list. Termination of servers can only carried out on the servers in this list. When a SAPS is terminated, it is then suppressed from the Active SAPS list.

4.1.6 Message Area

This area of the interface reports the success or failure of commands. Whenever it is possible, error messages give the reasons of failures in order for the administrator to modify its demand and try it again as quickly as possible.

4.2   ELSET-A system initialization

The Administration Tool is responsible for the initialization of the ELSET-A system. As the graphics workstation running the tool and the accelerator are networked via Ethernet, a protocol has been defined to start and stop the system remotely (figure 6).

The Administration Tool starts the initialization by sending via a TCP/IP connection a request to the Name Server process (ISP daemon) which then creates all the system processes under OS9. These are:

a]   the Pool Manager : process which handles commands from the Administration Tool to initialize the processor pool (resetting and booting the WKernel). It also keeps track of processor loads, processor states (reset/booted/started) and slot states.

b]   the Object Manager : keeps track of all data objects within the ELSET-A system. The information kept for each object description includes data type and characteristics as well as the location of the object and its decomposition properties.

42

Data required by the SAPS during execution are fetched with the aid of the Object Manager.

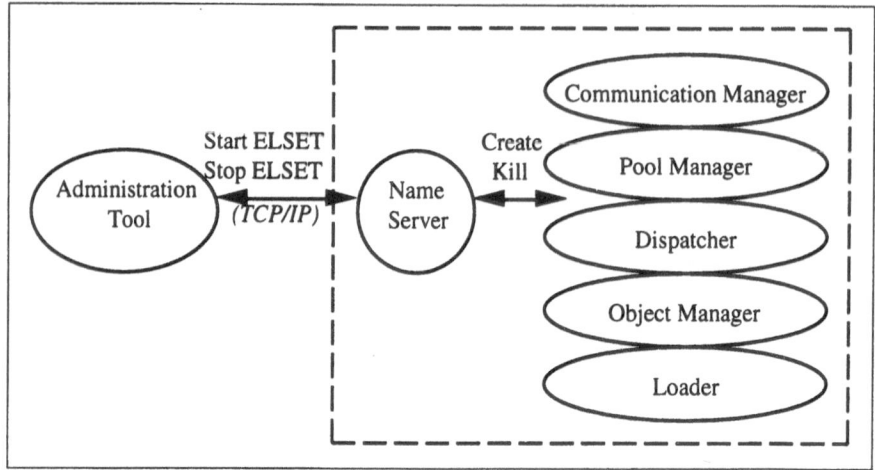

Figure 6. Start/Stop ELSET-A

c] the Dispatcher : carries out the distribution of the data among the workers of a parallel server.

d] the Loader : process is used for down-loading new servers onto the processor pool. It receives orders from the Pool Manager to down- load servers on a specific set of processors.

e] the Communication Manager : was introduced to improve the efficiency of the communications. Instead of having individual socket-based communication channels between the tools and each system process, a single socket-based channel is used to multiplex data. Once a message reaches the OS-9 system through a socket, the Communication Manager dispatches it to the destination process.

The Administration Tool is also responsible for the system termination. For that, it uses the same protocol used for initialization. The Name Server then terminates the OS9 processes of the ELSET-A system.

4.2.1 Communications

Once the ELSET-A system has been initialized (i.e. all OS9 processes created), a dedicated channel (TCP/IP socket) is created between the Administration Tool and the Communication Manager process. An RPC protocol has been implemented for communication on this channel.

Then according to the administrator's requests, coded commands for, for example, "Reset DSP 0", "Start SAPS test" are transmitted to the ELSET-A system, waiting for an acknowledgement which carries a status code (telling if the action has been correctly undertaken by the OS9 software). This is used afterwards to report the success or failure of the command in the Message Area of the user interface.

5 Command Tool

5.1 Description

The Command Tool (figure 7) handles running a user parallel application on the ELSET-A. The interface is based on a collection of X Window/OSF Motif widgets: windows, menus, buttons, text, fields. It is an Explorer™ like interface where modules are connected in sequence to define tasks.

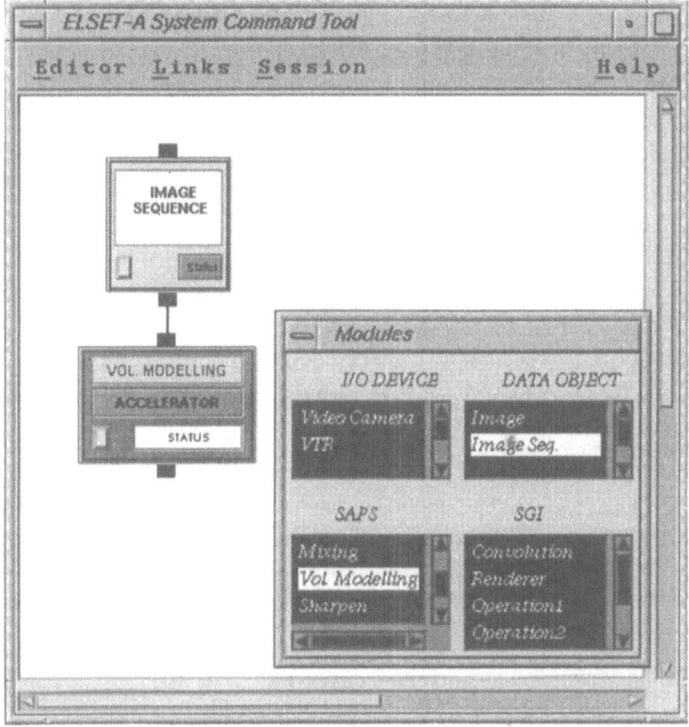

Figure 7. Command Tool

The Command Tool has three main components: a menu, a work area and a Module Browser. The menu consists of three pull-down submenus used for calling the Module Browser, managing the modules in the work area (cut/paste/copy), removing links between modules and running user-defined applications. Modules are selected from the Module Browser and then popped up in the work area to create flow maps.

5.2 Modules

The Module Browser is a file browser and selector that provides access to modules. Modules are the individual units in a map; fed with data, they make applications work. The idea is simply to select modules from the Module Browser, initialize them and connect them in order to define a flow map of the application (or session) to be executed on the accelerator.

As modules have different functionalities (e.g. modules for data attribution, for computation, etc...), they provide a means to set their properties (e.g. data file name, parallel server name, etc...). For this purpose, each module incorporates a square button in its bottom left corner when pressed opens the module's control window. Parameters required by a module must be specified there.

Furthermore, at the bottom right corner of modules, a status rectangle indicates the status of the related operation on the target machine. If that status changes to red then the module is in an error state.

There are four classes of modules: I/O Device, Data Object, Active SAPS and SGI modules.

5.2.1 I/O Device modules

I/O Device modules are used to control video I/O devices such as video cameras, VTRs, RGB Monitors. For example, a VTR module can be selected from the Module Browser and assigned to a VTR connected to the ELSET-A system. It provides then facilities to start, stop, rewind the VTR from the Command Tool.

5.2.2 Data Object modules

Data Object modules handle data in the system. They provide a means to associate data with I/O Devices and applications. Data objects are created in the system either from files or data from remote workstations or by using file-associated devices (video camera, VTR, etc...) connected to the frame buffer subsystem. Data objects can be as diverse as images, image sequences, scene descriptions, arrays, lists, etc...

Data Object modules have been defined for:

a]   on-line creation of data objects:

For example, connecting an I/O Device module such as a camera to a Data Object module 'Image Sequence' will create a new data object (image sequence) within the frame buffer during live shooting.

b]   browsing existing data objects:

As the frame buffer subsystem uses a specific file format for its data (DVS format), before transfer to the frame buffer subsystem, data objects must be converted into that format. This phase may be carried out off-line in order to register new data objects in the frame buffer before starting any parallel work on the accelerator.

Basically, the DVS file format is composed of two headers (although the second one is optional) describing the data in the file (name, size, data length, colour mode, etc...) and a set of arrays of data. For image sequences, each array is a simply a frame.

Convertion into the DVS format is undertaken either from the Command Tool or from another small visual tool developed earlier in the project: Studio [11].

Studio is an image viewer connected to the frame buffer that handles images and image sequences in formats such as RGB (Silicon Graphics image format), COST211 (used to exchange picture material in digital form on computer tapes) (figure 8). It also incorporates a converter between these different formats and provide a means for transferring DVS formatted data into/from the frame buffer for off-line data object creation.

Figure 8. Studio: Image sequence viewer

Furthermore, each object has a well defined data layout (i.e. object name, size, type of data, etc...). Therefore, Data Object modules incorporate parameter control windows used to set those properties. For example, for the Image Sequence Data Object module, the parameter control window contains a browser of existing files (figure 9), either from the SGI disk or the Frame Buffer (i.e. data objects).

c]   viewing data objects:

In the case of images, image sequences or scenes, it is also possible to directly view, on the graphics workstation, data from either the frame buffer or the host disk (which is very useful when working with a large database of data objects to pick up a particular one).

d]   provision of data to parallel servers and applications running on the host:

Selecting a data object within a Data Object module and connecting the output (or input) connector of this module to the input (or output) connector of an application module provides a means to feed the connected module with data. For example, connecting a Image Sequence Data Object module to a camera tracking server module means that the camera tracking will process the image sequence as input data. Then, another Data Object module may be connected downstream to the camera tracking module to store the camera tracking results into the frame buffer.

5.2.3 Active SAPS modules

Active SAPS modules refer to parallel servers running on the processor pool (this assumes that they have been previously started with the Administration Tool). These modules let then users incorporate SAPSs in their maps.

46

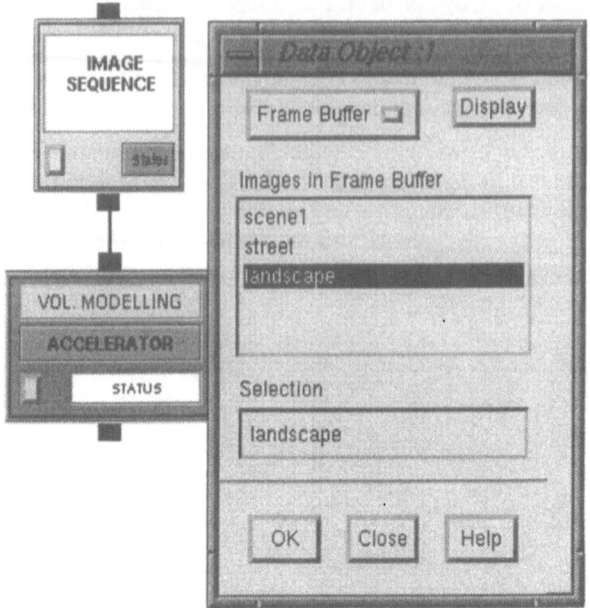

Figure 9. Selection of a data object from the frame buffer

5.2.4 SGI modules

SGI modules utilize the facilities provided by the graphics workstation. One can be used, for example, to pipe the result of a parallel server to a rendering process running on the Silicon Graphics.

5.3 Session

5.3.1 Example

The figure 10 shows an example of a connected module-based diagram defined for running a camera tracking on the accelerator on an input image sequence shot from a video camera. The results of the camera tracking are then pipelined to a renderer running on the host workstation (Silicon Graphics). The Data Object module 'Image Sequence' indicates that the sequence coming from the camera is stored within the frame buffer and then used as input of the camera tracking server.

5.3.2 Session coherence

When the session has been built, before to execute it on the ELSET-A system, an analyser checks the coherence of the task, such as verifying that all modules in the map were initialized in sympathy with their properties (e.g. object names set in

Data Object modules). The analyser stops whenever an error is found, an error message as clearly as possible is then popped up. It is then impossible to run the session on the ELSET-A system until all errors have been corrected.

Two types of errors may occur:

[1] - link errors: the first level of verification consists in determining whether all modules present in the work area have the correct number of connected input and output links. Indeed, if a SAPS module requires one input, it should have it to run correctly.

[2] - initialization errors: a second level verifies that the parameters of all modules (accessible through their respective parameter window) have all been set correctly (e.g.. data object module initialized with object name).

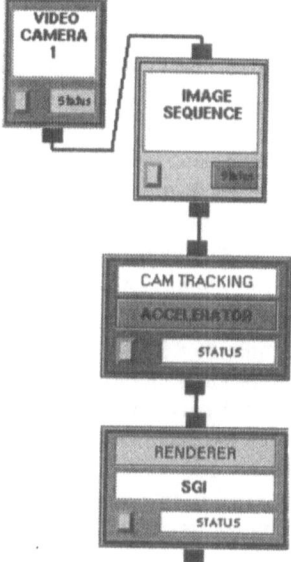

Figure 10. Example

5.3.3 SAPS execution

After having started with the Administration Tool, servers wait for service requests. A service request consists of a list of object ids related to a SAPS: it defines the input and output data. For example, an object id may be an input sequence name. The Command Tool therefore simplifies the building of service requests by hiding that level of work from users.

During the analysing phase, a service request is built. This service request contains all the informations regarding to the session (e.g.. input data names, SAPS identifier, etc...). This request is then sent to the Dispatcher under OS9 which carries out the distribution of the data between the copies of the SAPS on the processor pool and the collection of results.

5.4 Data Object management

Each data object module connected to the input ports of a SAPS module provides an input argument for the procedure executed by that SAPS, i.e., an object identifier is passed (one per data object) to the SAPS in the service request. Every identifier is associated with a data object that resides in the frame buffer.

Once the SAPS receives a service request with the object identifiers in it, it contacts the *object manager* for decomposition. It is the object manager that registers the required decomposition rules with the respective objects and creates the list of unit tasks with the respective data handles encapsulated in them. Every unit task is then processed by the SAPS in parallel; each data handle being associated with a different section of the object data. The decomposition specification file used by the object manager to decompose the data objects is developed as part of the server construction process.

The SAPS workers (the processes that provide the parallel service) use these data handles in accessing the data grains when a particular unit task is assigned to them. Different workers of a SAPS can read individual images from an image sequence as input data, and after carrying out the processing, they can write the processed images to form the output sequence. To the worker process which possesses a data handle, the way data is partitioned is transparent, e.g, an image sequence partition may correspond to a strip, or an image quadrant, or a full frame.

Two primitives, *GetData()* and *PutData()* are used to program the distribution of the data. GetData operation allows a SAPS process to copy a partition data associated with a particular input data handle into the specified local buffer. With the PutData operation a worker can invoke the copying of the data provided in a local buffer into the frame buffer associated with a particular output data handle. These primitives have been implemented using message passing protocols between the object manager and the SAPS workers. The object manager when receives a operation request message from the workers it initializes the respective I/O processor for a fast transfer of data between the frame buffer and the DRAM of the respective processor.

5.5 Communications

5.5.1 Connection to/disconnection from the ELSET-A system

At startup, the Command Tool attempts a connection to the ELSET-A system through the Name Server process (daemon) in order to establish a link to the OS9 ELSET-A software. The ELSET-A System Administration Tool should be already running (on the same or on another workstation) when a Command Tool is started. The Command Tool assumes indeed that the ELSET-A system has been initialized by the Administration Tool. If not, connection to the ELSET-A system fails and the Command Tool cannot be used until the system has been setup.

When the connection is accepted (as several Command Tools may run at the same time, up to five connections to the ELSET-A system are permitted), the Name Server process creates firstly an ISP Server (figure 11). The ISP Server is the system process that provides the services related to the usage of the ISP system (the

Intelligent Frame Buffer System). The Command Tool running on the graphics host is then used as a front-end to the ISP Server. The Name Server allocates then two ethernet port numbers, on which TCP/IP socket-based channels are created for communications with the ISP server. The Command Tool connects itself to those ports, establishing two separate channels to the ISP Server; one is used to exchange commands to control the ISP System, the other, data with the frame buffer. Finally a third channel is created between the Command Tool and the Communication Manager to send service requests for parallel applications.

Exiting the Command Tool results in the disconnection from the ELSET-A system. The Name Server kills then the ISP Server used by the Command Tool. Channels between the workstation and the OS9 machine are then freed.

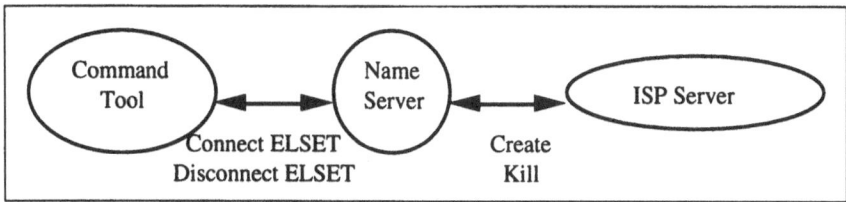

Figure 11. Connect/Disconnect ELSET-A

5.5.2 Video Device Library

The Video Device LIBrary (VDLIB) is a subroutine package used for controlling a video input/output device and for transferring data between the frame buffer of the video I/O device and the data arrays in the workstation memory from a remote machine. Commands and data are exchanged with the ISP System [8] via an ISP server process that serves the host program.

All control and transfer functions are performed by using a single subroutine, i.e. the function vdlib(). This function takes as the first parameter a function code which determine the actual function of the routine; the following parameters are then related to the function code.

Example: vdlib(CF_SDEV,1)

        selects device number 1

    vdlib(CF_BUIL,gscale,1,720,576)

        builds file "gscale" with one 720x576 frame

The Command Tool uses fully the Video Device Library to control the I/O devices connected to the ELSET™ system and manage files in the frame buffer. For example, selecting an image sequence from a Data Object module creates an attachment to that file under the ISP Server. That file is then considered as a current file by the ISP system for subsequent operations.

6 Conclusion

This paper has presented some X Window/OSF Motif visual tools for parallel server handling on the ELSET-A system's processor pool. These interfaces make the operations on the accelerator transparent to end-users.

The ELSET-A System Administration Tool lets the system administrator initialize and monitor remotely the processor pool. The Command Tool aims at running parallel applications on the accelerator. Its connected module-based interface provides facilities to define parallel sessions and start their execution.

These user interfaces have been widely used for testing the ELSET-A system. First, during the tests of the "home-made" kernel (WKernel) on the processors, the Administration Tool was a precious aid to reset the processors, boot and debug the kernel. Then, it was used to start and terminate very simple servers to check that the process management was correctly undertaken by the kernel.

The next step was to run "real" servers on the processor pool, which means starting servers that were using data from the frame buffer, computing these data and putting results into it. The Command Tool was therefore used to define the test applications by building the maps of the applications. It was pretty easy to manage objects in the frame buffer and provide data to servers by connecting Data Object and SAPS modules.

However, the current Command Tool lacks of flexibility, it only works with the existing modules. Future work will focus on the provision of a module editor to add custom modules to the tool.

7 Acknowledgements

This work was supported by the RACE II project R2052 "MONALISA". Partners in this project are Thomson CSF/LER, BBC, Daimler-Benz, DVS Digitale VideoSignale GmbH, Siemens AG, University of Balearic Islands, University of Hannover and VAP Video Art Production.

ELSET™ is a trademark of VAP Video Art Production Gmbh, Hamburg

Explorer™ is a trademark of Silicon Graphics, Inc.

References

[1]   C. J. Pavlakos, L. A. Schoof and al - A Visualization Model for Supercomputing Environments - IEEE Parallel and Distributed Technology, Vol. 1, No. 4, November 1993, pp.16-21

[2]   L. H. Jamieson, E. J. Delp - A Software Environment for Parallel Computer Vision - IEEE Computer, Vol. 25, No. 2, February 1992, pp.73-77

[3]   P. S. Utter, C. M. Pancake - Advances in Parallel Debuggers: New Approaches to Visualization - Theory Center Technical Report - Cornell University, New York 1989

[4]   J. Bley, W. Schmidt, G. Thomas - Short Market Report - RACE 2052 Internal Deliverable No. 7 Report, Septembre 1992

[5]   A.V. Sahiner, P. Le Floch, A. Nimmo, Y. Paker - A Parallel Accelerator for Generation of Virtual Studio Sets - Eight EuroGraphics Workshop on Graphics Hardware, 1993

[6]   OSF/Motif™ Style Guide - Open System Foundation - Prentice-Hall, Inc. - 1991

[7]   W. Schmidt - Real-Time Mixing of Live Action and Synthetic Backgrounds based on Depth Values - Monalisa Workshop Proceedings, 1994

[8]   ISP200-ISP400 Reference Manual, DVS Gmbh, Hannover 1992

[9]   P. Dibble - OS9 Insights - Microwave Systems Corporation, 1988

[10] A.V. Sahiner - A Computation Model for Parallelism: Self-Adapting Parallel Servers - Ph.D. Thesis, The Polytechnic of Central London, 1991

[11] P. Le Floch - Studio: A Tool for Image Sequence Handling, DESS Thesis, QMW London , 1993

P³I,
a Multi-Paradigm Real-Time Video Engine.

M.J.Colaïtis, J.L.Jumpertz, B.Chéron, F.Battini, B.De Lescure,
E.Gautier, B.Guérin, J.P.Geffroy
THOMSON-CSF/LER, Av. de Belle Fontaine, 35510 Cesson, FRANCE
Fax : (33) 99 25 43 34, Tel : (33) 99 25 42 00
e-mail : spi@ler.thomson.fr

Abstract

This paper is an overview of the hardware and software
architecture of the P³I project developed at THOMSON/CSF-LER.
P³I is a fully programmable experimental machine aimed at real-
time processing of video streams. The current prototype exhibits
good performances in terms of computational power with respect
to equipment cost and size, and attractive flexibility for new
applications development. A wide variety of processing used in the
field of the TV studio have been successfully implemented,
opening the way to new special effects.

1   Introduction

1.1   Why Programmable Real-Time Video Processing?

Real-time video processing ranges from as many domains as industrial vision, MPEG
coders, including video studio special effects and many others (defense, medical, ...).
These various applications exhibit different requirements in terms of computational
or communication power, but they share common hardships:
*   Time constraints are heavy (typically 40ms/picture).
*   Huge data rate (typically 10 to 300 Mbytes/s).
*   Geometrical parallelism inherent in images data structures : more than 100K
    pixels per image.
*   Temporal recurrence : some computation is done repetitively on each frame.
*   Memory requirements in relation with the temporal processing and with the
    need for real 2 D processing.
For years, due to the huge data-rate of the video signal, **dedicated hardware**
appeared to be the only way (in terms of equipment size and cost) to achieve
real-time video processing, making expensive the design of a new equipment. During
the second half of the 80's, an alternative approach, based on reusable **hardware**

building blocks and proprietary **video data-path** (see Imaging Technology [1] or Data Cube) has brought the possibility to shorten the development time of a new image processing hardware, the design of which consisting of assembling (and to some extent programming) pre-existing boards, each board implementing a given image processing function. Today, recent advances in the field of **parallel computing** show promising possibilities to allow fully programmable implementation of real-time image processing applications ([2], [3] and [4]).

At least two major advantages could be foreseen from this recent *"software based"* approach to video real-time processing :

- **Multi-applications** : the same "target" machine could be used by different applications, leading to shared development costs and to faster development time to market.
- **Flexibility** : equipment retro-fit could be as simple as software upgrades.

Back to 1990, Thomson-CSF/LER decided to investigate this approach by starting the design of an experimental programmable platform dedicated to video real-time processing : P^3I (Parallel Programmable Processor for Image processing). This paper presents the hardware and software main choices, and gives some figures on P^3I performances.

1.2   Outlines

In terms of computing power, the huge requirements (some tens of Gops) of real-time video processing lead to turn towards parallel processors. Optimizing both equipment and development costs (and size) while preserving efficient processing capabilities makes it mandatory to focus the design on the specificities of video real-time processing :

- **high data-rate** (image size * video-rate) not compatible with a standard bus structure and leading to intensive computations (but mainly with integer arithmetics),
- **Wide range of applications** leading to various kind of very heterogeneous algorithms, from highly repetitive number crunching low-level functions to complex (forky) high-level processing, operating on a restricted set of data,
- **inherent parallelism in the data structure** : more than some 100K pixels per image processed locally.

The choices made for the P^3I architecture reflect all the above mentioned features : P^3I is based on **a set of various heterogeneous computation units interconnected through a very high bit-rate data network**. Each computation unit is fully programmable and makes use of parallel processors, some of them being organised on SIMD[1] or MIMD[2] modes, and some of them being hardwired automatons with dedicated ALU or specialised-yet-programmable hardware(such as downloadable LCAs (XILINX, ALTERA, ...)[5]). The architectural choices of a given computation

---

[1] Single Instruction Multiple Data

[2] Multiple Instructions Multiple Data

unit have been made in order to reach an efficient and cost-effective implementation for a given class of image processing algorithms : SIMD is well suited to low level processing, such as filtering, FFT, ... while MIMD addresses medium and high level processing. This correspondence between algorithms levels and hardware architecture is a classical topic in the field of image processing (e.g. see [4] or [11]).

Before going further in the description of the P^3I hardware, we will answer first to the question which logically rises from this very short overview of P^3I : *"how can be programmed and to controlled this multi-paradigm architecture?"*.

Although this problem is a key issue for the future of parallel programming, an unified approach based on a multi-paradigm high level language (e.g. FORTRAN or C) compiler is obviously out of the scope of our project ; to be convinced, just consider the present state of maturity of such a super-compiler which has to take care efficiently of various types of parallelism... In the P3I design, we considered an alternative approach based on data-flow programming. Dataflow has been widely adopted as a model for reactive systems such as digital signal processing for 2 principal reasons. The first reason is that dataflow does not overly constraint the order of evaluation of the operations that make up the algorithm, permitting the available parallelism of the algorithm to be exploited. This advantage holds regardless of the application area. The second reason is that a graphical dataflow model, based on block diagram representation, is an intuitive model for the way that signal processing designers think about systems : operators act upon streams of data to produce additional streams of data. So, building a new image processing application consists of **assembling library functions**, only a few part of the application code being brand new, written from scratch. Recent development tools (e.g. PTOLEMY [6]) have taken advantage of this methodology, offering a comprehensive set of tools that allow the user to graphically define its application, to test and simulate it, etc...

Using this approach, P^3I shows 2 programming levels : (i) the application-level, and (ii) the function-level.

- Using a top-down approach, **application-level** describes how the different functions involved in the processing are cascaded together, what kind of data they exchange, what the conditions required to activate a given function are, ... A P^3I application program roughly looks like a data-flow netlist interconnecting function calls, merged with conditional clauses (Boolean Control Flow) allowing to invalidate some nets. The aim is to define the scheduling of the various tasks which are to be executed on P^3I. The execution model behind this scheduling is event-driven. Application-level is the domain of image processing experts, which should focus on the application itself and consequently, the machine should be *"hidden"* as much as possible.

- Because of the heterogeneity of the various computation units of P^3I, the **function-level** is splitted in as many parts as there are different kinds of units, each part making use of the native tools of the processors used within the unit. This level concerns the tasks to be executed on the various computation units of the machine : the image processing functions are coded and *optimized* as in a standard image processing library. This level is more complex than the previous one : it requires a more dedicated expertise in the field of algorithm parallelization and an in-depth knowledge of the structure of the given unit. Data parallelism is generally the programming model at this level.

2 Hardware

2.1 Global Architecture

Let us come back to the hardware architecture (see fig 1). As stated before, P³I is basically build around a collection of various heterogeneous functional units working concurrently in a task parallelism model. The problem to be solved here is twofold :
(i)   define a methodology to control all those units in terms of task scheduling and data flow (see part 3.1),
(ii)   specify a common hardware interface independent of the architecture of each functional units, including electrical and mechanical constraints, protocol considerations as well as physical and logical data format.

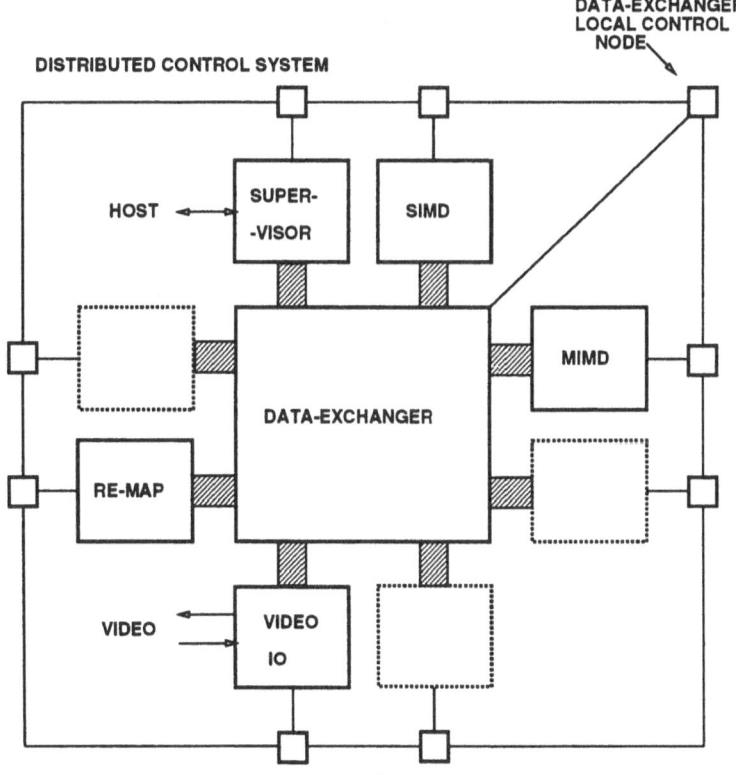

Figure 1 : P³I global architecture

Because of the multi-paradigm aspect of the processing units, the **distributed control**

system is the heart of P³I. Supporting the application-level programming methodology, the control system is in charge of scheduling of data transfers and processing within the machine ; the implementation is distributed and makes use of *local control nodes* based on Transputers [7] connected together by their serial links as a ring, each Transputer controls a given processing unit and communicates with its 2 neighbours (trough messages broadcasting). A distributed execution kernel supports dynamic run-time scheduling, making possible data-dependent decisions and optimized concurrency between the various computation units.

Assuming a control message length of 16 bytes and 8 simultaneous functional units, the maximum latency for a message broadcast is approx. 150 µs, while the maximum communication bandwidth of the ring is huge : 1200 messages per picture (40 ms). Furthermore, the distributed control system is in charge of other operations including bootstrapping of P³I, code downloading, application debugging, ...

Connected to the distributed control system, are the functional units, each of them being based on 2 main parts :

(i)   the **operational part** in charge of image processing or IO, ... which makes the specificity of a given unit

(ii)   the **communication-and-control node** in charge of inter-units operations (tasks control, data exchange, ...). The implementation of this part is "standard" for the various P³I units.

To ease the implementation of a "wide" variety of functional units, a generic **common interface** has been defined between those 2 parts. Being both hardware and software, this interface includes :

(i)   an attachment to the distributed control system based on the local control node,

(ii)   a high bandwidth synchronous data path (see 2.2. the data-exchanger).

The existing functional units implementing this interface are : the data exchanger, the supervisor, the real-time video IO channel, the MIMD processor, the SIMD processor and data re-mapping processor.

2.2   The Data Exchanger

The **data exchanger** is in charge of conveying pictures between the processing or IO units ; in the current version of P³I, the data exchanger is implemented with a 8 bidirectional ports dynamically reconfigurable synchronous cross-bar, each port having a bandwidth of 320 Mbytes/s. 4 communications channels can be active at a same time, broadcast mode is supported. Hosting up to 8 functional units (extensible to 16 if required), the control exchanger coupled to the control system provides a smooth interface between the processing units.

The data exchanger has a local control node, and is directly interconnected to the high bandwidth data paths of the other functional units.

The data exchanged by this unit are formatted on a packet basis without any video or image-like structure. A very simple protocol is implemented between the units involved in a data transfer. Executing a data transfer between 2 functional units of the machine can be seen as sending a packet from the "*mail box*" of the sender to the *"mail box"* of the receiver, the *"mail box"* mechanism being used in order to allow concurrency between data-transfer and processing. The overhead time needed for opening or closing a communication channel between 2 *mail boxes* is around 40 μs, while transferring a 512^2 1-byte image requires 800 μs.

2.3 The Supervisor

The **supervisor** is in charge of booting and testing the P^3I machine during the initialization phase, down-loading code from the host (a SUN workstation) and supporting the debugging of applications. During application run-time, the supervisor can be used as man-machine *"real-time"* interface.
The supervisor is able to access to the control ring and to the data exchanger.

2.4 The Real-Time Video IO Channel

The **video IO unit** is concerned by real-time video input and output. The IO unit transforms the video stream in the internal packet-like format of the data exchanger and performs buffering both on input and output in order to adapt the processing asynchronism to the synchronous requirements of real-time video.
Up to 4 simultaneous 8-bits inputs and outputs can be active at the same time on one IO unit. Channels can be grouped allowing up to 32 bits per pixel. The video format could be completely parametrized up to 1024^2 images, with a maximum clock rate of 36 MPixels/s. Colour images (RGB or YUV) are supported as well as monochrome ones.

2.5 The SIMD Image-Processor

The most powerful unit of the machine is the low-level image processor based on a 64 * 64 grid of a proprietary **SIMD 4-bit processors**. This unit is able to perform some tens of giga pixel-operations per second. For example, a Nevatia-Babu (6 5*5 convolutions) edge detector operates in less than 2 ms on a 512^2 picture, while 8-bit histogramming the same picture size requires 300μs.
An important part of the work done in the design of the SIMD processor was to study how to ease the application code development while preserving efficiency. This lead to an analyze of relationships between applications, compiler and architecture (refer to the software part), implying an important hardware counterpart in the SIMD control hierarchy as well as in the PE itself.

2.5.1 Overall Architecture

Figure 2 shows the overall architecture of the SIMD unit, including the connection to the data-exchanger (bottom) and to the control system.
Massively parallel video processing makes intensive use of memory to store temporal sequences of various sized pictures and intermediate results of computation. This is why the P^3I SIMD processing array is tightly coupled with dynamic RAMs (for their

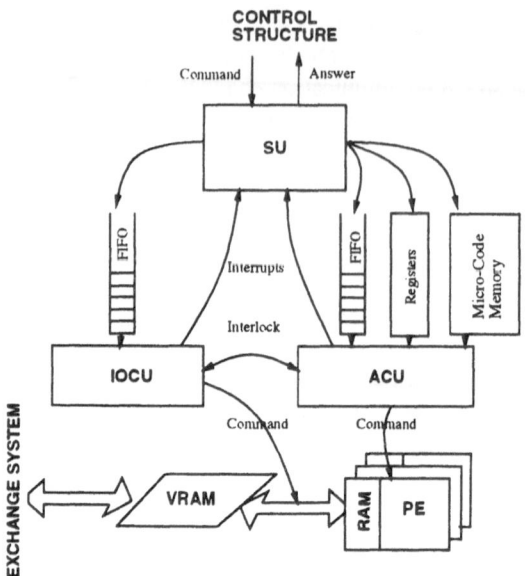

Figure 2 : SIMD global architecture

attractive size versus cost ratio). More precisely, VRAMs were chosen (Video RAMs see [10]) instead of DRAMS, thanks to their dual-port architecture, one of them being used directly by the array, while the other is concurrently accessed by the data-exchanger.

However, due to the slow access time of DRAMs, efficient processing (at high clock speed) could not be achieve. A memory hierarchy has therefore been introduced in the SIMD array : each PE has an internal fast static RAM tightly coupled (using cycle steal techniques) to the external dynamic RAM. This internal small RAM can be seen as a software driven data cache, the management of which being done using *decoupled* processing phases and load/store.

Due to this decoupled architecture, a dual array controller is used : the ACU (Array Control Unit) is in charge of processing the micro-code sequence, while the IOCU (IO Control Unit) supports the load/store mechanism. Those 2 low-level controllers are driven through FIFOs by the SU (Scalar Unit) which is in charge of (i) sequencing load/store and appropriate processing, (ii) solving virtuality of pictures size at run-time and (iii) scalar processing. The EXCU (Exchange Control Unit) controls IOs with the data-exchanger using cycle steal.

The SU is build around a MIPS R3000 processor. ACU, IOCU and EXCU are standard PLAs and RAMs devices.

2.5.2 The SIMD Processing Element

The SIMD array is based on a 64 * 64 array of 4-bit PE, the physical interconnection scheme being NEWS. 16 PEs are assembled on the same 1 μm CMOS ASIC die, each PE having an *internal* private 8 Kbits SRAM and an *external* 64 Kbits memory

(one 1 Mbits DRAM chip is shared by 16 PEs). The instruction rate is 20 Mips.
First, tradeoffs between functional requirements and the current state of VLSI
technology have to be achieved when designing a PE for massively parallel computer
. For example, as far as pictures are concerned, the memory issue is really a key-
point : flexibility and efficiency of processing tend to increase the size of local PE
memory, while current technology shows a clear limitation here [13]. In the P^3I
project, CMOS technology gave 3 major constraints :

(i)   the die size (in terms of the maximum number of implementable
        transistors),
(ii)   the power consumption and dissipation (operating clock frequency, number
        of transistor, packaging), and
(iii)   the maximum number of IO pins.

These *technological* considerations made it possible to sketch the main parts of the
PE : width of the ALU, internal buses and IO data-path, amount of memory, clock
speed, registers versus memory, number of memory ports, number of gates per PE,
... Concerning the functional requirements in terms of algorithms and computing
power, various architectural alternatives have been studied within the ranges fixed
by technology, each of those alternatives having the same ratio "*number_of_PEs* *
width_of_PE * *clock_frequency*".

Secondly, the ease of programming was also a considerable issue for the design of
the SIMD unit : this implied a *good* regularity and orthogonality in the architecture
of both the PE and the control strategy in order to allow efficient and as much as
possible automatic code generation and optimisation. This leads to choose a *good*
balance between the various parts of the PE or of the ACU, to use internal pipe-line
avoiding as much as possible delay-slots and resource conflicts (interlocks, bypass),
to use internal parallelism, ...

Finally, in terms of processing, the functional requirements came from an analysis
of the image processing algorithms themselves, leading to define the main computing
features including (see fig 3) :

• operations (ALU, shift, Boolean, multiplication, ...),
• local autonomy (instruction, addressing and partly communication),
• communications (4-bit wide, synchronous and asynchronous, NEWS and X-
  net),
• global operations (OR reduction), ...

2.6   The MIMD Image-Processor

More flexible but less powerful, a **MIMD unit** using 16 T800 INMOS Transputers
[7] is in charge of intermediate-level or high-level image processing. In the future,
the T800 will be replaced by T9000, when available or equivalent processors. For
intermediate-level processing, each T800 can be boosted by a coprocessor (such as
a DSP or programmable logic [5]).

Although the name of this unit being "the MIMD unit", actually this unit must be
seen as a *coarse grain* unit as regard to the fine grained so-called SIMD unit : the
programming model used for the MIMD unit could be either data-parallelism (closer

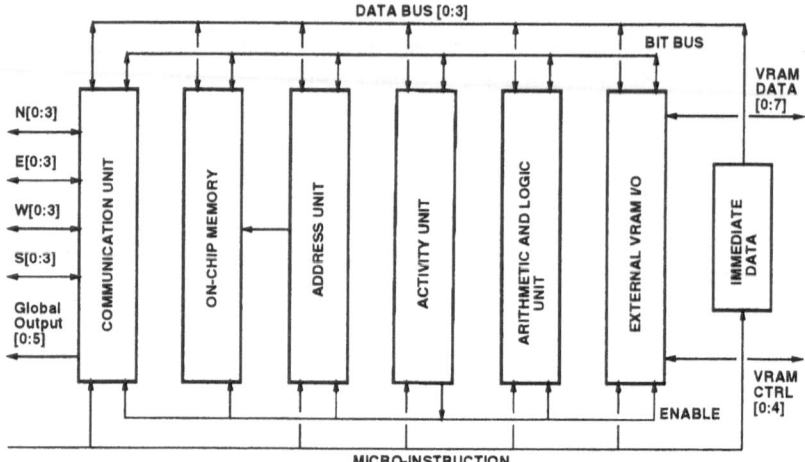

Figure 3 : SIMD PE Architecture

to SPMD[3] than MIMD) or task-parallelism. The idea behind this remarks about coarse grain comes from the implicit parallelism which can be found in image processing : as far as the "level" (see the taxonomy presented in 1.2.) of the processing algorithm increases, the amount of implicit parallelism decreases ; pixels being transformed into region attributes.

The MIMD unit is made of 16 Transputer cells connected to each other by their Transputer links and a serial cross-bar. These 16 cells are attached to the data-exchanger and to the control system. A Transputer cell is build around a T805, 32 Mbits of private fast DRAM, 8 Mbits of dual-ported VRAM (one port for the Transputer, the other one for data-exchange), a small dual-ported SRAM for the synchronisation with the control system, an interrupt controller and a small bus extension (to connect coprocessors using piggy-back boards).

The performance of the MIMD unit can be compared to that of a standard 16 Transputers based computer, but with a very small latency to start and stop processing tasks (the control is not made through links, but with dual-ported RAMS).

2.7 The Data re-Mapping Processor

The **re-mapping unit** is in charge of any regular image re-mapping (e.g. hierarchical versus cut-and-stack, mirroring, windowing, ...). This unit is based on hardwired address generators, shuffler controlled by programmable automatons and RAMs. It is interfaced to the local control node and the data-exchanger.

The corner turning of a standard 512 x 256 8-bits image requires between 0.4 ms and 2 ms depending on the complexity of the transformation.

Actually this unit being more parametrizable than programmable, it demonstrates the

---

[3] Single Program Multiple Data

ability to interface the P^3I machine with dedicated hardware instead of fully-programmable processors.

3 Software

As stated before, P^3I shows two levels of programming : (i) the application-level addressing all the heterogeneous *multi-machines* aspect of P^3I and based on a task-parallelism paradigm and (ii) the function-level which directly concerns the development of the various processing tasks on the various functional units of P^3I.

3.1 Application-Level

The two-levels programming model of P^3I (application and function-level) was not only designed for the programmer's convenience but it has a direct influence on the machine software architecture. Machine level software pilots the execution of local functions on P^3I's appropriate functional units and transfers data between these units, and therefore guarantees the correctness of application execution.

P^3I machine level software should have the following characteristics :

- a **highly effective utilization rate of every resource** of the machine (computing resources, data transfer resource). This means that these resources have to work simultaneously (macro-parallelism) as much as possible.
- a high level of flexibility in terms of **algorithmic control structures** (conditional branch, merge, inter-execution memorization, ...) in order to address the widest application class.

To reach both objectives, applications execution control on the P^3I machine relies on a dynamic data-flow strategy : a local function (task) can be activated when its inputs are all available i.e. when all local functions calculating these input data have completed execution. This fully dynamic strategy ensures that all local functions composing the application are calculated as soon as possible, whatever the local functions individual timings are.

P^3I applications consist in the repetitive execution of a given algorithm on an image input sequence. The ongoing execution may need previous results, thereby requiring data memorization between successive executions.

The internal programming language used for P^3I applications level is **SIGNAL**, an equational, data flow oriented language, built around a minimal kernel of basic constructs including data memorization (see [8] and Annex 2). The SIGNAL compiler checks the temporal consistency of the program and guarantees the absence of run-time deadlock. Then, based upon results of the SIGNAL compilation, the P^3I control compiler generates binary code for application scheduling. A P^3I **dedicated interactive graphical interface** is used to edit and debug the application, seen as an algorithmic graph of library functions (tasks) connected by data dependencies.

The system software architecture for the control processor of a given P³I functional unit is divided into 3 main components (see fig 4) :

- message services
- scheduling
- task execution (specific for each unit).

The message services process handles message routing between processes on the same unit or between different units. Client processes (scheduling and task execution) use the same communication ports for internal and external messages, having even no way to distinguish them.

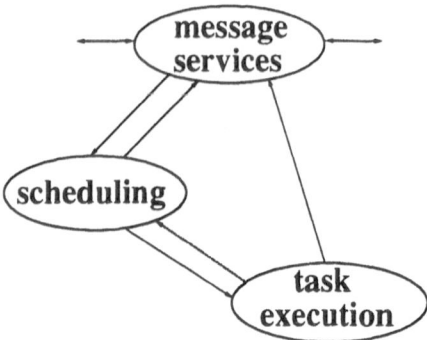

Figure 4 : System software architecture

The task execution process receives task execution commands from the scheduler, pilots execution of the required task on the functional unit (depending on the unit internal architecture), detects its completion and sends the "end of task" message to the schedulers of the appropriate units. The task execution process has no memory of the application internal state and can make no assumption about tasks execution ordering.

The scheduling process is the heart of the system. It manages the application internal state of its functional unit, i.e. the execution status of all tasks run on this unit and the value of all conditional events (clock signals) involved in the scheduling of these tasks. Roughly speaking, a task can be executed (activated) when :

- its predecessors have all completed execution for the current occurrence of the application (*tick*),
- its successors have all completed their execution for the previous *tick*.

The second condition does not result from data flow constraints, but from software pipe-line constraint. Software pipe-lining means simultaneous execution of several *ticks* on the machine, each unit interlacing execution of tasks belonging to different *ticks* ; it increases the effective utilization rate of the machine, hence, its performance.

3.2 Function-Level

The function-level programming follows a host-to-coprocessor model : each unit is scheduled by a main scalar processor called *"the local host"* (generally the local control system Transputer) in charge of *"calling"* parallel operations on the image processing part of the unit.

3.2.1 Programming the SIMD : LaPIN and P³C

Roughly speaking, the Scalar Unit (SU, refer to fig. 2) holds the code and micro code of single threaded tasks. From time to time, it receives commands from the top-level : *execute task XXX with the following arguments*. It executes them, then returns the results.

Executing a task can be divided into 3 parts :

• Compute the control-flow of the task

• Execute scalar instructions (hence the name Scalar Unit)

• Sends orders to the PE array through FIFOs, so that the PEs execute them.

So programming the SU is equivalent to program the whole SIMD unit : it includes all the ACU and PEs aspects. Programming the SU is done essentially by using one tool : P^3C (which stands for Pre Processor for C) which is today's compiler for LaPIN (LAnguage Parallele pour l'Image Numerique).

The objectives of P^3C/LaPIN are three-fold :

(1) Provide an interface between the SU and other units of P^3I,

(2) Provide basic common implementation and optimization tools,

(3) Implement some high level language constructs.

These 3 layers are roughly independent, and allow an easy and fast implementation of efficient tools on the SIMD unit. The key idea is that every language implemented on the SIMD should use level 1 and level 2 facilities ; a basic example of a higher level language is LaPIN itself. The sub-set of FORTRAN 90 compiler whose implementation is today under study (PhD [14]), addresses only the 2nd layer.

3.2.1.1 Level 1 : System Interface

The objective of this layer is to implement in an automatic and user-hidden way various interfaces between software running on the SU and other parts of the machine.

Roughly, this level involves the following items :

• **Automatic generation of system calls** : for instance, arguments and results passing from/to global sequencer is coded in the same way than normal function call, but actually involves system calls.

• **Automatic management of Micro-Code** : micro-code is the way Elementary Instructions (IE) that run on the PE are coded. IEs are called by the SU by issuing a system call. Micro-Code of IEs is written inside the LaPIN source using the /MACRO /ENDMACRO directive. Then P^3C extracts a micro-code file (xxx.ass), generates symbol tables, calls the assembler, edits links between micro-code and code, generates a single executable file.

• **Automatic generation of the top-level SIGNAL description of the process.**

3.2.1.2 Level 2: Intermediate Language

At this level, LaPIN is an intermediate language, which is designed more for automatic or painful hand-written generation than user-friendly coding.

This layer can be divided into 3 different tools :

(1) **RAM/VRAM management**. LaPIN handles transparently the VRAM/RAM memory hierarchy. The compiler generates memory swaps between VRAM

and RAM, and generates synchronisation signals between the ACU and the IOCU.

(2)   **Implementation of fundamental types.** At this level, no parallel data types are implemented. LaPIN has no understanding of what is an image or a matrix.

Nevertheless, parallel data-types must be described in terms of dynamic data structures held on the SU. They figure the format and properties of the parallel objects. The programmer communicates essential features of his class objects (such as memory use ...) by defining methods, which are (partially) evaluated at compile-time.

One must also code basic functions that handle its own defined parallel data types, such as arithmetics... (provided that these functions have a meaning for this data-type).

Overloading can be used to write several implementations of the same function for various data-types.

The programmer can extend compile-time error messages.

(3)   **Optimisation.** P^3C is able to do at this stage some local and global optimizations that do not require the interpretation of the semantic of the program. Placing theses optimizations in this layer allow their use whichever higher level language used later.

Supported optimizations include:

•   *Dynamic to static parameter passing between SU and ACU.* This minimizes the load of register write and betters register re-use.

•   *Constant propagation through function calls.*

•   *Dead-code elimination.*

•   *Micro-instruction concatenation.* This reduces the traffic between SU and ACU by grouping several instructions into one.

•   *Micro-instruction loop merging.* This allows to minimize the size of intermediate variables, reducing the amount of memory the task needs, and suppresses some loop instructions.

•   *Specialization of generic functions* to the actual type of their arguments.

3.2.1.3   Level 3 : Higher Level Language

The purpose of this level is to provide the user with a friendly and upgradable paradigm.

This layer relies on the implementation of data-types done using level-2 tools. The basic idea is that this level-2 layer can be completely hidden to the application programmer.

•   Simplified parallel data declarations and basic operations are provided by the implementation level.

•   Type, variable and function use can be checked.

•   A complete development environment is provided, including:
        → transparent library use
        → centralised compiler

      $\rightarrow$ simulation on workstation

      $\rightarrow$ runtime debug on P³I using dbg

      $\rightarrow$ emacs interface

- Polymorphic types can be used.
- Basic operators can be overloaded by procedures (user-friendly syntactic sugar).
- New operators can be defined (and implemented).
- Moreover, the language and compiler can be modified following users ideas
  ...

3.2.1.4 Example

Annex 1 shows an example of P³C and LaPIN.

3.2.2 Programming the MIMD Unit

Based on the T800 Transputer, the programming of P³I MIMD unit makes use of the common tool-set provided by INMOS for the development of Transputer applications, including OCCAM, C, ...
The link with the application level (SIGNAL) is based on tools developed by TCSF-LER to automatically generate the necessary information and encapsulation. Processing tasks are loaded dynamically and activated as requested by the scheduling. In the former ESPRIT project PADMAVATI [9], TCSF-LER had developed LELISP and Prolog interpreters as well as efficient message routing micro-kernels for the Transputer. These tools could be used on P³I MIMD.

3.2.3 Programming the Re-Mapping Unit

A comprehensive set of software has been developed to generate automatically the necessary parameters defining re-mapping function on the various automaton of this unit. This unix and X-Window based tool-set includes a mapping compiler and a simulator. The re-mapping functions are selected among a library and parametrized by various information including the size of the processed image, its format, ...

3.2.4 Programming the Real-Time Video IO Unit

Automatic time-base generators allow a complete flexibility in the definition of the various scanning standard used by P³I.

4   Where are we Now ?

A complete hardware mock-up and the basic system software are today operating. We are presently working on porting various video real-time applications on P³I, including image bit-rate reduction, target tracking and identification, special effects for TV studio, image synthesis, ...

In terms of basic performances, 2 major points have to be mentioned :

- A comparison has been made on real image applications on both the PE developed for P³I SIMD and the MasPar MP-1 PE (see [12]). The results show better performances of P³I PE as compared to MasPar's, for image applications.
- Concerning the use of SIGNAL for task parallelism, the development of complex applications (such as MPEG encoding or complex studio mixers), shows a real efficiency in terms of flexibility of application development and temporal dynamic load balancing.

Today's video real time demonstration applications include :

- MPEG 1 video encoding,
- Studio geometrical transform : zoom, rotation (2D and 3D),
- Complex studio key generation and mixing,
- Studio chroma key,
- 3D visualisation of surfaces,
- basic functions as edge extraction, 2D FFT, Distance Transform, 2D FIR, histogramming, Levialdi ...

The P³I SIMD node is able to perform some tens of giga pixel-operations per second. Table 1 shows execution time of a sample of well-known image processing functions performed on 512 * 256 images by the 4096 PEs P³I SIMD node. Tests made on those low-level image processing routines between the P³I SIMD network and a standard today workstation, show a performance ratio ranging from 500 to 2000 in favour of P³I. Figure 5 depicts the evolution of the performance ratio when the size of images are modified for some functions

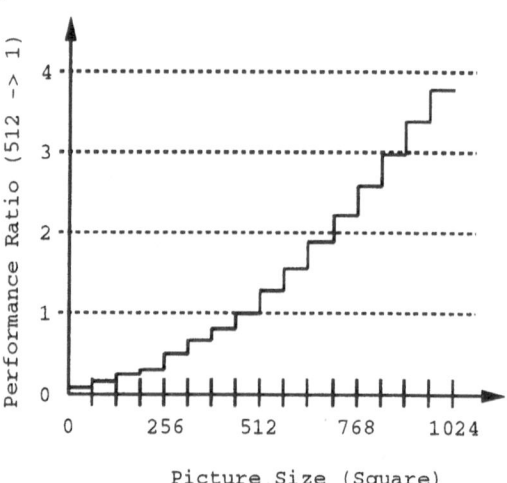

Picture Size (Square)

Figure 5 : Performance ratio

such as Nevatia's edge extraction or picture rotation. This figure is valid for square images and 512 sized images are taken as the unity reference (see [14] for more details).

We have presented how it is possible to take advantage of the specific features of low-level video real-time processing to build an efficient SIMD node for this kind of application. This architecture provides unchallenged performance and ease of use for a large range of applications, ranging from video-studio special effects to industrial vision. All the ideas beyond this paper have been implemented both in hardware and in software, and we would like to point out their simplicity and their cost-effectiveness.

Function	Execution time
Levialdi's shrinking (64 x 4 binary pixel-operations)	4.4 ms
2-D (5 x 5) general purpose FIR	580 µs
2-D averaging of a 5 x 5 window	740 µs
2-D variance on 5 x 5 window	1.8 ms
Temporal averaging ("true" multiplication and division)	370 µs
8-bits histogramming	200 µs
11 x 11 binary mask correlation	3.3 ms
25 x 25 binary mask correlation	14.5 ms
Nevatia-Babu edge detection (6 x (5 x 5) masks)	1 ms
Sobel's gradients edge detection	420 µs

Table 1 : Execution time of some processing functions (field size = 512 x 256)

5   Acknowledgments

This work was supported by the French Ministry Of Defense (SEFT, project P^3I) and the French Ministry of Industry (SERICS). The final realization of the P^3I machine, the implementation of its programming environment and the development of applications could not have been possible without the work of Marc Picart, François Roudier, Renaud Marigny, Yves Robin and Jean-François Lagardère.

References

[1]   Imaging Technology (1990) ITEX 150/151 programmers manual 47-515001-02, interpreters users manual 47-515103-01

[2]   S.Knight et al. (1988), *"The Princeton Engine : a real-time video system simulator"*, IEEE 0098 3063/88/0200 0285$01.00

[3]   N.Yagi et al. (1991), *"A programmable real-time video signal-processing system"*, SMPTE journal Nov. 91

[4]   G.Quénot and B.Zavidovique (1991), *"A data-flow processor for real-time low-level image processing"*, IEEE CICC, May 1991

[5]   P.Bertin et al. (1989), *"Introduction to programmable active memories"*, in *"Systolic array processors"*, p. 301-309, Prentice Hall

[6]   E.A.Lee et al. (1992), *"The Almagest, manual for Ptolemy version 0.3"*, University of California at Berkeley

[7]   INMOS (1989) The Transputer Databook

[8]   A.Benvéniste and G.Berry, *"The synchronous approach to reactive and real-time systems"*, IEEE vol 79 n°9 sept. 91.

[9]   F. Battini, P. Juré, *"ESPRIT Project P956 PADMAVATI final report"*, EEC internal report.

[10]   D.W. Blevins et al. (1989), *"BLITZEN : a highly integrated massively parallel machine"*, Journal of parallel and distributed computing, vol 8 - 1990.

[11]   V. Cantoni, S. Levialdi (1987), *"PAPIA : a case history"*, Parallel computer vision, academic press, 3-13.

[12]   J.R. Nickolls (1990), *"The design of the MasPar MP-1 : a cost effective massively parallel computer"*, Proceedings of COMPCON spring 90.

[13]   M.J. Colaïtis et al (1994), *"A Memory Management Scheme for Massively Parallel Video Real-Time Processing"*, Transputer 94, IOS Press, Amsterdam

[14]   Y.Robin (1994), *"Programmation et Compilation sur Architecture SIMD à Mémoire Distribuée dans un contexte de Traitement d'Images Temps-réel"* PhD thesis, Université de Rennes 1, Rennes (FRANCE).

Annex 1 : Programming example of the SIMD.

Here are the sources for a very simple program, that merely adds an inverted image to itself.

The sources "*invert.p3c*" and "*add.p3c*" listed here are library functions in the sense that they normally have to be developed once by experts and used by applications developers. The 1st include file "*image.h*" contains the definition of the main "*parallel*" objects used for this example, and the main methods (@*pixel()* and @*nibble()*) attached to these objects. The variables *NPEX* and *NPEY* define the array dimensions and can be evaluated at compile-time as well as at run-time for virtualization. The files "*invert.p3c*" and "*add.p3c*" concern library optimized routines ; each of them includes the LaPIN encapsulation of the routine and the assembly language source code.

Note   - The directive *implementation* which enables to overload the operator + by the method *add_im* for the corresponding objects.

            - The *USER_ERROR* system call allowing to handle error conditions at the library level.

The source "*demo.p3c*" is the core of the basic application implemented on P^{3}I SIMD.

file images.h

```
parallel  {
   int        address ;
   int        lines;
   int        columns;
   int        nibbles;
   @pixel() {
     return ((lines / NPEX)*
             (columns / NPEY));
   };
   @nibble() {
     return nibbles;
   };
} image ;

#define image_std(x,y,pel) \
   image(x IN (NPEX*4):(NPEX*8),\
         y IN (NPEY*2):(NPEY*8),\
         pel IN 1:6 )

#define image_cst \
   image ((NPEX*4):(NPEX*8),\
          (NPEY*2):(NPEY*8),\
           1:6 )
```

file invert.p3c

```
/MACRO ie_inversion
      (%R:source,  %R:result,
       %R:pixel, %R:nibble )()
       LOOP %R:pixel.
       LOOP %R:nibble.
       DJMP;
       MOVE (%R:source++) , %A;
       INITADD.
       NEGA (%R:result++).
       DJMP.
       CONT.
/ENDMACRO

public instruction inv
   (write image_cst Res,
    read   image_cst Im )
{
   ie_inversion(Im->address,
                Res->address,
                Res->pixel,
                Res->nibbles);
}
```

file add.p3c

```
/MACRO ie_add
  (%R:srce1, %R:srce2, %R:result,
   %R:pixel, %R:nibble )()
      LOOP %R:pixel.
      LOOP %R:nibble.
      DJMP;
      MOVE (%R:srce1++) , %A;
      MOVE (%R:srce2++) , %B;
      INITADD.
      ADDU (%R:result++).
      DJMP.
      CONT.
/ENDMACRO

public instruction add_im
   (write image_cst Res,
    read  image_cst Im1,
    read  image_cst Im2 )
{
 if (Im1->pixel != Im2->pixel)
   USER_ERROR(COMPILE_TIME,
           "Format of images");

 ie_add(Im1->address,
        Im2->address,
        Res->pixel,
        Res->nibble);
}
implementation(+,add_im);
```

file demo.p3c

```
#include <images.h>

public function demo
   (write image_cst Res,
    read image_cst Im )
{
  image_cst tmp;

  /* "procedural" call of inv */
  inv(tmp, Im);
  /* "operator" overload of + */
  Res = Im + tmp;
}
```

Annex 2 : SIGNAL programming example of P³I.

Here are the sources for a very simple program, that implements some basic functionalities of a 2 inputs video mixer, such as one used in a TV studio. Special effects are applied to the video streams (*image1..2*), depending on commands (*act_effect1..3*). The constant images *imcste1..2* are used as pixels and lines address within an image. The scanning parameters are : color images of size 512 x 256 at 50 Hz. The pragmas beginning by "->" are extensions to the original SIGNAL syntax, used for code generation and mapping for P³I. The first part of the example below shows the task parallelism : "(| *task1* | *task2* | ... | *taskn* |)" with data dependencies. The last part (section after "*where*") presents only the declaration of local variables ; local tasks with pointers to their respective executable files are not shown.

```
process EXAMPLE = ()
  { ? _image_ im_cste_effect2,im_cste_effect3
    ! }
  {-> init image : 1 -> imcste1.imp3i
   -> init image : 2 -> imcste2.imp3i
   -> init unit : IO_VIDEO -> (CODE_APPLI,Clr_512x256E_2i_init.bin)}

  (| {image1, image2} := IOV_IN {}              % Capture of 2 images %
                                                % Selection of effects %
   | {act_effect1, act_effect2, act_effect3} := EFFECT_SELECTION { }
                                                % Execution of effects %
   | i_effect1 := EFFECT1 {image1 when act_effect1,
                           image2 when act_effect1}

   | i_effect2 := EFFECT2 {image1 when act_effect2,
                           image2 when act_effect2,
                           im_cste_effect2}

   | i_effect3 := EFFECT3 {image1 when act_effect3,
                           image2 when act_effect3,
                           im_cste_effect3}
                              % Return one image selected from :
                       - active effects according to priority 1, 2, 3
                       - or initial capture if no effect is active %
   | IOV_OUT {i_effect1 default i_effect2 default i_effect3
                       default image1}
  |)

  where
    logical act_effect1, act_effect2, act_effect3;
    _image_ image1, image2;
    _image_ i_effect1, i_effect2, i_effect3

    function      % etc .... N o t   s h o w n   h e r e  .... %
                  % ........................................... %

end
```

Session 2: Analysis 1 – Tracking

Global Motion Estimation for Registering Real and Synthetic Images

G.A. Thomas
BBC Research & Development Department
Tadworth, Surrey, UK

Abstract

In order to allow image compositing using images from a moving camera, it is necessary to estimate the camera motion so that the effect of the motion on the inserted picture material may be modelled. In many situations, limiting allowable camera motion to pan, tilt and zoom is acceptable. This paper presents a method of deriving these parameters by global motion estimation from the camera image. A suitable motion estimation technique is identified and its development is described. A primary requirement of the technique is that it should be capable of real-time implementation on a DSP.

1 Introduction

Matteing and chroma-key are well-known techniques in frequent use in television production for combining real camera images with other images. When they are used, it is generally necessary to ensure that the camera remains stationary in order for the inserted picture material to remain in the correct position with respect to the foreground picture material. This places significant constraints on the use of these techniques. For example, it is not generally possible to have even a small degree of camera motion to follow the movements of the head of a presenter, since any picture material inserted electronically (such as a weather map, other graphic, or background scene) would not appear to move.

It is possible to attach mechanical sensors to the camera to measure parameters such as pan, tilt and zoom. These measurements can then be used to drive either a slave camera, a digital video effects unit (DVE), or a graphics computer generating a 3D background, to generate an image that moves in sympathy with the camera motion [1]. However, this solution is not always practical for several reasons. Operational constraints may make the use of such sensors inconvenient. Sensors cannot measure motion from causes such as an unsteady camera mounting, or from unsteadiness in film. They are also inapplicable if a scene is shot without the use of sensors but in post-production a decision is made to use a matte (for example, to conceal unwanted material in the scene). Careful calibration of the camera optics is required to relate measurements of pan and tilt (in units of degrees) and zoom (possibly in units of focal length) to the actual displacement of the image (in units of pixels and lines, and a scaling factor).

To allow matteing and keying to be used in the presence of camera motion in situations where mechanical sensors are inappropriate, a motion estimation algorithm is needed that can measure global image motion to a high degree of accuracy. This paper describes the development of such an algorithm, tailored to this application. If the algorithm is used in conjunction with a keying unit and a blue background, the background cannot be a uniform shade of blue, but must contain enough information to allow reliable motion estimation to be carried out. In such circumstances, the key signal can be used to indicate the areas of the image which correspond to background, so that the estimation process can ignore foreground areas. In applications where a blue background is not used, it is necessary to use other means to disregard areas having motion different from that to be tracked.

2 Motion Estimation Algorithm

2.1 Requirements

In the general case, movement of the background in a scene will be caused by the camera panning, tilting, zooming, rotating about the optic axis and translating in three dimensions. Therefore, seven parameters need to be measured to allow image material to be moved to match all possible camera movements.

However, in many situations, movement of the image background is due solely to panning, tilting and zooming of a fixed camera, causing horizontal and vertical translation and change of scale in the image. Measurements of these three global image motion parameters are therefore sufficient to allow a keyed-in image to be moved appropriately.

There are two effects that prevent these camera motions from appearing exactly as translations and a change of scale in the image, although generally the deviations are small and can be ignored. Firstly, imperfections in the camera optics can cause geometrical distortion of the image. Secondly, the image becomes stretched slightly at the edges, because the distance from the sensor to the lens is greater at the edges than at the centre. Both these effects are only likely to become significant when using wide-angle lenses. Neither effect should be confused with perspective (or 'keystoning'), which changes the size of objects as a function of their distance from the camera, but not as a function of camera angle or zoom; perspective effects do not interfere with the motion estimation operation.

There are considerable advantages to be gained by limiting the scope of the method to the determination of pan, tilt and zoom. Firstly, any method that uses image analysis to measure both camera translation and rotation will generally require that material having a wide range of distances from the camera is visible at all times, so that motions such as panning and horizontal translation may be distinguished reliably. This is likely to be difficult to arrange in many operational situations. Secondly, the computational processes involved in the calculation of general camera movement are complex and time-consuming, involving for example the solution of non-linear simultaneous equations. Since it is desirable for the selected algorithm to be capable of real-time implementation using hardware based on general-purpose computer equipment, complex calculations should be avoided.

To allow the translation and scale change of the image to be measured, there must be sufficient detail present in the background. In many applications, the background may be a blue screen, to allow a key signal to be generated by analysing the *RGB* values of the video signal. Clearly, a plain blue screen cannot be used if camera motion information is to be derived from the image, since it contains no detail. Thus it is necessary to use a background that contains markings of some sort, but is still of a suitable form to allow a key signal to be generated. The key signal provides a convenient means for removing foreground objects from the image before the motion estimation process, so that the motion of foreground objects will not confuse the calculation.

2.2 Existing Methods for Measuring Translation and Scale Change

Several methods are known for measuring translation and scale change in an image. Approaches based on techniques such as block matching [2] provide a means of measuring global translation. Change of scale may be determined by further analysis of vectors measured at many locations within the image. An alternative approach, described in [3], is to measure translation and scale change simultaneously using a technique based on differentials. Reference [4] shows how such an approach may be extended to include measurement of rotation about the image centre; however the measurement of rotation is unlikely to be relevant for a studio camera as most camera mounts prohibit such movement.

An approach that allows translation and scale change to be measured simultaneously was attractive, so the algorithm described in [3] was studied and developed further to match the needs of the application described here. This algorithm measures the translation and scale change by computing the spatial and temporal luminance gradients at many points in successive images. A set of over-determined linear simultaneous equations is formed (one equation per point) relating the measured gradients to the motion parameters. The least-squares solution of these equations is then calculated, giving estimates of the motion parameters. A more detailed description of the algorithm is given below.

The first stage of the algorithm is to apply a two-dimensional spatial low-pass filter to the image signal. This is necessary to ensure correct functioning of the algorithm, because of the assumptions made about smoothly-varying luminance that are inherent in the method of differentials.

A large number of equations are then derived, forming an over-determined set of linear simultaneous equations that may be solved to yield values for zoom and displacement that minimise the squared error summed over all the equations.

Each equation relates the spatial luminance gradients at a point (x, y) in the image to the temporal gradient (frame difference), using the translation x_t, y_t and scale factor m. The equations have the form

$$g_t = g_x x_t + g_y y_t + (m - 1) . (g_x x + g_y y)$$ [1]

where g_x, g_y, g_t are the horizontal, vertical and temporal luminance gradients,
x_t, y_t, m are the horizontal and vertical translation and scale change,
x, y are the coordinates of the pixel in the current image.

Without reproducing the full derivation here, it is easy to show that this equation has the correct form. The luminance difference caused by horizontal motion is clearly given by the product of the horizontal luminance gradient and the horizontal displacement. Similarly, the product of the vertical luminance gradient and the vertical displacement will give the contribution to the inter-frame luminance difference caused by vertical motion. These two contributions correspond to the first two terms in the equation [1] above.

To find the contribution to the luminance difference caused by the scale change, the effect of the horizontal and vertical translations caused by the scale change can be considered separately. The horizontal translation, caused by a scale change of a factor m, at points with a horizontal coordinate x is simply $(m - 1) x$, where the centre of expansion is $x = 0$. For example, if there is a scale change of a factor of two $(m = 2)$, then a point that was four pixels away from the centre of expansion $(x = 4)$ will now be eight pixels away, a move of four pixels. The contribution to the inter-frame difference signal caused by this horizontal displacement is the product of the displacement and the horizontal luminance gradient, which is therefore $(m - 1) x g_x$; this is the third term in equation [1]. Similarly, the contribution from the vertical component of the scale change is $(m - 1) y g_y$, the last term in the equation.

References [3] and [4] show that some account may be taken of second order terms in the Taylor expansion of the image by taking g_x and g_y to be the average of the gradients measured in the preceding and current images, rather than simply the gradients in the current image. This approach for considering second order terms was originally proposed in [5]. The gradients may be measured by calculating the difference between the luminance signal at pixels immediately to the left and right of the pixel in question; this method is commonly used in gradient-based motion estimation algorithms.

2.3 Development of the Chosen Method

To adapt the method of [3] for the application described here, several changes were made. The object of these was to reduce the computational requirement of the method and to prevent any significant accumulation of motion estimation error.

To reduce the amount of computation, the number of simultaneous equations generated was limited to those from a subset of pixels. A further reduction in computation was achieved by replacing the iterative estimation strategy proposed in both [3] and [4] with the use of a single iteration for each measurement, starting with a prediction of the motion based on preceding measurements.

The algorithm was then modified to measure image motion relative to a given reference image, rather than between consecutive images. This technique was adopted instead of one based on performing measurements between consecutive images so that motion estimation errors would not accumulate. Initially, the reference image is that viewed by the camera when it is placed in a known orientation. Only when the degree of overlap between the present image and the stored reference image becomes small is the present image adopted as the new reference for future measurements. Discarded reference images may remain in memory (subject to memory size) to be re-used if the camera returns later to a previous orientation. This helps to reduce further the accumulation of estimation error that could occur each time a new reference image is adopted.

Figure 1 shows a block diagram of the camera motion estimation system, as it would be used with a blue background. A single-component signal is formed which allows the variations in the blue background to be seen. This signal is then low-pass filtered. A key signal is generated to allow the foreground objects (whose motion will not necessarily correspond to that of the background) to be blanked out. The stored reference image is transformed by predicted values of translation and zoom before measuring the translation and scale change between it and the incoming image. If the prediction is perfect, no motion will be seen; however any acceleration in the camera motion or errors in previous measurements will cause an apparent net motion.

In applications where a blue background is not being used, the key generator is not required and another method must be used to distinguish between foreground and background motion. A possible approach has been proposed [3], based on the formation of a histogram of separate motion estimates for a number of blocks in the picture, to identify the dominant motion.

3 Testing the Algorithm

The algorithm described above was tested both on synthetic and real images. Figure 2 shows the measured displacement for a sequence containing artificial movement, corresponding to a camera pan to the right at a speed of 1.5 pixels per frame, followed by a pan back to the left, returning to the starting position. The improved accuracy obtained when using the first image in the sequence as the reference image, compared with making all measurements between adjacent frames, is clearly visible. Indeed, the line corresponding to measurements made with respect to the first image in the sequence lies almost on top of the line showing the true movement.

The accuracy of the motion estimates for real sequences (whose true motion was unknown) was tested by superimposing an image of a grid on the sequence, moved according to the estimated camera parameters. This test revealed the effects of lens distortion in the camera, referred to earlier. While the grid stayed firmly locked to the image in the central part of the picture, small deviations were apparent near the edges. The fact that the motion estimates were accurate for the central area suggests that the distortion around the edges tended to cancel during the motion estimation process. Had the image of the grid been pre-distorted to match the distortion of the camera lens, it seems likely that it would have appeared rigidly locked across the whole frame.

In order to test the algorithm with a blue background, a cloth was constructed consisting of a checkered arrangement of squares of two slightly different shades of blue. Experiments were conducted to establish whether the blue shades chosen differed to a sufficient extent for reliable motion estimation to be performed. It was found that sufficiently accurate measurements could be made by simply using the luminance signal as the input to the motion estimation process, despite a luminance difference of only 10 grey levels between the two shades.

It was also verified that a simple key generator worked satisfactorily when the checkered background was used. However, since the two blue shades used differed in luminance level, it did not prove possible to reproduce shadows cast by actors on the blue background without the appearance of the checkerboard pattern. Should such shadows be required, alternative blue shades or the use of a better keying unit may rectify the problem.

Some short test sequences were shot showing actors and objects in front of the blue background and it was verified that accurate camera motion parameters could be determined, using the key signal to mask out the foreground. A still image was translated and zoomed according to the measurements and the resulting image sequence was keyed into the original test sequence. This resulted in a sequence showing actors in the foreground and an electronically-generated background that maintained its correct position in relation to the actors as the camera panned, tilted and zoomed.

4 Processing Power Requirements

The software developed was benchmarked to determine the processing power required for real time implementation. The main parameter of the algorithm that controls the tradeoff between accuracy and processing power is the number of image points (and therefore equations) used. It was found that accurate measurements could be made on a range of picture material (including the blue checkered cloth) with as few as 900 measurement points, arranged as a rectangular grid of 30x30 points. Tests showed that a workstation based on an R3000 processor could perform this computation at a rate of up to 50 images per second (excluding any overheads for image capture). Low-pass filtering of the signal before measurement is best implemented in dedicated hardware, and was not included in the benchmarking. The horizontal component of the filter can conveniently be implemented using analogue circuitry before the image signal is digitised.

5 Conclusion

In order to allow matteing and keying in the presence of camera motion, a motion estimation algorithm has been developed to measure global image motion to a high degree of accuracy. This approach provides an alternative to the use of mechanical sensors on the camera mounting; such sensors can be inconvenient to use and are inapplicable in many post-production situations. The algorithm requires no user interaction and will work with most normal picture material; it does not require the presence of designated marker points in the scene. For situations where the camera image consists largely of a blue background, it is necessary to use a form of background that contains sufficient variation to allow the motion estimation process to operate. The camera motion estimation algorithm has been designed so that it requires no more processing power than that available on a typical modern workstation, although specialised hardware may be needed to provide real-time image acquisition.

Acknowledgements

The author would like to thank the BBC for permission to publish this paper. This work has been supported by RACE project R2052 'MONA LISA'. This paper is based upon [7], published by the IEE.

References

1. Enami, K. 1993. Desk Top Program Production (DTTP) - A Scenario of Studio Digitalization. 18th International Television Symposium, Montreux, June 1993.

82

2. Uomori, K., Morimura, A., Ishii, H. 1992. Electronic image stabilisation system for video cameras and VCRs. *SMPTE Journal*, Vol. 101 No. 2, pp. 66-75, Feb. 1992.

3. Hoetter, M. 1989. Differential estimation of the global motion parameters zoom and pan. Signal Processing, Vol. 16, No. 3, March 1989, pp. 249-265.

4. Wu, S.F., Kittel, J. 1990. A differential method for simultaneous estimation of rotation, change of scale and translation. Signal Processing : Image Communication 2, Elsevier, 1990, pp. 69-80.

5. Bierling, M. 1985. A differential displacement estimation algorithm with improved stability. 2nd International Technical Symposium on optical and electro-optical applied science and engineering, Cannes, December 1985.

6. Weston, M. 1988. Fixed, adaptive and motion-compensated interpolation of interlaced TV pictures. 2nd International Workshop on Signal Processing for HDTV (L'Aquila, Italy), 29 Feb. - 2 March 1988.

7. Thomas, G.A. 1994. Motion-compensated matteing. IBC'94 (Amsterdam, The Netherlands), IEE Conference Publication No. 397, pp. 651-655, September 1994.

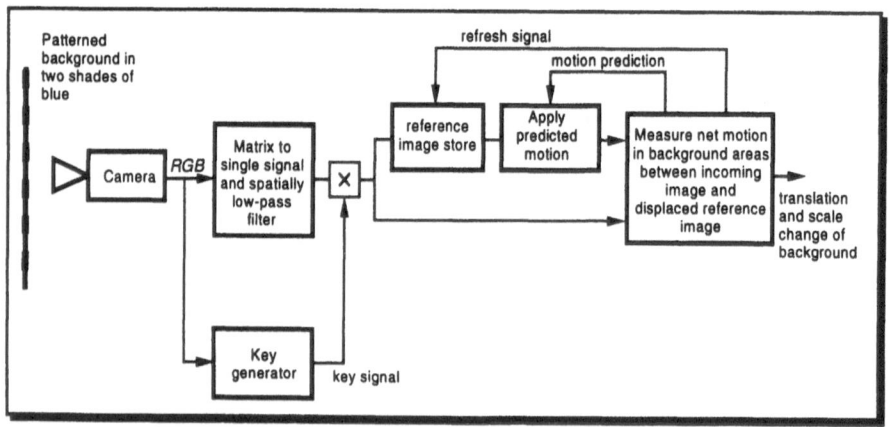

Figure 1. Block diagram of camera motion estimation system

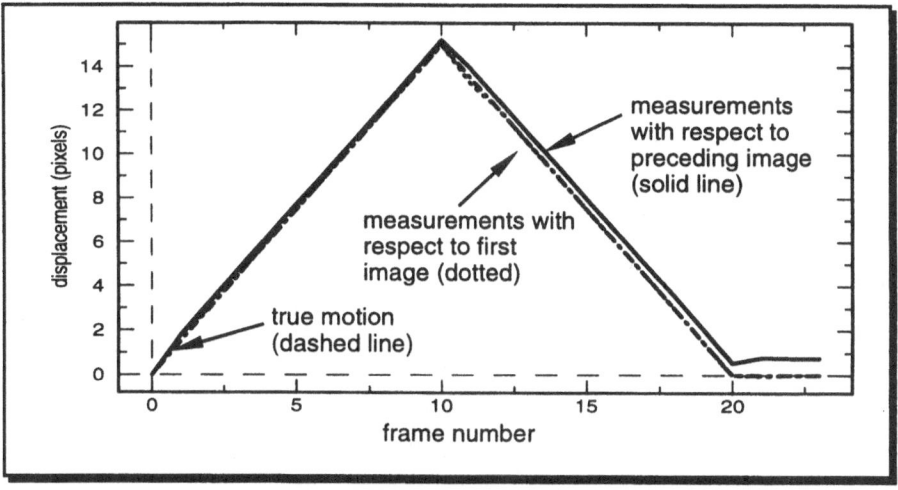

Figure 2. A comparison of measurements made with and without a fixed reference image

Real-Time Camera Tracking Server on the ELSET Accelerator

D Routsis, P Le Floch, A V Sahiner

Dept. of Computer Science, Queen Mary and Westfield College, Univ. of London

G Thomas

BBC, London

1. Introduction

A Camera Tracking subsystem plays an important role in any system that attempts to use synthetic images in video and TV production. In the ELSET™ demonstrator for the RACE 2052 MONA LISA project [1] such a subsystem drives a virtual camera to generate a synthesized 3-D background that moves in sympathy with the motion of the real camera.

The camera tracking subsystem estimates the camera parameters (pan, tilt, and zoom) by image analysis using the sequence of images from the camera. These parameters are then fed to a graphics process that generates the synthetic background from the correct viewpoint in real-time. This is then mixed with the real foreground, giving the final result of real actors and props with an artificial background or even foreground objects.

The frame-grabbing [2], camera tracking and mixing are done on a specially built hardware accelerator called the ELSET-A [3]. The rendering is done on a graphics workstation.

This paper describes the implementation of real-time camera tracking on the multiprocessor hardware accelerator that is part of the ELSET™ demonstrator.

2. System Architecture

The camera tracking subsystem has been implemented as a real-time server on the ELSET accelerator. The accelerator consists of an intelligent frame buffer, a mixing unit and a pool of high performance processors.

A Motorola 68040 processor based controller manages all the activities of the frame buffer system. It is equiped with RS232, Ethernet and SCSI interfaces to connect the ELSET-A to host computers and networks. It also acts as a host for the processor pool boards.

The processor pool consists of four Motorola DSP96002-based VMEBus processor boards. Each processor board has two DSP processors (operating at 40 MHz with a peak performance of 60 MFlops) and two DbeX (peripheral expansion bus) interfaces which are used for data transfers in and out of the frame buffer.

2.1. Pool Processors

The DSP96002 is a powerful floating point digital signal processor operating at 40 Mhz clock [5]. At peak, it can carry out 20 million instructions per second (MIPS) or 60 million floating point operations (MFlops) per second. It has a highly parallel instruction set, allowing up to two floating point operations plus two data transfers plus an instruction fetch in a single instruction cycle. It also has two identical independent external memory expansion ports, allowing two data transfers in parallel in the same instruction cycle. Other features include nested hardware DO loops, pipelining by overlapping the fetch, decode and execute cycles of instructions.

The DBV96 boards[4] have two on-board DSP96002 processors each operating at 40 MHz. A simple block diagram of the board can be seen in figure 1.

The two DSP96002 have one of their buses (the A-bus) connected. This shared bus is called the global bus. The two processors share on the global bus 256 KWords of 32-bit static RAM (SRAM) and 4 MWords of 32-bit dynamic RAM (DRAM). The B-bus of each DSP96002 are connected to local banks of 256 KWords of 32-bit SRAM and a 256 Kbyte bootstrap EPROM.

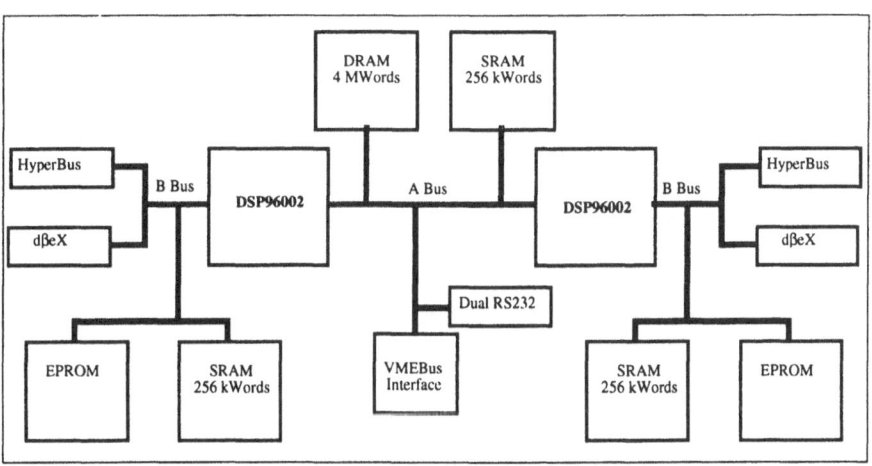

Figure 1. The DBV96 Board

In terms of memory management DSP96002 supports a flexible memory mapping scheme where the physical memory can be mapped on 3 different logical memory spaces: program memory, X data memory, Y data memory and L data memory. These are 32 bits wide and all can be accessed independently from each other. The X and Y data memories may also be referenced together as a single 64 bits wide memory space (the L data space).

In our implementation the A-bus is assigned to Y memory and the B-bus is assigned to both X and P memory spaces. This mapping has allowed the utilisation of a section of local (0 wait-state) SRAM banks as program memory. The remaining section coupled with the global SRAM bank is used for kernel data area and stack space, and the global DRAM is shared by the two DSPs for application data memory.

2.2. System Software

The ELSET software consists of a collection of system and application software modules which are supported by three separate operating environments [6]. These are:

1) Unix, running on the host graphics workstation.
2) OS-9, running on the 68040 frame buffer control processor.
3) W-Kernel, running on the processor pool.

Unix, as a universally used operating environment, provides a convenient front end to the ELSET system, bringing in the benefits of open systems. The user interface to the ELSET system runs on the Unix workstation and is OSF/Motif based. There is no separate interface for the ELSET-A accelerator, all its functionalities are accessed via the workstation.

OS-9 is a real-time multitasking operating system running on the 68040 frame buffer control processor. It serves as system administrator, supervisor and resource manager on the VME-bus system which is the backbone of the ELSET-A accelerator. It provides the host environment for the utilisation of the intelligent frame buffer, the processor pool and the mixing subsystem. OS-9 has TCP/IP and NFS interfaces with Unix.

W-Kernel is a light-weight operating system kernel that runs on each processor in the processor pool. It supports parallel servers and an object-oriented access to the frame buffer. It provides process creation and management functionalities for parallel server execution on the processor pool. It also incorporates a communications layer for the DBV96 to OS-9 communications, and supports a library for programming parallel servers on the processor pool. Communication between OS-9 and W-Kernel is via the VME bus and the Host Interface (HI) of the DSPs.

2.3 Camera Tracking Server

The utilization of the processor pool as an accelerator is based on the SAPS (Self-Adapting Parallel Servers) model for parallelism [7]. This model allows computationally heavy procedures to be accelerated by configuring and running them as parallel servers For the implementation of the camera tracking system, however, due to the real-time requirements, the capabilities of the server built are coupled with real-time video management capabilities specific to this application. The organisation of the camera tracking software is shown in Figure 2. The camera tracking server consists of two components: the manager and the worker. Since the performance analysis done prior to the implementation has shown that real-time performance can be achieved on a single processor, the server has been implemented as a single-worker server.

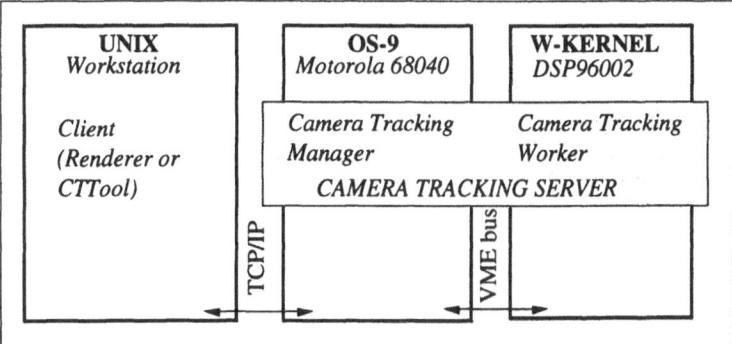

Figure 2. Camera tracking server

The application proper (the actual camera tracking algorithm) is executed by the worker running on one of the pool processors. The access to the incoming frame sequence by the worker is programmed using data object capabilities of servers which have been built as part of the SAPS model implementation. The worker communicates with the camera tracking manager running on the 68040 control processor under OS-9. The manager carries out the following administrative jobs:

a] Starting and stopping the worker
b] Fetching the estimated camera parameters from the worker and passing them to the client
c] Initialising the frame grabbing activity
d] Initialising the frame buffer I/O processor for data distibution to the worker
e] Synchronising the worker activities with the availability of the frames. For this purpose, the I/O processor that connects the DSP board to the frame buffer is programmed to automatically signal the manager whenever a new frame from the camera input is available.

Communication between the client and the manager (Unix and OS-9) takes place via TCP/IP sockets. Communication between the manager and the worker (OS-9 and W-Kernel) is via two mechanisms: either the VME bus (the DSP shared memory and the on-board interprocessor communication registers are both mapped on the VME address space) or the Host Interface (HI) of the DSPs.

3. Camera Tracking Application

The application program that is executed by the camera tracking worker has originally been developed by BBC (coded in C language) and it has been tested in a number of simulations [8]. This program measures the image motion relative to the first image in a sequence. Running it on the DSP processors in real-time (25 frames/sec) has required the analysis and optimisation of the code.

The program is based on an algorithm that measures the translation and scale change between two consecutive images in a sequence by computing the spatial and temporal luminance gradients at many points arranged on a rectangular grid (will be referred to as the lattice in the rest of the paper) [9,10]. A set of over-determined linear simultaneous equations is formed (one equation per point) relating the measured gradients to the motion parameters. The least-squares solution of these equations is then calculated, giving estimates of the motion parameters for pan, tilt and zoom. The size of the lattice is critical both in terms of the camera tracking functionality and the computational time required.

The algorithm uses a fixed reference image for the measurements and can update this image when the camera moves to a significant extent. The data consists of 360x288 resolution images which are obtained from the normal 720x576 PAL resolution by using only one of the two fields and subsampling horizontally at a1:2 ratio. Only the luminance signal is used.

3.1. Optimization

As a first step the C code which had been used in simulations was compiled to run on a DSP with the Intermetrics' Intertools 96002 C compiler [11]. The benchmarks showed that optimization was required for real-time performance. To achieve this we first have analysed the algorithm using the performance analysis tool kit, Case Vision, running on a SGI Indy. The results are shown in figure 3.

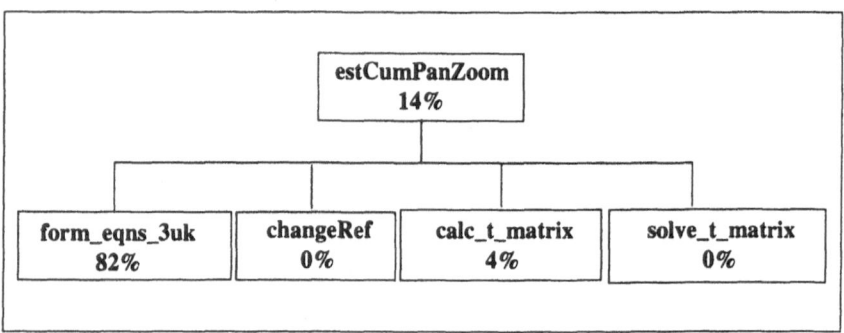

Figure 3. Performance analysis results

As can be seen, the software spends practically all its time in three routines. form_eqns_3uk() forms the set of simultaneous equations by computing the luminance gradients. calc_t_matrix() multiplies the matrix holding the coefficients of the equations by its transpose in order to obtain a normalised equation matrix. estCumPanZoom() is the main routine.

It was decided to hand-optimise the form_eqns_3uk() and calc_t_matrix() routines using assembly language. We decided not to optimize estCumPanZoom() because, firstly, it includes no time-critical code (e.g. loops) and, secondly, as the main routine, it was quite probable that modifications and improvements would need to be made to it, something much easier to do in C than in highly-optimized assembly code.

The two routines were therefore optimized using a combination of techniques. The first group of techniques have involved taking advantage of the advanced features of the DSP96002 chip. These can be listed as:

    a]   Hardware DO loops.

b] Using modulo-addressing. This effectively confines a pointer in an area of memory, so that it automatically 'wraps around', avoiding costly code to do the same explicitly.

c] Using fast inline code instead of a function call for divisions. (A division can be done in only 7 machine instructions.)

d] Using pipelined parallel DSP instructions (e.g. multiplication and addition within the same instruction). Such instructions are especially useful for matrix multiplication, as in `calc_t_matrix()`. In fact, the inner loop of the matrix multiplication consists of only two machine instructions.

e] Replacing C math functions such as `floor()` by single machine instructions. (We had found that a lot of time was spent on function call overheads.)

f] optimising `if` statements like the following:

```
if (current[offset]    > KEY &&
current[offset+1] > KEY &&
current[offset-1] > KEY &&
current[offset+xdim] > KEY &&
current[offset-xdim] > KEY )
```

Two specific features of the DSP96002 were particularly useful in optimising such statements. Firstly, the automatic register updates are faster than indexed addressing. In fact, a post-increment by 1 or N costs no additional clock cycles, while an indexed access costs two additional clock cycles. Therefore, post-increment and -decrement instructions were used in conjunction with parallel moves to update the pointer at no additional cost. Second, the special 'sticky' LR flag in the Status Register (SR) was used for the comparisons. This has the particular property that it is cleared for a non-negative result, but, unlike the usual CPU flags, once cleared it stays cleared regardless of the results of any following instructions. This means that all comparisons can be done one after the other, and the result tested only once at the end. This allows us to use only one conditional jump instruction right at the end, instead of 5 that would normally be needed. (Jump instructions have a high overhead, especially on a pipelined architecture such as on the DSP96002.)

As a result of the optimisation the statement listed above was brought from 41 down to 8 machine instructions, while another one was brought down from 93 to 14.

The second family of techniques involved more 'traditional' methods of optimization, such as:

a] Moving constant calculations outside loops.

b] Rewriting calculations to reduce the number of instructions. For example, the calculation of variable x:

```
x = ((float)i + 0.5) / nx * xlen + xpos;
```

can instead be rewritten in recursive form as:

```
x(i+1) = x(i) + xlen / nx
```

with $x(0) = 0.5 * xlen / nx + xpos$
$xlen/nx$ is calculated only once and held as a local variable, so updating x can be done using only one addition each time through the loop instead of two additions, a multiplication and a division, as in the original calculation. It must be noted that, not all instruction removals are for good, though. A similar attempt for simplification was made for the x_d and y_d variables. The resulting code, however, was actually slower than the original. This was finally traced to the fact that additional temporary variables were needed, which in turn meant doing more memory accesses. Memory accesses are slow, so the resulting code, despite containing less instructions, was slower.

Finally, the code was written to maximise the use of parallel instructions and register variables. Memory accesses are especially costly, as most of the data is in the DRAM which has wait states, so they must be avoided if at all possible. This meant in several cases re-arranging the order of calculations to take advantage of values that have already been loaded from memory in registers, and using as many register variables as possible. There are currently no registers that could be used for storage of data (including offset registers and even, in one case, a modifier register) that remain unused.

4. Benchmarks and Tests

A number of experiments have been carried out to evaluate the optimisation results. In an early experiment we have used computer generated test data to compare the timings obtained using the original C code and the optimized assembler code. Figure 4 shows the respective curve plots for time vs the number of analysed frames. The size of the lattice used in this experiment was 30x30 which is assumed to be minimum for acceptable results.

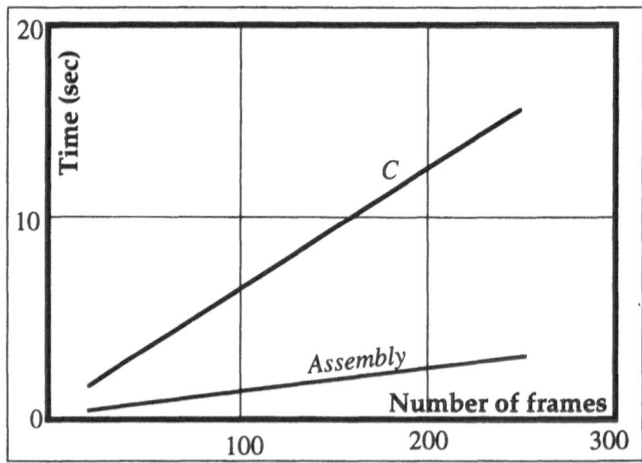

Figure 4. Optimisation Benchmark

It has been observed that the overall speed-up by optimisation was from 61.1 msec/frame to 10.6 msec/frame, which is approximately 5.8 times. The breakdown was as follows: for the `calc_t_matrix()` routine a x2.7 speed increase and for the `form_eqns_3uk()` routine a x6.4 speed increase. The reason the improvement for the `calc_t_matrix()` routine was significantly smaller is that, firstly, calculations in it are straightforward and only arithmetical, so the code produced by the compiler was already fairly good and, secondly, that it was inherently memory-bound so the memory accesses time were accountable for a large proportion of the elapsed time.

4.1. Frame Buffer Usage

As the next step in benchmarking we have used a 200 frame sequence shot by the BBC. The sequence was stored in the frame buffer and the camera tracking worker was programmed to access the individual frames one by one for analysis. Only one field from every PAL resolution frame was required to carry out the task. During the processing, each frame was copied into the DSP memory as an array of integers, 32-bit word per pixel. Loading the frame as an array of floating point numbers would have simplified the camera tracking software as it uses floating point arithmetic, but this method was much slower and the overhead would have been more than the benefit from avoiding conversions from integers to floating point numbers in the camera tracking module itself. The chosen method gives a total time of 19.7 msec for loading each 360x288 frame. After this, we have benchmarked the whole process (loading a frame, then performing camera tracking on it). The results are shown in figure 5.

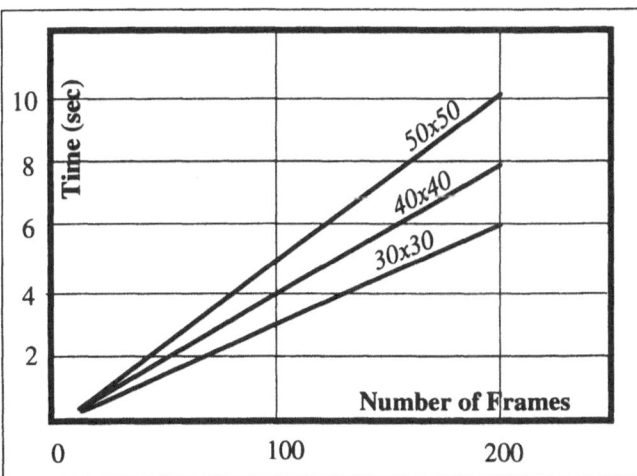

Figure 5. Benchmarks with BBC test sequnce

For a 30x30 lattice, the whole process takes 30.3 msec/frame, which is well within the limits for real-time processing (40 msec/frame). For a 40x40 lattice, the total

time is 39.2 msec/frame, which is again within the limits of real-time. Finally, a 50x50 lattice gives 50.3 msec/image, failing to satisfy the real-time requirement.
These results have shown that the camera tracking software can perform in real-time using a lattice of points of up to about 40x40 size.

4.2. Testing with Studio Equipment

After the initial benchmarks with sample image sequences proved to be satisfying, the whole system was tested with a real camera. The test setup consisted of a broadcast quality camera mounted on a tripod, a camera control unit, an analog low-pass filter with a cutoff frequency of 1.6 MHz and a TV analog to digital converter connected to the frame buffer. The low-pass filter is used for noise reduction purposes. Frames were stored in a 3-frame circular buffer in the intelligent frame buffer. A monitor connected to the frame buffer via a TV digital to analog converter provided feedback on the camera output.
The camera tracking process ran on ELSET-A and provided the camera pan, tilt, and zoom estimations to the server running under OS-9. A terminal connected to OS-9 provided a continuous display of these parameters.
As a test background, a cloth was used consisting of a chequered arrangement of 40x40 cm squares of different shades of blue. Storing multiple images was tested by making enough memory available for the storage of 20 images (1 current + 19 reference images).
The results were very encouraging and certainly demonstrated the system's capability of real-time performance. The camera panned, tilted and zoomed and the parameters listed on the monitor followed with no noticeable delay. We were able to pan, tilt and zoom freely starting from an initial position; and the estimates we obtained when we had moved the camera back to that initial position showed that the acculmulation of error was negligable.

5. The CTTool

The Camera Tracking Tool (CTTool) is a OSF/Motif based user interface developed on the host graphics workstation. It is implemented as a client of the camera tracking server and it is initially used as a testing tool. It gives visual feedback on the measured camera parameters and allows calibration of the camera tracking software. A screen dump is shown in figure 6.
The pan window and the tilt window together display in real time the pan, tilt and zoom angles of the camera as estimated by the camera tracking software.
The pan window, for example, gives a top view of the camera. The angle drawn represents the zoom angle, i.e. the camera angle of view. The dotted line in the middle of the angle represents the camera axis and therefore the pan angle. The values of the pan and zoom angles are also displayed numerically at the top of the window. The same applies for the tilt window, which is a side view of the camera. The zoom angle is repeated in both windows; it is the same in both of course.

On the right side of the CTTool window, there are the start, stop and reset buttons, as well as the pan, zoom and tilt edit fields. The edit fields are used to specify the initial camera angles (the pan, tilt and zoom angles at the moment that camera tracking is started).

The user can start and stop the camera tracking process with the start and stop buttons. The reset button allows a 'quick restart', with the initial camera angles reset.

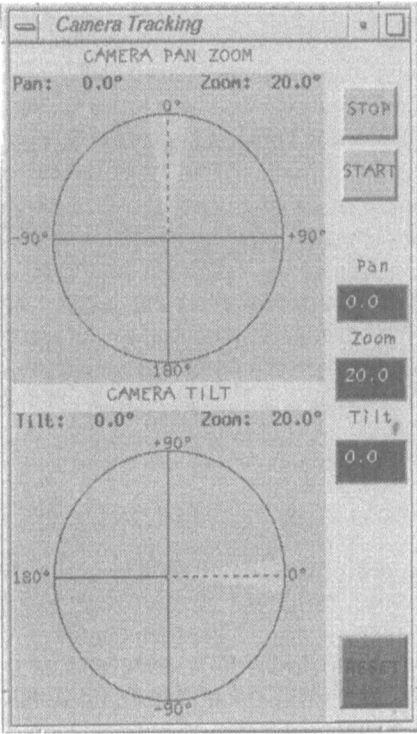

Figure 6 The CTTool

6. Conclusions

The implementation of the camera tracking server on the ELSET accelerator has involved on one hand the optimisation of the application code, and on the other hand the development of software tools to handle the real-time control and synchronisation aspects of a working camera tracking system. The software developed specifically for the camera tracking software has been successfully coupled with the SAPS model software for data distribution purposes. The WKernel environment which has been developed for supporting parallel servers on the DSP processors has also proved to be effective in providing support for this kind of real-time application.

A user interface tool has also been developed, providing visual feedback on the measured camera parameters and allowing calibration of the camera tracking software.

The system has recently been tested in a TV studio environment for a virtual news studio set-up. The server has successfully provided the client rendering process running on an 8 processor SGI Onyx. These early experiments have proved that the system can be used in live TV productions as well as for post-production purposes. There is however, room for improvements: one option that we are currently looking into is increasing the lattice size for better accuracy. This requires an improvement in processing speed which can be achieved by splitting the processing of the frames between the two processors of each procesor board. This is possible by dividing the frame into two halves and distributing them to the processors accordingly. This scheme should substantially speed up processing, since forming the equations and multiplying by the transpose matrix takes up the major part of processing time. We have experimented in overlapping the data input and processing using both of the processors on the DBV96 board. However, this scheme has not delivered any improvement because of the overhead introduced by the shared memory usage. We are also investigating on possible schemes for using the local zero wait state SRAM banks on the DBV96 processor boards to store application data to improve the data access rates on the system.

References

1. MONALISA Partners   Functional specification for ELSET System Demonstrator, November 1992.
2. Schmidt W. Accelerating hardware and frame buffer, DVS, Monalisa Internal Report R2052/DVS/WP42/DR/009/I/b1, September 1993.
3. Sahiner A.V., Le Floch P., Nimmo A., Paker Y. A Parallel Accelerator for Generation of Virtual Studio Sets, EuroGraphics, August 1993.
4. DBV96 VME floating-point DSP user's guide Issue 2.0, Loughborough Sound Images Ltd., 1992.
5. DSP96002 IEEE Floating-point dual-port processor user's manual, Motorola Inc., 1989.
6. Sahiner A.V. System software for acceleration, integration of hardware and benchmark tests, Queen Mary & Westfield College, London, Monalisa Internal Report R2052/QMW/WP43/DR/I/001/b1, September 1993.
7. Sahiner A.V. A computation model for parallelism: Self-Adapting Parallel Servers, Ph.D. Thesis, The Polytechnic of Central London, 1991.
8. Thomas G.A. Motion - Compensated Matteing, IBC '94, Amsterdam, 16-20 September 1994. Proceedings to be published by the IEE.

9. Hoetter M. Differential estimation of the global motion parameters zoom and pan, Signal Processing, Vol.16 No.3, March 1989, pp. 249-265.

10. Wu S.F. and Kittler J. A differential method for simultaneous estimation of rotation, change of scale and translation, Signal Processing: Image Communication 2, Elsevier, 1990, pp. 69-80.

11. Intermetrics [1992] Intertools 96002 C compiler/assembler reference manual, Intermetrics Microsystems Software Inc., 1992.

Tracking and Recognition of Face Sequences

S.Gong†, A.Psarrou‡, I.Katsoulis†, P.Palavouzis†

† Department of Computer Science, Queen Mary and Westfield College,
University of London, Mile End Road, London E1 4NS, UK

‡ School of Computer Science, University of Westminster,
New Cavendish Street, London W1M 8JS, UK

Abstract

In this work, we address the issue of encoding and recognition of face sequences that arise from continuous head movement. We detect and track
a moving head before segmenting face images from on-line camera inputs.
We measure temporal changes in the pattern vectors of eigenface projections of successive image frames of a face sequence and introduce the
concept of "temporal signature" of a face class. We exploit two different
supervised learning algorithms with feedforward and partially recurrent
neural networks to learn possible temporal signatures. We discuss our
experimental results and draw conclusions.

1 Problem Statement

Face recognition is important for the interpretation of facial expressions in applications such as intelligent man-machine interface and communication, intelligent visual surveillance, teleconference and real-time animation from live motion
images. There have been many computer models proposed for machine-based
recognition of face images [21, 17, 4]. Among them, the eigenface approach,
initially introduced by Sirovich and Kirby [19, 9] for face image coding and then
adopted by Turk and Pentland [21] for classification, extracts principal local and
global hidden "face stimuli" that are significant in recognition. The distinctive
features of this method are: the eigenvectors reflect the statistical properties of
face images they represent; they capture more global "signatures" of the faces
and therefore, more tolerant and immune to local variations. Because face recognition is commonly subject to a wide range of changes in viewing angle and facial
hair as well as to partial occlusion and blurring, the eigenface method is computationally more robust [12] and biologically more plausible than other template
matching techniques that are based on the detection of visible local facial features
and the representation of face models by geometric measures of such features, for
example the location and size of eyes, nose and mouth as well as their distance.
Eigenfaces also provide an attractive mechanism for the transmission of coded
image sequences through networks. However, there is a fundamental problem
with the existing eigenface models. Current eigenface models only recognize
single face images that have been taken from a strict narrow view angle, most
commonly a frontal view. This substantially limits its robustness and effectiveness [15]. For example, two face images of the same face class (i.e. an individual)

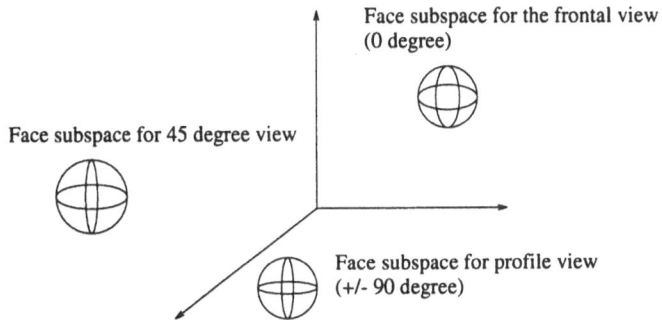

Figure 1: *The face space and sub-spaces associated with different view angles.*

are more likely to be identified with different classes if the difference in viewpoint is large.

Temporal information of time sequences provides important constraints in recognition. We introduce the concept of "temporal signature" in face recognition. Instead of recognizing single "snapshots" of a face, a sequence of face movement is taken into account for a coherent interpretation. In the rest of this paper, we briefly describe in section 2 the computation of pattern vectors following the notion of Turk and Pentland [21]. In section 3, we address the issue of head tracking and segmentation of face images. We describe two different types of neural networks that are designed to learn temporal characteristics in face sequences in section 4. We draw our conclusions in section 5.

2   Face Representation

With eigenface approach, a face image can be represented as a linear sum of a set of *eigenfaces*. These eigenfaces are normalized eigenvectors which are the principal components of a "face space" and they characterize distinctive variations in facial appearance. In general, for a set of M face images that have an unified size N, where $N = m \times n$ and (m, n) are the width and height of an image, a N-dimensional face space can be defined where face images are points in this hyperspace (see figure 1).

2.1   From Eigenfaces to Pattern Vectors

Given a set of face images $\Gamma_1, \Gamma_2, \ldots, \Gamma_M$, an average image can be computed as:

$$\Psi = \frac{1}{M} \sum_{i=1}^{M} \Gamma_i \tag{1}$$

and a new set $\Phi_1, \Phi_2, \ldots, \Phi_M$ is given by $\Phi_i = \Gamma_i - \Psi$. This simply translates the original face images by Ψ in the face space [1]. Then the principal components

---

[1]For calculating eigenvectors, Φ_i are computationally more stable since their values are much smaller compared with those of Γ_i.

of the new face space given by Φ_i are the eigenvectors of the following covariance matrix:

$$C = \frac{1}{M} \sum_{i=1}^{M} \Phi_i \Phi_i^T = AA^T$$

where $A = [\Phi_1 \Phi_2 \ldots \Phi_M]$ and C are $N \times N$ matrices. For a typical image size [2], computing the N eigenvectors of C is computationally hard. However, since the number of the face images is much smaller than the dimension of the face space ($M \ll N$), there only exists $M - 1$ nontrivial eigenvectors with the remaining ones associated with negative or zero eigenvalues. Now, if we consider V_i to be the eigenvectors of matrix $A^T A$ whilst $A^T A$ is only a $M \times M$ matrix, i.e. $(A^T A)V_i = \lambda_i V_i$ where λ_i are the eigenvalues, then $A(A^T A)V_i = A(\lambda_i V_i)$, which means $(AA^T)(AV_i) = \lambda_i(AV_i)$ and AV_i are the eigenvectors of $C = AA^T$. Therefore, the eigenvectors of C are given by:

$$U_i = AV_i = [\Phi_1 \ldots \Phi_k \ldots \Phi_M] \begin{bmatrix} v_1^i \\ \vdots \\ v_k^i \\ \vdots \\ v_M^i \end{bmatrix} = \sum_{k=1}^{M} v_k^i \Phi_k \tag{2}$$

where ($i = 1, \ldots, M - 1$) and v_k^i is the kth element of V_i. Then the eigenfaces are the normalized eigenvectors with image pixel values. For a given set of eigenvectors U_k, a face image Γ can be projected onto the eigenvectors by:

$$\omega_k = \frac{U_k^T(\Gamma - \Psi)}{\lambda_k} \qquad k = 1, \ldots, M' \tag{3}$$

where Ψ is the average face image given by equation (1), λ_k are the eigenvalues and $M' \leq M - 1$ [3]. Now, we have a weight distribution vector $\Omega = [\omega_1 \omega_2 \ldots \omega_{M'}]$ known as the *pattern vector* of Γ. A face image can therefore be represented by its pattern vector and the first M' eigenfaces of the face space. If we regard the eigenfaces as the basis set of the face space, then $\omega_k \in (-1, 0) \cup (0, 1)$. Now, for all the face images in the given set that belong to the same face class (i.e. an individual), one computes an average pattern vector $\overline{\Omega}$. This can be regarded as the "signature" of that face class. For a new face image, one calculates the Euclidian distance ε between its pattern vector and the $\overline{\Omega}$ of a known face class $\varepsilon = \| \Omega - \overline{\Omega} \|$. Then, this face image can be identified with the known face class if ε falls within a given threshold.

So far we have assumed that face images are taken from a very similar view. In reality, face images appear from different views (e.g. face image frames arise from continuous head movements). With the method described, two face images of the same class but with large view difference are more likely to be associated with two different classes. This is because that eigenfaces do not explicitly register any three-dimensional facial structure and images are not differentiated in any way if they are taken from different view angles. For face images with

---

[2] For an image size of 256×256, the dimension of the face space N is 65536.

[3] With $M' < M - 1$, the representation is approximate.

large view difference, the number of eigenfaces required has to be large enough in order to cope with the vast face space due to the number of samples needed for individual view angles of each face class. Our experiments show that for just 4 face classes, if 5 common views are taken into account, 30 face images are used to represent one view of each class, to calculate only the first 120 eigenfaces of the face space (having $600 - 1$ meaningful eigenfaces) required over 18 hours of computation on a typical workstation plus over 100MB of memory space. This is computationally very expensive, even just for 4 people. One obvious solution to the problem is to divide the face space into a set of sub-spaces where each sub-space is associated with a typical view angle. However, with such an approach, it is not obvious how to associate an unknown face image to any of the face sub-spaces unless an exhausted projection of the given face image into all sub-spaces is carried out. This again requires expensive computation. In the following, however, we first address the issue of getting face images.

3　Segmentation of Face Images

In order to encode face images by eigenfaces, it is necessary to obtain face images in the same size from the camera input. If large areas in the images that are used to form a face space contain background rather than face information, the extracted eigenfaces would say more about the statistical properties of the background than that of the faces. Camera inputs need to be processed in order to locate, track and segment only the face images.

3.1　Bootstrapping the Region of Interest

The first step of the computation requires the detection of a "region of interest" (ROI), assuming only one head movement in a given scene being of our interest. This bootstrapping process is based on the information of motion detected in the images. Accurate and consistent estimation of visual motion is hugely time consuming [5]. For real-time processing, we apply two filtering techniques that only compute partial motion and detect possible temporal change respectively. We show that such information is sufficient for the purpose of locating the ROI.

3.1.1　Detection and estimation of movement

With a spatio-temporal Gaussian filter:

$$G(x, y, t) = u(\frac{a}{\pi})^{3/2} \exp^{-a(x^2 + y^2 + u^2 t^2)}$$

where u is a time scaling factor and a gives the width of the filter as $w_m = \frac{2}{\sqrt{a}} = 2\sigma\sqrt{2}$, a symmetric second order temporal edge operator is given by [1]:

$$m(x, y, t) = -(\nabla^2 + \frac{1}{u^2}\frac{\partial^2}{\partial t^2})G(x, y, t) \tag{4}$$

By convolving image frames $I(x, y, t)$ of a temporal sequence with this operator $m(x, y, t) \otimes I(x, y, t)$, spatio-temporal zero-crossings can be located in the output images $S(x, y, t)$. For avoiding the computational complex of a three-dimensional

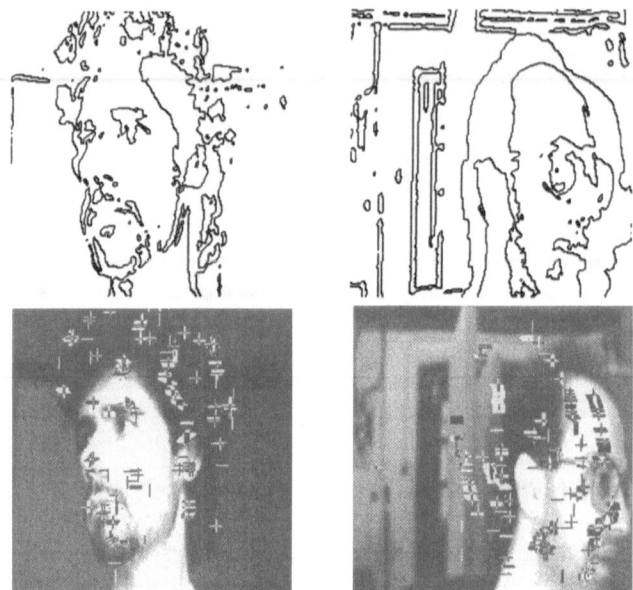

Figure 2: *The spatio-temporal zero-crossings of images from two different sequences and the corresponding normal visual motion.*

convolution, the above operator can be approximated by three one-dimensional operations in x, y and t independently [1, 13]. As a result, the temporal filtering takes place over 8 image frames in time, i.e. it can only start from the eighth frame of a sequence. With the output $S(x, y, t)$, one can calculate the normal components of visual motion along the spatio-temporal zero-crossings. For accuracy, however, the convolution window size w_m requires to be ≥ 8 so that the output image $S(x, y, t)$ is linear over a $3 \times 3 \times 3$ neighbourhood. That means the computation of the normal motion at any given time requires at least 3 successive image frames. Therefore, it starts at the 10th frame of a sequence. Now, let $S_{ijk} = S(x + i, y + j, ut + k)$ be in a three-dimensional cubic neighbourhood of a zero-crossing point (x, y, t) in S, then a least-squares fitting of S_{ijk} to a linear polynomial $f_{ijk} = f_0 + f_x i + f_y j + f_z k$ gives:

$$f_x = \tfrac{1}{18} \sum_{ijk} i S_{ijk}, \quad f_y = \tfrac{1}{18} \sum_{ijk} j S_{ijk}, \quad f_t = \tfrac{1}{18} \sum_{ijk} k S_{ijk} \tag{5}$$

As a result, the spatio-temporal gradient of S at (x, y, t) estimates the normal visual motion as:

$$(\dot{x}_\perp, \dot{y}_\perp) = \frac{-u f_z}{f_x^2 + f_y^2}(f_x, f_y) \tag{6}$$

Figure 2 shows the effect of applying such a filter to image sequences. It is necessary to point out, though, that this spatio-temporal filter measures continuous motion that lasts for more than eight image frames. When the head movement is rapid and head position changes significantly in less than eight frames, the computed visual motion field gives a poor indication of head positions.

In order to address rapid head movements, an additional fast motion detector is introduced. This process does not measure any visual motion but it copes well

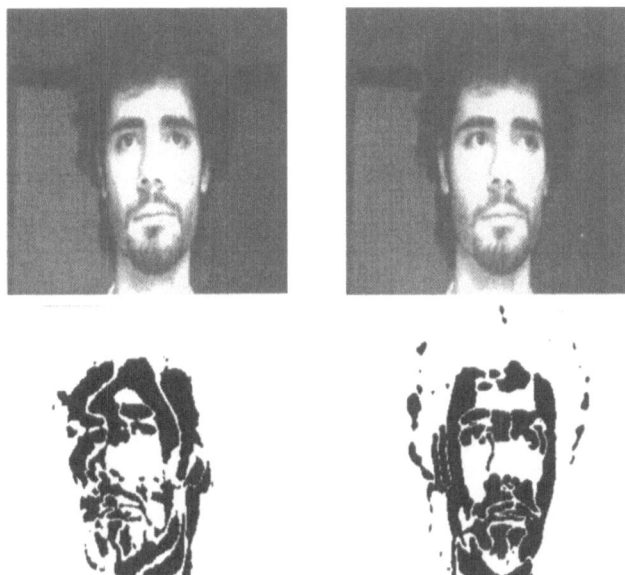

Figure 3: *Top: Two successive image frames of a sequence. Bottom left: The result of subtracting the spatio-temporal filtered two frames. It shows that information about the movement of the head (i.e. turning from left to right) is evident whilst the location of the head in the current frame is unclear. Bottom right: The subtraction of spatially filtered image frames which gives more accurate indication of the head position.*

with large temporal changes in fewer image frames. By subtracting two spatially Gaussian smoothed [4] successive image frames in a sequence, we obtain images that only contain regions of temporal change (see figure 3). This operation can be sensitive to sudden changes in lighting conditions and the output of a subtraction is subjected to a threshold that is often heuristic.

3.1.2   Initialization of ROI

In the outputs of the motion detectors described above, one marks the locations of movement. The boundaries of moving regions can then be grouped and segmented. With a single ROI, this can be easily done by determining the extreme location of moving pixels. For multiple regions of interest, Gong and Buxton [7] demonstrated an adaptive segmentation algorithm based on Bayesian belief networks. After finding out the approximate boundaries of a ROI, an elliptic active contour is initialized with its centre, major and minor axes being determined by the distance between the left and right, the upper and lower boundaries. There are a number of advantages in using an active ellipse over the more traditional active snakes based on splines. Studies by Torr *et. al.* [20] show that whilst they share a common feature for small number of parameters, ellipse does not suffer from two common drawbacks of other snakes, i.e. part of a snake often gets left behind so the curve straddles front and back of the contour it tries to follow, and a snake sometimes crosses itself or folds and partially collapses onto itself.

---

[4] Palavouzis gives detailed discussions on not using spatio-temporally smoothed images [13].

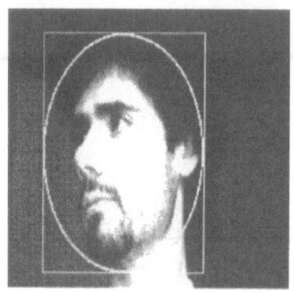

Figure 4: *Initialization of an active elliptic contour based on the detection of movement in image frames.*

Figure 4 shows two examples of initializing a ROI by ellipse.

3.2 Head Tracking

Fitting an ellipse with the initialization process in every frame is unreliable and inconsistent since individual points in visual motion are often fragmented in time. Robust tracking requires continuous updating of the parameters of the elliptic contour. We apply Kalman filters [8] to model the dynamics of these parameters and to predict future movement of an ellipse in order to provide more accurate estimation of its position in time. A Kalman filter is a recursive, linear optimal filter for state estimation in dynamic systems. A system state can be a single variable or a vector that describes the characteristics of the system. For an active ellipse, it has four temporal parameters (ignore the orientation for the time being). Assuming that the position of an ellipse is uncorrelated with the length of its axes, a dynamic system can be used to describe both coordinates of the centre of an ellipse with its position, velocity and acceleration. For the x coordinate (similar for y), an update condition is given by:

$$\begin{bmatrix} x \\ \dot{x} \\ \ddot{x} \end{bmatrix}_{k+1} = \begin{bmatrix} 1 & \Delta t & \Delta t^2/2 \\ 0 & 1 & \Delta t \\ 0 & 0 & 1 \end{bmatrix} \begin{bmatrix} x \\ \dot{x} \\ \ddot{x} \end{bmatrix}_k + \begin{bmatrix} 0 \\ 1/2 \\ 1 \end{bmatrix} \mathbf{v}_{acc} + \begin{bmatrix} 1 \\ 0 \\ 0 \end{bmatrix} \mathbf{v}_{pos}$$

where $\mathbf{v}_{acc}$ and $\mathbf{v}_{pos}$ are noise covariances for assumptions about constant acceleration and position estimation, and a measurement model is given by $\mathbf{z}_{k+1} = \mathbf{x}_{k+1} + \mathbf{w}$, where $\mathbf{x}_{k+1}$ is the actual state vector at time t_{k+1} and $\mathbf{w}$ is a noise covariance vector for measurement errors. $\mathbf{z}_{k+1}$ is the observation vector at time t_{k+1}. For updating the major and minor axes of an ellipse, we use a different dynamic system where its state is the length of one of the axes. The update condition for the major axis (similar for the minor axis) is:

$$l_{k+1} = l_k + v_l$$

where v_l is the noise measure for constant length assumption and the measurement model is $z_{k+1} = l_{k+1} + u$, where u is an error measure in the measurement of length.

Setting parameters is rather crucial for a Kalman filter to perform. The noise and error covariances are usually determined by experiments. Our experiments show that the appropriate values for $\mathbf{v}_{acc}$ and $\mathbf{v}_{pos}$ are between $(1.5, 2.0)$ whilst $\mathbf{w} = [2, 0.5, 0.2]$, $v_l = 10$ and $u = 4$. Palavouzis gives a detailed description and analysis on tuning the Kalman filters [13]. We take the average of the normal optic flow field given by equation (6) as an estimation for the ellipse's velocity and the temporal difference between velocities of successive frames as the estimation for acceleration. Consequently, the Kalman filters are initialized at the 11th frame and start to update at the 12th frame of an image sequence. The results of a tracking process can be seen in figure 5.

Figure 5: *Two snap shots of the head tracking process.*

4 Recognition of Face Sequences

Temporal information in time sequence provides important constraints in recognition [6, 18]. To divide a face space in time not only overcomes the ambiguity in mapping a target image with its corresponding sub-space since they share a time reference, but also takes the continuity in the temporal changes of face images into account. Instead of recognizing any single "snapshot" of a face, a temporal sequence of face movement is taken for recognition. In the following, we give details about our neural network approach for dividing a face space in time.

4.1 A Feedforward Neural Network Classifier

A key factor that needs to be considered when applying feedforward neural networks (FFNNs) is the training time required to learn efficient information from a set of training patterns. Past experiments in applying FFNNs to learn face images [10] have shown to be computationally expensive because mapping face images to neural networks requires vast amount of training in order to capture meaningful information. However, the eigenface representation enables the pattern vectors to be used in place of images. This hugely reduces the dimension of patterns involved in training.

We divide the face-space of face sequences into a set of temporal sub-spaces that correspond to groups of possible face orientations associated with time. We capture a set of sequences of continuous head movements in front of a stationary camera. Each sequence has M image frames. Every image frame in a sequence contributes to one group of possible head orientations associated with a given time (see figure 6). We compute the pattern vectors of each sub-space and

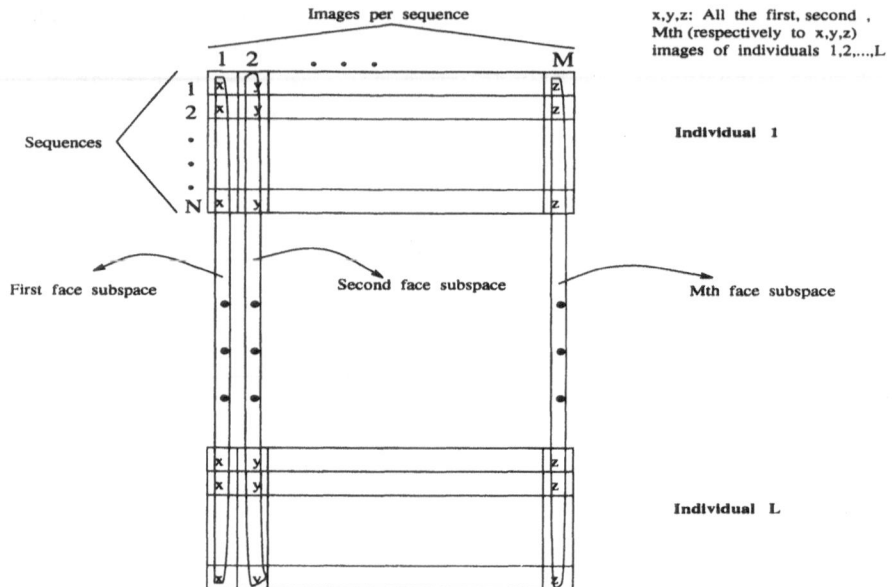

Figure 6: *M temporal face sub-spaces for a feedforward neural network classifier.*

train independently *M* FFNNs in order to encode the sequences with *M* subspaces. During training, pattern vectors of a specific time instance are applied to a network and are classified into different face classes. During recognition, the network is presented with a pattern vector of a face image from a sequence not included in the training set. The output units of the trained networks are further connected with a fixed value of 1.0 to form a fourth layer (see figure 7). These connections are only between units that represent face classes of the same individual and are used to give an overall vote based on the sum of the individual responses of the FFNNs. In addition, the units of the last layer are biased with a value of -2.0 in order to reduce the activation of the unlikely candidates. In order to recognize a new face sequence, a sequence of pattern vectors are calculated by projecting each frame of the face sequence into the corresponding sub-space in time. Each pattern vector is applied to the input units of the corresponding FFNN. The output of each of the FFNN signifies the probability of the face image to be recognised as one of the known face classes at the given time. The overall vote for a known face class is determined by the most "popular" outputs of all the FFNNs in time throughout the sequence.

4.1.1 Training

Each of the FFNNs used here is trained by back-propagation [16], a supervised learning algorithm in which a desired response is provided for a given input. The difference between the actual and the desired response gives an error measure:

$$E[w] = \frac{1}{2} \sum_{\mu\iota} (t_\iota^\mu - O_\iota^\mu)^2$$

where w is the weight matrix of a connection, t is the teaching output of the net-

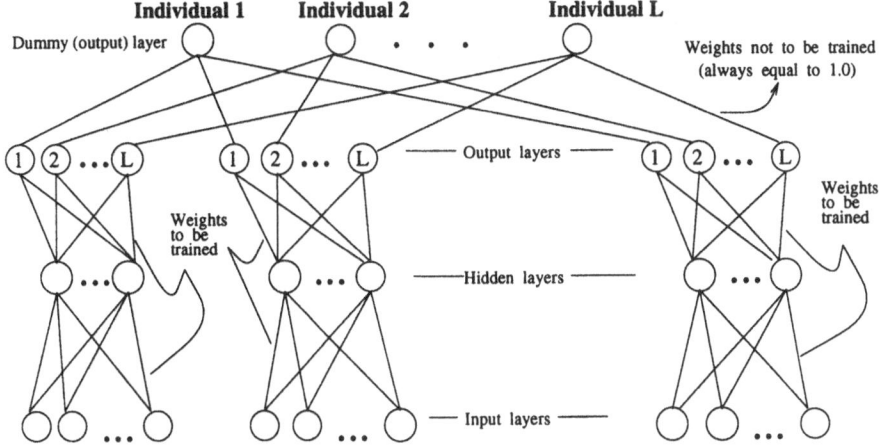

Figure 7: *The design of a feedforward neural network classifier.*

work and O is the computed output. Back propagating this error measure from each output unit to the input layer allows the network to learn the association between the pattern vectors and the face classes. The aim of the propagation is to update connection weights as follows:

$$\Delta w_{ij}(t+1) = \eta \delta_j o_i + \mu \Delta w_{ij}(t) \tag{7}$$

$$\delta_j = \begin{cases} (f_j'(net_j) + c)(t_j - o_j) & \text{if } j \text{ is an output unit} \\ (f_j'(net_j) + c)\sum_k \delta_k w_{jk} & \text{if } j \text{ is a hidden unit} \end{cases} \tag{8}$$

where:

1. η is a learning rate parameter and typically, $\eta \in [0.1, 1.0]$.
2. μ is a momentum measure which specifies the level of influence from the previous weight change allowed in the current change. This avoids oscillation problems common with the regular back-propagation algorithm when the error surface has a very narrow minimum area. Typically $\eta \in [0, 1.0]$.
3. c is a flat spot elimination value, a constant added to the derivative of the activation function in order to allow the network to pass flat spots on the error surface. Typically $c \in [0, 0.25]$ but most often 0.1 is used.
4. t_j is a teaching value whilst o_j is a computed value for output unit j. net_j is the net input received by unit j.
5. f is the activation function. The logistic activation function is used for the hidden layers.

4.1.2 Experiment 1

We take 21 face sequences of 5 image frames for five individuals. The sequences are from *continuous left-to-right or right-to-left* head movements. Among these 105 face sequences (525 face images in total), 90 sequences (18 for each individual) were used to train the networks and the remaining 15 (3 for each individual) were used for recognition. Five face sub-spaces were created and for each sub-space, we calculated the best 30 eigenvectors (out of 89). The training set for each network consists of 90 pattern vectors that are computed by projecting 90 images at a given time onto the corresponding 30 eigenfaces. Each network has 30 input units, 15 hidden units and 5 output units. Each network was trained after 60 epochs. After training, the output of the five networks were combined to a fourth layer. The fourth layer consists of 5 units with one for a face class. The network was evaluated using 18 sequences that were not used in training. Among them, 15 sequences are from head movements of known individuals whilst 3 sequences are from unknown individuals. The network was able to *correctly classify all* sequences with the recognition phase taking less than one second. One of the main features of the recognition phase is that often with miss-identified face classes at specific time frame, the overall recognition is correct.

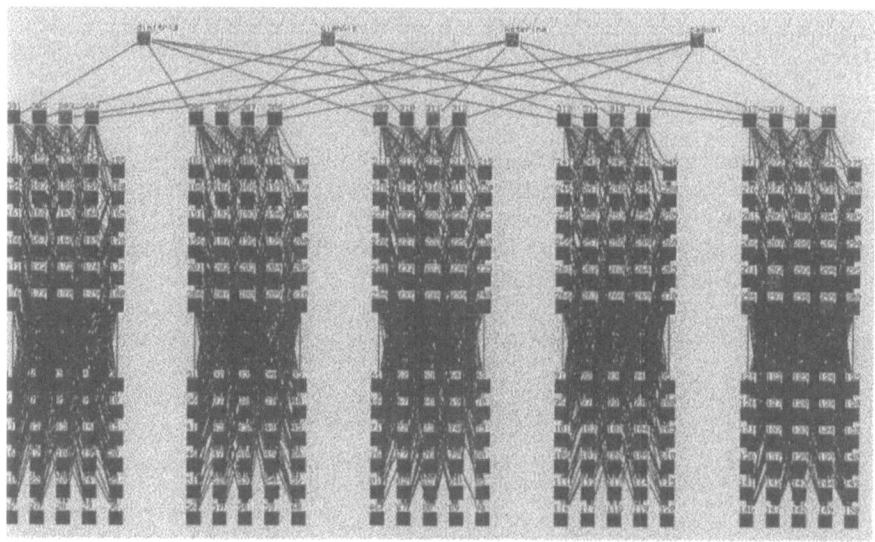

Figure 8: *A feedforward neural network for learning temporal face sub-spaces.*

4.1.3 Experiment 2

Again we take 34 face sequences of 5 frames for four individuals. However, the sequences now are from *continuous unconstrained* head movements with *varying lighting conditions*. Among these 136 face sequences (680 face images in total), 120 (30 for each individual) were used to train the networks and the remaining 16 (4 for each individual) were used for evaluation. With the same number of eigenfaces used in experiment 1, each network has 30 input units. However, we now have 30 hidden units and 4 output units (see figure 8). The training of each network required 200 epochs and the fourth layer consists of 4 units. The network was evaluated using 20 sequences that were in the training set. Among them, 16 sequences are from known individuals and 4 are unknown. The network was able to *classify correctly 18 out of the 20* sequences.

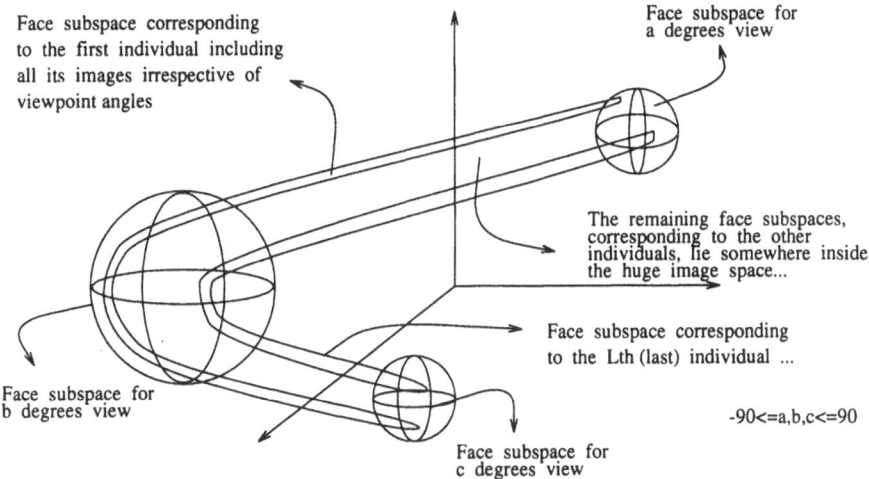

Face subspace corresponding
to the first individual including
all its images irrespective of
viewpoint angles

Face subspace for
a degrees view

The remaining face subspaces,
corresponding to the other
individuals, lie somewhere inside
the huge image space...

Face subspace corresponding
to the Lth (last) individual ...

Face subspace for
b degrees view

-90<=a,b,c<=90

Face subspace for
c degrees view

Figure 9: *Face sub-space for face classes.*

4.2 Learning Temporal Signatures in Face Sequences

Following the success in our early experiments with the FFNN classifier, we now
consider an explicit measure of the temporal change in the pattern vectors of
successive frames of a face sequence. We regard this as a "temporal signature"
of a face class. This temporal change between successive pattern vectors in time is
given by their Euclidian distance: $\varepsilon =\parallel \Omega_t - \Omega_{t+1} \parallel$ where $t = 1, 2, \ldots, M' - 1$.
With this approach we divide a face space to sub-spaces that correspond to
individual face classes. Therefore, each sub-space contains the information of
one face class with different view angles arisen from continuous head movements
(see figure 9). In the following, we describe our experiments in learning temporal
signatures of face sequences by partially recurrent neural networks.

Partially recurrent neural networks (PRNNs) are networks with mainly feedforward connections, but also include a carefully chosen set of feedback connections either from the hidden or output layer. They are very attractive for
learning and predicting temporal changes in time sequences [2, 3, 11, 14]. Given
L set of face sequences of M frames for L face classes, we compute the pattern
vectors of each face class and train independently L PRNNs.

4.2.1 Training

A partially recurrent neural network shown in figure 10 is based on the Elman's
architecture [3]. Such networks consist of (1) four sets of units: the input, hidden,
output and context units, (2) a set of feedforward connections and (3) a set of
fixed feedback connections (at 1.0) from the hidden to the context units. The
goal of these connections is to copy the activation values of the past hidden units
to the context units [5]. The networks are trained with the back-propagation
algorithm introduced in section 4.1.1. We train each of these networks with
the patterns vectors of successive image frames of sequences. Given that the

---

[5] The activation of the context units is initially (at time $t = 0$) set to 0.5.

activation of the hidden units of a network is **h**, then the activation of the units of the network at time t can be represented as:

$$
\begin{aligned}
\text{input units} &= \Omega(t) \\
\text{hidden units} &= \mathbf{h}(t) \\
\text{output units} &= \Omega(t+1) \\
\text{context units} &= \mathbf{h}(t-1)
\end{aligned}
$$

A network is trained to associate its input pattern vector $\Omega(t)$ to its output pattern vector $\Omega(t+1)$ and therefore it learns to *predict* the successive pattern vector of every frame in a sequence. This is because that the context units hold a copy of the activations of the hidden units from the previous time step and thus help to remember the past internal state. At the same time, the hidden units "encode" the pattern vectors and the layer interconnections build an internal representation of the relationship between successive pattern vectors of a sequence.

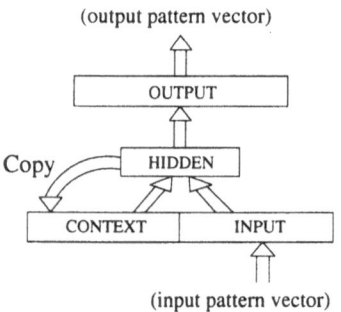

Figure 10: *Recurrent network for a face class.*

4.2.2 Experiment 3

We take 10 face sequences of 5 frames for 3 individuals to create 3 face sub-spaces. For each sub-space, we use the first 20 eigenfaces (of total 49) and compute 50 pattern vectors to train 3 PRNNs in order to model the temporal signatures of faces. Each network has 20 input units, 30 hidden units, 30 context units and 20 output units. The networks were trained after 6000 epochs. After training, the networks were tested for the following task: <u>Recognizing John</u>.

Now, we use "John", "Pascal" and "Katerina" to refer to the PRNNs of the face classes. We then take a new face sequence of John, Sequence-John, and compute 3 pattern vector sequences by projecting the frames of Sequence-John to the 3 face sub-spaces. Each pattern vector sequence is then applied to the PRNN associated with the corresponding sub-space and the Euclidian distance between successive outputs of the PRNN is computed. In figure 12, we show the Euclidian distance between the successive pattern vectors of Sequence-John, and compare them with the Euclidian distance between the successive outputs of PRNN "John", "Pascal" and "Katerina" respectively. It is shown that the Euclidian distances of Sequence-John are much closer to the Euclidian distances of "John". More importantly, it is not difficult to notice that the gradients of the Euclidian curves for Sequence-John and model "John" are very similar. This

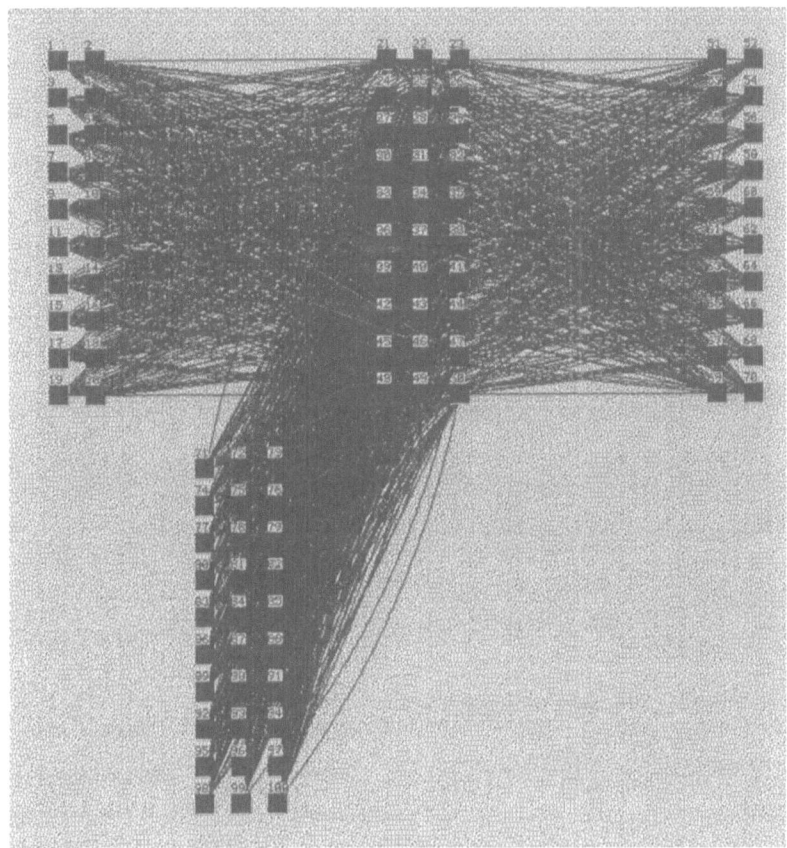

Figure 11: *An Elman recurrent neural network for learning temporal signatures.*

suggests that a measure of the ratio of the temporal change in the pattern vectors of face sequences gives a form of temporal signature for a dynamic face.

5 Conclusion

In this work, we presented a novel approach to face recognition. To address the problems with existing eigenface based classification models, we introduced a *dynamic face recognition* approach that exploits the temporal information in face appearance by first classifying face changes according to time and second measuring the temporal changes in the pattern vectors of face sequences. This enables us to effectively classify face images from a moving head that spans across large view angles with respect to the camera. With this approach, instead of recognizing any single "snapshot" of a face, a temporal sequence of face movement is taken into account for a coherent interpretation. More specifically, with a head tracking system that consists of temporal subtraction, spatio-temporal filtering and active ellipse tracking with multiple Kalman filters, face images of head moving sequences were successfully segmented continuously in indoor light-

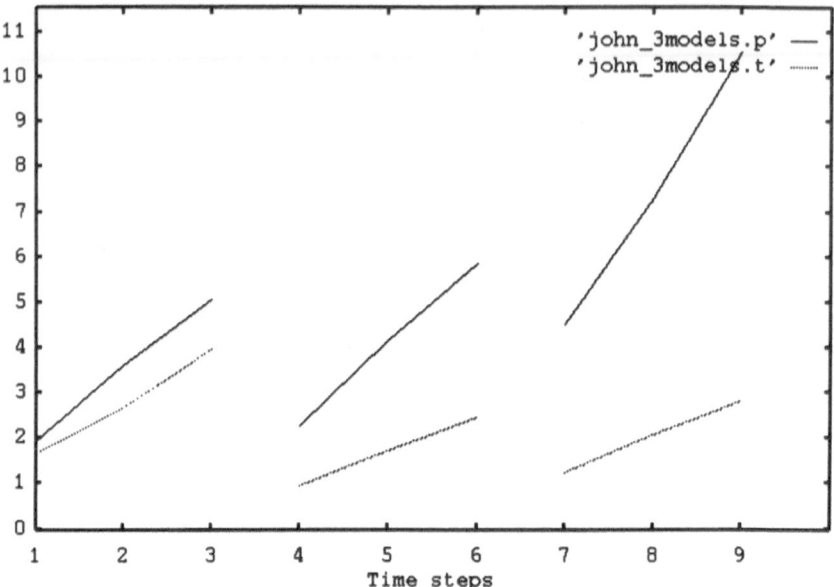

Figure 12: *The Euclidian distance between successive pattern vectors that belong to Sequence-John and the Euclidian distance between the outputs of model "John", "Pascal" and "Katerina" respectively.*

ing conditions. By applying a set of partially recurrent Elman neural networks and a 4-layered feedforward neural network over 150 training sequences, two different supervised learning strategies have been exploited to learn the temporal characteristics of face images with large view differences (over 45°) arisen from continuous head movements. We exploited the concept of temporal signature in face recognition with limited experimental results. The current systems achieves an over 90% success rate with 40 different test sequences of known and unknown individuals.

References

[1] B.F. Buxton and H. Buxton. "Monocular depth perception from optic flow by space time signal processing". *Proceedings of the Royal Society of London*, B-218, 1983.

[2] A. Cleeremans. "Finite state automata and simple recurrent networks". *Neural Computation*, 1, 1989.

[3] J. Elman. "Finding structure in time". *Cognitive Science*, 14, 1990.

[4] M. Fleming and G. Cottrell. "Categorization of faces using unsupervised feature extraction". In *IJCNN*, San Diego, California, 1990.

[5] S. Gong. *Parallel Computation of Visual Motion*. PhD thesis, Department of Engineering Science, Oxford University, 1989.

[6] S. Gong. "Visual observation as reactive learning". In *SPIE International Conference on Adaptive and Learning Systems*, Orlando, Florida., 1992.

[7] S. Gong and H. Buxton. "Bayesian nets for mapping contextual knowledge to computational constraints in motion segmentation and tracking". In *BMVC*, Guildford, Surrey, England, 1993.

[8] R. Kalman. "A new approach to linear filtering and prediction problems". *ASME Journal of Basic Engineering*, 1960.

[9] M. Kirby and L. Sirovich. "Application of the Karhunen-Loeve procedure for the characterization of human faces". *PAMI*, 12(1), 1990.

[10] T. Kohonen. *Self-organization and Associative Memory*. Springer-Verlag, Berlin, 1989.

[11] M. Mozer. "Neural net architecture for temporal sequence processing". In A. Weigend and N. Gershenfeld, editors, *Predicting the Future and Understanding the Past*. Addison-Wesley Publishing, 1993.

[12] A. O'Toole, H. Abdi, K. Deffenbacher, and D. Valentin. "Low-dimensional representation of faces in higher dimensions of the face space". *Optical Society of America*, 10(3), 1993.

[13] P. Palavouzis. *Head Tracking for Face Recognition*. Master's thesis, Department of Computer Science, QMW, London, 1994.

[14] A. Psarrou and H. Buxton. "Motion analysis using recurrent neural networks". In *ICANN*, Sorrento, Italy, 1994.

[15] G. Robertson and I. Craw. "Testing face recognition systems". In *BMVC*, Guildford, Surrey, England, 1993.

[16] D. Rumelhart, G. Hinton, and R. Williams. "Learning representations by back-propagation errors". *Nature*, 223, 1988.

[17] F. Samaria. "Face segmentation for identification using hidden markov models". In *BMVC*, Guildford, Surrey, England, 1993.

[18] M. Seibert and A. Waxman. "Adaptive 3D object recognition from multiple views". *PAMI*, 14(2), 1992.

[19] L. Sirovich and M. Kirby. "Low-dimensional procedure for the characterization of human faces". *Optical Society of America*, 4(3), 1987.

[20] P. Torr, T. Wong, D. Murray, and A. Zisserman. "Cooperating motion processes". In *BMVC*, Glasgow, Scotland, 1991.

[21] M. Turk and A. Pentland. "Eigenfaces for recognition". *Journal of Cognitive Neuroscience*, 3(1), 1991.

Session 3: Analysis 2 – Stereoscopic Imaging

Depth Estimation from Stereoscopic Image Pairs Assuming Piecewise Continuos Surfaces

Lutz Falkenhagen
Institut für Theoretische Nachrichtentechnik und Informationsverarbeitung
Universität Hannover, Appelstr. 9A, 30167 Hannover, Germany
Email: falkenhagen@tnt.uni–hannover.de

Abstract

An algorithm for estimating reliable and accurate depth maps from stereoscopic image pairs is presented, which is based on block–matching techniques for disparity estimation. By taking neighboring disparity values into account, reliability and accuracy of the estimated disparity values are increased and the corona effect at disparity discontinuities is avoided. An interpolation of disparity values within segmented regions of homogeneous disparity enables the computation of dense depth maps by means of triangulation.

1 Introduction

Depth estimation is used in applications like 3D–modelling of natural objects [1] [2], 3D–remote handling and quality control [3]. Depth information is obtained by a triangulation of corresponding image points with known stereoscopic camera parameters. Therefore, the coordinate difference between corresponding image points, called disparity, has to be estimated. Applying common block–matching techniques for disparity estimation, the correspondence of image points is evaluated using the cross correlation or mean absolute difference of corresponding image blocks [4]. To increase the reliability of disparity estimates, large block sizes have to be chosen. On the other hand, large block sizes decrease the accuracy of disparity estimation. Hierarchical block–matching combines both, accuracy and reliability, but gives rise to corona effects at disparity discontinuities [5].

The goal of this contribution is to overcome the contradictory requirements of accuracy and reliability and to avoid the corona effect. The hierarchical block–matching will be substituted by a non–hierarchical block–matching technique, which uses small block–sizes in order to provide accuracy and to avoid the corona effect. Neighboring disparity estimates are considered in order to provide reliability. A cost function for a maximum–likelihood estimator will be developed that combines block–matching with a consideration of neighboring disparity estimates.

In low textured areas and in areas which are only visible in one image, disparity cannot be estimated. These areas, called disparity gaps, have be interpolated in order to obtain dense depth maps. Therefore an interpolator has to be developed that preserves disparity discontinuities.

Chapter 2 presents the developed disparity estimation algorithm. The computation of dense depth maps from disparity is explained in Chapter 3. Depth estimation results are

116

presented for the image sequence 'aqua', a stereoscopic image sequence acquired by the RACE–DISTIMA project [6], and compared to common disparity estimation based on block–matching in Chapter 4 . Chapter 5 concludes this paper.

2 Disparity estimation

2.1 Model of the Stereoscopic Camera System

In the course of disparity and depth estimation, a pinhole camera model based on the central projection of diffuse illuminated and diffuse reflecting spatial points in the image plane is applied. No lense distortion is considered. Each camera is defined by its position $\vec{C}$, its optical axis $\vec{A}$ and its image plane, which is determined by two perpendicular vectors $\vec{H}$ and $\vec{V}$. The camera is therefore called CAHV–camera [7]. The projection of a spatial point $\vec{P}_S = (P_{Sx}, P_{Sy}, P_{Sz})$ into the image plane of a CAHV–camera can be computed using equation (1).

$$\vec{P} = \begin{pmatrix} P_h \\ P_v \end{pmatrix} \quad \text{with} \quad P_h = \frac{(\vec{P}_S - \vec{C}) \cdot \vec{H}}{(\vec{P}_S - \vec{C}) \cdot \vec{A}} \quad , \quad P_v = \frac{(\vec{P}_S - \vec{C}) \cdot \vec{V}}{(\vec{P}_S - \vec{C}) \cdot \vec{A}} \tag{1}$$

For DISTIMA image sequences, only the intrinsic and relative extrinsic camera parameters are known, which is sufficient for depth estimation. The absolute camera parameters needed for the CAHV–camera model can therefore be chosen arbitrarily for one of the cameras. Here, the left camera is arranged in the center of the coordinate system and the right camera is positioned with respect to the known relative camera parameters (Fig. 1). Due to the emulation of human vision in DISTIMA, both cameras are arranged horizontally with a base length b and their optical axes have a small convergence angle ϕ. The focal length of both cameras is identical.

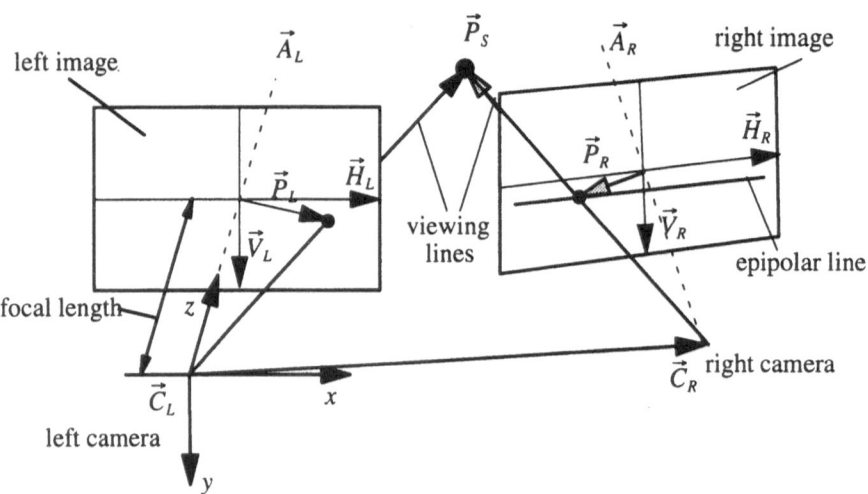

Fig. 1: Model of the stereoscopic camera system

When depth shall be estimated, the spatial position of a point has to be reconstructed from to known image coordinates of its projection in the stereoscopic image planes. The spatial position of the point is the intersection of both viewing lines. If the viewing lines are skewed, the spatial position is assumed to be located at the point with minimal distance to both viewing lines.

The direction of the viewing lines is determined using the CAHV–camera parameters and the image coordinates. Evaluating the projection equation (1) the direction appears to be the following vector product.

$$\vec{S} = \left(\vec{A} \cdot \vec{P}_h - \vec{H}\right) \times \left(\vec{A} \cdot \vec{P}_v - \vec{V}\right) \tag{2}$$

The vector $\vec{M}$ links both viewing lines at the location of minimal distance.

$$\vec{M} = \vec{C}_R + \lambda \cdot \vec{S}_R - \vec{C}_L - \mu \cdot \vec{S}_L \tag{3}$$

Therefore $\vec{M}$ has to be perpendicular to both viewing lines $\vec{S}_L, \vec{S}_R$.

$$\vec{M} \cdot \vec{S}_L = 0 \ , \qquad \vec{M} \cdot \vec{S}_R = 0 \tag{4}$$

Based on condition (4), λ and μ are computed with equation (5).

$$\lambda = \frac{\vec{C}_L \cdot \vec{S}_L + \mu \cdot \vec{S}_L{}^2 - \vec{C}_R \cdot \vec{S}_L}{\vec{S}_L \cdot \vec{S}_R} \tag{5}$$

$$\mu = \frac{\left((\vec{C}_L - \vec{C}_R) \cdot \vec{S}_R\right) \cdot \left(\vec{S}_L \cdot \vec{S}_R\right) - \left((\vec{C}_L - \vec{C}_R) \cdot \vec{S}_L\right) \cdot \vec{S}_R{}^2}{\vec{S}_L{}^2 \cdot \vec{S}_R{}^2 - (\vec{S}_L \cdot \vec{S}_R)^2}$$

Finally the spatial position is determined using equation (6).

$$\vec{S}_P = 0.5 \cdot \left(\vec{C}_R + \lambda \cdot \vec{S}_R + \vec{C}_L + \mu \cdot \vec{S}_L\right) \tag{6}$$

This equation will be used for the computation of depth maps from disparity maps.

2.2 Disparity Estimation Constraints

The entity of disparity estimation is the search for corresponding image features in a stereoscopic image pair. Corresponding image features are projections of the same object feature into both image planes. Due to physical laws of image acquisition, a number of constraints for matching features can be derived. These constraints are mainly applied in feature based disparity estimation algorithms, where luminance features are extracted from the images in a first step and the disparity of these features is estimated in a second step [4].

In most area–based disparity estimation algorithms, not all of these constraints are considered, because disparity is estimated for each image point or block of image points independently. In the following, these constraints are explained.

2.2.1 Epipolar Constraint

With the applied camera model an image point $\vec{p}_L$ results from the central projection of a spatial point $\vec{P}_S$ into the left image plane. The viewing line is the connection of the spatial point $\vec{P}_S$ and the center of the camera $\vec{C}$. The projection of the viewing line into the other image plane results in the epipolar line (Fig 1). Therefore the corresponding point in the right image plane $\vec{p}_R$ has to lie on the epipolar line, which reduces the search area of the disparity estimation to one dimension.

Under the assumption of a small convergence angle between both optical axes and a horizontal arrangement of the cameras, the epipolar line is approximately horizontal.

2.2.2   Extended Continuity Constraint

Under the assumption of large objects with a smooth surface shown in the stereoscopic image pair, the disparity varies continuously in most parts of the image. Disparity discontinuities are allowed at object boundaries only. Therefore, disparity discontinuities have to be detected and involved in the disparity estimation algorithm.

2.2.3   Disparity Gradient Limit

The possible disparity gradient is limited, because disparity changes coincide with depth changes and therefore with an occlusions of object parts in one of the images in case of high gradients. Assuming horizontally arranged cameras, for the left disparity map an upper disparity gradient of size +1 and for the right disparity map a lower disparity gradient of –1 results. The disparity gradient limits are given in equation (7).

$$- \infty < \frac{\partial d_h}{\partial h} \leq +1 \quad \text{for the left disparity map}$$

$$- 1 < \frac{\partial d_h}{\partial h} \leq +\infty \quad \text{for the right disparity map}$$

(7)

2.2.4   Monotonic Ordering Constraint

With a defined order of points along a line in one image of the image pair, the corresponding points have to occur in the same order in the other image. This constraint will be of interest when the scan line oriented disparity estimation algorithm is introduced.

2.2.5   Luminance constraint

Correspondence analysis is disturbed by camera noise. For a reliable disparity estimation, the local luminance variance σ_{lh}^2 within the compared image blocks in direction of the epipolar line has to be clearly higher than the camera noise variance σ_n^2. Therefore correspondence analysis is restricted to points $\vec{P}$ with high local luminance variance σ_{lh}^2.

$$\sigma_{lh}^2 = \frac{1}{b} \sum_{i=-b2}^{b2} \left[\frac{1}{b} \sum_{j=-b2}^{b2} I^2(P_h-j; P_v-i) - \left(\frac{1}{b} \sum_{j=-b2}^{b2} I(P_h-j; P_v-i) \right)^2 \right] \gg \sigma_n^2 \quad (8)$$

with b = blocksize and b2 = (blocksize–1) / 2

2.3   Disparity Estimation considering Directly Neighboring Disparity Values (DN–Cost Function)

In order to estimate a dense disparity map for an image, for each point of the image a corresponding point is searched in the other image. This pair of points is denoted as candidate pair. In common area–based algorithms, each possible corresponding point, denoted as candidate, is evaluated using the luminance difference or the cross correlation of surrounding image blocks. For reliable estimation, large block sizes from 11x11 pel to 17x17 pel are needed for block–matching or in the first level of hierarchical block–matching. These block sizes giving rise to corona effects at disparity discontinuities, e.g. at object boundaries [5] and leading to less accurate disparity estimates, if no further estimation with smaller block sizes is applied.

Some of the estimation constraints mentioned in Chapter 2.2 cannot be taken into account, when disparity is estimated for each point independently. Therefore a simultaneous disparity estimation for all points along one scan line has been proposed [8]. There, a maximum likelihood cost function is employed, evaluating the luminance difference of the candidate pair and the disparity change along the scan line. This cost function is minimized for each scan line using a dynamic programming strategy. With this method all mentioned estimation constraint expect the extended continuity constraint are considered.

The first of the two presented cost functions is based on [8], but evaluating the Normalized Cross Correlation NCC (9) of a candidate pair instead of the luminance difference.

$$NCC(\vec{P}_L; \vec{P}_R) = \frac{\sum_{i=-b2}^{b2} \sum_{j=-b2}^{b2} \left(I_L(P_{Lh}\text{-}i; P_{Lv}\text{-}j) - \bar{I}_L\right) \cdot \left(I_R(P_{Rh}\text{-}i; P_{Rv}\text{-}j) - \bar{I}_R\right)}{\sqrt{\sum_{i=-b2}^{b2} \sum_{j=-b2}^{b2} \left(I_L(P_{Lh}\text{-}i; P_{Lv}\text{-}j) - \bar{I}_L\right)^2 \cdot \sum_{i=-b2}^{b2} \sum_{j=-b2}^{b2} \left(I_R(P_{Rh}\text{-}i; P_{Rv}\text{-}j) - \bar{I}_R\right)^2}}$$

with $\bar{I}$ = mean luminance of a block   (9)

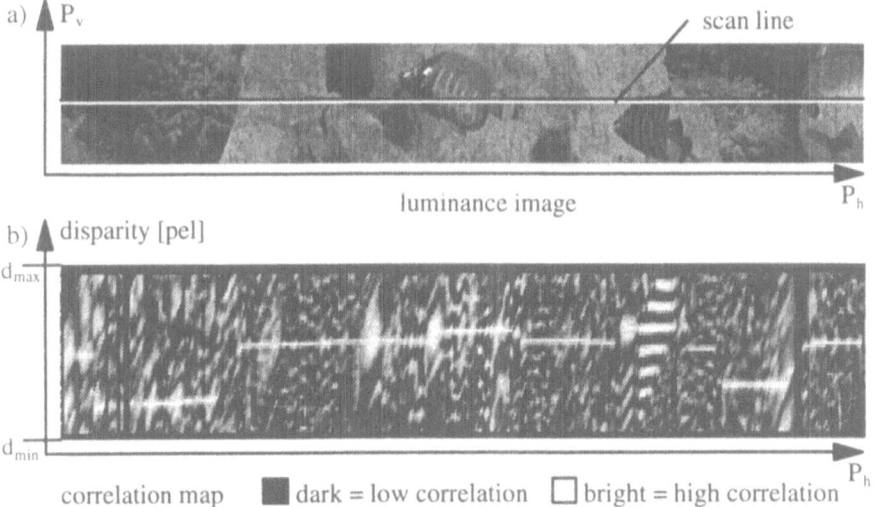

Fig. 2:   a) Horizontal slice of an image from the DISTIMA test sequence
'aqua' with a selected scan line
b) Correlation map of the selected scan line, showing the NCC between
each point along the scan line and each candidate on the epipolar line

In order to estimate the disparity for a scan line, a NCC map is computed, specifying the NCC for each possible candidate pair. Possible candidates are image points within a fixed disparity range. A cross correlation map for two scan lines of the test image pair 'aqua' is shown in Fig. 2, where bright horizontal lines indicate probable areas of continuos disparity. Based on the correlation map a cost map is computed applying a cost function for each candidate pair.

2.3.1 Evaluation of the DN–Cost Function

A dynamic programming strategy is applied to find the maximum likely disparity estimates for each scan line. With this strategy the cost of the candidate pairs are computed one after another starting with $h_j = 1$ and $d = d_{max}$. The cost for each candidate pair is composed of two summands, a local cost and the cost of the most probable predecessor.

For each candidate pair three possible predecessors are evaluated using (10), which have a maximum disparity difference of $\Delta d = \pm 1$ (see Fig. 3). Depending on the disparity difference the local cost is a fixed cost C_{change} for changed disparity or a matching cost C_{match} for constant disparity. The predecessor that leads to the minimal resulting cost is chosen and its position is stored additionally, in order to find the most likely way for the whole scan line.

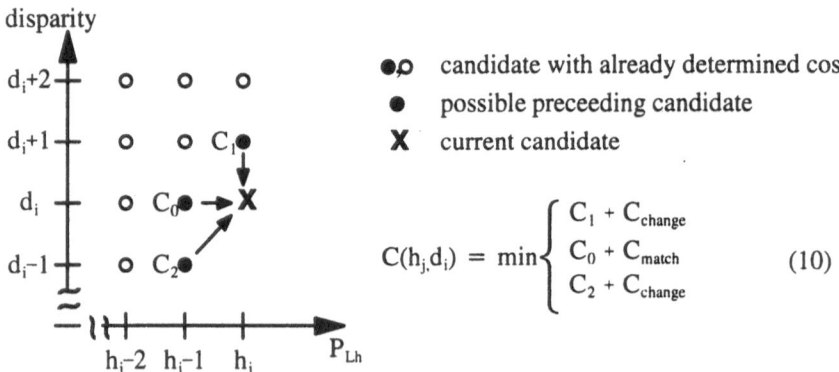

Fig. 3: Computation of the cost map with the DN–cost function

When the complete cost map of a scan line is computed, the disparity candidate with the lowest cost is searched at the last pel of the scan line. Starting from this candidate the disparity values along the scan line are determined backwards, using the path that is stored for each cost element pointing to the predecessor.

2.3.2 Elements of the DN–Cost Function

The cost for a change in disparity C_{change} depends on the probability of an object boundary $P_{boundary}$ and on the image noise variance σ_n^2. $P_{boundary}$ depends on size of the objects in the scene and is determined by the mean number of object boundaries along a scan line of the image related to the number of pels in each scan line. $P_{boundary}$ is of size 0.95 –0.98. In [8] the following cost value is derived.

$$C_{change} = \ln\left(\frac{1 - P_{boundary}}{P_{boundary}} \cdot \frac{1}{\sqrt{2\pi\sigma_n^2}}\right) \qquad (11)$$

On the other hand a matching cost C_{match} has to be derived, evaluating constant disparity along the scan line. This cost value depends on the NCC of the candidate pair and has to be adapted to the size of C_{change}, which is related to the noise variance of the luminance signal. Therefore the NCC is scaled in the range of the luminance values.

$$C_{match} = 255 \cdot \frac{1 - NCC^2}{4 \cdot \sigma_n^2} \qquad (12)$$

2.4 Disparity Estimation considering an Extended Neighborhood (EN–Cost Function)

The DN–cost function derived in Chapter 2.3 does not consider all estimation constraints. An extended maximum likelihood cost function is presented in this Chapter that considers additionally the extended continuity constraint. This constraint requires the examination of more than three preceding candidates. The examination is still limited to candidates in the same scan line and the new maximum likelihood cost function is minimized for each scan line using dynamic programming.

The EN–cost function is composed of three cost terms. The first cost term is the cost of the predecessor. The second cost is the cost for matching probability of a candidate pair. This cost term is similar to the one in the previous cost function, but is considered independently on the disparity change. In the previous cost function, this term was considered only in the case of constant disparity.

The third cost term $C_{penalty}$ evaluates the disparity change with respect to the predecessor. Due to the resolution of disparity, changes are limited to integer values. The evaluation of disparity changes in the left disparity map is listed below.

- Case 1: $\quad \Delta d = 0 \Rightarrow C_{penalty} = 0$
  Continuous disparity due to an object surface parallel to the image plane.

- Case 2: $\quad \Delta d = \pm 1 \Rightarrow C_{penalty} = C_{inclination}$
  Continuous disparity change due to the inclination of an object surface with increasing or decreasing distance to the camera

- Case 3: $\quad -\infty < \Delta d < -1 \Rightarrow C_{penalty} = C_{discontinuity}$
  Disparity discontinuity due to a transition from an object in the foreground to an object in the background.

- Case 4: $\quad +1 < \Delta d < +\infty \Rightarrow C_{penalty} = C_{discontinuity} + \Delta d \cdot C_{occlusion}$
  with $\Delta d = d(h_0) - d(h_0 - \Delta d)$
  Disparity discontinuity due to a transition from an object in the background to an object in the foreground, considering possible occlusions.

Because of the asymmetric disparity gradient limit, two different kinds of disparity discontinuities have to be considered. These discontinuities are denoted as Case 3 and Case 4 in the list above. For rising disparity, a discontinuity coincides with an occluded area in the right image. As a result, disparity is undetermined in the left image within a range of Δd preceding image points. In the cost function this is considered by taking $C(h_0-\Delta d, d_0+\Delta d)$ as a possible predecessor. An additional penalty is required, evaluating the number of skipped disparity estimates. For falling disparity, a discontinuity does not coincide with an occlusion.

The cost map is determined in a similar manner as in the previous algorithm. In contrast to the previous cost function, where three predecessors have been evaluated for each candidate, the number of possible predecessors is now predestinated by the disparity range.

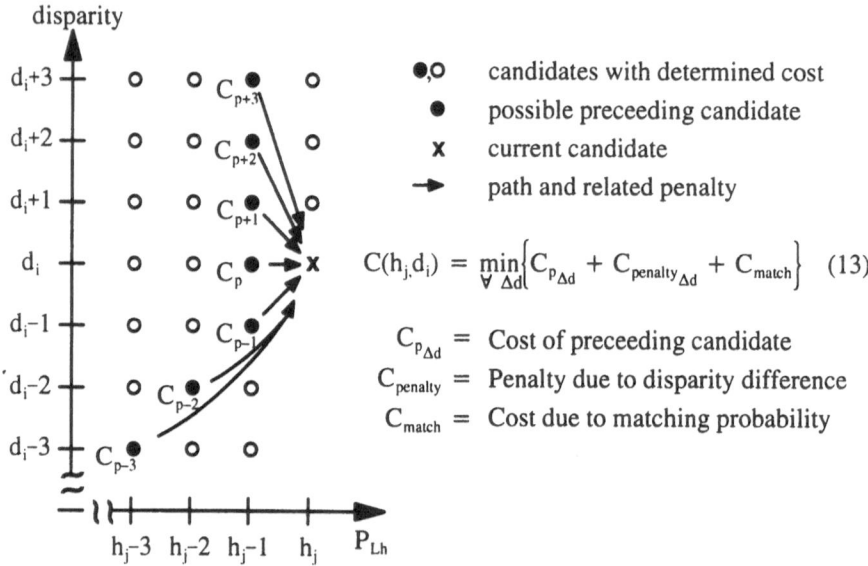

Fig. 4: Computation of the cost map with the EN–cost function

The computation of the cost of a single candidate pair is illustrated in (Fig. 4). In this Figure, each point is one element of the cost map. From each predecessor an arrow points to the current candidate, which coincides with a penalty depending on the change of disparity. The reason for the asymmetric arrangement of possible candidates is the asymmetric disparity gradient limit.

The quality of disparity estimation depends to great extent on the penalty terms of the EN–cost function (13). These penalty terms have been optimized with respect to the penalty term of the DN–cost function C_{change} using the DISTIMA test sequences.

$$C_{inclination} = C_{change}$$
$$C_{discontinuity} = 4 \cdot C_{change}$$
$$C_{occlusion} = 4 \cdot C_{change}$$
(14)

3 Computation of a Dense Depth Map

Disparity cannot be estimated in low textured areas and in areas which are visible in one image only. These disparity gaps shall be interpolated without a smoothing of disparity discontinuities. Additionally the corona effect of block–matching shall be compensated.

3.1 Segmentation of Regions of Homogeneous Disparity

With the applied disparity estimation algorithm, disparity is estimated in pel resolution. Because of the disparity gradient limit introduced in Chapter 2.2.3 and the disparity resolution, all disparity estimates with an absolute disparity difference to their neighbors below 2 pel shall be merged into one region of homogeneous disparity. The resulting regions are therefore not limited to a certain amount of different disparity values, but to a maximum absolute disparity gradient of 1.

The segmentation is carried out in several steps. Initially, all neighboring points with equal disparity are merged into regions of constant disparity. In a second step neighboring regions with a maximum disparity difference of one are merged. In order to compensate single disparity estimation failures, a minimum connection of 10 pel between these regions is additionally required. In a third step small labels are assigned to the neighbor with the most similar disparity, which guarantees a minimum size of regions. Undetermined regions are treated as occlusions and are therefore ascribed to the deepest neighbor, which is the one with the lowest disparity.

Even with the small block–sizes of the developed disparity estimation algorithms, the corona effect of block–matching is apparent in the disparity maps (Fig. 5b). Under the assumption that object boundaries and therefore disparity discontinuities coincide with luminance edges, the corona effect of block–matching is compensated by adapting region boundaries to neighboring luminance edges. The maximum size of the corona is half of the block–size. Therefore luminance edges in this area around region boundaries are detected by evaluating the luminance gradient. Both, luminance edges and region boundaries are then dilated and afterwards skeletonized, resulting in a new region boundary in the middle between their original position. When this method is applied iteratively, the region boundaries are successively adapted to neighboring luminance edges (Fig. 5d).

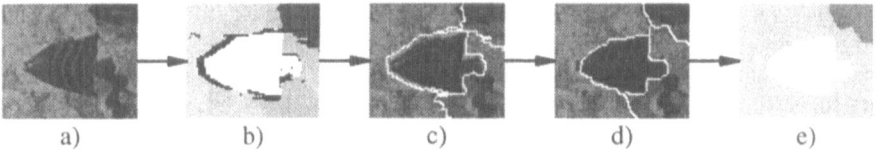

a)   b)   c)   d)   e)

Fig. 5:   a) Part of DISTIMA image 'aqua'
b) Estimated disparity map (dark = low disparity, bright = high disparity)
c) Segmentation into regions of homogeneous disparity
d) Adaptation of region boundaries to neighboring luminance edges
e) Interpolated disparity map with corona compensation

3.2   Disparity Interpolation

In order to compute dense depth maps, disparity gaps have to be interpolated. Disparity discontinuities are not effected, because disparity is interpolated within segmented regions of homogeneous disparity only.

For interpolation purposes, the disparity estimates of a segmented region are approximated by a thin plate. The finite element method is used to minimize the energy of the thin plate, which is connected to the disparity values with springs of different force. The force of the springs is controlled by the reliability of the estimated disparity, which is the NCC in the proposed method. Springs of no force are applied to disparity gaps. In addition springs of no force are applied to region boundaries, because disparity estimation is unreliable due to the corona effect there. The hierarchical interpolation algorithm minimizing the energy of the thin plate is based on [9].

The reliability of disparity estimation is enhanced before the interpolation, using a disparity verification between the left and right disparity map. With this verification all disparity estimates that differ more than 1 pel from their corresponding disparity estimate in the other disparity map are neglected (15).

$$|d_L(h_i; v_j) - d_R(h_i - d(h_i; v_j); v_j)| \leq 1 \tag{15}$$

This verification enables also an assessment of disparity estimation, because the remaining disparity estimates can be treated as correct disparity values.

3.3   Depth Computation from Disparity

With known extrinsic camera parameters depth is computed from disparity. Therefore each point of the interpolated disparity map is evaluated using equation (6).

4   Results

The developed algorithms have been examined using DISTIMA stereoscopic image sequences. In this paper the results for image sequence 'aqua' are presented, which are typical for the results obtained with other image sequences. Image sequence 'aqua' has TV resolution and is 2 seconds long. The first image pair and results are presented in (Fig. 6).

Disparity has been estimated for each field of 'aqua', applying block–matching, The DN–cost function and the EN–disparity estimation use block sizes of 5x5 pel. An example of the disparity estimation results is given in (Fig. 6). To compare the three different estimation algorithms, the amount of correct disparity estimates is evaluated. The correctness is verified using (15). For 25% of the image, no disparity can be estimated, because the luminance constraint is not fulfilled of the points are only visible in one of the images of an image pair. For the remaining 75% disparity can be estimated. The part of verified disparity values rises from 65% applying block–matching to 70% with the new approaches. The difference between both new approaches is below 1%. The increased number of correctly estimated disparity values shows the result from the increased reliability of the developed algorithm. Even the consideration of an extended neighborhood increases the reliability slightly, so that the usage is only recommended if the computation time is not relevant. Applying the proposed algorithm increases the computational effort by a factor of 2 in the case of the DN–cost function and by the factor of 3 in the case of the EN–cost function when compared to block–matching.

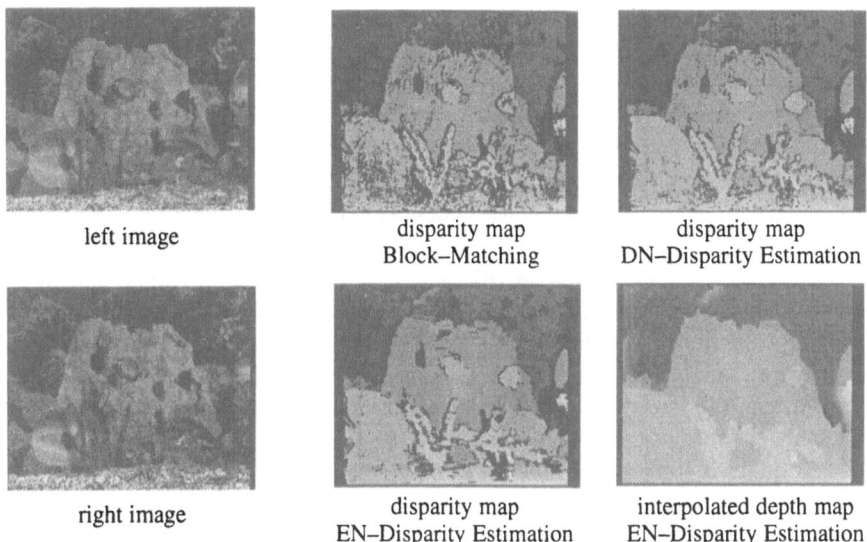

left image	disparity map Block–Matching	disparity map DN–Disparity Estimation
right image	disparity map EN–Disparity Estimation	interpolated depth map EN–Disparity Estimation

Fig. 6: Depth and disparity estimation results for a DISTIMA image pair 'aqua'

5 Conclusions

In this contribution, an algorithm for reliable and accurate disparity estimation has been developed that avoids the corona effect of block–matching at disparity discontinuities. Therefore, a maximum likelihood estimator for two corresponding lines of a stereo-scopic image pair has been developed that evaluates neighboring disparity estimates. Under the assumption of horizontally arranged cameras, corresponding lines, which are also called epipolar lines, are according scan lines.

For the evaluation of neighboring disparity estimates a cost function and a cost minimization procedure has been developed that considers the following disparity estimation constraints. Each picture element (pel) of one scan line corresponds exactly to one pel of the epipolar line. Corresponding pels have to occur in the same ordering in both scan lines. These constraints are fulfilled by applying dynamic programming for the minimization of the cost function. The disparity gradient in horizontal direction is limited between $[-\infty ; +1]$, which reduces the amount of possible neighboring disparity values. With the extended disparity continuity constraint, large objects are assumed and disparity discontinuities are allowed at object boundaries only. Therefore penalty terms evaluating disparity changes between neighboring disparity values are applied that cause continuos disparity to be favoured. The correspondence measure between two pels is the cross correlation of corresponding image blocks. Two cost functions have been derived, which differ in the number of considered neighbors. The first algorithm evaluates only direct neighboring disparity estimates (DN–cost function), which enables the consideration of all constraints except the extended continuity constraint. The second algorithm evaluates an extended neighborhood (EN–cost function), which enables the consideration of all constraints.

Block sizes between 11x11 pel and 17x17 pel are chosen for block–matching or in the first level of hierarchical block–matching, in order to give reliable results. With the new cost functions the necessary block size for reliable disparity estimates is reduced to 5x5 pel. Due to the reduced block size disparity can be estimated more accurate compared to block–matching and the corona effect at disparity discontinuities can be reduced effectively compared to hierarchical block–matching. Reliability is ensured by the consideration of neighboring disparity values. The reliability of disparity estimates is verified by comparing disparity estimates of the left disparity map with corresponding disparity estimates in the right disparity map. Disparity values that do not match are deleted in the disparity map. Disparity is only be estimated, when the local luminance variance in direction of the epipolar line is much higher than the camera noise variance. Disparity estimation result for DISTIMA image sequence 'aqua' are presented. In this sequence, approximately 75 % of all image points are visible in both images and fulfill the luminance constraint. Averaged over the 50 frames, the percentage of verified disparity values is increased from 65% using block–matching to 69% using the DN–cost function and 70% using the EN–cost function. Verifications using other DISTIMA image sequences provided similar results. Applying the proposed algorithm increases the computational effort by a factor of 2 in the case of the DN–cost function and by the factor of 3 in the case of the EN–cost function when compared to block–matching.

In order to compute dense depth maps, disparity gaps have to be interpolated without a smoothing of disparity discontinuities. Therefore the disparity map is segmented into regions of homogeneous disparity. The developed segmentation algorithm subdivides the disparity map, which is estimated with integer resolution, into regions of equal disparity values in a first step. It is assumed that disparity changes between neighboring pels of a continuos surface are limited to ± 1 pel. Therefore, in a second step neighboring regions with a disparity difference of ± 1 are merged. The remaining corona effect of block–matching is compensated during segmentation by adapting segmented region boundaries to neighboring luminance edges using an iterative dilation and skeletonization technique. Disparity values inside the corona are not considered during interpolation. Therefore the corona effect is avoided in the resulting depth map.

Beside its usage in DISTIMA, the presented algorithm has successfully been applied to modelling of 3D natural objects from multiple views in the RACE–MONA LISA project [2] and modelling of buildings from stereoscopic image sequences [10].

6 References

[1]   R. Koch, "Model–Based 3D Scene Analysis from Stereoscopic Image Sequences", ISPRS '92, Vol. 29, Part B5, Washington, October 1992, pp. 427 – 437.

[2]   Niem, W., Buschmann, R., "Automatic Modelling of 3D Natural Objects from Multiple Views", European Workshop on Combined real and synthetic image

processing for broadcast and video productions, 23–24. 11. 1994, Hamburg, Germany.

[3] L. Falkenhagen, A. Kopernik, M. Strintzis, "Disparity Estimation based on 3D Arbitrarily Shaped Regions", RACE Project Deliverable, R2045/UH/DS/P/023/b1

[4] A. Koschan, "Eine Methodenbank zur Evaluierung von Stereo–Vision–Verfahren", Ph. D Thesis, Technische Universität Berlin, Berlin, Germany, 1991.

[5] M. Bierling, "Hierarchische Displacementschätzung zur Bewegungskompensation in digitalen Fernsehbildsequenzen", Ph. D Thesis, Universität Hannover, Hannover, Germany, 1991.

[6] B. Choquet, A. Poussier, "Selection of short existing test sequences", RACE Project Deliverable, R2045/CCETT/WP3.1/DS/T/004/01

[7] Y. Yakimovski, R. Cunningham, "A System for Extracting 3D Measurements from a Stereo Pair of TV Cameras", CGVIP, Vol. 7, 1978, pp. 195 – 210.

[8] Cox, I., Hingorani, S., Maggs, B., Rao, S., "Stereo without Regularisation", NEC Research Institute, Princeton, NJ, USA, Oct. 1992.

[9] D. Terzopolus, "The computation of visible surface representation", IEEE Trans. Pattern Analysis and Machine Intelligence, Vol. 10, pp.417–438, USA, 1988.

[10] Koch, R., "3–D Scene Modelling from Stereoscopic Image Sequences", European Workshop on Combined real and synthetic image processing for broadcast and video productions, 23–24. 11. 1994, Hamburg, Germany.

3–D Scene Modeling
from Stereoscopic Image Sequences

Reinhard Koch

Institut für Theoretische Nachrichtentechnik und Informationsverarbeitung
Division "Automatic Image Interpretation", Chair Prof. C.-E. Liedtke
Universität Hannover, Appelstrasse 9A, 30167 Hannover, Germany
email: koch@tnt.uni–hannover.de

Abstract

A vision–based 3–D scene analysis system is described that is capable to model complex real–world scenes like buildings automatically from stereoscopic image pairs. Input to the system is a sequence of stereoscopic images taken with two standard CCD Cameras and TV lenses. The relative orientation of both cameras to each other is estimated by calibration. The camera pair is then moved throughout the scene and a long sequence of closely spaced views is recorded. Each of the stereoscopic image pairs is rectified and a dense map of 3–D surface points is obtained by area correlation, object segmentation, interpolation, and triangulation. 3–D camera motion relative to the scene coordinate system is tracked directly from the image sequence which allows to fuse 3–D surface measurements from different view points into a consistent 3–D scene model. The surface geometry of each scene object is approximated by a triangular surface mesh which stores the surface texture in a texture map. From the textured 3–D models, realistic looking image sequences from arbitrary view points can be synthesized using computer graphics.

1   Introduction

The rapid progress in the development of powerful computer graphics hardware and software enables users in a wide range of applications to gain a better insight into processes by visual simulation. Suppliers of flight and driving simulators as well as landscape and city planners are interested to simulate photo–realistic views of the environment. Architects and city planners for example construct new buildings with CAD systems and are interested to visualize their impact onto the existing environment beforehand. Complete realism, however, is possible only if the buildings to be constructed are placed inside a 3–D reconstruction of of the real environment. It is therefore necessary to reconstruct the existing environment as a 3–D model of the real scene with as little effort as possible [1]. One possible approach is to obtain a complete 3–D scene description by evaluating images of the scene.

Automatic evaluation of all scene properties, camera position and 3–D object geometry as well as photometric surface mapping, for the purpose to reconstruct 3–D scene models for visualization, are discussed in this contribution. To overcome the problem of simultaneous estimation of object geometry and camera position, a calibrated stereoscopic image sequence is recorded. From each image pair the geometry is measured and from the sequence information relative camera motion can be extracted. All measurements obtained from the image sequence need then to be integrated into a consistent 3–D scene model that contains not only the scene geometry but also texture maps of the object surface. Visual simulations of the scene from this complete scene model can be performed using computer graphics methods [2].

This approach is mostly data driven and models the 3–D scene directly from the recorded image sequence in a bottom–up process. It can be complemented by the model–driven approach by Grau and Tönjes [3] that uses high level semantic information about the scene contents to constrain the modeling problem in a top–down process.

The paper is organized as follows. Chapter 2 discusses the concept of the scene analysis system. Chapter 3 treats the measurement of object geometry from a single image pair whereas in Chapter 4 motion estimation and sequence accumulation is discussed. Chapter 5 concludes with some results of scene reconstruction.

2   Concept of 3–D Scene Modeling

The structure of the scene analysis process is shown in Fig. 1. The upper part consists of the image analysis pipeline that computes a model scene M_k from a stereoscopic image pair L_k, R_k at time instant k. The pipeline computes a complete surface model for the current view point k through image rectification, correspondence analysis, scene segmentation, depth interpolation, and surface mesh generation. The model is represented by a triangular surface mesh that stores the surface geometry in its control points **P** and the color from the input images as texture maps on the triangle surfaces.

Sequence information is included into the analysis pipeline by camera motion tracking and 3–D model accumulation. The camera motion is computed directly from the

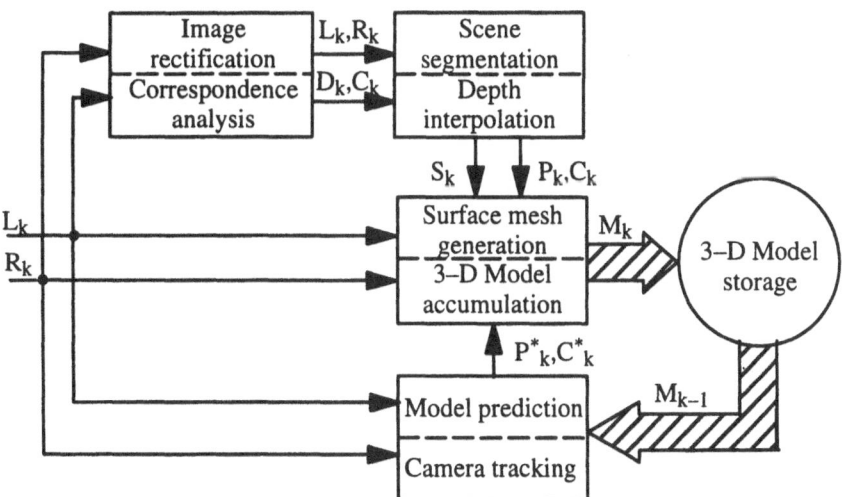

L_k: Left image D_k: Disparity map S_k: Segmentation map
R_k: Right image C_k: Confidence map P_k: Depth map M_k: 3–D Scene model
k: Index indicating the actual time frame $^*k$ = data predicted from model M_{k-1}

Fig. 1: Structure of 3–D scene analysis from stereoscopic sequences.

130

spatio–temporal image intensity gradients. Once the new camera position is known, the geometry of the existing scene model M_{k-1} can be predicted into the current camera position at frame k and merged with the new depth measurements to yield a refined scene model M_k. Merging is performed by computing an optimal estimate from the predicted surface geometry $\mathbf{P}^*_k$ and the newly measured geometry $\mathbf{P}_k$ with a Kalman filter for each control point $\mathbf{P}$.

3   3–D Surface Modeling from an Image Pair

Stereoscopic image analysis allows to compute a 3–D surface model of the scene for each image pair through correspondence analysis. For each pixel in the left image the corresponding pixel in the right image is searched for and stored in the disparity map D_k. As quality measure for the best match the cross correlation of a small block circumscribing the pixel is evaluated in combination with dynamic programming to search for the optimum disparity. The quality of the match and therefore the quality of the disparity value is recorded in a confidence map C_k. For a detailed description of the correspondence analysis please refer to the literature [4],[5]. As an example of disparity estimation the correspondence analysis for the scene HOUSE is shown in Fig. 2. Fig. 2a contains the left image of a stereoscopic image pair taken from the scene and Fig. 2b and 2c display the disparity and confidence map computed from the scene.

The correspondence analysis yields a disparity map based on local depth measurement only. These measurements are corrupted by noise and must be merged to regions that describe physical object surfaces. Based on similarity measures the segmentation divides the viewed scene into smooth object surfaces. As similarity measure the estimated disparities as well as grey level statistics are used to group pixels into regions of similar surface orientation. The region boundaries are then corrected from the grey level image with a contour approximation by assuming that physical object boundaries most often create grey level edges in the image.

In order to obtain an efficient 3–D surface description and to treat hidden surfaces properly, the scene depth is represented by a triangular surface mesh. For each surface the depth map is approximated by triangular, planar surface patches. The triangular mesh was chosen because it is capable to approximate arbitrary surface geometries

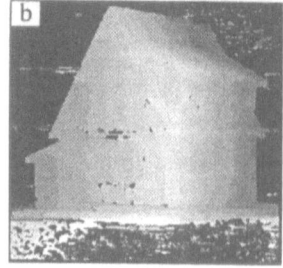

left original image

disparity map
(dark = far from camera,
light = near to camera)

confidence map
(dark = low confidence,
light = high confidence)

Fig. 2:   Stereoscopic disparity analysis of image pair "HOUSE".

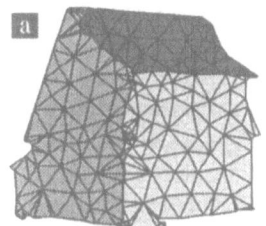  

| Triangular surface mesh of walls and roof | texture mapping of scene texture | synthesized image from new view point |

Fig. 3: Triangulation, texture mapping and image synthesis.

without singularities. The geometric surface model computed for the scene HOUSE is shown in Fig 3a with each surface having another color. On the surface of each triangular patch the original texture is stored in a texture map from which naturally looking views can be synthesized through texture mapping, as shown in Fig. 3b for the original and in3c for a new view point.

4 Image Sequence Fusion

For each image pair of the sequence a disparity map D_k is calculated independently by stereoscopic analysis together with its associated confidence map C_k. The model geometry can be enhanced when multiple views of the scene are processed and fused together. The goal of sequence accumulation is therefore to fuse the depth measurements from the image sequence into a consistent 3–D scene model to improve estimation quality. This implies the need to estimate the camera positions for all view points.

4.1 Estimation of 3–D Camera View Point

The camera position can be derived directly from the spatial and temporal image gradients as long as the relative camera motion is small between consecutive image frames [6], [7]. It is computed by tracking the relative motion of the 3–D objects visible to the camera and then adjusting the camera position accordingly.

An object is defined as a rigid 3–D surface in space that is spanned by a set of N control points. Six motion parameters are associated with the object. Object motion is defined as rotation of the object control points around the object center followed by a translation of the object center, measured between two successive image frames k–1 and k. The object center $\mathbf{G}$ is the mean position vector of all N object control points. Each object control point $\mathbf{P}_{i(k-1)}$ at frame k–1 is transformed to its new position $\mathbf{P}_{i(k)}$ in frame k according to the general motion Eq. (1) between frame k–1 and k.

$$\mathbf{P}_{i(k)} = \underline{R} \cdot (\mathbf{P}_{i(k-1)} - \mathbf{G}) + \mathbf{G} + \mathbf{T} \tag{1}$$

$\mathbf{T} = (T_x, T_y, T_z)^T$ = translation vector, $\mathbf{G} = \sum_{i=1}^{N} \frac{\mathbf{P}_i}{N}$ = component center

$\underline{R}$ = matrix of rotation vector $\mathbf{R} = (R_x, R_y, R_z)^T$

The only information available to the analysis system is the surface texture projected onto the camera target throughout the image sequence. From this sequence the motion parameters have to be derived. Assume a scene with an arbitrarily shaped, moving textured object observed by a camera during frames k–1 and k. The object moves between frame k–1 and k according to the general motion Eq. (1) with motion parameters $\mathbf{R}$ and $\mathbf{T}$. A control point on the object surface $\mathbf{P}_{(k-1)}$ holds the surface intensity I_1, which is projected onto $\mathbf{p}_1$ in the image plane at frame k–1. $\mathbf{P}_{(k-1)}$ is moved to $\mathbf{P}_{(k)}$, still holding I_1 that is now projected onto $\mathbf{p}_2$ in image frame k. In image frame k the surface intensity I_1 is projected at image position $\mathbf{p}_2$, whereas the image intensity at point $\mathbf{p}_1$ has changed to I_2.

The image displacement vector $\mathbf{d} = \mathbf{p}_2 - \mathbf{p}_1$ is called optical flow vector and describes the projection of the observation point displacement $\mathbf{P}_{(k)} - \mathbf{P}_{(k-1)}$ onto the image plane. When assuming a linear dependency of the surface texture between I_1 and I_2 and a brightness constancy constraint between frame k–1 and k it is possible to predict I_2 from I_1 and its corresponding image intensity gradients and hence to estimate $\mathbf{d}$ from the measurable difference $I_2 - I_1$. I_2 is measured at position of $\mathbf{p}_1$ at frame k, where I_1 is taken from image position $\mathbf{p}_1$ at frame k–1. When approximating the spatial derivatives as finite differences the optical flow vector $\mathbf{d} = (d_x, d_y)^T$ can be predicted from the spatial image gradients $\mathbf{g} = (g_x, g_y)^T$ and the temporal image intensity difference $\Delta I_{p1} = I_2 - I_1$ between frame k and k–1 at $\mathbf{p}_1$ in Eq. (2):

$$\Delta I_{p1} = \mathbf{g}^T \cdot \mathbf{d} = g_x \cdot d_x + g_y \cdot d_y = g_x \cdot (p_{2x} - p_{1x}) + g_y \cdot (p_{2y} - p_{1y}) \quad (2)$$

In Eq. (2) $\mathbf{d}$ is related to intensity differences. Substituting the perspective projection of $\mathbf{P}_{(k-1)}$ and $\mathbf{P}_{(k)}$ for $\mathbf{p}_1$ and $\mathbf{p}_2$ in Eq. (2) yields a direct geometric to photometric transform that relates the spatial movement of $\mathbf{P}$ between frame k–1 and k to temporal intensity changes in the image sequence at $\mathbf{p}_1$.

$$\Delta I_{p1} = f \cdot g_x \cdot \left(\frac{P_{(k)x}}{P_{(k)z}} - \frac{P_{(k-1)x}}{P_{(k-1)z}} \right) + f \cdot g_y \cdot \left(\frac{P_{(k)y}}{P_{(k)z}} - \frac{P_{(k-1)y}}{P_{(k-1)z}} \right) \quad (3)$$

With this approach, rigid 3–D object motion can be estimated directly from the image sequence when the object shape $\mathbf{P}_{(k-1)}$ is known. Assuming that rotation between successive images is small, $\underline{R}$ can be linearized and $\mathbf{P}_{(k)}$ is substituted in Eq. (3) as a function of the unknown parameter $\mathbf{R}$ and $\mathbf{T}$ as derived in Eq. (1):

$$\Delta I_{p1} \cdot P_z^2 = f \cdot g_x \cdot P_z \cdot T_x + f \cdot g_y \cdot P_z \cdot T_y - [\Delta I_{p1} \cdot P_z + f P_x g_x + f P_y g_y] \cdot T_z$$
$$- [\Delta I_{p1} \cdot P_z \cdot (P_y - G_y) + f P_x \cdot g_x \cdot (P_y - G_y) + f P_y \cdot g_y \cdot (P_y - G_y) + f P_z \cdot g_y \cdot (P_z - G_z)] \cdot R_x$$
$$+ [\Delta I_{p1} \cdot P_z \cdot (P_x - G_x) + f P_x \cdot g_x \cdot (P_x - G_x) + f P_y \cdot g_y \cdot (P_x - G_x) + f P_z \cdot g_x \cdot (P_z - G_z)] \cdot R_y$$
$$+ [f P_x \cdot g_y \cdot (P_x - G_x) - f P_z \cdot g_x \cdot (P_y - G_y)] \cdot R_z$$
$$\text{with } (P_x, P_y, P_z)^T = P_{(k-1)}. \quad (4)$$

Eq. (4) contains a linear dependency of the motion parameter $\mathbf{X} = (\mathbf{T}, \mathbf{R})^T$ with the image gradients ΔI and $\mathbf{g}$ and can be solved when many independent control points $\mathbf{P}_i$ are evaluated using linear regression. Solving the system of equation (4) for all observation points simultaneous is accomplished by minimizing the squared error of intensity differences ΔI. The confidence of the motion estimation can be computed as motion parameter covariance $\underline{C}_\mathbf{X}$ from the solution as well.

4.2 Fusing Depth Measurements from Multiple View Points

Depth measurements are improved by weighted depth accumulation from the motion compensated sequence of depth maps. An optimum estimate $\hat{P}_k$ and covariance $\hat{C}_k$ of the model control points is computed throughout the sequence by applying a Kalman filter to each control point of the surface. The Kalman filter exists of three phases: measurement, prediction, and update. Details can be found in the literature [8],[9].

<u>Measurement</u>: For each control point of the model surface at the current frame k a depth measurement $\mathbf{P}_k$ is computed from the analysis pipeline together with a confidence value C that expresses the measurement accuracy. A point covariance $\underline{C}_{Pk}$ can be computed from the confidence value C and the camera uncertainty $\underline{C}_X$.

<u>Prediction</u>: A Prediction $\mathbf{P}^*_k$ of the new point position is made based on the motion model of the objects as defined in Eq. (5) from the old control point $\mathbf{P}_{k-1}$. The point covariance $\underline{C}^*_{Pk}$ is predicted as well by the motion model in Eq. (6). This prediction propagates the existing model control points from M_{k-1} to the current frame k.

$$P^*_k = \underline{R} \cdot (\hat{P}_{k-1} - G) + G + T \tag{5}$$

$$\underline{C}^*_{P_k} = \underline{R} \cdot \hat{\underline{C}}_{P_{k-1}} \cdot \underline{R}^T \tag{6}$$

<u>Update</u>: The new control point measurement is fused with the predicted old control point position by the Kalman filter. The Kalman gain $\underline{K}$ is computed from the covariance matrices and the optimum new control point position and covariance matrix is derived in Eq. (8) and (9).

$$\underline{K}_k = \underline{C}^*_{P_k} \cdot \left(\underline{C}^*_{P_k} + \underline{C}_{P_k}\right)^{-1} \tag{7}$$

$$\hat{P}_k = P^*_k + \underline{K}_k \cdot (P_k - P^*_k) \tag{8}$$

$$\hat{\underline{C}}_{P_k} = \underline{C}^*_{P_k} - \underline{K}_k \cdot \underline{C}^*_{P_k} \tag{9}$$

Fig. 4 shows the result of sequence accumulation for the scene HOUSE. A 3–D model of the house was generated and images were synthesized from a new view point by rotating the camera to 45 degrees from above. Fig. 4a displays the result of modeling from a single image pair. The model shape appears rough due to measurement errors. In Fig. 4b the result of image fusion from five different view points is shown. The model geometry is much smoother because of the temporal filtering. This result can still be improved when spatial interpolation is used to smooth the measurements as shown in Fig. 4c.

Image pair modeling   Depth fusion from 5 views   Spatio–temporal interpolation

Fig. 4:   Results of temporal and spatial filtering (synthesized views).

5 Conclusion

A system for automatic 3–D scene analysis was discussed. The system is capable to analyze a complex real scene from an arbitrarily moving stereoscopic video camera system. It segments the scene into smooth surfaces and stores the 3–D geometry of the scene in a 3–D scene model, including surface texture. Camera motion is tracked throughout the sequence and measurements from different view points are integrated to improve the model geometry.

The system was tested with a variety of scenes. An example of a more complex scene with many objects is the scene STREET in Fig.5a. The scene depth was computed (Fig.5b), the scene was segmented into different objects (Fig.5c) and a 3–D model of the main scene objects are was generated and synthesized (Fig.5d).

Applications of the system are expected in many areas like automatic model generation for driving simulators, architecture visualization, or realistic image synthesis for computer generated television production.

Left original image

Disparity map (dark = far from camera, light = near to camera)

Triangular mesh of main scene objects, superimposed onto the left image

Synthesis of the main scene objects from the 3–D surface model

Fig. 5:   3–D Modeling of image pair STREET.

Acknowledgement

This work was supported by a grant of the German postal service TELEKOM.

References

[1] Durisch, P. Photogrammetry and Computer Graphics for Visual Impact Analysis in Architectur. Proceedings of ISPRS Conference 1992, Vol. 29, B5, pp. 434–445.

[2] Koch, R. Automatic Modelling of Natural Scenes for Generating Synthetic Movies. In: Vandoni, C.E. and Duce, D.A. (ed.) Eurographics Association 1990. Elsevier Science Publishers B.V. (North–Holland).

[3] Grau, O., Tönjes, R. Knowledge Based Modelling of Natural Scenes. European Workshop on Combined real and synthetic image processing for broadcast and video productions, 23–24. 11. 1994, Hamburg, Germany.

[4] Falkenhagen, L. Depth Estimation from Stereoscopic Image Pairs Assuming Piecewise Continuos Surfaces. European Workshop on Combined real and synthetic image processing for broadcast and video productions, 23–24. 11. 1994, Hamburg, Germany.

[5] Cox, I., Hingorani, S., Maggs, B., Rao, S. Stereo without Regularisation. British Machine Vision Conference, Leeds, UK, David Hogg & Roger Boyle (ed.), Springer Verlag, 1992, pp. 337–346.

[6] Koch, R. Automatic Reconstruction of Buildings from Stereoscopic Image Sequences. Eurographics '93, Barcelona,Spain, 1993.

[7] Koch, R. Dynamic 3D Scene Analysis through Synthesis Feedback Control. IEEE Trans. Patt. Anal. Mach. Intell., Special issue on analysis and synthesis 1993. Vol. 15(6):556–568.

[8] Brammer, K, Siffling, G. Stochastische Grundlagen des Kalman–Bucy–Filters. R. Oldenbourg Verlag, München, 1985.

[9] Brammer, K, Siffling, G. Kalman–Bucy–Filter: Deterministische Beobachtung und stochastische Filterung. R. Oldenbourg Verlag, München, 1985.

The Usage of Turntable Sequences for Disparity/Depth Estimation

Thomas Riegel, Raphael Haermens
Siemens AG, ZFE ST SN 22
81730 Munich, Germany

1 Introduction

For the modelling of natural objects various approaches are known. Buschmann/Niem [1] developed an algorithm for the automatic modelling of isolated objects with convex shapes using silhouettes from multiple views of the object. One major drawback of this approach is its limitation on modelling objects with concavities. One way to overcome this restriction is to integrate depth information into the convex volume model. This additional information can be obtained by disparity/depth estimation using the same images. The aim of this contribution is to describe the individual steps which are necessary to calculate a depth value for each pixel of the object in each perspective view.

After starting with a short description of the turntable environment the image rectification process for transforming the turntable images into (almost) ideal stereo images pairs is explained. The main part of the paper deals with the engaged stereo matching technique to produce dense disparity maps. The last section of this paper explains how the depth information is calculated.

2 Acquisition of a turntable sequence

The environment for taking the images consists of a platform, a diffuse lighting and a CCD camera. After placing the object onto the platform, the turntable is rotated and still pictures are captured (Figure 1). Besides measuring the rotation angle of the platform a camera calibration is performed. Thus for each image the focal length, the orientation of the optical axis, and the position of the focal point relative to a world coordinate system is obtained.

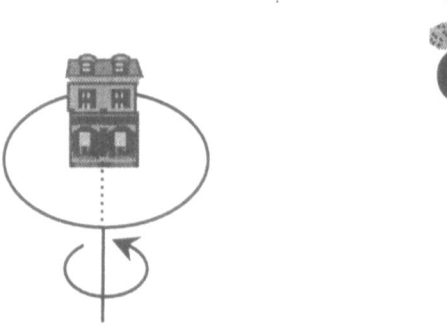

Figure 1: Turntable environment

Choosing a small rotation angle (from 1 to 10 degree) allows it to treat two successive images as a stereo image pair. Figure 2 shows a schematic drawing of the corresponding stereo camera arrangement, with the inclination angle α, the elevation angle ϑ, and the baseline b.

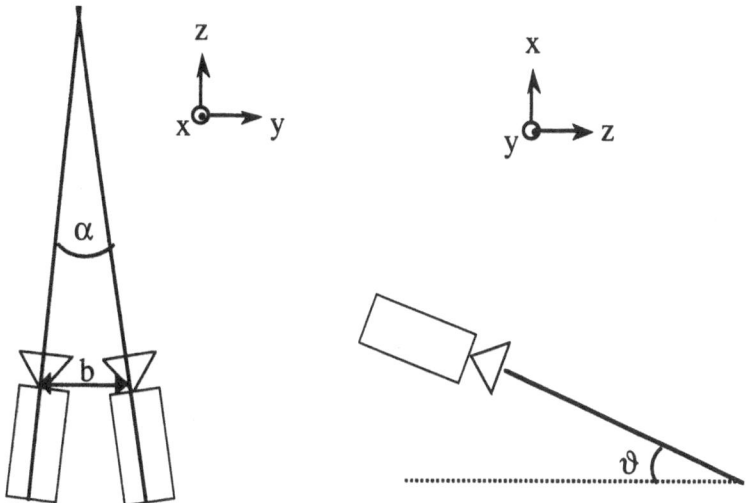

Figure 2: Corresponding stereo camera arrangement

For recovering depth from stereo images a correspondence needs to be established between features from the left and right image that correspond to the same physical feature in space. Then, employing the camera calibration results, the depth can be reconstructed using triangulation. The matching is achieved by local search procedures and can be governed by the imaging (epipolar line) geometry. The epipolar constraint assures that the corresponding match of a point in the left image belongs to a straight line (epipolar line) in the right image. The above camera arrangement (general case) yields stereo images with non parallel epipolar lines (Figure 3).

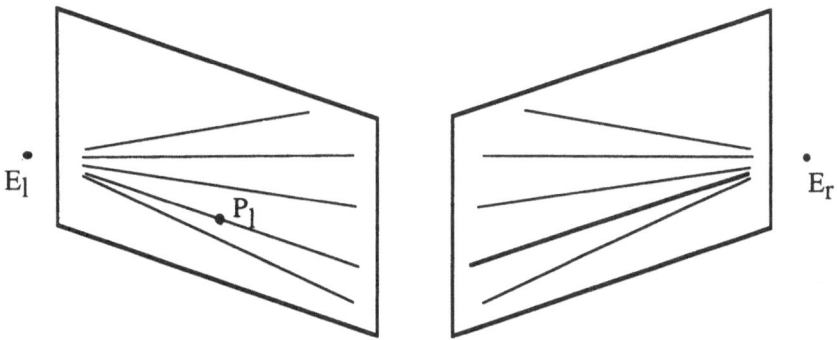

Figure 3: The bundle of epipolar lines (general case)
The bold line in the right image is the corresponding epipolar line to the Point P_1 in the left image

3 Rectification of turntable images

Since a dense depth/range map is required an area-based disparity estimation technique has to be employed. Area-based stereo techniques use correlation among brightness (intensity) patterns in the local neighbourhood of a pixel in one image with brightness patterns in a corresponding neighbourhood of a pixel in the other image. Due to the non parallel epipolar lines the cross-correlation measure has to be calculated on "distorted" neighbourhoods. This may lead to an erroneous measure and therefore to an inaccurate disparity estimation. To avoid this, the stereo images have to be rectified.

The way to achieve this is depicted in Figure 4. The undistorted images - as they would have been captured with aligned cameras (inclination angle $\alpha=0$) - are calculated from the original images. The positions of the focal points S_l and S_r, and the focal length f remains unchanged. By this the positions of the (rectified) image planes are determined. Thus for every pixel in the (rectified) image plane B the corresponding position of it in the original image plane A can be computed (intersection point of the line from the focal point to pixel in B with image plane A). The following parameters are necessary for that calculation:

Camera orientation:	Focal length	f
	Inclination angle	$\alpha = 2 \bullet \varphi$
Chip parameter:	Centre of image	M_x, M_y
	Effective Pixel size	dx, dy

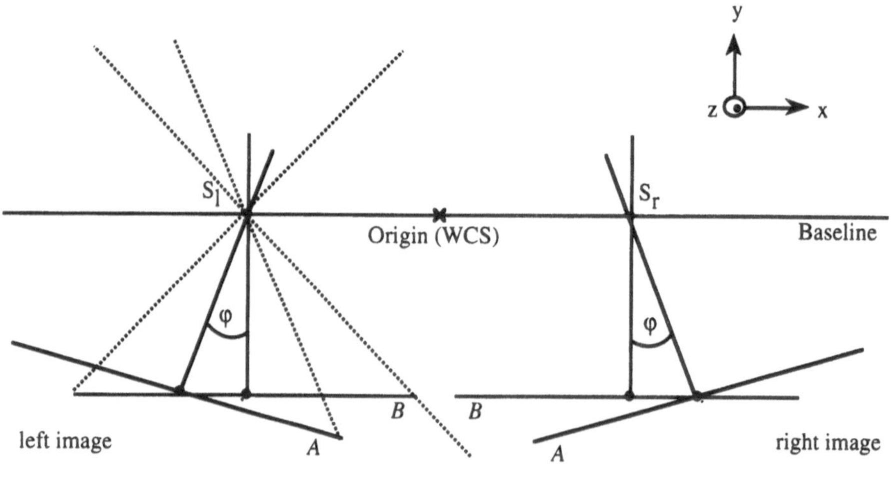

A: Image plane of original images, B: rectified image planes, WCS: world coordinate system

Figure 4: Rectification of turntable images

Due to the virtual rotation of the camera, pixel at the right border of the rectified image can not be calculated, whereas image parts on the left side of the original image get lost. It is obvious, that the size of these parts depends on the inclination angle. This can be avoided by shifting the image planes B in x direction by a suitable amount. Using a bilinear interpolation for the resampling yields good results.

Figure 5 shows two rectified successive images of the "Buggy" turntable sequence used as stereo image pair. The turntable sequence has been captured with an inclination angle of 5 degree.

Figure 5: Left and right rectified image of the "Buggy" turntable sequence.

In principle rectifying the original stereo images allows to compensate the distortions in the image geometry. Nevertheless lens distortions, calibration errors, and the resampling are influencing more or less the result, so that not really ideal stereo images with parallel lines can be expected. But under normal conditions the search space in the y direction can be reduced to ±1 line. This alleviates the disparity estimation regarding the computational effort as well as the quality of the result.

When computing the depth information from the disparity maps, the horizontal shift during the rectification has to be taken into account.

4 Disparity estimation

For the disparity estimation a modified version of an algorithm developed by Geiger et al. [2] has been applied. To model the stereo matching process a Bayesian approach is used defining an "a priori" probability for the disparity field, based on a weak smoothness assumption allowing discontinuities, uniqueness of matching and an occlusion constraint. These constraints are enforced through a cost function which is evaluated on a series of possible matching positions. The position which fulfils best the criteria will be chosen as the probable matching candidate. Each possible solution of the disparity field is represented as a path through the matching space (Figure 6a) and the optimal matching path is selected by a dynamic programming technique.

The basic algorithm works only with ideal stereo images, namely with the cameras having no inclination to each other and being aligned. In such case, the epipolar lines are horizontal and there is one-to-one correspondence with each other.

140

In cases where slight misalignment exists and the epipolar lines don't coincide with the scan lines, the algorithm gives false results. To solve this problem a vertical search has been added. Instead of following strictly an epipolar line, the y-search is added to the horizontal x-search to compensate for the epipolar line inclination. This method is more general and applicable to many cases where the camera parameter measurement contains error. Consequently another optimisation criterion was included in the dynamic programming cost, namely the vertical displacement correlation.

The vertical search requires the dynamic programming to find an optimum matching path in a 3-dimensional space (Figure 6b) unlike the previous algorithm which was calculating optimum matching path in a 2-dimensional space (Figure 6a). The new algorithm, although computationally more expensive, allows flexibility in disparity calculation for the case of misaligned cameras and cameras inclined to each other.

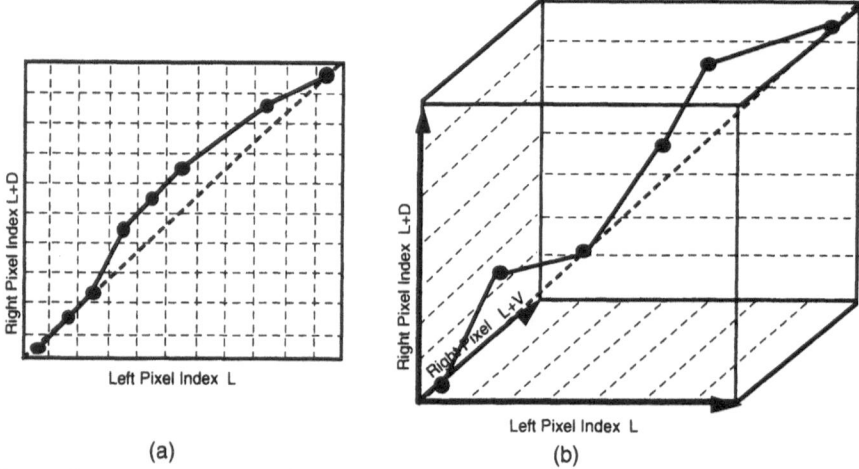

(a)   (b)

Figure 6 : (a) An example of optimum path finding using dynamic programming in 2-d space as in [2], (b) Modified algorithm : an example of an optimum path in 3-d space using dynamic programming. D denotes the horizontal disparity and V denotes the vertical displacement.

For the control of the selection of the best displacement vector the Frame Difference (FD) is used, which is essentially the luminance differences between two corresponding local neighbourhoods. In Figure 7, is shown, the matching window designed for the FD calculation for a pixel (n, m). It matches a large pattern in the horizontal direction (9 pixels wide) and also takes into account the neighbourhood above and below the pixel (± 1 pixels).

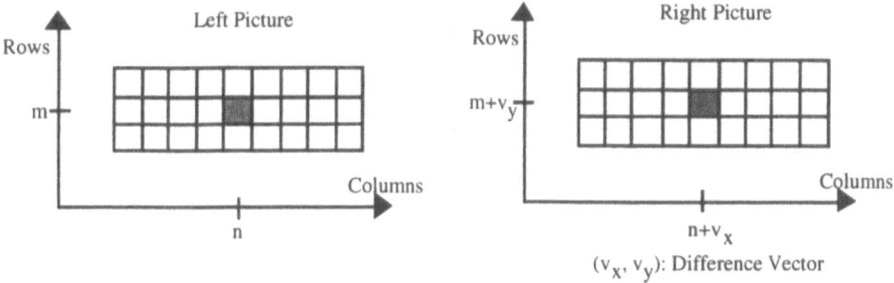

Figure 7: Window used for the calculation of the FD for picture point (n,m)

The point (n, m) in the first image is displaced by vector (v_x, v_y) in the search image where v_x and v_y, take values within the search range determined by a preceding fast block matching. For each vector (v_x, v_y) the FD is evaluated as:

$$FD_{n,m}(v_x, v_y) = \frac{c}{N} \sqrt{\sum_{i=n-\tau}^{n+\tau} \sum_{j=m-1}^{m+1} \left(W_l(i,j) - W_r(i+v_x, j+v_y) \right)^2} \qquad (1)$$

where:

n, m: pixel coordinates

(v_x, v_y):   displacement vector

$2\tau + 1$:   width of the window in the x-direction

$N = (2\tau + 1) \cdot 3$:   number of pixels in the window

c: normalisation constant

$W_l(i, j)$:   luminance value at i, j

For determination of discontinuities there is a function which punishes possible disparity jumps along a raster line. For each point n in row m there are many possible disparities $D_{n,p,q}$ where (p,q) are the coordinates of the possible matches (column and row respectively) in the right picture. For each possible disparity there is a $FD_n(v_x, v_y)$ calculated with equation (1). If x is defined as the difference between disparities:

$$x = \left| D_{n-1,p1,q1} - D_{n,p2,q2} \right| \qquad (2)$$

then a function $f(x)$ is required as the cost function to penalise for possible disparity jumps.

Geiger et al in [2] have proposed:

$$f(x) = \mu \sqrt{x} + \varepsilon |x|, \quad f'(x) = \frac{\mu}{2\sqrt{x}} + \varepsilon, \quad x \geq 0 \qquad (3)$$

as the cost function for disparity jumps (Figure 8a) and the derivative of the above for smaller disparity jumps (Figure 8b). It has been empirically determined that the values $\mu=0.3$ and $\varepsilon=0.15$ give acceptable results.

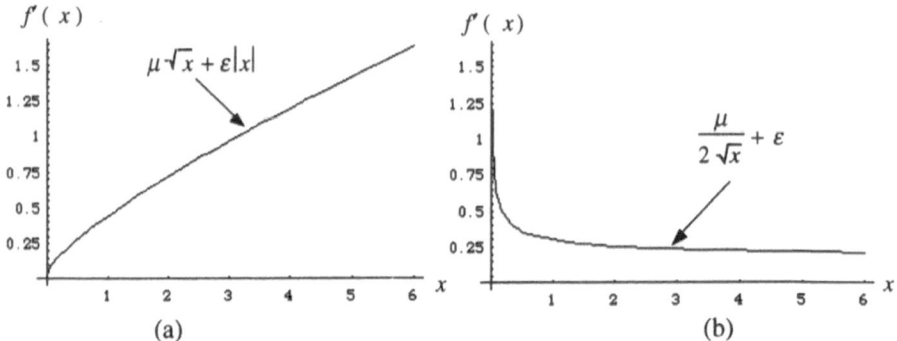

(a)   (b)

Figure 8: The cost-function $f(x)$ for disparity jumps x and for smaller disparity jumps x

Figure 9 shows the segmented disparity/depth map of the "Buggy" (the gray values have been equalised for display purposes). Since the wooden buggy has been placed in front of a blue screen for an easy segmentation, the lack of texture information in the background makes it impossible to achieve reliable disparity values. Therefore the disparity map has been masked by the segmented buggy. Due to the horizontal shift within the rectification procedure a value of 206 has to be added to the estimated disparity value.

Figure 9: Disparity image (equalised gray values)

5 Recovering Depth

Due to the prior rectification, the recovery of the depth information is reduced to the conventional parallel axis stereo geometry. By considering similar triangles and using the estimated disparity map, the world coordinates $P(x, y, z)$ of a point $P_l(x_l, y_l)$ can be easily obtained as

$$x = \frac{bx_l}{d}, \qquad y = \frac{by_l}{d}, \text{ and } \qquad z = \frac{bf}{d}$$

where b is the stereo baseline, f is the effective focal length of the camera and d is the disparity value between the matched pair of points $P_l(x_l, y_l)$ and $P_r(x_r y_r)$.

The disparity values of the "Buggy" (cf. Figure 9) are in the range from 212 to 200 (a disparity value of 1 corresponds to a z-value of 0.78 cm, i.e. the depth values of the "Buggy" lie in the interval between 1.56 m and 1.65 m). Figure 10 depicts the calculated disparity map as a terrain map.

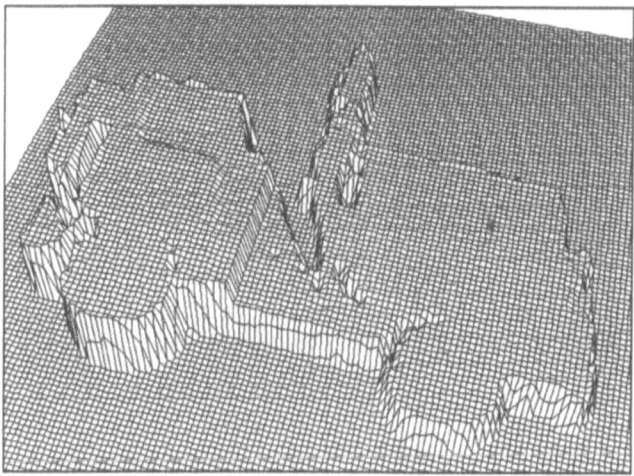

Figure 10: Terrain map of "Buggy"

Applying the above method to all turntable images yields a set of range images. The range information can be used directly to improve the shape regarding concavities by fusing it with the 3-d volume model of the object. Another approach is to fuse multiple successive range maps by means of Kalman-Filtering to a more confident one and use this information for a further shape refinement. The second approach is followed by P. Robert [3] to model indoor background scenes.

144

6 Conclusion

A promising chain for computing dense disparity/range maps from turntable images has been shown. The rectification of the images makes it easier to estimate the disparity as well as to recover the depth information from the disparity image. The new engaged disparity estimation algorithm, although computationally more expensive, allows flexibility in disparity calculation for the case of slight misaligned cameras. The recovered depth values are of good quality and suited for improving the 3-d volume model regarding concavities.

References

1. Buschmann R., Niem W. Automatics Modelling of 3D Natural Objects from Multiple Views, European Workshop on Combined Real and Synthetic Image Processing for Broadcast and Video Production, 23./24. 11. 94, Hamburg
2. Geiger D., Landendorf D., Yuille A., Sandini G. Occlusions and Binocular Stereo Proc. of Second European Conference on Computer Vision - ECCV '92, Santa Margherita Ligure, Italy 18-23 May 1992
   Springer-Verlag, Berlin 1992, ISBN 3 540 55426 2, pp.425-433
3. Niem W., Buck M., Kummerfeld G., Chevalier L., Robert P. 3D Shape and Textuure Estimation, Deliverable #11, RACE 2052 - MONA LISA

Session 4: Analysis 3 – 3D Automatic Modelling

Joint Estimation of depth maps and camera motion in the Construction of 3D Models from a Mobile Camera

Ph. Robert, F. Ogor
Thomson Broadband Systems
Cesson-Sévigné - France

Abstract

A vision-based 3D scene analysis system that is capable to model real world scenes automatically from an image sequence has been developed in the MONALISA project. Input to the system is a sequence of images taken by a standard CCD camera. The camera motion is unknown. The output is a facet model that can be exploited for image synthesis of virtual viewpoints. In this paper, emphasis is placed on the image sequence processing for the estimation of both depth maps and camera motion.

1.   Introduction

Within the scope of vision-based 3D modeling, the estimation of accurate 3D data from a set of observations is a key factor, and it has been extensively studied in the last years. In particular, two ways have been investigated: depth from motion [1][2], in which a unique camera captures the scene, and dynamic stereovision [3][4] in which the mobile acquisition system is composed of two or more cameras. In both cases, the algorithms often operate in an on-line incremental fashion: the estimates become more accurate as new observations are integrated. Such a process requires to manipulate uncertainty. Among the techniques that include a noise model, the Kalman filtering has been used for 3D reconstruction of features [4] as well as of dense depth maps [2]. In the latter case, the camera motion is known and simply horizontal; it was generalised to any known camera motion in [5]. Some works tackled the problem of joint estimation of motion and structure from monocular images and image features [6][7]. More recently, several authors proposed to solve this problem from uncalibrated cameras: in case of orthographic projection [8], and perspective projection [9].

The main characteristic of our system is that both the problems of 3D reconstruction and camera motion are tackled in the context of a dense description of the scene[10] captured by a moving monocular camera. Within the scope of 3D scene modeling for image production, such an approach suits a surface-based description of the scene. In the next section, the system framework is presented. The main modules are then described in the following sections emphasizing the estimation of both camera motion (section 5) and depth maps (section 6). Experiments results are shown in section 7.

2. System Framework

The system is illustrated in figure 1. The process can be decomposed into three phases.

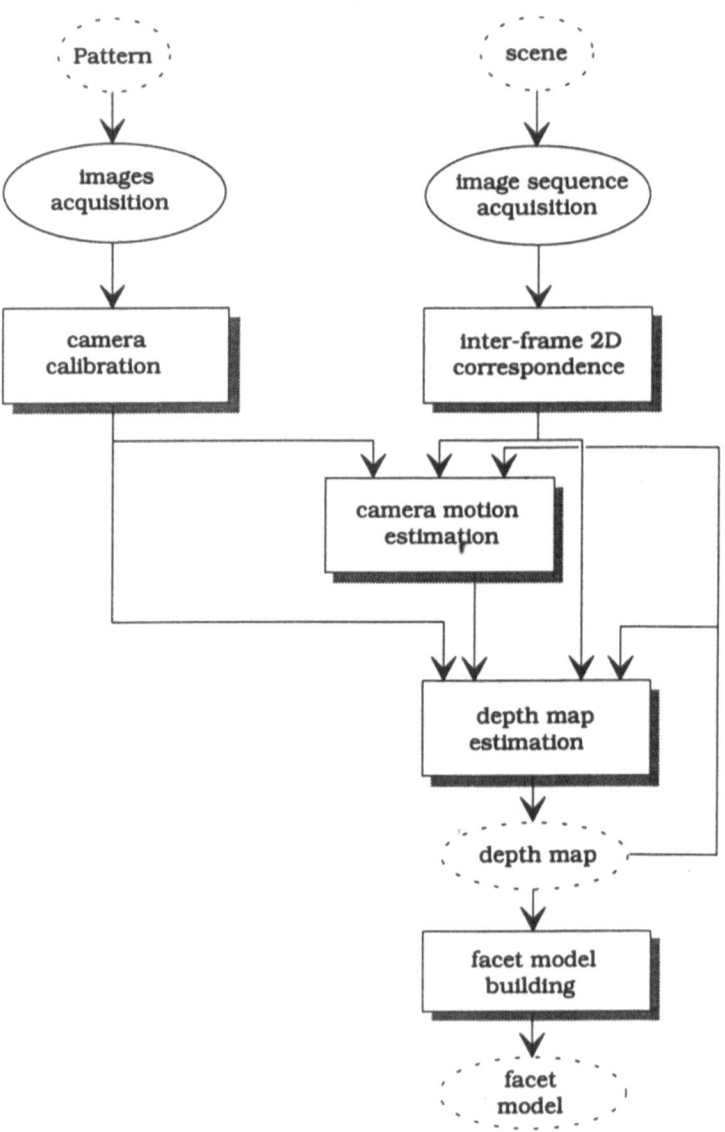

figure 1: system framework

The first phase corresponds to the acquisition of the images of the scene by means of the mobile camera, and of images of a pattern dedicated to the camera calibration.

The second phase concerns the 3D reconstruction phase via the processing of the image set and the application of the triangulation principle. The input of this phase is the set of selected images. The output provides two types of information: 3D information represented as a set of depth maps, each depth map corresponding to a viewpoint, and the position of the camera in the 3D space. This phase can be itself decomposed into several steps.

In the first step, the correspondence between pixels of successive images is estimated: it relates the pixels in two successive images corresponding to the same 3D point. An optical flow estimator was developed.

A recursive loop applied along the image set allows then to estimate both the camera motion and the depth map corresponding to each viewpoint. In this loop, this 3D information at viewpoint t_i is estimated by relying on the optical flow estimated between images t_i and t_{i-1}, and on the 3D information available at time t_{i-1}.

In particular, the camera motion estimator relies on the depth map recovered at time t_{i-1} (except for the first pair where an initial procedure is required). It was supposed while setting the equations that the camera rotation between two successive views is small. This requirement is quite reasonable in our context of acquisition.

The depth map is estimated at each instant t_i via the extended Kalman filtering that allows to take into account both the current observation (optical flow at t_i) and the depth map estimated at t_{i-1}.

In an off-line process called calibration (see section 3), the intrinsic camera parameters are estimated. These parameters are supposed to be constant in all images. They are then used in the reconstruction loop.

The last phase is the construction of the facet model from the set of depth maps. The depth data are integrated in a unified facet representation via a recursive Delaunay triangulation. This phase is not presented in this paper.

3. Camera Calibration

The calibration phase precedes the scene data processing. The objective is to estimate the camera intrinsic parameters that are supposed to be fixed all along the acquisition phase. Before entering into more details, let us first establish the equations relating the 3D scene to the image.

Let us consider a 3D coordinate system $R_a(O_a, x_a, y_a, z_a)$ in which the scene can be described (figure 2) and the camera 3D coordinate system $R_{ci}(O_{ci}; x_{ci}; y_{ci}; z_{ci})$ attached to the viewpoint i. Let us consider a 3D point of the scene M described by $M_a = (x_a, y_a, z_a)^t$ in R_a and $M_{ci} = (x_{ci}, y_{ci}, z_{ci})^t$ in R_{ci}. The relation between M_a and M_{ci} is described by the following equation:

$$M_{ci} = R_{ia} \cdot M_a + \overrightarrow{T_{ia}} \tag{1}$$

in which R_{ia} is a 3x3 rotation matrix and $\overrightarrow{T_{ia}}$ is a 3-component translation vector. During the acquisition phase, this transformation evolves as the camera moves.

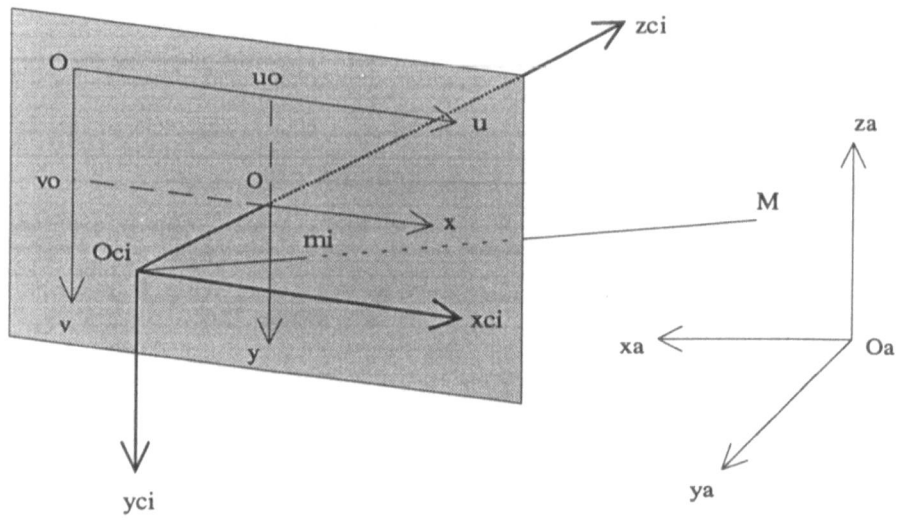

figure 2: camera model

The camera model used in this system is the classical pinhole model : the image m of the point M is obtained by the perspective projection. According to this transformation, the relation between $m_{ci}=(U_i,V_i)^t$ in R_{ci} and M_{ci} is given by:

$$\begin{cases} U_i = \dfrac{x_{ci}}{z_{ci}} \\[2mm] V_i = \dfrac{y_{ci}}{z_{ci}} \end{cases} \tag{2}$$

The image formation model is described in the present case by a linear model: this model links the pixel coordinates $(u_i,v_i)^t$ in $R_p=(O,u,v)$ of m to its coordinates $(U_i,V_i)^t$ in R_{ci} as follows:

$$\begin{cases} u_i = u_0 + f_u \cdot U_i \\[2mm] v_i = v_0 + f_v \cdot V_i \end{cases} \tag{3}$$

u_0, v_0, f_u, and f_v are supposed to be fixed for all the acquired images.

The relation between the 3D point M_a in R_a and the corresponding pixel m expressed in R_p can be now derived by juxtaposing the successive transformations described above:

$$
\begin{pmatrix} s_i.u_i \\ s_i.v_i \\ s_i \end{pmatrix} = \begin{pmatrix} f_u & 0 & u_0 \\ 0 & f_v & v_0 \\ 0 & 0 & 1 \end{pmatrix} \cdot \begin{pmatrix} \overrightarrow{r_{1ia}} & t_{xia} \\ \overrightarrow{r_{2ia}} & t_{yia} \\ \overrightarrow{r_{3ia}} & t_{zia} \end{pmatrix} \cdot \begin{pmatrix} x_a \\ y_a \\ z_a \\ 1 \end{pmatrix} = A_i \cdot \begin{pmatrix} M_a \\ 1 \end{pmatrix} \qquad (4)
$$

where $\overrightarrow{r_{1ia}}, \overrightarrow{r_{2ia}}$ and $\overrightarrow{r_{3ia}}$ are line vectors of the rotation matrix, and t_{xia}, t_{yia} and t_{zia} are the components of the translation.

The objective of the calibration can be now explicited: in the present case, it consists in identifying the camera intrinsic parameters, i.e. in the simple linear model of equation (3), u_0, v_0, f_u, and f_v. For this purpose, images of a known pattern are acquired. Considering a set of points on the pattern which coordinates are known in R_a (attached to the pattern), and their corresponding projections on the image expressed in R_p, the matrix A_i can be estimated by a least square method [11]. In the present case, the intrinsic parameters are then recovered from A_i.

The relation between the pixel coordinates (u,v) and (U,V) is now identified (it is independent on the viewpoint i). In the next sections, the image points coordinates will be expressed by (U_i, V_i) in R_{ci}.

4. 2D correspondence

2D correspondence between two successive images is seen as a pixel 2D motion measurement problem. The estimator used in our experiments is detailed in [12]. Its main characteristics are the following:
- differential approach [13]: the motion estimation is based on the recursive differential equation; based on a multiresolution and multipredictions approach, it

estimates the 2D motion of each pixel in t_i $\overrightarrow{d} = (d_u, d_v)^t$;

- 2D variance map: a variance vector $\sigma^2_{di} = \sigma^2(\overrightarrow{p}; t_i) = (\sigma^2_u, \sigma^2_v)^t$ is associated to each motion vector; this variance is obtained by modeling the local DFD surface obtained with the motion estimate. The variance is related to the surface parameters, depending on the surface curvature and on the DFD value. This variance expresses the quality of the estimated motion and is exploited in the subsequent functions of the system.
- smoothing: the motion is supposed to be locally smooth (except on the discontinuities); an iterative local smoothing filter is applied on the motion field at each resolution level; this filter takes into account the variance attached to each vector.

5. Camera Motion Estimation

As explained in the system framework presentation (section 2), the role of this step is to estimate the camera motion between two successive images. Two modules must be distinguished: a first one has been developed in order to estimate the camera motion between the two first views, for which only the optical flow and the intrinsic parameters are available. For the following views, information about the scene is available, and the module developed in this case exploits this knowledge. We first present the basic equation used in this process (section 5.1). Then, the estimation method is presented in the two cases: first pair of images (section 5.2) and next pairs (section 5.3).

5.1 Equations

Let us come back to the equations presented in section 3. The relation between a 3D point M expressed in any coordinate system R_a, and its projection m expressed in R_{ci} has been explicited (equation (4)). We now consider the transformation between two successive images, that is the basis of our reconstruction system.

Let us consider two successive viewpoints at t_{i-1} and t_i, and the image points m_{i-1} and m_i of a 3D point M. The relation between the image points in t_{i-1} and t_i (i.e. R_{ci-1} and R_{ci}) of the same 3D point M can be established from the equations defined in section 3.

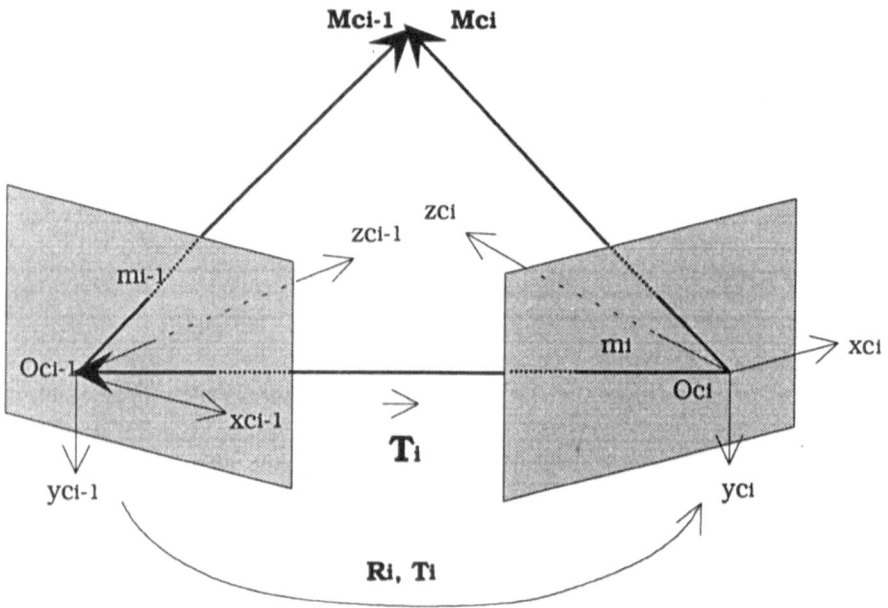

figure 3 : relation between two successive viewpoints

First, the relation between the camera coordinates of M in t_i $M_{ci}=(x_{ci},y_{ci},z_{ci})^t$ and its coordinates in t_{i-1} $M_{ci-1}=(x_{ci-1},y_{ci-1},z_{ci-1})^t$ is the following:

$$M_{ci} = R_i \cdot M_{ci-1} + \vec{T}_i \qquad (5)$$

or equivalently (decomposing R_i and $\overrightarrow{T}_i$ in a three-components vector) :

$$
\begin{pmatrix} x_{ci} \\ y_{ci} \\ z_{ci} \end{pmatrix} = \begin{pmatrix} \overrightarrow{r_{1i}} \\ \overrightarrow{r_{2i}} \\ \overrightarrow{r_{3i}} \end{pmatrix} \cdot \begin{pmatrix} x_{ci-1} \\ y_{ci-1} \\ z_{ci-1} \end{pmatrix} + \begin{pmatrix} t_{xi} \\ t_{yi} \\ t_{zi} \end{pmatrix}
\tag{6}
$$

This equation can be easily modified using equation (2) to obtain this new expression:

$$
z_{ci} \cdot \begin{pmatrix} U_i \\ V_i \\ 1 \end{pmatrix} = z_{ci-1} \cdot \left\{ R_i \cdot \begin{pmatrix} U_{i-1} \\ V_{i-1} \\ 1 \end{pmatrix} + \frac{\overrightarrow{T_i}}{z_{ci-1}} \right\}
\tag{7}
$$

from which the third component z_{ci} can be written:

$$
z_{ci} = \left\{ \overrightarrow{r_{3i}} \cdot \begin{pmatrix} U_{i-1} \\ V_{i-1} \\ 1 \end{pmatrix} + \frac{t_{zi}}{z_{ci-1}} \right\} \cdot z_{ci-1}
\tag{8}
$$

This relation provides the depth component z_{ci} at t_i from the image point $(U_{i-1}, V_{i-1}, z_{ci-1})$ via the transformation (R_i, T_i). It will be used in the depth estimation procedure (section 6). The 2D components (U_i, V_i) in R_{ci} can be derived by replacing z_{ci} in (7) by its expression in (8):

$$
U_i = \frac{\overrightarrow{r_{1i}} \cdot \begin{pmatrix} U_{i-1} \\ V_{i-1} \\ 1 \end{pmatrix} + \frac{t_{xi}}{z_{ci-1}}}{\overrightarrow{r_{3i}} \cdot \begin{pmatrix} U_{i-1} \\ V_{i-1} \\ 1 \end{pmatrix} + \frac{t_{zi}}{z_{ci-1}}} \quad \text{and} \quad V_i = \frac{\overrightarrow{r_{2i}} \cdot \begin{pmatrix} U_{i-1} \\ V_{i-1} \\ 1 \end{pmatrix} + \frac{t_{yi}}{z_{ci-1}}}{\overrightarrow{r_{3i}} \cdot \begin{pmatrix} U_{i-1} \\ V_{i-1} \\ 1 \end{pmatrix} + \frac{t_{zi}}{z_{ci-1}}}
\tag{9}
$$

This equation relates (U_i, V_i) to (U_{i-1}, V_{i-1}). This relation depends on the camera motion, described by R_i and T_i, and on the depth component z_{ci-1} of (U_{i-1}, V_{i-1}).

A quite reasonable hypothesis has been introduced in order to simplify this equation: the rotation is supposed to be small. From this hypothesis, the rotation matrix is now written [14] as:

$$
R_i = \begin{pmatrix} 1 & -\Omega_{zi} & \Omega_{yi} \\ \Omega_{zi} & 1 & -\Omega_{xi} \\ -\Omega_{yi} & \Omega_{xi} & 1 \end{pmatrix}
\tag{10}
$$

Ω_{xi}, Ω_{yi}, and Ω_{zi} are the rotation components respectively around the x_{ci}, y_{ci}, z_{ci} axes. Introducing this new expression in (9) leads to:

$$\begin{cases} U_i = \dfrac{U_{i-1} - \Omega_{zi}.V_{i-1} + \Omega_{yi} + \dfrac{t_{xi}}{z_{ci-1}}}{-\Omega_{yi}.U_{i-1} + \Omega_{xi}.V_{i-1} + 1 + \dfrac{t_{zi}}{z_{ci-1}}} \\[3em] V_i = \dfrac{\Omega_{zi}.U_{i-1} + V_{i-1} - \Omega_{xi} + \dfrac{t_{yi}}{z_{ci-1}}}{-\Omega_{yi}.U_{i-1} + \Omega_{xi}.V_{i-1} + 1 + \dfrac{t_{zi}}{z_{ci-1}}} \end{cases} \tag{11}$$

This is the basic equation of the system used for the camera motion estimation. The use of this equation is quite suitable for the representation of the 3D information as a depth map. The motion components are defined by: $\vec{x} = (\Omega_{xi};\Omega_{yi};\Omega_{zi};t_{xi};t_{yi};t_{zi})^t$. The observation is the quadruplet $(U_{i-1},V_{i-1},U_i,V_i)$ that is derived from the optical flow and equation (3). Armed with this equation, we can now consider the camera motion estimation between two successive images. Practically, the position of the camera at t_i will be refered to its position at the previous instant t_{i-1} (defined by R_i and T_i), and the initial reference will correspond to the camera reference of the second viewpoint in the image sequence. Two important cases are to be distinguished depending on whether the depth is known or not.

5.2 3D Motion Estimation for the first pair

For the first pair of images (t_1,t_2), no information about the scene is available. The camera motion is estimated by eliminating the component z_{ci} in equations (11) leading to the following unique equation (i=2):

$$(U_1 - \Omega_z.V_1 + \Omega_y.(1 + U_2.U_1) - \Omega_x.V_1.U_2 - U_2) . (t_z.V_2 - t_y) -$$
$$(\Omega_z.U_1 + V_1 - \Omega_x.(1 + V_2.V_1) + \Omega_y.V_2.U_1 - V_2) . (t_z.U_2 - t_x) = 0 \tag{12}$$

In this equation, the rotation and translation components are linked in a non-linear manner, that is solved by an iterative procedure. The translation cannot be recovered exactly: only its direction can be estimated. To recover the exact scale of the scene supplementary information should be introduced. But, for the present purpose, it is not required to know the exact scale.

Three steps can be distinguished in this phase:

Selection of the correspondence points
    Starting from t_2, for which the correspondence map with regard to t_1 is available, the quadruplets (U_1,V_1,U_2,V_2) can be formed. In fact, only a subset of relevant points is selected. These points are selected by means of the variance information

attached to the optical flow: only the points with both horizontal and vertical variance components below a given threshold are selected.

Initialisation of the 3D motion parameters

In order to make the iterative process converge towards the exact motion, an initialisation process is introduced. It is based on a set of simple 3D motion models corresponding to typical movements for which a subset of the six parameters is supposed to be close to zero, and therefore is not considered in the model. These models are:

- translation only
- ty and Ω_x (rotation around an axis parallel to the x_c (horizontal) axis)
- tx and Ω_y (rotation around an axis parallel to the y_c (vertical) axis)
- tz and Ω_y (motion along the z_c axis with a possible rotation around the y_c (vertical) axis).

Practically, most of the camera motions can be assigned to one typical motion among this set. These models equations are derived from (12) by setting the right parameters to zero. It leads to linear equations that are solved by a least square method. The best initial estimate is the one that minimises the reprojection error (reported in section 5.3).

Recursive estimation

The criterion to be minimised in the estimation has been chosen as:

$$f(\overrightarrow{x}) = \sum_{\overrightarrow{p}} r^2(\overrightarrow{x};\overrightarrow{p}) \tag{13}$$

where $r(\overrightarrow{x};\overrightarrow{p})$ corresponds to the left side of equation (12) in which one translation component that is different from zero (according to the initialisation) is set to 1. The minimisation of the criterion is solved by the Levenberg-Marquardt numerical method [15]. Outliers are rejected at each iteration: these are points which the reprojection error is above a given threshold (see section 5.3).

5.3 3D Motion Estimation for the next pairs

For the next pairs, the depth component in t_{i-1} is available. Therefore, the motion parameters are estimated by means of the linear equations (11) and a least square method. The module of the translation is computed relatively to the scale of the model fixed in the processing of the first pair.

The points used for the estimation are selected from the variance maps corresponding to the optical flow and to the depth map z_{ci-1} (see section 6). Moreover, the distribution of the selected points should be homogeneous. In order to guarantee this homogeneity, the variance map is first decomposed into a set of adjacent rectangles, in which a fixed number of points must be selected.

The estimation process is repeated several times. At each time, an error is computed on each point and is used as point rejection criterion. This rejection procedure is the same as in the case of the first pair. It is required because among the selected points, some (few) can remain erroneous. This procedure requires the following steps:
- first, the depth component z_{ci} is computed from equation (20) derived from (11)
- then, the 3D reconstructed point is reprojected on t_i, i.e. (U_{ir}, V_{ir}) are derived from equation (11)
- the distance between (U_{ir}, V_{ir}) and (U_i, V_i) is computed
- if this distance is above a threshold, the point is rejected in the further iterations.

6. Estimation of the depth maps

The Kalman filtering is used for reconstructing the depth component at each viewpoint t_i. This tool allows to estimate recursively a vector as new observations become available. In the present case, the objective is to recover the 3D information that is represented as a depth map $z_{ci}(u;v)$, from the observation given by the optical flow $\vec{d_i}(u;v)$ and the variance $\sigma_{di}^2(u;v)$. The depth map and the optical flow are linked by the equations (11). As this equation is non linear, the integration is performed using the extended Kalman filtering. In the following, the Kalman filtering is first briefly presented, and then extended to the non linear case.

Let us consider the **state vector** z_{ci} to be estimated and the observation given by the 2D vector $\vec{d_i}$. The discrete-time evolution model is described by the following equation:

$$z_{ci} = F_i \cdot z_{ci-1} + G_i + \eta_i \qquad (14)$$

where η_i is a white noise such that $E[\eta_i] = 0$ and $E[\eta_i.\eta_i^t] = Q_i$, and F_i is the evolution matrix. The term G_i is the command parameter. F_i and G_i are explicited in the equation (8).

The **a priori model** corresponds to the initial knowledge of the system, where the initial state vector is noted z_{ci} and the associated covariance matrix is noted P_i.

Let us consider the equation linking the state vector z_{ci} and the observation vector that is called $\vec{o_i}$ for the moment. This equation is called the **measurement model** and is noted $f(\vec{o_i};z_{ci}) = 0$. In the linear case, the measurement equation links $\vec{o_i}$ and z_{ci} as follows:

$$\vec{o_i} = H_i \cdot z_{ci} + \vec{\varepsilon_i} \qquad (15)$$

where $\vec{\varepsilon_i}$ is a white noise such that $E[\vec{\varepsilon_i}] = 0$ and $E[\vec{\varepsilon_i}.\vec{\varepsilon_i}^t] = W_i$, and H_i is the observation matrix.

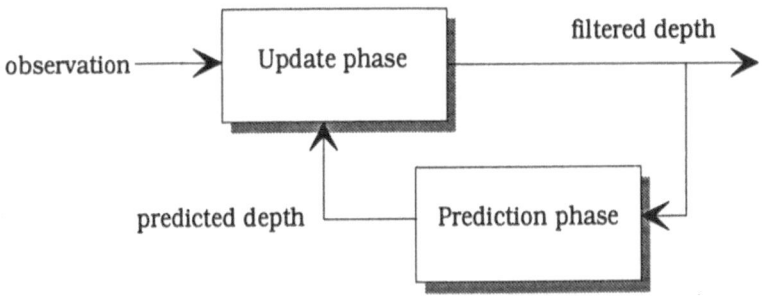

figure 4 : Kalman filtering principle

From the initialisation given by the a priori model, the temporal filtering process is decomposed in two main steps (figure 4) :

- **Prediction** of the state vector and of its covariance, defined by the evolution model equation:

$$
\begin{cases}
z_p = F_i \cdot z_{ci-1} + G_i \\
\sigma_p{}^2 = F_i{}^2 \cdot \sigma_{i-1}{}^2 + Q_i
\end{cases}
\tag{16}
$$

In this way, both a depth prediction map and a variance one are built at t_i by scanning the estimated maps at t_{i-1}. $(u_p;v_p)$ are the pixel coordinates of the prediction in t_i. They are computed via equations (11)and (3) followed by a simple interpolation to fit in a pixel.

- **Updating** the state vector from the predicted state vector and from the observation:

$$
\begin{cases}
z_i = z_p + K_i \cdot (\vec{o_i} - H_i \cdot z_p) \\
\sigma_i{}^2 = (1 - K_i \cdot H_i) \cdot \sigma_p{}^2
\end{cases}
\tag{17}
$$

where K_i is the Kalman gain:

$$
K_i = \frac{\sigma_p{}^2 \cdot H_i{}^t}{H_i \cdot \sigma_p{}^2 \cdot H_i{}^t + W_i}
\tag{18}
$$

However, if the equation $f(\vec{o_i};z_{ci}) = 0$ of the measurement model is non linear, it must be first linearised. It is the case here where the measurement model is described by $f(\vec{d_i};z_{ci}) = 0$. This equation can be established by adopting the procedure presented in section 5.1, by inverting the equation (5) as follows:

$$M_{ci-1} = R_i^{-1} . M_{ci} + R_i^{-1} . \vec{T_i} \qquad (19)$$

R_i is given in (10). R_i^{-1} is derived by changing Ω_{xi}, Ω_{yi}, Ω_{zi} respectively in $-\Omega_{xi}$, $-\Omega_{yi}$, $-\Omega_{zi}$. The new translation $\vec{T'_i}$ can be then simply derived from R_i and $\vec{T_i}$. It leads to the following equation:

$$
\begin{cases}
U_{i-1} = \dfrac{U_i + \Omega_{zi}.V_i - \Omega_{yi} + \dfrac{t'_{xi}}{z_{ci}}}{\Omega_{yi}.U_i - \Omega_{xi}.V_i + 1 + \dfrac{t'_{zi}}{z_{ci}}} \\[4mm]
V_{i-1} = \dfrac{-\Omega_{zi}.U_i + V_i + \Omega_{xi} + \dfrac{t'_{yi}}{z_{ci}}}{\Omega_{yi}.U_i - \Omega_{xi}.V_i + 1 + \dfrac{t'_{zi}}{z_{ci}}}
\end{cases}
\qquad (20)
$$

The measurement model $f(\vec{d_i};z_{ci})=0$ is then:

$$
\begin{cases}
d_{ui} - fu . U_i - fu . U_{i-1}(z_{ci}) = 0 \\
d_{vi} - fv . V_i - fv . V_{i-1}(z_{ci}) = 0
\end{cases}
\qquad (21)
$$

in which $U_{i-1}(z_{ci})$ and $V_{i-1}(z_{ci})$ are expressed in equation (20). Supposing that a good estimate z_p of z_{ci} is available, f can be expanded in the vicinity of $(\vec{d'};z_{ci})$ ($\vec{d'}$ is the true motion vector):

$$f(\vec{d'};z_{ci}) = 0 \approx f(\vec{d_i};z_p) + \partial f_d(\vec{d_i};z_p) . \vec{\delta d} + \partial f_z(\vec{d_i};z_p) . (z_{ci} - z_p) \qquad (22)$$

in which $\partial f_k()=\partial f()/\partial k$. The measurement equation remains the one described by equation (15), where:

$$
\begin{aligned}
\vec{o_i} &= -f(\vec{d_i};z_p) + \partial f_z(\vec{d_i};z_p) . z_p \\
H_i &= \partial f_z(\vec{d_i};z_p) \\
\vec{\varepsilon_i} &= \partial f_d(\vec{d_i};z_p) . \vec{\delta d}
\end{aligned}
\qquad (23)
$$

The covariance matrix of the noise W_i is:

$$E[\vec{\epsilon_i} \cdot \vec{\epsilon_i}^t] = W_i = \partial f_d(\vec{d_i};\vec{z_p}) \cdot \sigma^2_{di} \cdot \left(\partial f_d(\vec{d_i};\vec{z_p})\right)^t \qquad (24)$$

where :
$$\sigma^2_{di} = \begin{pmatrix} \sigma^2_{ui} & 0 \\ 0 & \sigma^2_{vi} \end{pmatrix}. \qquad (25)$$

The temporal filtering process described by equations (16) and (17) remains the same. All the pixels are processed in the same way. A spatial median filter is then applied to the depth map in order to suppress the isolated erroneous points. The next section presents some evaluation results of this scheme.

7. Experiments

Experiments were carried out on synthetic image sequences and on a set of real image sequences corresponding to various scenes. The camera motion estimator for the first pair was tested on various sequences and motions. These tests show the capability of the method to estimate different types of motion (not reported here: see [10]). Results are presented below in order to show the performance of the reconstruction loop and the interest of the Kalman filtering.

7.1 Synthetic images

In order to quantify the performance of the system, a CAD model called *cube* was designed, and images were synthesized by simulating a camera moving around the cube. An image is presented in figure 6a. The sequence which results are reported below was obtained with the following camera motion: $\Omega_x=\Omega_z=0$, $\Omega_y=3.6°$, $t_y=0$, $t_x/t_z=32$. Tests on the estimation loop were carried out in the following three configurations (see figures 5):
  - as described above;
  - without the Kalman filtering (refered as "no Kf" in the figure)
  - the camera motion is estimated and displayed in the figure, but the true motion is used for 3D reconstruction (refered as "km" in the figure)
Figure 5a displays the rotation components, while the translation components are reported in figure 5b. All Ω_z, Ω_x, t_y and t_z are close to zero, and only the components of the complete loop are shown. The interest of the Kalman filtering appears through the display of t_x and Ω_y. The error cumulated on the successive Ω_y estimates is about 9.5° for a 360° total rotation around the cube, and about 39° without Kalman filtering.

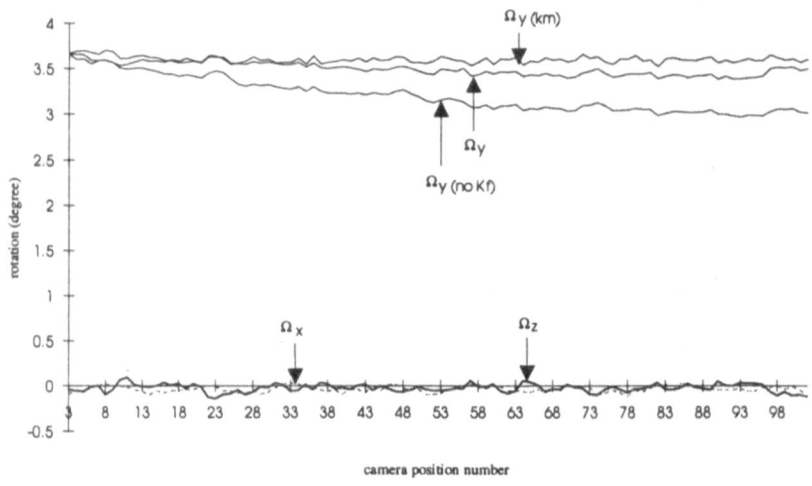

figure 5a

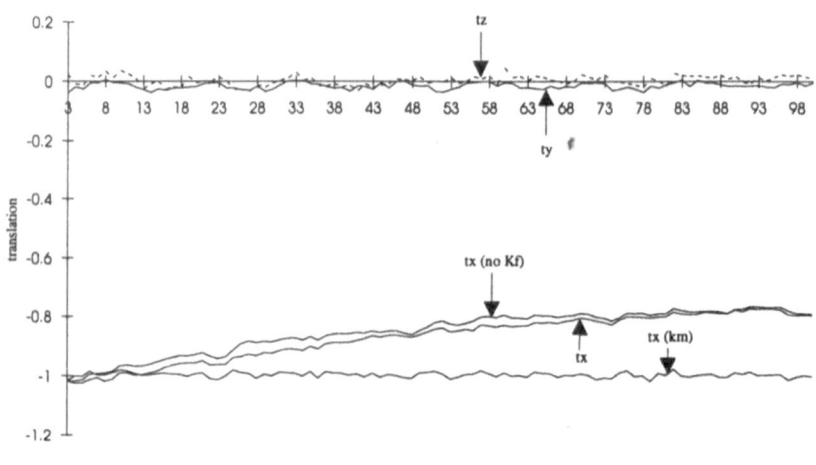

figure 5b

Figure 6a (up-left) shows an original image. The corresponding depth map is displayed in figure 6b (up-right), the variance map in figure 6d (bottom-right) and the difference map between the ideal and measured depth maps is displayed in 6c (bottom-left). The large errors (white regions) in the depth map are located mainly in the new areas.

figure 6: results on the sequence *Cube*

7.2 Real images

The images below present results on the sequence *Carton* (figure 7). Images of the first and last viewpoints with the corresponding depth and variance maps are displayed showing the evolution of the reconstruction phase.

8. Conclusions

A system for the construction of 3D models from a mobile camera was briefly presented. This system is based on the joint estimation of depth maps and camera motion along the sequence. Emphasis was placed on this part of the system. A recursive loop allows to estimate camera motion from the current knowledge of the scene (except for the first pair for which a special procedure was developed), and then to build the current depth map by means of a Kalman filter.

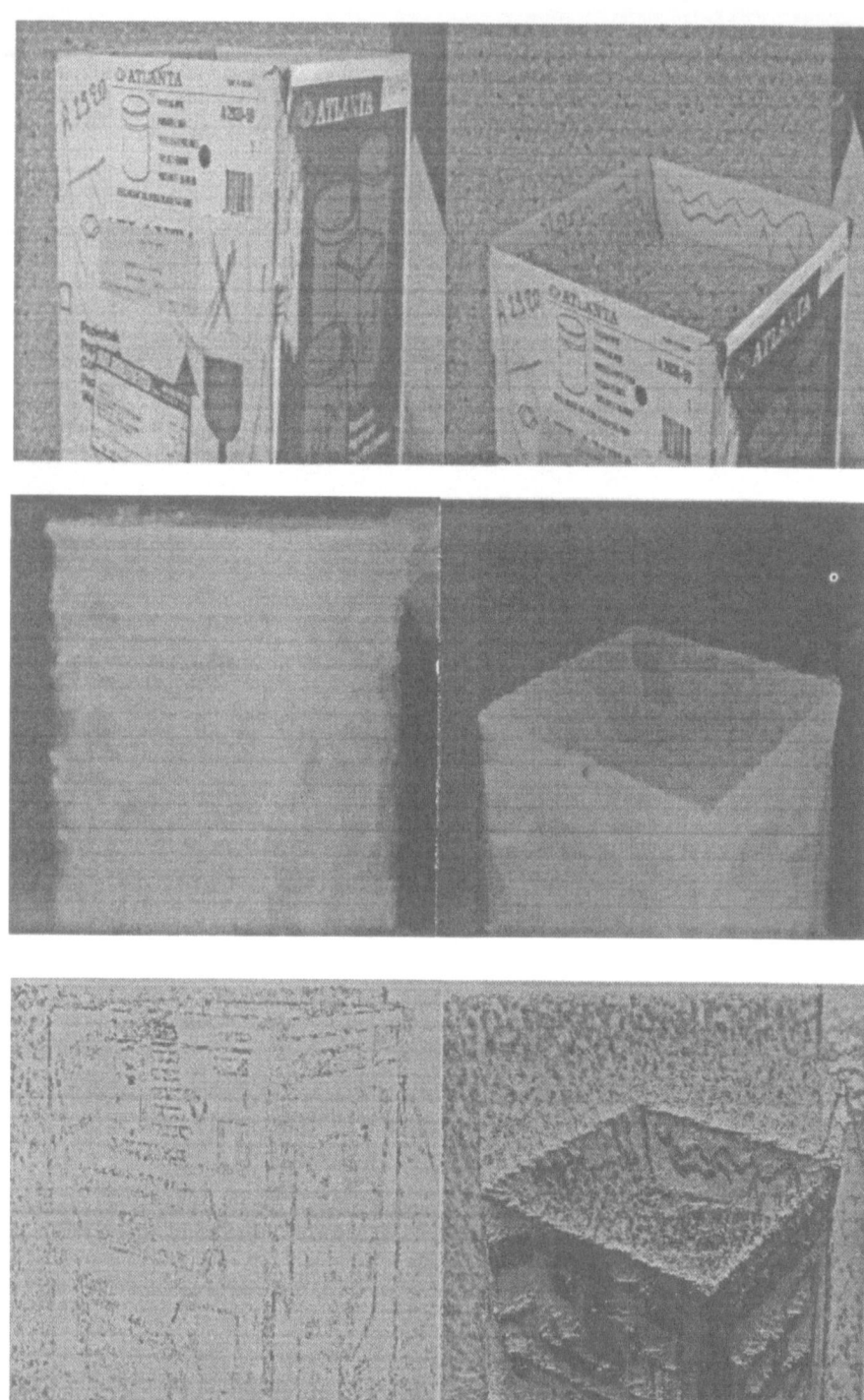

figure 7:results on the sequence *Carton*

References

1. Aggarwal J.K., Nandhakumar N.: On the computation of motion from sequences of images - A review, Proc. of the IEEE, vol.76, n°8, August 1988.
2. Matthies L., Kanade T.: Kalman filter-based algorithms for estimating depth from image sequences, Image Understanding Workshop, 1988.
3. Ayache N., Faugeras O.: Building, Registrating and Fusing Noisy Visual Maps, The International Journal of Robotics Research, vol.7, n°6, December 1988.
4. Koch R.: Automatic reconstruction of buildings from stereoscopic image sequences, EUROGRAPHICS'93, vol.12, n°3, 1993.
5. Heel J.: Temporal surface reconstruction, Technical report 1296, MIT Artificial Intelligence Laboratory, May 1991.
6. Boukari B.: Reconstruction 3D récursive de scènes structurées au moyen d'une caméra mobile-Application à la robotique, Rapport de thèse-Note CEA N 2634-1990.
7. Broida T., Chellappa R.: Estimating the kinematics and structure of a rigid object from a sequence of monocular images, IEEE PAMI, vol.13, n°6, June 1991.
8. Tomasi C., Kanade T.: Factoring image sequence into shapes and motion, Proc. of IEEE Workshop on Visual Motion, Princeton, NJ, october 1991.
9. Szeliski R.: Recovering 3D shape and motion from image steams using non-linear least squares, Journal of Visual Communication and Image Representation, n°1, March 1994.
10. Ogor F.: Construction de modèles 3D à partir d'une caméra mobile, Thèse de l'Université de Rennes I, Septembre 1994.
11. Faugeras O., Toscani G.: The calibration problem for stereo, Proc. of CVPR, 1986.
12. Lemonnier B.: Approche intégrative de l'analyse du mouvement et de la reconstruction 3D dans les séquences d'images, Thèse de l'Université de Rennes I, Mai 1993.
13. Robert Ph., Cafforio C., Rocca F.: Time/space recursions for differential motion estimation, SPIE symposium, vol.594, image coding, Cannes, Dec.1985.
14. Fang J.Q., Huang T.S.: Solving three-dimensional small rotation motion equations : uniqueness, algorithms and numerical results, in CVGIP, vol.26, 1984.
15. Fletcher R.: Practical methods of optimization, a Wiley Interscience Publication, 1987.

Scene Reconstruction based on penta-ocular Image Sequences for 3D-Imaging

Robert Skerjanc
Heinrich-Hertz-Institut GmbH
Einsteinufer 37, 10587 Berlin, FRG
e-mail: skerjanc@hhi.de

1 Introduction

We present a new technique for 3D-scene modelling based on stereo and motion analysis of penta-ocular image sequences. Scene modeling is the most critical part of any image analysis-synthesis procedure. Apart from coding applications, the proposed approach is intended to be used for the realisation of a viewpoint-depending virtual camera that can be located at arbitrary positions within the original camera array. With virtual cameras it will be possible to create any number of perspective views needed, e.g. for the reproduction of smooth motion parallax in multiview 3DTV systems[1,5-8] or for the recovery of eye contact in video conferences[2]. This framework is also essential for image capturing of natural scenes for Virtual Environment concepts or for further approaches as Vision Like Television VLTV[3].

The solution of the correspondence problem is carried out more dependably by combination of stereo and motion information. Supporting disparity estimation by motion information is common practice now. Although being an ill posed problem as well, motion estimation is done independently from disparity analysis. We suggest to combine both tasks into a single one, and to additionally exploit the advantages of a multi-ocular camera rig. This has the avantage that disparity can support motion estimation and vice versa with regard to common optimization criteria.
An imaging system for any kind of scenes requires a stereo and motion matcher that must cope with arbitrary shaped bodies. As opposed to indoor scenes, this presents new problems in the implementation of segment based approaches. On the other hand, accuracy of absolute depth estimation is less important to the demand, that every part of a synthesized image should be *subjectively* error-free.

In our approach the modelled scene is represented by 3D line segments and their temporal conduct within several frames. We assume that flaws in synthesised views are less visible, if neighbouring image features show certain common behaviour. The features are treated as being dependent on each other with respect to spatial position and motion according the coherence principle in a 4D space.

2 The penta-ocular Approach

The use of a multiocular camera rig should not only be regarded as glueing several binocular matching algorithms side by side in order to broaden the camera basis and to uncover occluded areas. By using additional cameras we are able to explore the optimum of information, considering all possible pairings at the same time. To sum up, the benefits of using more than two cameras are: (1) Additional epipolar constraints are available for the elimination of erroneous matches, even of periodic structures. (2) Matching of horizontal features is possible. (3) Detection and uncovery of occlusions is possible. (4) Consistencies of matches between sub constellations support the reliability of final matches.

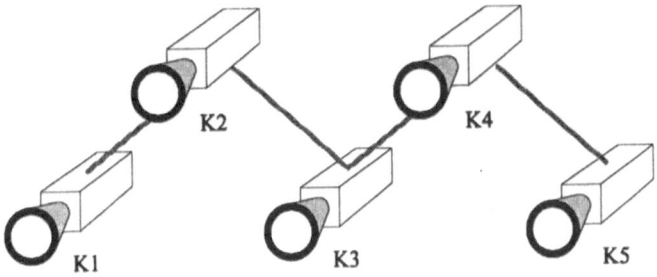

Fig. 1. The penta-ocular camera rig

In this example, five cameras are arranged in a zigzag manner (Fig. 1). The cameras are calibrated to have coplanar image planes in order to simplify the analysis.

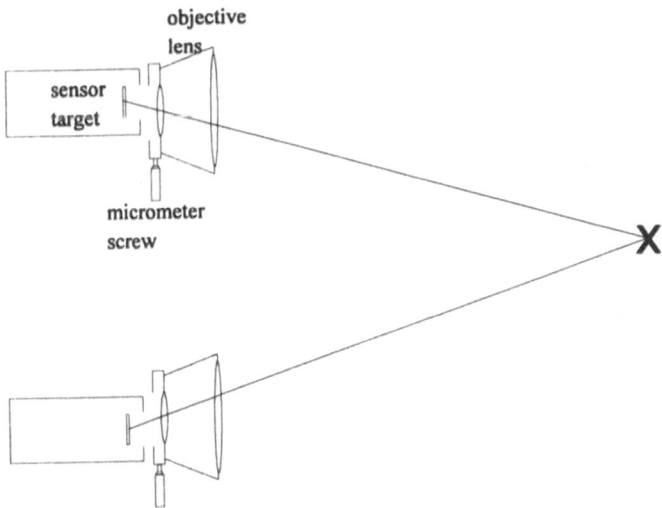

Figure 2: Principle of shifted lenses to enlarge the common view section of near objects

Unfortunately, with increasing camera base the common section of the scene seen by all cameras will shrink. For this reason we use camera lenses which may be laterally shifted with respect to the camera sensor (Fig. 2). With this we get a common section of the scene like using converging camera axes, but without any keystone distortions. The advantages of parallel epipolar lines are preserved in this way.

Fig. 3 shows a hierarchy of camera constellations, here every group represents a bi-, tri-, tetra-, or penta-ocular subgroup of the total five cameras. Note that they are the same cameras as in the constellation of Fig. 1.

Correspondences found in all constellations have to fulfil the epipolar and local similarity constraints of the cameras involved. The uppermost group is the complete penta-ocular constellation. In this constellation the probability of erroneous matches is low, or in other words, there is a small quota of positive false results (Grimson '81). On the other hand many correspondences cannot be found due to the strict penta-ocular constraint, resulting in a high probability of negative false results. Looking at constellations with less cameras, this ratio of positive/negative false results changes. More candidates are available in the lower levels because of the smaller difference in perspectives. However the probability of wrong matches raises because they have to be validated with less views (more positive false matches).

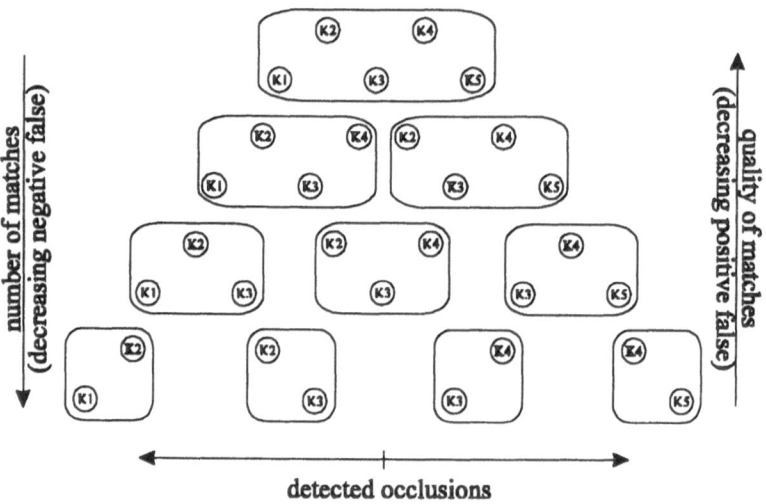

Fig 3. Sub-constellations of the camera rig shown in Fig. 1

Each sub-constellation of the penta-ocular camera rig is a source of 3D data. Assuming groups of adjacent cameras, we get a total of $\binom{5}{2} = 10$ sources of 3D data, each of them providing 3D segments with different shaping of quality and quantity.

3 The 4D-Model

The 4D model represents the current estimate of the scene and the temporal conduct within upto five time frames. The constituents of the model are the 3D segments delivered by all camera sub-constellations as intraframe relations (disparity). This model includes matches of higher levels with a quality measure associated as well as the matches of lower levels (these last ones are less reliable but are they able to supply occluded regions). Using triangulation, each match candidate represents two 3D co-ordinates at the endpoints of the line segments along with their positional uncertainties. If the model contains this 3D segments at least at two successive frames, we are able to determine the motion component of the 4D model as inter-frame relations.

At the very first step, the 4D model is based on a coarse estimation of disparity and motion comparing local features like epipolar constraints, similar slope, similar contrast etc. Thus, we search for corresponding segments for each camera constellation at a given frame (stereo analysis), and for corresponding segments of each camera in a given sequence of frames (motion analysis).

This estimate is then going to be improved by exploitation of the coherence principle explained below. For the application of the coherence principle it is essential to have a good estimate of the neighbours of a 3D segment. This selection is done by an agglomerate hierarchical clustering algorithm.

4 The Coherence Principle

Our method of simultaneously solving the correspondence problem regarding disparity and motion uses the coherence principle suggested by Prazdny[4]. As he suggests, the coherence principle means that "the world is not made of points chaotically varying in depth but of (not necessarily opaque) objects each occupying a well defined 3D volume". He develops a binocular matching algorithm which regards a discontinuous disparity field as a superposition of a number of several interlaced continuous disparity fields each corresponding a to piecewise smooth surfaces. For the matching of pixels, he minimized differences of disparities according to some neighbourhood criteria.

Instead of calculating in 2D, we suggest to extend the coherence principle to derive a 4D scene model based on the spatial and temporal relationships of 2D features found in multiocular sequences. We argue, that each point in the world consists of objects occupying a well defined 3D-motion also. With that assumption, we are able to put forward following principles:

a) Local coherence: Adjacent *features* of a cohesive body belong to a *common 3D-surface*. This surface is locally defined by a regression plane, minimising the variance σ_p^2 of the Euclidean distance of the features to this plane.

b) Body motion coherence: Adjacent features of a cohesive body have *common 3D-motion*. This claims for a minimum of variance σ_m^2 of motion vectors of the neighbours.

c) Image motion coherence: Images of a moving body feature represent a *common 3D-motion* if they are taken by cohesive cameras. The variance σ_M^2 of 3D-motion within a camera sub-constellation and within several frames has to be a minimum.

The solution of the correspondence problem according to these principles gives a scene model which obeys a minimum of the variances σ_p^2, σ_m^2, and σ_M^2 in four dimensions (x,y,z,t) of features in relation to their immediate 3D-neighbours. In our case the appropriate 4D model contains 3D line segments of consecutive frames and their temporal assignments. Using the standardized variances $\tilde{\sigma}_i^2 = \dfrac{\sigma_i^2}{\varepsilon_i^2}$ (with the current uncertainties in the denominator), the sought 4D model that is optimised in the meaning of the coherence principle meets the demand

$$\tilde{\sigma}_p^2 + \tilde{\sigma}_m^2 + \tilde{\sigma}_M^2 \rightarrow \min.$$

We use an iterative relaxation algorithm that selects correspondences of any camera sub-constellation, minimising the variances of the location and the motion variables for every 3D segment in the 4D model. Up to five time frames are computed in one shot in order to reconstruct the temporal behaviour of the scene.

5 Discussion and Conclusions

The suggested method of image analysis has a quite complex structure due to the four-dimensional data structure being used. Altogether up to 25 images have to be simultaneously processed. This is justified by the fact, that the more picture information, the better the quality of reconstruction we get. At a next step, a subjective evaluation will show, how many cameras actually are needed. This is maily dependent on the scene content, the conditions of viewing and the constraints for the positioning of the cameras (e.g. if the cameras have to be placed around a video monitor). For subjective evaluation of synthesised intermediate views a multiview experimental system is available at our labs. This set-up realises a motion parallax stereoscopic display, where both eyes are able to see synthesised pictures of virtual cameras.

One can expect difficult conditions at applications like 3DTV with motion parallax, where the observer is enabled to move his head within a camera base of about 50 cm or more. It should be taken into consideration, that a scene reconstruction from images having a viewing angle 20° or more is extremely hard to perform. What makes this algorithm handy in the sense of computation time is the use of line segments as matchable features.

The algorithm has been tested on trinocular motion sequences and synthetic penta-ocular sequences. The simulations with real trinocular sequences (typical video-communication scene) have been carried through within approx. 2 minutes on a DEC Alpha workstation, processing three time frames in one shot. Due to difficul-ties with calibration of a pentaocular camera rig with shift objectives, the tests on pentaocular real sequences were not carried through to its conclusions.

This work is supported by grants of the BMFT referenced as TK 463/8 "3D-Techniken für Fernsehen und Bildkommunikation (3DFB)". The author assumes responsibility for the contents of this paper.

6 References

1. Pastoor S. Human Factors of 3D displays in advanced image communication. *Displays*, vol. 14, No. 3, 1993

2. Kellner B. et al. Bildtelefon mit Blickkontakt? Technische Möglichkeiten und empirische Untersuchungen. (in german), *ntz*, Bd. 38, Heft 10, 1985

3. Boerger G. Human Factors Problems with "Vision-Like Television" (VLTV). *Proc. of the 12th Int. Display Research Conference (Japan Display '92),* October 12-14, 1992, Hiroshima, Japan.

4. Prazdny K. Detection of Binocular Disparities. *Biological Cybernetics* 52, 1985, pp. 93-99.

5. Skerjanc R. Liu J. A three camera approach for calculating disparity and syn-thesizing intermediate pictures. *Signal Processing: Image Communication* Vol. 4, 1991, No. 1, pp. 55-64.

6 Skerjanc R. Liu J. Computation of Intermediate Views for 3DTV. Theoretical Foundations of Computer Vision, *Mathematical Research* Vol 69, Akademie Verlag Berlin, pp. 191-202, 1992.

7. Skerjanc R. Combined motion and depth estimation based on multiocular image sequences for 3DTV. *SPIE Stereoscopic Displays and Virtual Rality Systems*, Feb-ruary 1994, San Jose, USA, pp. 35

8. Liu J. Skerjanc R. Construction of Intermediate Pictures for a Multiview 3D Sys-tem. *SPIE/IS&T's Symp. on Electronic Imaging*, February 1992, Proc. 1669, San Jose, USA.

C3D™: a Novel Vision-Based 3-D Data Acquisition System

J.P. Siebert and C.W. Urquhart
The Turing Institute and
Computing Science Department, University of Glasgow
77-81 Dumbarton Road, Glasgow G11 6PP, Scotland.

Abstract

This paper reports on the development of C3D, a computer-based product for constructing 3-D surface models of real world 3-D objects, e.g. a model of a human face, from stereo image pairs. C3D is a GUI-based computer program that converts the implicit 3-D information contained within the stereo image pair into an explicit 3-D surface model in a standard CAD file format. Hence, C3D extracts automatically the 3-D information from a stereo pair of images which have been frame-grabbed (digitised) into a computer and then builds a 3-D surface model. This surface model can then be edited using standard CAD packages or manipulated within virtual reality environments in the usual way.

1 Introduction

While 3-D visualisation and virtual reality systems have revolutionised the manipulation and use of 3-D information respectively, users of these systems encounter a major bottle-neck in the construction of surface models of existing objects. In an industrial context, many pre-CAD objects exist and require to be captured in three dimensions to allow design upgrades. C3D was conceived to provide a fast and cost effective route to capturing 3-D surface models of these classes of objects for applications ranging from industrial design, virtual reality and graphic arts to stereo biometrics (human body modelling) for pre-surgical planning.

1.1 Background

The core technology required for C3D was primarily developed with support from the UK Joint Funding for Information Technology scheme under the Active Stereo Probe (ASP) project, IED3/1/2109, which was lead by the Turing Institute and completed in July of 1993. This research work was further developed under the UK Department of Trade and Industry Small firms Merit Award scheme to produce a technology demonstrator. The goal of the current C3D project is to integrate this core technology into a 3-D data conversion product prototype. Hence, it is anticipated that this prototype will culminate eventually in the development of a

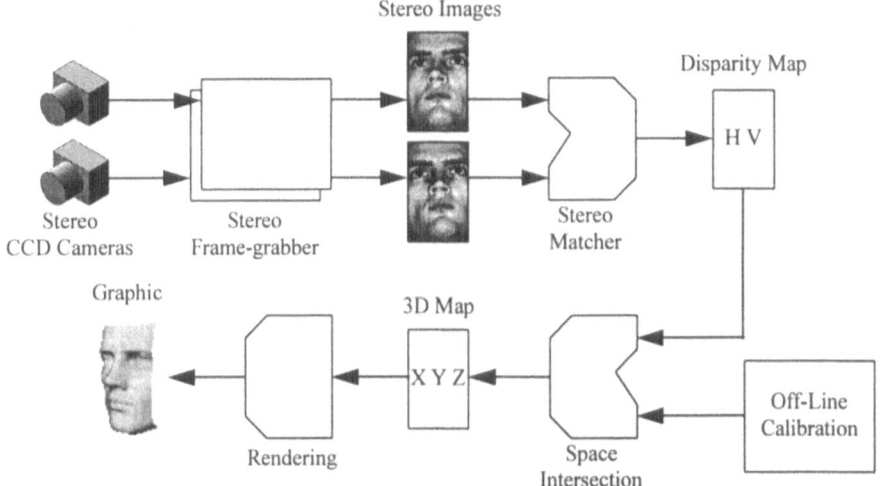

Figure 1. The complete C3D processing chain.

complete "shrink-wrapped" product. Currently, the prototype system serves as the basis for further research and custom development work by the Turing Institute.

1.2 Technical Approach Adopted

The technical approach to surface model construction proposed in C3D employs a correlation-based scale-space automatic stereo matching algorithm to determine the displacements, or parallaxes, between stereo image pairs of objects to be modelled. As these parallaxes reveal the 3-D structure of objects within stereo image pairs, photogrammetric analysis can be applied to the parallaxes to compute the 3rd dimension of interest. Hence, this 3-D information can be converted into a format compatible with, for example, standard packages such as the Silicon Graphics "Inventor" graphics information format. Figure 1 outlines the complete C3D processing chain.

Image capture hardware and object illumination have been accomplished by utilising the binocular sensor head developed under the ASP project as described fully in [1], [2].

2 An Overview of C3D

Currently, C3D has been implemented using the TK/TCL [3] GUI development toolkit which produces X-Windows compatible code running under UNIX. C3D is a modular program that enables the user to perform image acquisition, stereo matching, photogrammetry and calibration, 3-D surface construction and also 3-D surface visualisation within a single operating environment. These facilities are described further in the following sections.

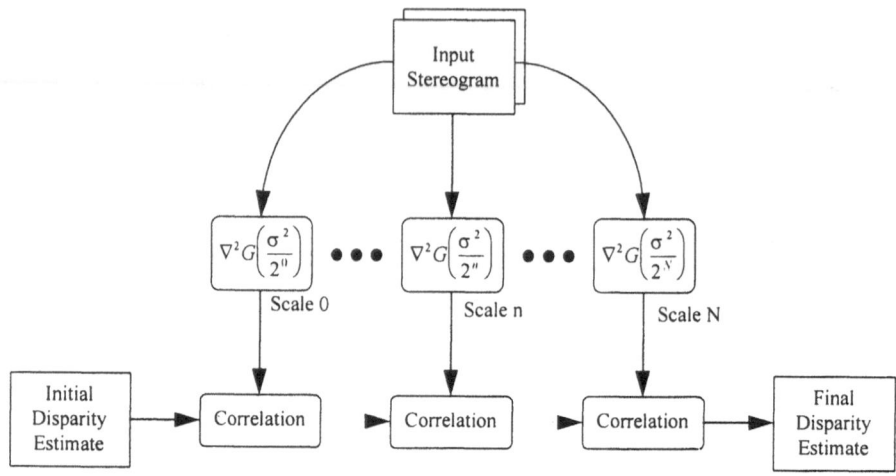

Figure 2. Schematic of the C3D stereo matching algorithm.

2.1 Image Capture and Scene Illumination

Image capture is provided by commercially available frame digitisation hardware (DataCell S2200) hosted within a SUN SPARCstation. The binocular sensor head is connected to the red and green channels of the frame grabber. This configuration allows live red-green anaglyph display of objects being digitised and synchronised capture of stereo image pairs. It is also possible to input stereo pairs from existing image files.

In order to ensure that the stereo image pairs of the object being digitised contain a uniform spatial distribution of high frequency *image energy* or "texture", the scene is bathed in "textured light" [4] during image capture. A second image is captured of the scene using "plain" illumination to provide a surface reflectance map which is later "draped" over the digitised surface during a subsequent photo-realistic rendering stage for 3-D visualisation. Illumination switching is accomplished by means of a computer controlled slide projector.

2.2 Stereo Matching

The Turing Institute's proprietary signal matching algorithm is used to determine correspondences between the stereo image pairs, the detailed operation of which is discussed in [5]. This algorithm builds a scale-space image pyramid of octave separated image spatial frequency bandpasses. Image matching proceeds at the *top* of the pyramid, at the coarsest image resolution using area correlation to generate a low resolution map of horizontal and vertical inter-image parallaxes. This low resolution map is "expanded" by Gaussian filtering to the size of the next lower (higher resolution) level in the image pyramid and matching then proceeds as before. However, in this case the parallaxes held in the expanded low resolution map are now used as the starting point where the correlation search proceeds. Hence as the correlator is now operating at a higher image resolution than before, the correlation search process is now *refining* the estimates of parallaxes found at the previous level of resolution in the pyramid. This matching strategy is repeated for each remaining level in the input image pyramid until the pyramid *base* (containing the highest resolution bandpass images) is reached whereupon matching is complete. The C3D matching process is outlined in figure 2.

Clearly, for this coarse-to-fine matching strategy to succeed, image energy must be present in each of the spatial frequency bandpasses of the input stereo pair. Hence the need for texture projection when the inherent image resolution prohibits capturing fine surface texture of objects (e.g. low resolution images of human skin) or where the objects are man-made and lack surface texture, i.e. are smooth. In these cases, the low spatial frequency nature of bland naturally illuminated surfaces would not provide any image information to enable the correlator to identify unique correspondences between the pixels of the input stereo pair images. Hence, by projecting texture onto these surfaces, it is possible to ensure that there is adequate image matching energy at all levels of the matching pyramid and thereby provide accurate parallax recovery over the interiors of smooth inherently featureless surfaces. A match confidence map is also generated as a result of the matching process and gives a pixel-by-pixel map of the estimated confidence of the recovered parallax maps.

It is possible for match errors to occur at *occlusions*, where a local image feature is visible in one of the images of the stereo pair, but *occluded* in the other. Although these errors could be corrected manually after model construction, we have found that the range image filtering operation makes this, at least superficially, unnecessary. Accordingly, the results presented in section 3 have been achieved without such manual intervention. The most satisfactory method for dealing with occlusions is to fuse together several 2.5-D surfaces recovered by the system in such a manner as to omit the portions of these depth maps which contain occlusions and merge those areas which are unoccluded. This could be achieved by utilising the match confidence map to label those recovered surface areas suffering from the effects of occlusion and thereby omit these areas (since occluded regions return poor match confidence scores).

2.3   Photogrammetry and Calibration

The DLT (Direct Linear Transform) [6] method of system calibration has been integrated into the C3D program to allow the operator to configure the system to the geometry of the cameras, i.e. vergence angle, baseline separation, relative orientation, focal length of lenses etc., used for stereo capture. A grid comprising an 8×8 matrix of circular rods of varying length (measured to 50 microns tolerance) serves to calibrate the system. The centre-points of these rods are located automatically within stereo image pairs captured of the grid using an implementation of Cumani's method [7] of circle centre finding. The current overall accuracy of the calibration of the order 0.2 mm in planimetry and 0.5mm in elevation for a camera baseline separation of 0.3m and object distance of approximately 2m. However, we are currently researching more advanced photogrammetric techniques to improve this result considerably, as described in section 4.

2.4   3-D Representation

The basic 3-D representation takes the form of an elevation image, where each pixel in the image represents a height value. Image processing operations have been included such as Gaussian smoothing and rank order sifting to allow the recovered elevation field to be filtered. It is then possible to convert the elevation field into a polygon model.

Two approaches are possible to achieve polygonisation. A surface polygon grid can be produced by simply treating pixels as the vertices of polygons. This is a convenient representation since the number of polygons that comprise a surface can be controlled by building a Gaussian pyramid from the height field map. The desired resolution can then be selected by extracting the appropriate level in the pyramid for direct polygonisation.

A better approach to polygonisation has been investigated which comprises selecting a matching confidence threshold above which height field pixels are accepted and below which they are rejected. Those accepted pixels are then Delaunay triangulated to deliver a mesh of variable polygon density depending on the local match confidence.

Polygon complexity control has been developed but not yet fully integrated into the system and could be applied to either the regular or triangulated grids. This comprises a standard polygon relaxation algorithm to reduce automatically the polygon density based on merging adjacent co-planar polygons (or near-coplanar polygons) into single polygons. Polygon merging takes place if the merged polygon is within a surface displacement error threshold when compared to the un-merged polygons. Clearly, it would be desirable to combine the merging and triangulation algorithms together to exploit directly the confidence information associated with the height field in a single algorithm that outputs a triangulated polygon grid of the desired complexity based on the best (most confident) set of vertices.

2.5   Visualisation

In order to visualise polygon surface models, a fast surface rendering algorithm has been incorporated into the system to allow this data to be displayed as either a shaded surface model or rendered with one of the input stereo images "draped" over the surface to give a photo-realistic perspective view. Conversion programs have been developed to allow this data to be exported in either DXF format or Silicon Graphics Inventor format.

3   Results

Figure 3 shows two stereo pairs of images acquired using the Active Stereo Probe: one captured while the subject was illuminated with textured light, and the other, captured immediately afterwards, under normal non-textured illumination. The images shown are a 512×320 pixel region extracted from the original full 576×768 pixel images. The surface model recovered using the C3D package is shown in figure 4 as a wire frame, a Gouraud shaded surface and a surface rendered (surface "draped") with the left image from the normally illuminated stereo pair.

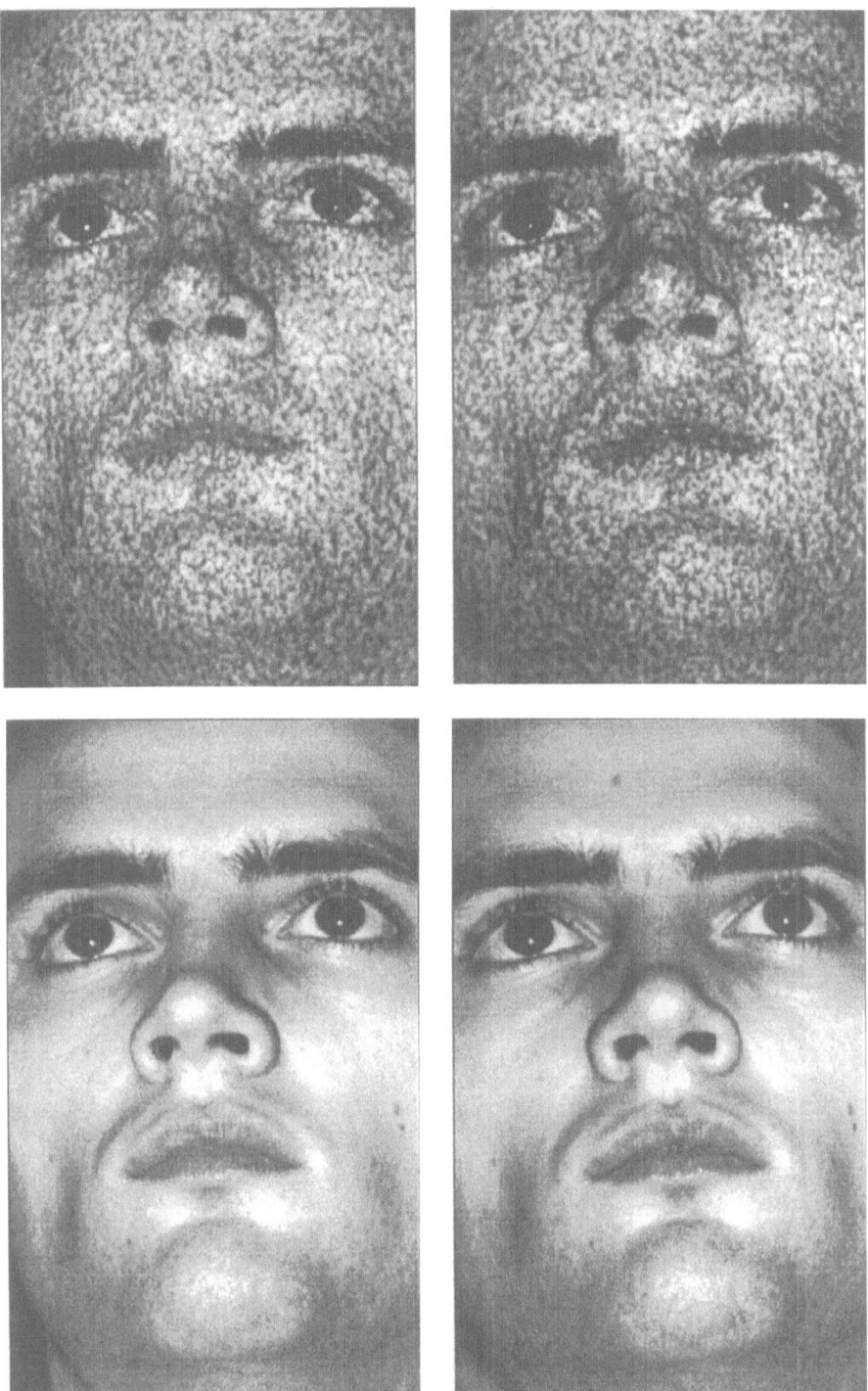

Figure 3. Input images. Top: stereo pair captured under textured illumination. Bottom: stereo pair captured under normal illumination.

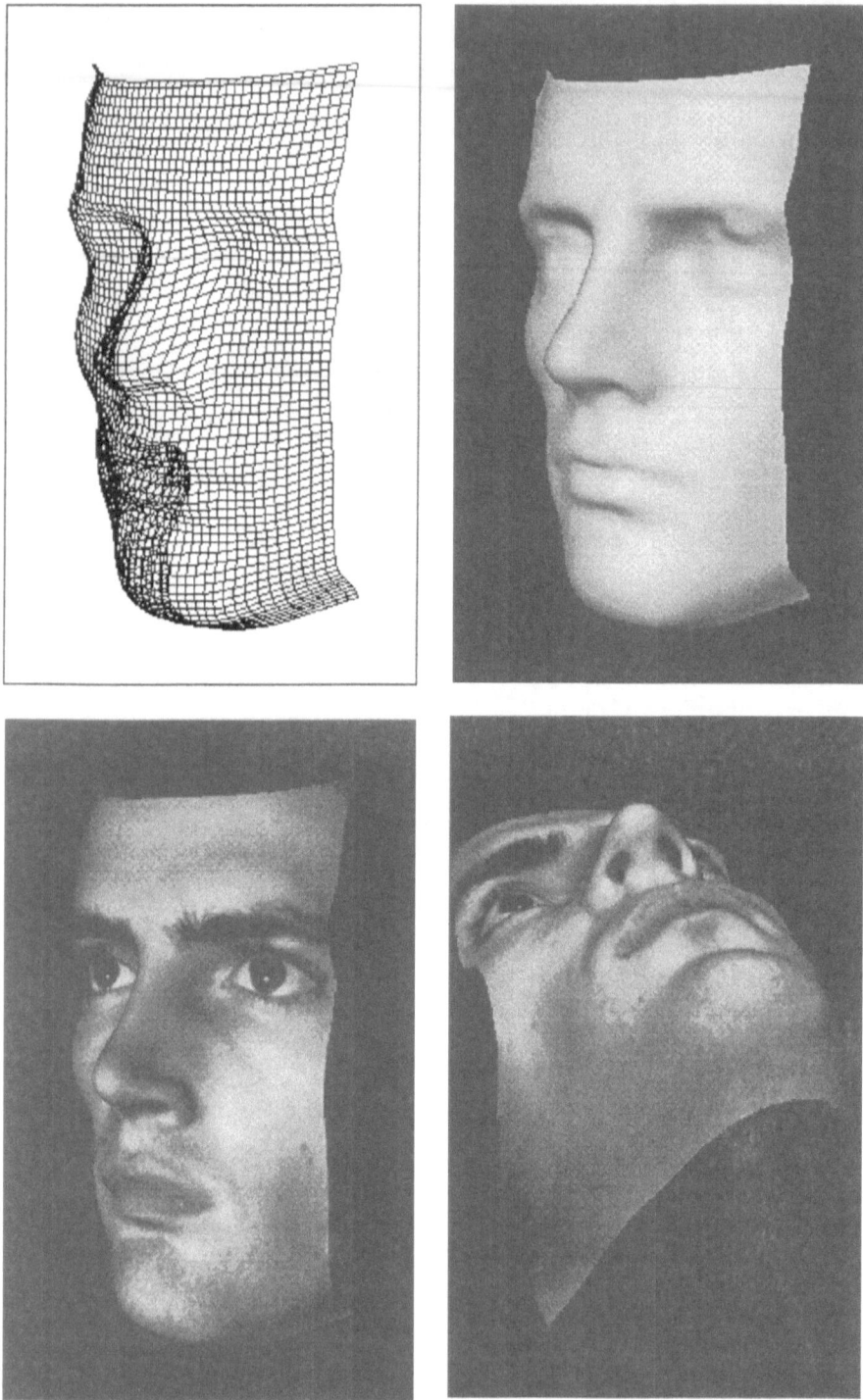

Figure 4. Recovered surface model. Top: wire frame and Gouraud shaded. Bottom: rendered.

Figure 5. A conventional *film* camera equipped with a commercial stereo adapter attachment

4   Future Extensions

Currently, we are extending C3D both in terms of the image sources that it can accommodate and also the photogrammetric operations it provides.

We are also developing a variety of sensor heads ranging from high resolution DFCs (Digital Frame Camera) to low cost single chip cameras. High resolution cameras offer the possibility of capturing whole human torsos in a single shot process, since skin pore texture can be resolved and matched at an appropriately high image sampling density. Accordingly, automatic matching of high resolution stereo image pairs obviates the need for textured illumination of the subject. To this end we have recently investigated stereo-pair image capture by means of a conventional *film* camera equipped with a commercial stereo adapter attachment, as shown in figure 5. Kodak's PhotoCD digitisation service is used to obtain 3k × 2k digital images of each film frame, providing stereo pairs of sufficient (1.5k × 2k) resolution to allow images of human face subjects to be matched *without* texture projected illumination. Figure 6 shows a typical stereo-pair captured using this method and figure 7 shows two rendered views of the resultant 3-D surface models constructed by C3D.

Single chip cameras can be utilised in multiple-stereo pairs to provide cost-effective all-round views of objects/subjects. We also intend to provide a GUI based

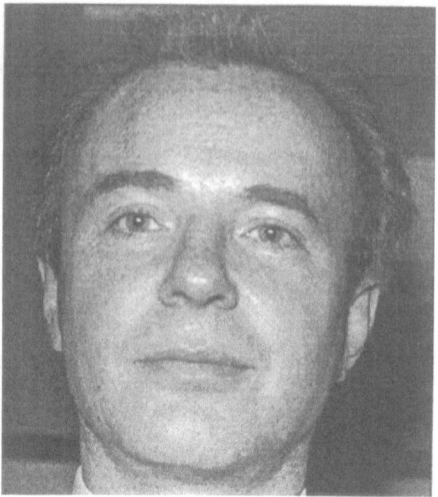

Figure 6. A stereo-pair of images captured using the equipment shown in figure 5 and digitised via Kodak's PhotoCD service.

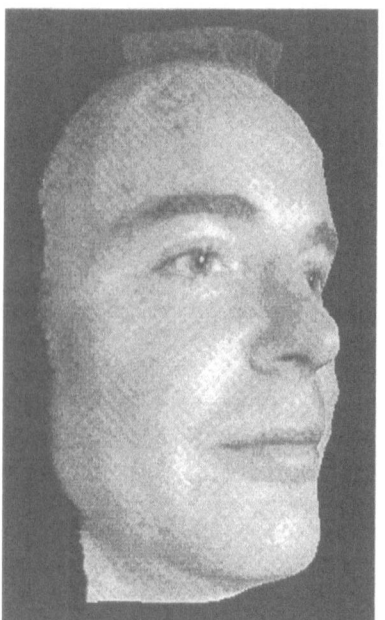

Figure 7. Two rendered views of the resultant 3-D surface model constructed by C3D from the stereo-pair images in figure 6.

interface to allow input of *ground control* points in order to accommodate stereo image pairs which have been captured from uncalibrated camera sources.

We have developed, but not yet integrated into C3D, a *bundle adjustment* [8], [9] photogrammetry package. Using bundle adjustment we expect to improve considerably our calibration and model accuracy. We shall also use bundle adjustment to fuse multiple stereo image pairs into a single 3-D surface model. In this case, we shall investigate both manual and automatic selection of tie-points between the stereo image pairs, using scale-space signal matching in the automated case. It may also be possible to use bundle adjustment in conjunction with scale-space matching to recover 3-D surface models from digitised high resolution cine sequences such as 70mm film.

5 Conclusions

The essential innovation of C3D is to provide a cost effective software tool for generating 3-D models from stereo images using automatic stereo matching. While manual methods for model construction do exist, these manual methods are laborious, time consuming and are dependent on the skill of the operator for the final model quality. Precision automatic stereo matching employed within C3D provides for far greater model complexity and accuracy than could possibly be achieved by hand entered digitisation methods.

The principal technical challenge of the project has resided in devising and implementing a software architecture that both efficiently and seamlessly integrates stereo image capture, stereo image matching, photogrammetry, surface model construction and visualisation of this model. The human-computer interface challenge has been to devise a system that can harness the sophisticated algorithms and techniques developed under the ASP project within a simple-to-use yet powerful and productive software product.

In conclusion, the results presented demonstrate the technical viability of utilising stereo images for 3-D digitisation of human subjects. Two exciting implication stem from this development. Firstly, automated 3-D digitisation need no longer be highly costly as is the case for mechanically scanned systems such as laser stripers, since our system need only comprise a stereo pair of cameras (we have demonstrated C3D using only a conventional *film* camera) and a workstation to process these images. Secondly, data capture times are now restricted only by shutter speeds (electronic or mechanical) opening the possibility of capturing 3-D surface models of subjects *in motion.*

6 References

1. Urquhart C.W. and Siebert J.P. Development of a Precision Active Stereo System. In: *Proceedings of the IEEE International Symposium on Intelligent Control,* Glasgow, Scotland, August 1992, pp. 354-359.

2. Urquhart C.W. and Siebert J.P. Towards real-time dynamic close range photogrammetry. In: *Proceedings of SPIE Videometrics II*, Boston, U.S.A., September 1993.

3. Ousterhout J.K. *Tcl and the Tk Toolkit.* Addison-Wesley Publishing Company, Reading, Massachusetts, U.S.A., 1994.

4. Siebert J.P. and Urquhart C.W. Active Stereo: Texture Enhanced Reconstruction. *Electronics Letters*, 26, 7 (March 1990), pp. 427-430.

5. Jin Z.P. and Mowforth P.H. *A Discrete Approach to Signal Matching*. Research Memo TIRM-89-036, The Turing Institute, Glasgow, Scotland, January 1989.

6. Abdel-Aziz Y.F. and Karara N.M. Direct Linear Transformation from Comparator Coordinates into Object Coordinates in Close-Range Photogrammetry. In: Proceedings of the ASP Symposium on Close-Range Photogrammetry, Illinois, USA, January 1971, pp. 1-18.

7. Cumani A. *et. al.* High Accuracy Localisation of Calibration Points for Dimensional Measurements by Image Processing Techniques. In: *Proceedings of the Fifth International Conference on Advanced Robotics,* Pisa, Italy, 18-22 June 1991, pp. 1761-1765.

8. Karara H.M. (ed.). *Handbook of Non-Topographic Photogrammetry*, 2nd edition. American Society for Photogrammetry and Remote Sensing, Falls Church, VA., 1989.

9. Slama C.C. (ed.). *Manual of Photogrammetry*, 4th edition. American Society of Photogrammetry, Falls Church, VA., 1980.

Automatic Modelling of 3D Natural Objects from Multiple Views

Wolfgang Niem, Ralf Buschmann
Institut für Theoretische Nachrichtentechnik und Informationsverarbeitung
Universität Hannover, Appelstr. 9A, D–30167 Hannover, Germany
email: niem@tnt.uni–hannover.de, buschman@tnt.uni–hannover.de

Abstract

An algorithm for the fast automatic construction of a 3D model of any real object using images from multiple views is presented. The images are taken from a real object rotating in front of a stationary calibrated CCD TV camera. The presented algorithm generates the object shape in a first step. For that purpose an effective implementation of the method of occluding contours is used to obtain a convex volume model of the object. This model is refined in order to detect shape concavities by using additional depth information from disparity estimation and finally approximated by a triangle mesh. In a second step the texture is estimated from the image sequence and projected onto the surface model to obtain natural looking models. Results with real image sequences have confirmed the suitability of the developed algorithm even for the modelling of real objects with highly detailed and complex surfaces.

1 Introduction

The objective of this work is the development and refinement of algorithms for modelling arbitrary shaped 3D objects using multiple perspective views from different viewpoints. Fields for applications are computer animation used in TV production, architecture simulation, as well as driving and flight simulators. For all these applications the generation of the virtual scene can be facilitated by providing a large library of model objects. It is important that the acquisition of the model objects can be done with simple equipment and in reasonable time.

One way of constructing a virtual 3D–model is the evaluation of multiple views. For a turntable with the real object rotating in front of a stationary calibrated camera Busch [2] describes a technique which can be divided into three steps. In a first step a rough volume model is estimated using the silhouettes of the real object applying the method of occluding contours [3],[8],[9],[10],[11]. The surface of the volume model is approximated by a triangular mesh in a second step and in a third step the real object texture is projected onto this surface model to obtain a natural looking model.

One drawback of this technique is the volume modelling algorithm which is only suited for simple–shaped convex objects and uses an inefficient volume representation. Further it shows deterioration of edges in the 3D model and the simple method for texturing of the surface model leads to visible defects of the texture.

In order to overcome the described drawbacks three new approaches are investigated.

The first approach exploits a new volume representation during volume modelling. Further an algorithm for the detection of object concavities which can be integrated into the volume model is developed. The second approach aims the representation of the volume model by a triangular mesh which is realized by considering 3D–edge information. A method for the integration of texture information from different images is proposed in a third approach in order to reduce texture distortion.

Section 2 describes the system calibration and the camera model used for the modelling process. Section 3 deals with volume modelling. Section 4 explains the surface modelling method. Section 5 describes the texture estimation technique. Section 6 presents and discusses results obtained with the developed new algorithm.

2 System Calibration and Camera Model

The environment used for this work consists of a stationary CCD TV camera in front of a turntable, which can be rotated in controlled steps. The background is of uniform colour in order to facilitate the segmentation of the real object against the background. Before the acquisition of a real object on the turntable can be started, the system has to be calibrated in order to obtain position, orientation and focal length of the camera. For that purpose, a precisely known test pattern consisting of black circles on a white background is placed on the turntable as shown in Fig. 1. The detection of the corresponding ellipses in the image taken by the CCD camera and the subsequent estimation of all parameters describing the acquisition process is performed using a calibration method like the one proposed by Tsai [13].

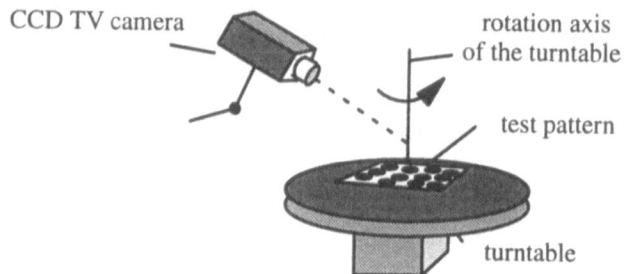

Fig. 1 Arrangement for system calibration

For the processing of the input images, the real camera must be represented by a mathematical model. A camera model, which is suited for 3D–modelling applications, is the one introduced by Yakimovski and Cunningham [14]. It assumes the camera to be geometrically linear, an assumption which is reasonable, considering the linear sensor array and the high quality of the used lens. Thus, it is possible to use the laws of central projection for the object acquisition.

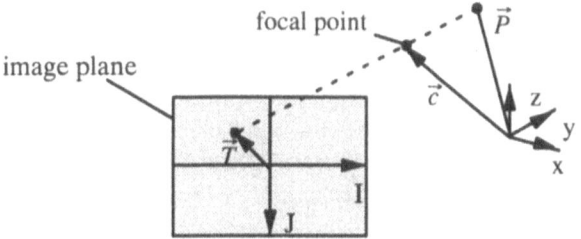

Fig. 2 Projection of a real–world point $\vec{P}$ into an image point $\vec{T} = (I, J)$

Denoting

$\vec{c} = (c_x, c_y, c_z)^T$: vector to the focal center
$\vec{a} = (a_x, a_y, a_z)^T$: unit vector in the direction of the optical axis
$\vec{h} = (h_x, h_y, h_z)^T$: unit vector parallel to the horizontal axis of the image plane
$\vec{v} = (v_x, v_y, v_z)^T$: unit vector parallel to the vertical axis of the image plane
$f:$: focal length of the camera

the projection (Fig. 2) of a point $\vec{P}$ into the image point $\vec{T} = (I, J)$ can be performed as

$$ I = \frac{(\vec{P} - \vec{c}) \cdot \vec{h}}{(\vec{P} - \vec{c}) \cdot \vec{a}} \cdot f \quad ; \qquad J = \frac{(\vec{P} - \vec{c}) \cdot \vec{v}}{(\vec{P} - \vec{c}) \cdot \vec{a}} \cdot f \qquad (1) $$

3 Volume Modelling

The developed algorithm for the construction of a volume model consists of three steps. In a first step a bounding volume is estimated using the object silhouettes; in a second step additional depth information from different viewpoints is fused and in a third step the fused depth information is integrated into the volume model to reduce modelling errors (Fig. 3).

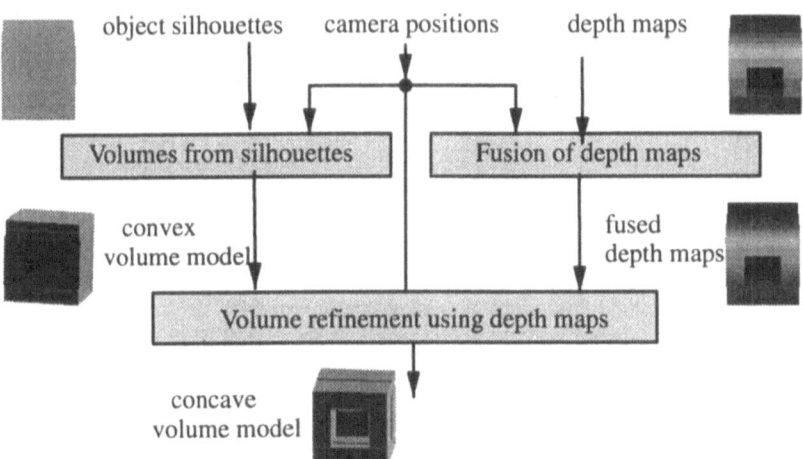

Fig. 3 Block diagram of the developed algorithm for volume modeling

3.1 Volumes from silhouettes

An approach for the construction of volume models using multiple views was first described by Martin and Aggarwal [7]. They introduced the method of occluding contours which uses the object silhouettes and the related camera parameters to construct a volume model of the real object. A key point in performing this method is a proper volume representation, characterized by low complexity and suitability for a fast computation of volume models.

In this work, the volume is decomposed into pillar–like volumes (pillars) which are built of elementary volume cubes of the finest resolution. Each of those pillars is completely described by the position of the center points of the cubes on the top and the bottom of the pillar as shown in Fig. 4. The complexity of this representation is proportional to the object surface area.

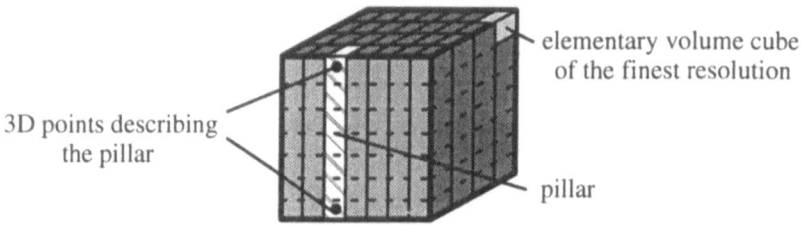

Fig. 4 Volume representation using pillar–like volume elements (pillars)

The volume modelling algorithm starts with the definition of an initial volume cube that surely contains the object. The algorithm works as follows:

1. Segmentation of the input image to get the object silhouette
2. Projection of the 3D points describing the pillar into the image plane with the silhouette (Fig. 5a)
3. Connecting the resulting image points with a 2D line (Fig. 5b)
4. Subdividing and reducing the 2D line into new line segments by eliminating the pixels outside the silhouette (Fig. 5c)
5. Subdividing and reducing the pillar corresponding to the pixels describing the new 2D line segments (Fig.5d)

Applying those steps consecutively to each pillar, the approximation of the volume model represented by a set of pillars will improve for each processed silhouette.

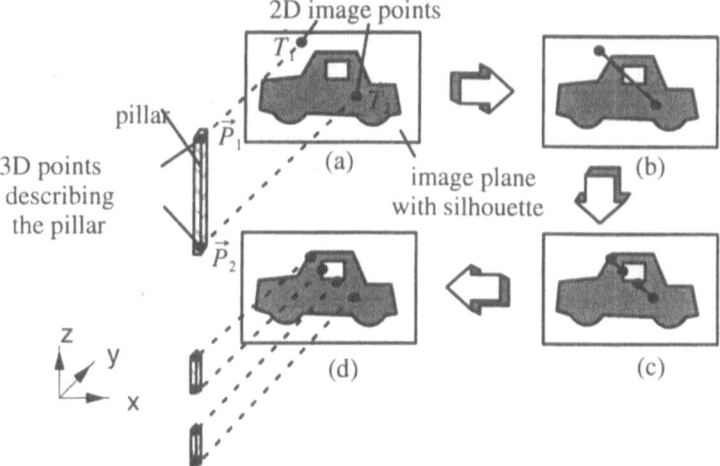

Fig. 5 Volume construction using pillars
(a) Projection of the 3D points $\vec{P}_1$, $\vec{P}_2$ into the image plane with the silhouette
(b) Connecting the resulting 2D image points with a 2D line
(c) Subdividing and reducing the 2D line into new line segments by eliminating the pixels outside the silhouette
(d) Subdividing and reducing the pillar corresponding to the pixels describing the new 2D line segments

The application of this algorithm can lead to the following two modelling errors: a) errors due to the restriction of the algorithm to convex objects and b) errors caused by the finite number of views used for the volume modelling. In Fig. 6 these two errors are shown exemplary.

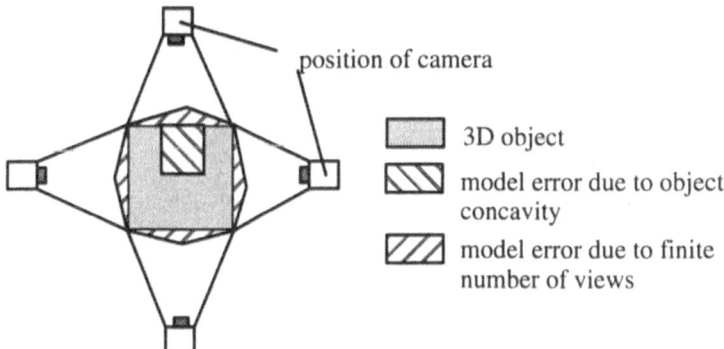

Fig. 6 : Two dimensional description of the resulting volume model

186

3.2 Integration of depth information

To overcome the principal inability of the above described volume modelling technique to model objects with concave shape additional information about the distance of the objects surface to the image plane is needed. This distance information, in the following called depth information, is stored in depth maps where a depth value is assigned to each pel. To obtain the depth maps active methods like laser scanner or structured light as well as passive methods like several disparity estimation techniques exist. Here the application of disparity estimation techniques is possible as the camera parameter, the 3D geometry between camera and turntable, and the rotation angle of the turntable between two successive images are exactly known. Thus two successive images can be viewed as one stereo image pair, and after rectification standard disparity estimation techniques can be used. As for active methods always additional equipment is needed, in this work a disparity estimation technique is used which is described in detail in [4]. This technique does not only estimate disparity values but also assigns a reliability value to each disparity value.

In general the depth maps estimated by active methods or by disparity estimation are inaccurate due to measurement errors and due to their restricted amplitude resolution. In the following a method is presented which describes how the accuracy of depth maps and their reliability can be increased by fusing depth maps from different viewpoints.

In a first step the depth of a surface element of the object is determined by considering the different depth values estimated from neighbouring viewpoints from which the surface element can be seen. Therefor at first a reference depth map is chosen. Then the 3D point represented by the assigned depth value z_1 of a pel $\vec{T}(x_1,y_1)$ of a neighbouring depth map is transformed into the reference depth map resulting in a 2D point $\vec{T}(x_0,y_0)$ and the depth value z_0' (Fig. 7).

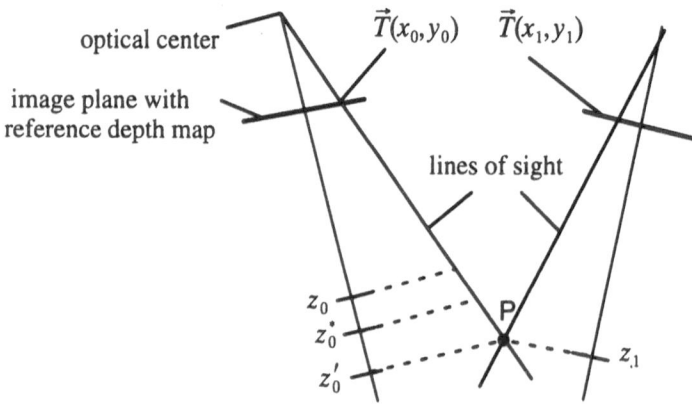

Fig. 7 Fusion of depth maps
P represented by the depth value z_1 of a pel $\vec{T}(x_1,y_1)$ of a depth map is transformed into the reference depth map resulting in $\vec{T}(x_0,y_0)$ and the depth value z_0'. The mean depth value of z_0 and z_0' denoted $\dot{z}_0$ is assigned to $\vec{T}(x_0,y_0)$.

If the difference between the assigned depth value of $\vec{T}(x_0, y_0)$ in the reference map z_0 and z_0' is below a predefined threshold, the mean depth value of z_0 and z_0' denoted $\overset{\cdot}{z_0}$ is calculated and assigned to $\vec{T}(x_0, y_0)$ considering their assigned reliability value.

The threshold avoids wrong correspondences for object surface elements which are visible from one viewpoint, but which are hidden in the neighbouring viewpoint. This procedure is repeated for each pel of each neighbouring depth map. In this way the depth measures of neighbouring depth maps are exploited to result in a more reliable and more accurate fused depth map.

In a second step an interpolation of the depth values assigned to neighbouring surface elements is performed, as neighbouring surface elements are likely to have similar depth values. Using physical surface models (membrane and plate) [12] a method for the smoothing of depth maps has been developed. In order to avoid errors due to smoothing at object edges, the edges are estimated during the smoothing process and considered as discontinuities in the physical models. The spatial interpolation process has thus been defined as a non–convex optimization problem. The optimization is performed using the GNC (Graduated Non–Convexity) algorithm, which has original-ly been developed for the reconstruction of luminance images [1]. Simulations have shown that especially the physical plate model in conjunction with the GNC algorithm can be recommended for the spatial interpolation process.

To enable the modelling of concavities the fused depth maps are used to refine the volume model. For each pel of each viewpoint the voxels are eliminated along the line of sight up to the assigned depth values in the fused depth maps. Modelling errors may now occur due to inaccurate depth information (too large depth values) and due to the limited number of viewpoints. The limited number of viewpoints leads to errors in areas of hidden surfaces (Fig. 8).

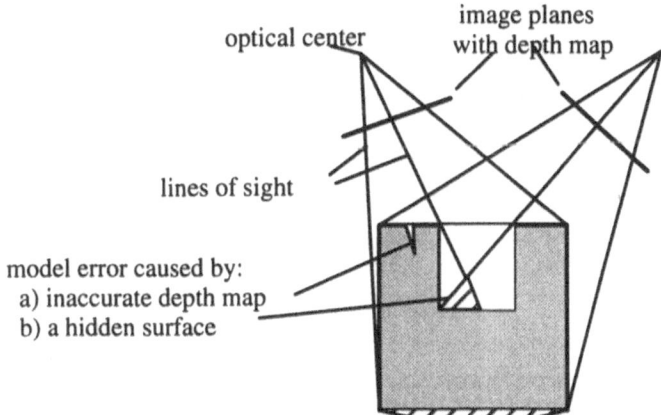

Fig. 8 Modelling of concavities by the use of depth maps
    In the visible surface area the concavity is carved out by eliminating the vol-
    ume elements along the line of sight of each picture element up to its assigned
    depth measure. Model errors caused by inaccurate depth maps and hidden sur-
    face are shown.

4 Surface Modelling

The synthesis algorithms used in computer animation work with surface models. Thus the volume representation must be transformed into a surface model. For that purpose the surface of the volume model is approximated by a triangle mesh. A mesh growing algorithm is used which allows a local adaptation of the volume model surface by adapting the size of each triangle patch according to a tolerable approximation error. This results in smaller triangles in surface regions with high curvature and larger triangles in surface regions with low curvature.

Starting with a single triangle placed on the volume model surface, or with a set of triangles located at 3D edges of the volume model, further triangles are constructed at each open edge until the whole volume model is covered with a mesh (Fig. 9).

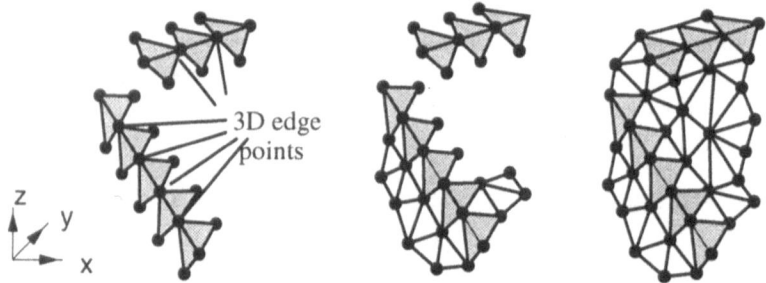

Fig. 9 Approximating the volume model by a triangle mesh

For the construction of the triangle mesh the following quality criteria have to be taken into consideration. These criteria can be divided into two groups. The criteria in the first group control the properties of each new single triangle, whereas the criteria in the second group evaluate the local neighbourhood of the triangle to form a regular mesh.

Criteria for single triangles are:

1. The distance between the triangle surface and the assigned surface voxels of the volume model must be within a tolerance to fulfill a given approximation quality. This leads to a generation of large triangles in planar areas and to small triangles in areas with large curvature.
2. The triangles should be equilateral and all angles should be larger than a given minimum angle. This avoids slim triangles which would lead to a direction dependant formability of the mesh.
3. The maximum size of the triangles is restricted to provide a high formability even in planar regions of the object surface.

Criteria for the mesh:

4. The distance of a new vertex to all edges of existing triangles should be larger than a given minimum triangle height. This avoids the need to fill the gap within the triangles with a slim triangle.
5. A gap between neighbouring triangles with an angle less than 80° will be closed directly, if allowed by the other criteria. This improves the symmetry of the mesh.

6. A gap between neighbouring triangles with an angle between 80° and 120° will be closed by symmetrical insertion of a new vertex. This is not really needed, but like criterion 5. improves the symmetry of the mesh forcing all angles to be between 40° and 80°.

7. If a new triangle overlaps an existing triangle, the new vertex will be fixed to the nearest vertex of the existing triangle, in order to avoid further overlapping. This is also how the mesh is closed. The recognition of overlapping triangles is very complex.

8. If no new triangle can be added to an existing edge, then the surface of the object is very uneven in this area and can not be approximated by a triangle with the given edge length. The edge has to be divided to enable the building of smaller triangles.

5 Texturing

The geometric model of the real object is not sufficient for applications in the field of computer animation. For natural looking 3D models the model texture is of great importance. To meet this goal a texturing algorithm has been developed which estimates the texture for each surface triangle from the input image sequence.

The principle to bind texture information to a single surface triangle is explained in Fig. 10. By using the cahv–camera parameters the vertices of a surface triangle are projected into the camera plane with the original image. The clipped rectangular image part containing the projected triangle is defined as texture map.

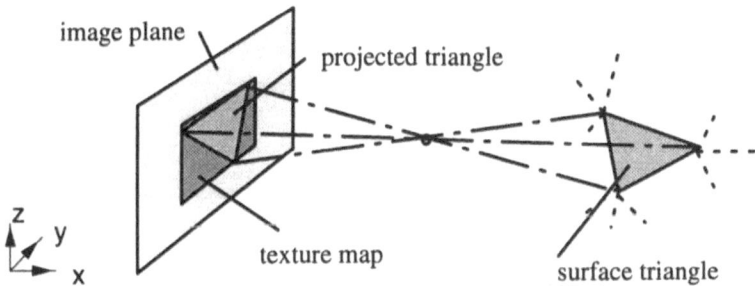

Fig. 10 Binding a texture map to a surface triangle

The quality of the final texture depends on illumination and the resolution of the CCD camera. Furthermore the correct binding of the texture to the 3D surface model is influenced by the accuracy of camera position relative to the object and by shape errors. All these influencing factors have to be taken into account in the texturing process in order to obtain a model with low distortion of texture.

The proposed texturing method is divided into three steps:

1. *Grouping triangles to surface regions textured from a common image.*(Fig. 11a)
   As the texture at boundaries between surface regions textured from different
   images is probably distorted, those regions should be as homogeneous as possible
   in order to reduce the total length of boundaries. Furthermore, the assignment of
   a triangle to a surface region depends on its texture resolution, which is defined
   as the ratio of pixel elements per surface unit and should be tolerable within a surface region.

2. *Local texture filtering of the boundaries between the surface regions.* (Fig. 11b)
   This is achieved by a newly developed filter which blends the texture between
   neighbouring triangles of different surface regions. This results in a local blurring
   effect, which is less conspicuous then the blocking effect occurring without filtering.

3. *Synthesis of texture for surface triangles not visible in any image.* For that purpose
   a filter has been developed which uses the texture from visible triangles.

(a)   (b)

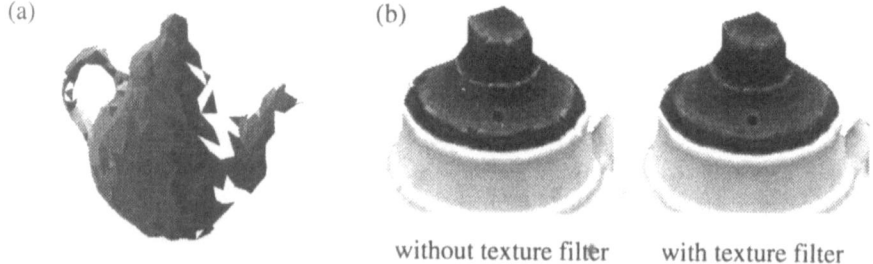

without texture filter   with texture filter

Fig. 11 (a) Grouping triangles to surface regions (b) effect of the texture filter

6 Results

The described algorithm was tested on a number of real 3D objects. For that purpose,
the real object was placed on a turntable and the turntable was rotated in 10^0 steps.
For each of the 36 views, a 720 x 576 image was taken from the real object with a
stationary calibrated CCD camera. The rotation angle accuracy of the turntable was
about 0.05^0. The processing of the volume was performed using a resolution in space
of 160^3 unit cubes for the bounding box of each real object.

Input sequences were taken not just from simply shaped objects but also from natural
objects with complex surfaces.

Fig. 12–14 show exemplary synthezised projections of the automatic generated models from a dinosaur, asterix and a wooden car. The results show a quality which is
sufficient for computer animation in case of the complex convex models asterix and
dinosaur. In case of the concave model of the wooden car the quality is lower which
can be traced back to errors in the depth maps.

Fig. 12 Synthetic generated projections of the model "asterix"

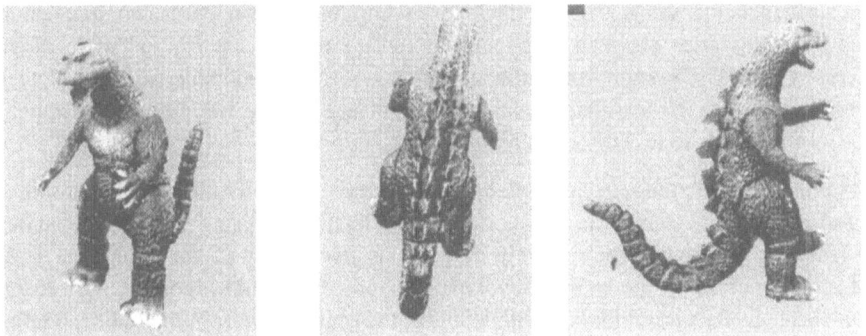

Fig. 13 Synthetic generated projections of the model "dinosaur"

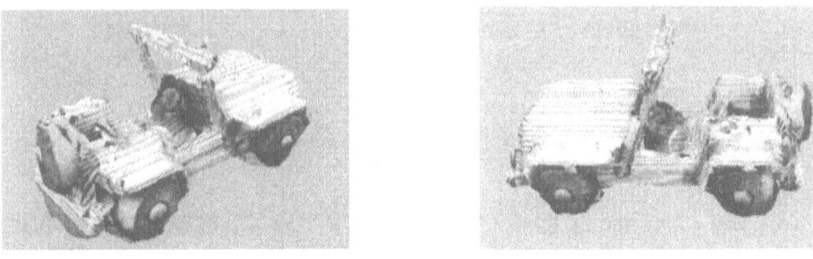

Fig. 14 Synthetic generated projections of the model "wooden car"

7 Conclusions

A complete process chain for the automatic modelling of 3D natural objects from multiple views is presented.

Based on a new volume representation the full resolution accuracy of the object silhouettes during volume modelling is exploited. The new volume representation furthermore allows a fast and simple realisation of the method of occluding contours. In order to enable the modelling of concave objects, additional depth information obtained by disparity estimation is integrated into the convex volume model.

The representation of the volume model by a triangular mesh is realized by considering 3D–edge information. Vertices of the triangular mesh can explicitly be set to 3D–edge coordinates in the initialization phase of the algorithm, which leads to reduced deterioration of edges in the final surface model.

For the texturing of the surface model a new method using all available images is proposed. Neighbouring triangles describing the surface of the 3D model are grouped to a surface region which is textured with one common image in a first step. In a second step the boundaries between neighbouring surface regions are filtered with a local texture filter. The texture for surface regions which are invisible in any image is synthesized from the texture of neighbouring surface regions in a last step. Applying this method leads to less distorted textured models.

Results with real image sequences have confirmed the suitability of the proposed algorithm for convex objects with complex and detailed surfaces. Though the quality of resulting concave models mainly depends on the quality of the integrated depth information. Due to the newly developed texture estimation algorithm the virtual models receive a natural look. Small details of the object which could not be modelled in the 3D geometry are well represented in the texture.

In future work the system will be extended by the facility to model outdoor objects by steering a camera around the object.

8 Acknowledgements

This work was supported by the RACE II project R2052 "MONA LISA". Partners in this project are Thomson Broadband Systems, BBC, Daimler Benz, DVS Digitale Videosysteme GmbH, Queen Mary & Westfield College, Siemens AG, University of Balearic Islands, and VAP Video Art Production GmbH.

9 References

[1]   A. Blake, A. Zisserman. *"Visual Reconstruction"*, MIT Press, 1987

[2]   H. Busch, "Ein Verfahren zur Oberflächenmodellierung dreidimensionaler Objekte aus Kamerabildfolgen", *Ph.D. thesis, Universität Hannover*, 1991.

[3]   C. H. Chien and J. K. Aggarwal, "Identification of 3D objects from multiple silhouettes using quadtrees/octrees ", *Comp. Vision, Graphics, and Image Processing* 36, 1986, pp. 256–273.

[4]   L. Falkenhagen, "Depth Estimation from Stereoscopic Image Pairs assuming Piecewise Continuos Surfaces", *European Workshop on Combined real and synthetic image processing for broadcast and video productions*, Hamburg, Germany, November 1994.

[5]   J.D. Foley et al., *"Computer Graphics: Principles and Practice"*, Addison Wesley, 1992.

[6]   Koch, R., "Automatic Reconstruction of Buildings from Stereoscopic Image Sequences", *Eurographics '93*, Barcelona,Spain, 1993.

[7]   W. N. Martin and J. K. Aggarwal , "Volumetric Descriptions of Objects from Multiple Views" ,*Trans. on Pattern Analysis and Machine Intelligence*, Vol. PAMI–5, 1983, pp. 150–159.

[8]   D. Meagher, "Geometric modelling using octree encoding", *Computer Vision, Graphics, and Image Processing*, Vol 19, 1982, pp. 129–147.

[9]   W. Niem, "Robust and Fast Modelling of 3D Natural Objects from Multiple Views", *SPIE Proceedings "Image and Video Processing II"*, Vol. 2182, 1994, pp. 388–397.

[10] M. Potmesil, "Generating octree models of 3D objects from their silhouettes in a sequence of images", *Computer Vision, Graphics, and Image Processing* 40, 1987, pp. 1–29.

[11] R. Szeliski, "Rapid Octree Construction from Image Sequences", *CVGIP: Image Understanding*, Vol. 58, No 1, July, pp. 23–32, 1993.

[12] D. Terzopoulos, "The Computation of Visible–Surface Representations", *IEEE Trans. on Pattern Analysis and Machine Intelligence*, Vol. 10, No. 4, July 1988.

[13] R. Y. Tsai, "A Versatile Camera Calibration Technique for High–Accuracy 3D Machine Vision Metrology Using Off–the–Shelf TV Cameras and Lenses", *Journal of Robotics and Automation*, Vol. RA–3. No.4, August 1987, pp. 323–344.

[14] Y.Yakimovsky, R. Cunningham, "A System for Extracting Three–Dimensional Measurements from a Stereo Pair of TV Cameras", *Computer Vision, Graphics, and Image Processing*, Vol. 7, pp. 195 –210, 1978.

Session 5: Analysis 3 (Continued)

Synthesis 1

Modelling Buildings from Single Images

Matthias Buck
Daimler-Benz AG, Research Centre Ulm
D-89013 Ulm, Germany

1 Introduction

In this paper, we describe an approach for the reconstruction of the 3D shape and texture of outdoor objects like buildings from a set of 2D images. This procedure is called '3D modelling' in the following, because the result is a 3D model of the analysed object. The modelling of outdoor objects is different from the modelling of indoor objects and other small objects in several aspects. When taking input images, the camera position, the object's illumination, and the object background are quite under control in studio environments, but not in outdoor situations. In outdoor situations, the set of possible camera views is restricted due to other objects occluding the object of interest, or because the camera cannot be placed everywhere. Fortunately, typical outdoor objects, in particular buildings, have certain properties, which can be used as constraints during the object's analysis and modelling phase. In [1] parallelism and orthogonality for the interpretation of perspective images are studied. [4] proposes a symmetry constraint for the same purpose.

2 Model Assumptions

The most important assumption we are using is, that the geometry of the modelled objects is based on a set of planar surface elements, the boundaries of which are straight lines. Further, it is assumed that the walls of a building are vertical, and that there are horizontal structures, e.g. rows of windows, visible on these surface elements. Further it is assumed, that the camera used for taking the 2D views of the object is a pinhole camera, which performs a central perspective projection from the 3D world onto the 2D image plane. It is known, that perspective projections lead to typical distortions in the projection image. In particular, a set of parallel lines in 3D is projected in the 2D image to a set of lines which intersect at one common point, called the vanishing point. The location of the vanishing point in the image plane is related uniquely to the orientation of the set of parallel lines in the 3D world. Mathematical details on this perspective projection can be found in [2, 5]. This leads to the modelling approach described in the following, which has already been implemented and verified by computer simulation.

3 Modelling Approach

The approach uses a set of few perspective views of the object to be modelled, which are taken by a calibrated camera. From each view, a partial 3d model is reconstructed. This set of views has to be selected properly to allow the subsequent analysis steps. Of course, all parts which should be included in the final model have to appear in one of these input images. The different views must overlap, so that the partial models, which are derived from each input image, can be linked appropriately.

The modelling procedure is divided into two complementary methods, one for the vertical faces of the building, and a second one for the roof. Both methods, which are described in the following two sections, are basing on the inversion of the perspective projection to recover the object's 3d geometry.

Generally, the 3d orientation of a plane is uniquely determined by two non-parallel 3d vectors. The method of inverting the perspective projection recovers the orientation of such a vector by analysis of the vanishing point, which corresponds to a set of parallel lines of that direction. Thus, two vanishing points determine the 3d orientation of a plane. In the case of rectangular surface elements, the two vanishing points can be obtained from the two pairs of parallel sides. To increase the numerical robustness, it is useful to take more than two parallel lines into account, e.g. in the case of buildings when there are several parallel rows of windows on a planar surface element.

With this method, the 3d geometry of planar surface elements can be recovered only up to a scale parameter. Under the assumption, that surface elements which adjoin in the 2d image also do so in 3d, the scale parameters of the individual surface elements can be adjusted appropriately. This leads to a 3d geometry, which is determined up to one global scale parameter.

Once the 3d geometry has been recovered, the texture maps of the surface elements are extracted from the 2d image, and their distortions are corrected according to the parameters of the perspective projection. These texture maps are used later on for the highly natural visualisation of the final model.

4 Modelling of Vertical Building Walls

We assume, that the building's walls are vertical planes. Consequently, the 3d orientation of each wall can be uniquely determined by knowledge of just one vanishing point, in particular the one which corresponds to the horizontal structures on that wall (e.g. rows of windows).

Thus, the following steps have to be taken to obtain a 3d model of the visible parts of a building from a given perspective view:

1. segmentation of the planar surface elements in the 2d image
2. determination of the horizontal vanishing point for each wall
3. reconstruction of the 3d geometry and extraction of the texture maps

The first step is hard to be done fully automatically, in particular, because buildings frequently are surrounded by other buildings. Therefore a segmentation module automatically extracts line structures in the 2d image, and proposes a segmentation into surface elements. This segmentation now can be confirmed by the user, or modified by selecting some of the automatically extracted lines.

In the second step, the straight lines inside each wall segment are analysed in the 2d image, and the corresponding vanishing points are estimated. This is achieved by grouping the lines which intersect at one common point. The intersection point of the biggest set of lines is proposed as the vanishing point. Again, this point can be confirmed or modified interactively. Now the 3d geometry and the texture maps can be recovered. An example of an input image is shown in fig. 3, and the corresponding partial model, which was derived from it, is depicted in fig. 2.

Fig. 1: Original camera image

Fig. 2: The corresponding 3d model which was derived from fig. 3

Fig. 3: A combined model which has been derived from about 20 images

Finally, the partial models which have been derived from the individual perspective views as described above, are linked to one complete model. This is done by using several matching criteria, which make sure that the overlapping parts of two adjacent partial models coincide up to a certain error threshold. The overlapping parts of the partial models must be consistent in their topologies and geometries (shape or aspect ratio of the overlapping walls and angles between adjacent walls) as well as in the corresponding texture maps.

All possible overlapping positions are tested according to these criteria to find the correct constellation. If the matching process cannot identify a unique solution, user interaction is required to choose one of the proposed solutions.

In fig.3 a model is depicted, which has been reconstructed from about 20 perspective views.

Complementary to this modelling procedure for the vertical front faces (walls) of a building, a different approach has been designed to model specific parts like e.g. the roof. This approach is designed to work with a data base consisting of suitable templates, and is described in the following paragraph.

5 Modelling of Roofs using Templates

For the modelling of building walls we assumed, that the walls can be described as a set of vertical rectangular surface elements. This assumption is true for the main body of most buildings. However, there are parts of buildings, for which this assumption does not hold, in particular for the roofs. For these parts, a method based on template matching can be applied, which is described in the following.

The great majority of real roofs can be divided into a few sets of basic geometries, which we call templates in the following. Templates are generic geometric descriptions, which can consist of elements like vertices, edges, faces or even 3d primitives like cubes or cylinders (CSG, constructive solid geometry). These descriptions are generic because they don't contain a precise description of a particular geometry, but a description of a class of geometries. Scaleable parameters allow to adapt the generic model to the particular properties (e.g. length of edges, angles) of a given object.

The modelling process using such generic templates consists of the following steps:

1- extract elements (edges, vertices etc.) from the real image
2- determine properties and relations among these elements
3- match the extracted data with the templates
4- select the template which corresponds best to the input data and
  establish correspondences between image elements and template elements
6- adapt the template to the actual properties (sizes, angles etc.)

In general, the template description consists of two parts. One part contains the 3d properties of the underlying geometric structure, and the other part contains the properties of this structure in a 2d projection. Depending on the 3d properties, there can be several 2d descriptions, corresponding to different projections which lead to principally different 2d geometries (so called 'aspects', [6]).

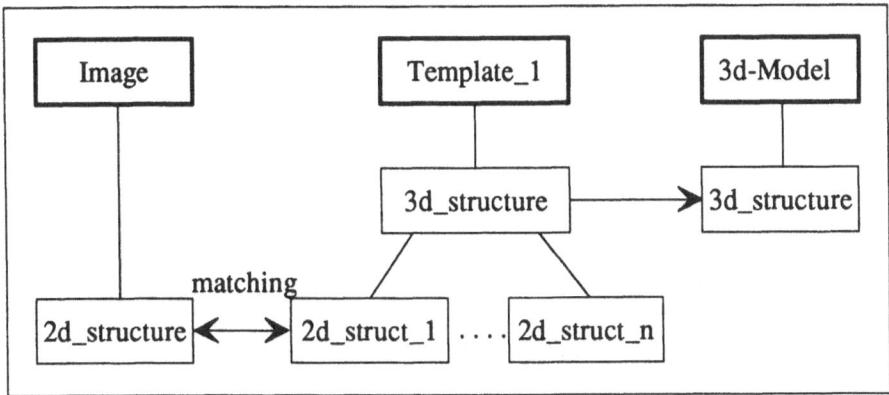

Fig. 4: 3d reconstruction by template matching

The matching (step 3) between the elements extracted from the image and the template structures is performed on the level of 2d structures. The evaluation of these correspondences leads to the identification of one of the templates (or of none, if there is no satisfying correspondence). In step 6, the 3d-part of the template is 'customised', i.e. its parameters are set according to the properties of the image elements. This procedure is illustrated in fig. 4.

In the context of the reconstruction of 3d geometry from 2d perspective views, as described in [5], there is another possibility. Through the identification of a suitable template, it is sufficient to determine certain relationships between the 2d elements identified in the image. In particular, it is sufficient to identify sets of edges which belong to common planar surface elements like triangles or rectangles. With this information, the 3d structure of such surface elements can be recovered by inverting the perspective projection.

5.1 The template structures

As the template matching method is used for the modelling of roofs in our application, we give examples from a set of 'roof templates' we are using, i.e. the templates 'saddle roof', 'hipped roof', and 'tent roof' (see fig. 5).

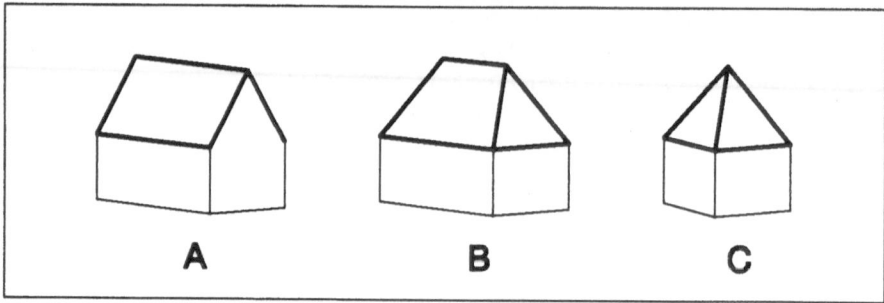

Fig. 5: Some roof types: (a) saddle roof, (b) hipped roof, (c) tent roof

Each roof template consists of a set of lines (edges), for which certain properties and certain relations are specified. Of course, these specifications always allow a range of values (e.g. for distances or angles), or equivalent formulations like 'clockwise' or 'counter clockwise'. As already mentioned, the relations between the edges of the templates have to be given separately, once for the 3d structure of the object class, and for each of the 2d projections of all principal views. In the case of the saddle roof, the template consists of 7 lines (D1 - D7, see fig. 6). The corresponding 3d properties for this type of roof are:

- D1, D2, D3, D4 form a slanted rectangle
- D1, D5, D6, D7 form a slanted rectangle
- both rectangles are oriented symmetrically

Which of these lines are visible in a perspective view depends on the particular view. Some typical views are shown in fig. 6

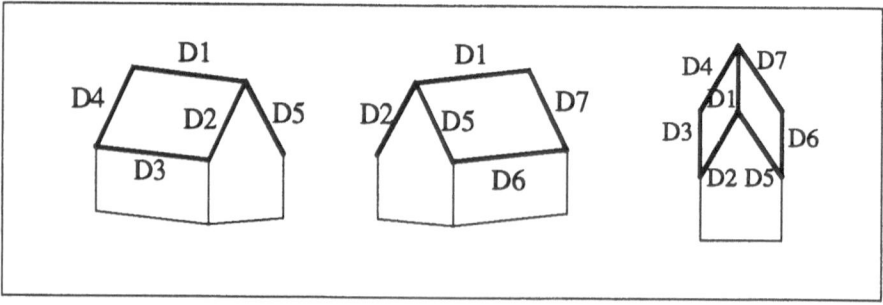

Fig. 6: Principal views of a building with a saddle roof

The relations which describe the 2d structure A in fig. 5 are:

	D5	D4	D3	D2
D1	d,c	d,c	p,v	d,c
D2	d,c	p	d,c	-
D3	-	d,c	-	-
D4	-	-	-	-

where
  d = minimal distance between endpoints
  p = enclosed angle
  c = corner type (upper left, lower left, upper right, or lower right)
  v = vertical distance

For each of the used relations, a fuzzy cost function is defined, which indicates how well the lines extracted from the input image match the corresponding properties of the template. The general form of such fuzzy functions is shown for example for the relation d (distance of endpoints) in fig. 7. In this case, endpoint distances up to d1 pixels produce no costs, and distances of more than d2 pixels produce maximal costs.

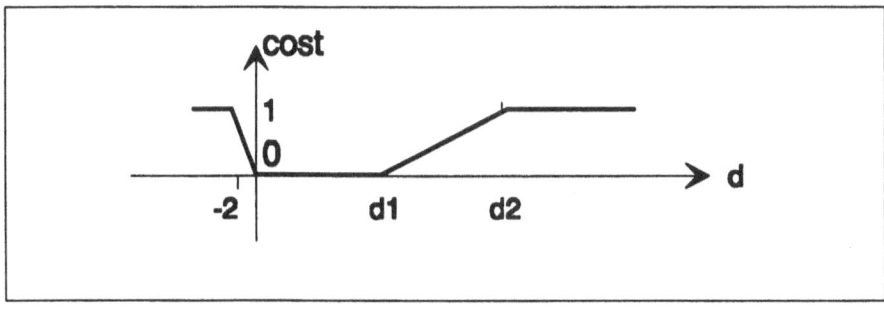

Fig. 7: The fuzzy cost function for the relation 'distance of endpoints'.

5.2 Matching

In this section, we describe the matching procedure which is used to determine the assignment of the lines in the image to those of the templates. In other words, the task is as follows: given one template, each of the lines in the image could correspond to each of the lines in the template. This leads to a great number of combinations. For each such combination, a cost value can be determined, which is a goodness criterion. The combination with the lowest cost is selected. If there are several templates, this procedure has to be done for each template, and the interpretation with the lowest of all costs is selected. This is not a trivial task, because the number of possible interpretations can be enormous: With the simple template of 5 Lines, and 100 lines in the image, its already $9 \cdot 10^9$.

To reduce the number of combinations, it is useful to restrict the set of lines which can be identified with a certain template line by some criterion, a possible range of length values, a possible range of orientations etc. However, if the object in the input image can be of any size, length criteria are not very useful, and often orientation criterion don't reduce the number of possibilities only slightly, either.

So this type of matching is only feasible with an efficient graph search algorithm. One of the most efficient ones is the so called A^*-algorithm (for details, see [7]).

The result of the matching procedure is an identification of some lines from the input image with template lines, and a cost value for this selection.

5.3 3D reconstruction

In our example, the matching process identified some of the lines, which have been extracted from the input image, as elements D1 ... D5 of the template. From this correspondence in 2d follows the conclusion, that the identified lines have certain 3d properties. In particular, it is assumed that the 4 lines in the input image, which correspond to D1 ... D4, make up a slanted rectangle in 3d. The intersections of these 4 lines correspond to the perspective projections of the vertices of this rectangle. By inversion of the perspective projection, the 3d shape and orientation of this rectangle is recovered, and the corresponding texture map is extracted from the 2d image. Together with the symmetry assumption in the 3d template, even the hidden surface of the roof could be hypothesised.

5.4 Experiments

The method was tested with line structures which have been extracted automatically from camera images, as well as with synthetic line structures. Fig. 8 shows a synthetic line structure, whereas in fig. 9 those lines are shown which have been identified by the template matching algorithm as elements of the roof templates shown in fig. 5.

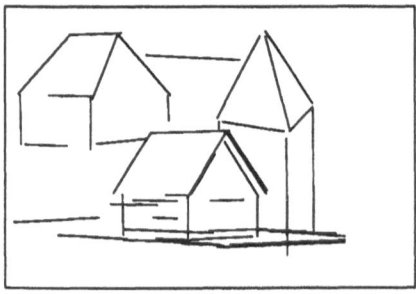 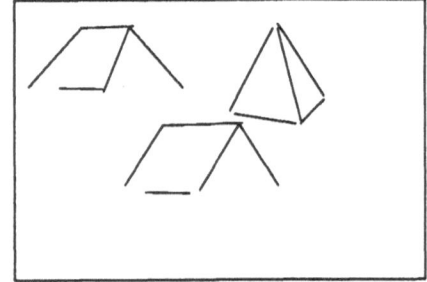

Fig 8: A synthetic line structure showing buildings with roofs

Fig 9: The lines of fig. 8 which correspond to one of the roof templates shown in fig. 5

Figs. 10 - 13 illustrate an example using a real camera image. An enlarged portion of the original input image, showing a house with a saddle roof, is depicted in fig. 10. The corresponding line structure is shown in fig. 12. These lines have been determined in the course of the segmentation of the building walls, and consist of automatically extracted contour lines, as well as of segmentation results (e.g. the vertical line in the center of the front face).

Fig 10: A camera image of a building with a saddle roof

Fig. 11: The corresponding 3d model, shown from a new viewing position

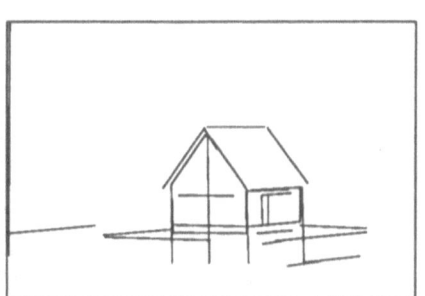

Fig 12: The extracted line structure

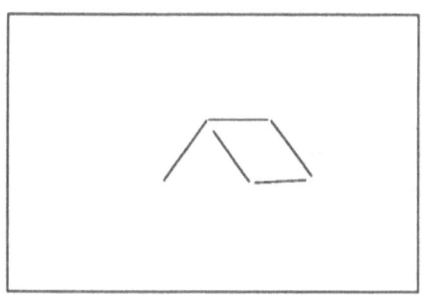

Fig. 13: The lines matching the correct template for the roof

The result of the template matching procedure is given in fig. 13. It shows those lines which correspond to the saddle roof template. Now that the visible part of the saddle roof has been identified in the 2d image, the corresponding 3d model is reconstructed using the inverse perspective projection. The resulting 3d model, including the vertical surface elements, is shown in fig. 11 from a different viewing position. The back side of the roof could have been included as well according to the symmetry of this type of roof. This however was not done in the shown example.

6 Results and Summary

The presented method uses automatic methods to perform the different modelling steps (e.g. the extraction of line structures, the analysis of vanishing points, the reconstruction of the 3d geometry, or the matching of roof templates). However, it allows the user to confirm the automatically proposed intermediate results, or to override them and do the necessary modifications. This makes the approach flexible, and capable of handling even difficult image material. Difficult situations just require more user interaction.

The results obtained with a set of test images of real buildings show that this approach is appropriate, if the objects shown in the input images meet the modelling assumptions. The quality of the reconstructed geometry of the modelled objects is so accurate that differences to the real object geometry are hardly visible. The extracted textures on the object surfaces correspond with good accuracy to the real object appearance. Their resolution of course is limited by the resolution of the original input images from which they were taken. This means, that the object models should be used in virtual scenes in a way that doesn't require a much higher resolution than the one provided by the images used for analysis and modelling. For example, if the virtual camera is placed much closer to the object than the real camera was, the resolution of the texture maps will not be sufficient in terms of detail.

The approach for the modelling of roofs, based on template matching, leads to a reliable recognition with the used test material, which contained only few examples. It has to be evaluated, however, with a greater test data set.

References

[1] S. T. Barnard: Interpreting perspective images
Artif. Intelligence, 21, 1983, pp. 435-462.

[2] J.D. Foley et al.: Computer Graphics: Principles and Practice
Addison Wesley, 1990.

[3] M. Buck, R. Buschmann, G. Kummerfeldt: 3D Shape and Texture estimation
RACE Project R2052, MONA LISA Deliverable no. 4, 1992

[4] F. Ulupinar, R. Nevatia: Constraints for Interpretation of Line Drawings under Perspective Projection
CVGIP: Image Understanding, Vol. 53, No. 1, 1991, pp. 88-96

[5] W. Niem, M. Buck, G. Kummerfeldt, L. Chevalier, P. Robert: 3D shape and texture estimation, RACE Project R2052, MONA LISA Deliverable no. 11, 1993

[6] Koenderink, J.J.; van Doorn, A.J.: The internal representation of solid shape with respect to vision, Biol. Cybernetics 32, 211 - 216, 1979

[7] N.J. Nilsson: Principles of artificial intelligence
Springer Verlag Berlin-Heidelberg-New York, 1982

Knowledge Based Modelling of Natural Scenes

Oliver Grau and Ralf Tönjes

Institut für Theoretische Nachrichtentechnik und Informationsverarbeitung

Division "Automatic Image Interpretation", Chair Prof. C.–E. Liedtke

Universität Hannover, Appelstrasse 9A, 30167 Hannover, Germany

E–mail: grau@tnt.uni–hannover.de, toenjes@tnt.uni–hannover.de

Abstract

A knowledge based approach for the automatic generation of 3D models from stereo images is presented. Two different application fields are shown: The modelling of houses and the modelling of landscapes from aerial images. The models are used for computer graphic applications. A human observer is in possession of a priori knowledge about the scene. To meet his expectations and thus to improve realism the presented approach employs explicit knowledge. The knowledge base is exploited to derive constraints for surface reconstruction and to complete partially occluded models.

1 Introduction

For visualization of synthetic scenes 3D models are required from which new simulated views can be computed. Applications such as flight and driving simulators, architecture and landscape visualization and film industry have a high demand for realistic models. Quantity, precision and the kind of models ask for methods that automate the model generation of real objects and are applicable to outdoor scenes, i.e. do not require active sensors or special illumination.

An approach for generating realistic 3D models of natural scenes based on photogrammetric stereo [1,2,3] is presented. Reconstruction of a 3D model from 2D projections is an inverse and underconstrained mathematical problem. Two kinds of solutions for this problem can be distinguished: 1. the data driven integration of data from multiple sources (multiple sensor, multiple views, multiple methods) and 2. the use of knowledge in a model driven approach.

The data driven 3D modelling attacks the ambiguity by assuming simple, i.e. smooth surfaces [1,2]. 3D reconstruction is achieved bottom–up by consecutive grouping of depth measurements to a fixed kind of surface primitive like a triangular patch [2] or a Bézier or NURBS patch.

The knowledge based or model driven approach incorporates a priori knowledge about the scene in the 3D modelling process. The reconstruction is achieved mainly top–down by generating hypotheses about the scene from the knowledge base and testing the hypotheses with the data. Further on the model driven and the data driven approach can be integrated. In this case the data driven phase of the modelling process is controlled by the knowledge based system. An advantage is that the system can limit the parameter space and select more specific surface primitives, e.g. either polygons or splines.

Another important application of the knowledge based system is the completion of the 3D model to obtain a plausible model for the human viewer even when no image information is available. These cases are caused by occlusions or insufficient image resolution.

In the presented approach the scene objects are modelled by using a polygonal mesh for the geometry and mapped texture for fine sub–structure.

The principal goal, a realistic looking scene, can be reached in two ways: The first approach is to model the objects as precise as possible and with the maximum level of detail. The other approach is to take care of what is important for the impression of a human viewer. The latter approach leads to more compact models, a common requirement for many applications, and can be achieved by the use of knowledge in the modelling process. Chapter 2 explains the general kinds of knowledge applicable for the modelling of 3D objects and how these are processed in the presented scene analysis system AIDA.

The chapter 3 describes the use of knowledge in the application of modelling houses. The chapter 4 describes an other application field, the knowledge based modelling of landscapes. The paper terminates with a conclusion.

2 Using explicit Knowledge for 3D Modelling

Five processing steps can be distinguished in the presented approach for the modelling of 3D objects:

    I.   Interpretation of the signal

    II. Deriving constraints from the knowledge base

    III. Reconstruction of the object geometry using the obtained constraints

    IV. Completion of object parts not supported by the signal (optional)

    V. Texturing of the 3D model

The interpretation of the signal assigns a meaning to the scene content represented in its 2D image projections. This part of the AIDA system is an image understanding system [7,6]. The assignment of meanings in terms of the generic model description is necessary for the selection of the proper constraints (step II) that can be applied for the reconstruction of the object surface (step III) and optional the completion of the object parts which are not visible (step IV). In the last step of the modelling process the images are projected onto the reconstructed object surface and stored in a texture map to obtain a photorealistic model.

Both kinds of knowledge the (generic) description of the model used in step I and the constraints used in step II can be formulated in a single knowledge base as a semantic net. The following section describes the used formalism.

2.1 Representation of the Knowledge

In AIDA the knowledge is mainly represented as semantic nets [4,5] implemented in a frame–like structure. Semantic nets have been applied to a number of image and signal understanding problems [5,6]. Each node of the net is represented by a frame, which can be considered as a collection of attributes. Further the frames constitute the concept of inheritance, a basic feature of object oriented programming. In the part of the semantic net that describes the generic world model, the nodes are called concepts, while the nodes describing the objects found in the scene are called instances. The edges or links of the semantic net form the relations between the nodes.

The is–a link connects a general node with a specialization, like flat roof as special kind of roof. The concept of inheritance in semantic nets is realized by this type of link. For example a flat roof has all the attributes of the general concept roof except these that are defined different in the flat roof node. Further a flat roof inherits all links from roof. If for example roof has a part–of link to chimney, then flat roof has this link too.

The right side of figure 1 shows a part of a semantic net describing a small scene. The scene is composed of parts, indicated by the part–of links from the sub objects to the parent node. The links can have attributes like the condition that there are more or equal than four parts or that a link is optional. So a "car" is optional in figure 1 and must not be present in the scene.

Another important link is the concrete–of link introduced by the ERNEST system [6]. It links two conceptional layers or levels of abstraction. In figure 1 the node "wall" is connected by a concrete–of link with the node "polygon". The link assigns a concrete geometric realization to "wall". Currently three conceptional layers are implemented in AIDA: The semantic scene layer, the geometric 3D layer and the 2D layer.

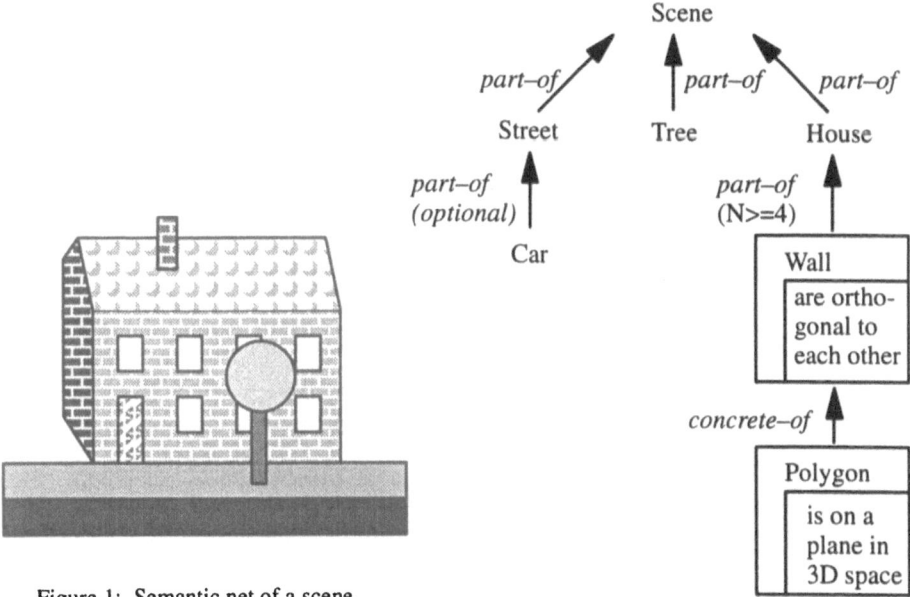

Figure 1: Semantic net of a scene

Following the concrete–of links from the top level nodes, the scene specific semantic of an object is transformed to a geometric or photometric concrete realization in the image data.

The last principal link type is the instance–of link. This link is established at the interpretation phase of the analysis and connects an instance supported by the signal with a concept in the generic model description. The next section gives a short outline of the algorithm that performs the interpretation.

2.2   Interpretation of the Signal

The AIDA system employs a graph processing algorithm to instantiate nodes and links, i.e. to assign a meaning to the signal. The algorithm is based on the speech and image analysis system ERNEST [6] extended by some features needed for the 3D scene analysis. The problem independent control strategy is implemented as a small set of rules for instantiation guided by an modified A* graph search algorithm to select the optimal instance.

In a model driven phase hypotheses for the appearance of a wall in the image are generated, judged, and the most probable is selected. The algorithm is also applicable for a bottom–up analysis. In this case the initial goal is not a node of the top conceptional layer like "house", but a node from a lower layer like "2D polygon". In both cases the algorithm stops if the scene is fully interpreted.

An important feature of the interpretation system is that it limits the parameter space of segmentation and low level search algorithms in the model driven phase. If a new view of the scene is analyzed, the position of already found objects can be predicted thus reducing the search area.

The assignment of the semantic nodes in the lowest conceptional layer to the image data is achieved by image segmentation or provided by a human operator. In the first case the system represents an image understanding system. The presented approach supports both ways. The goal is to create a system that works fully or nearly automatic, but in cases the system fails a human supervisor should have full control of all system components. Another point of view of the system is, that it offers the flexibility of an interactive system, but assists the operator in laborious and difficult tasks and minimizes the interactions neccessary.

2.3   Knowledge based Surface Reconstruction

The most important application of using knowledge in the modelling of 3D objects is to obtain a better conditioning of the surface reconstruction. The goal is to reconstruct the depth information, which is irreversible lost in the projection of a surface and can be reconstructed only noisy and unreliable with local depth measurement techniques like shape from X, e.g. shape from stereo.

A model driven approach offers several possibilities for the use of geometric constraints which can be formulated as explicit knowledge and in general the demand of independent depth measurements can be reduced significantly. The following constraints are used in the presented approach:

a) The most specialized surface primitive is selected. E.g. a plane polygon is used to model a wall.

b) Geometry is restricted by spatial relations. E.g. the walls of a house are forced to be orthogonal to each other.

c) Knowledge about the object structure like connections of sub–parts is exploited. E.g. two roof parts should be closed at the peak.

The used geometric constraints are application dependent. In the chapters 3 and 4 some examples for the two presented application fields will be explained in detail.

2.4 Knowledge based Completion of Models

The model reconstructed from the image data may be incomplete due to lack of signal caused by occlusions or insufficient image resolution. The knowledge base provides the missing parts. Selection of the right model from the knowledge base is achieved by image interpretation. Model completion employs different kinds of knowledge:

a) Knowledge about the object structure is used to add invisible parts like occluded backwalls of houses or in aerial images invisible edges of forests.

b) The geometric and photometric features of the parts without signal are obtained from the generic model and further restricted by the detected parts of the object. E.g. the texture of the wood edge depends on the visible adjacent part of the wood.

3 Knowledge based 3D Modelling of Houses

Houses are composed of very regular geometric structures with several spatial relations, like plane polygons which are orthogonal to each other. These facts are common knowledge for a human observer. Hence he will not accept a model that has rounded edges or non planar walls. In a knowledge based approach the geometric relations are used to improve the realism of the 3D models.

This application takes full advantage of the AIDA knowledge representation. A semantic net contains a prototype for houses, their components and the applicable geometric constraints.

Figure 2 shows the use of the knowledge that the wall geometry represents a polygon in 3D space. The local depth measurement performed by a stereo disparity estimator is noisy (Fig. 2 b), because of quantization and failure in locations where no texture is present. It is known that the regarded wall lies on a plane. Hence a regression for all disparity measurements within the marked wall region is performed. Given the disparity each image point p_i can be reprojected to a 3D point P_i according to the used camera model. The regression weighted with the certainty yields a more accurate estimation of the plane wall. The regression integrates the depth measurements of several stereo image pairs assuming known camera position.

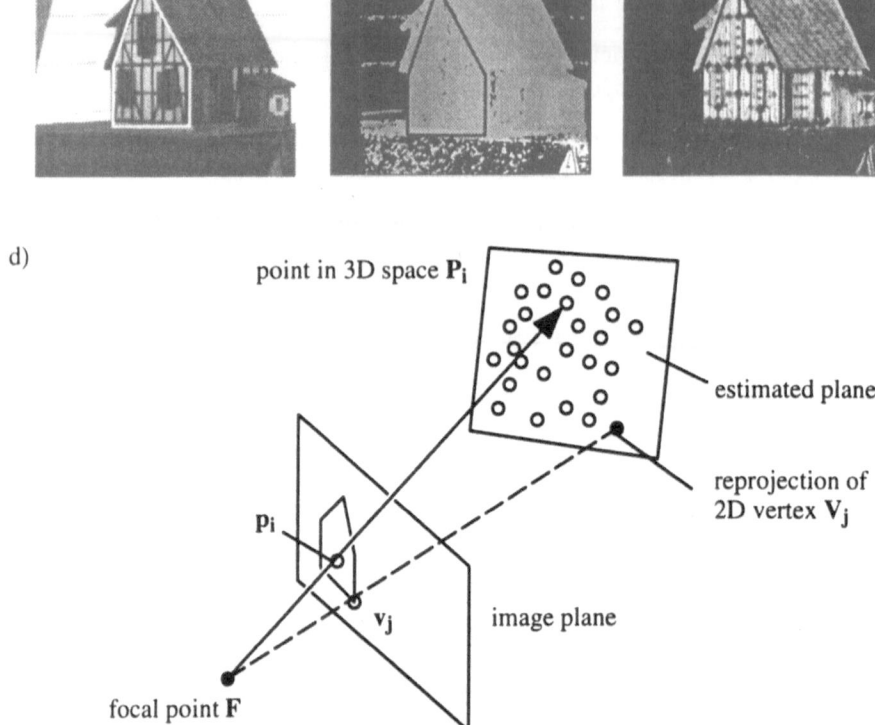

Figure 2: (a) Luminance image with marked region, (b) noisy disparity map, (c) certainty map of the disparity measurements, (d) and regression over all region points

To get a polygon in 3D as a first step the vertices of the 2D polygon are reprojected onto the 3D plane and form a 3D polygon. The reprojection is found as the point of intersection of the line of sight from the focal point $\mathbf{F}$ through the image plane at the vertex $\mathbf{v_j}$ and the estimated 3D plane.

After the reprojection of all polygons the knowledge about connections of sub–parts is exploited. This is explicitly formulated for the walls and the roof of the house. A spatial relation introduces the constraint that the neighboring polygons meet at the line of intersection of their 3D planes. This constraint yields closed models.

3.1 Results

The figure 3 shows the result of the presented modelling approach. Only three stereo pairs from different views were used to model the house from a laboratory scene. The model is only composed of a small number of polygons. The walls are typically modelled as one plane polygon and are connected at the line of intersection as outlined in the previous section. The knowledge base used consists of a semantic net with 41 nodes and 64 links. The net is able to represent simple houses like the one depicted in figure 3.

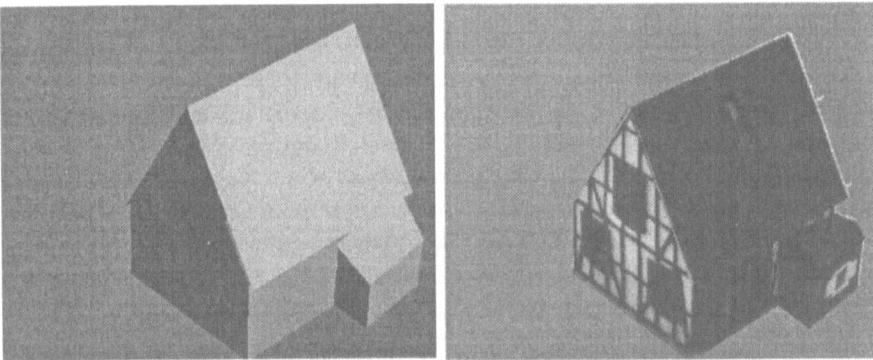

Figure 3: Synthesized view of the model in (a) shaded and (b) textured presentation

Since currently no automatic segmentation methods of the 2D polygons in the image are implemented, the region must be marked manualy. However, no high accuary is required because of the regression of the 3D plane and the calculation of the intersecting polygon edges.

4   Knowledge based 3D Modelling of Landscapes

Conventional landscape modelling ignores the object meaning and applies only stereo matching techniques to construct a terrain model. However this approach hardly works for complex scenes and fails when a high level of detail is required. Natural culture (wood, trees) and man made objects (buildings, roads) are not modelled or appear faulty. A human observer is in possession of a priori knowledge about the scene and expects height steps at the edges of forests and roads to run continuously. To obtain more realistic models this a priori knowledge must be integrated in the modelling process using image segmentation and interpretation.

a)   b)   c)

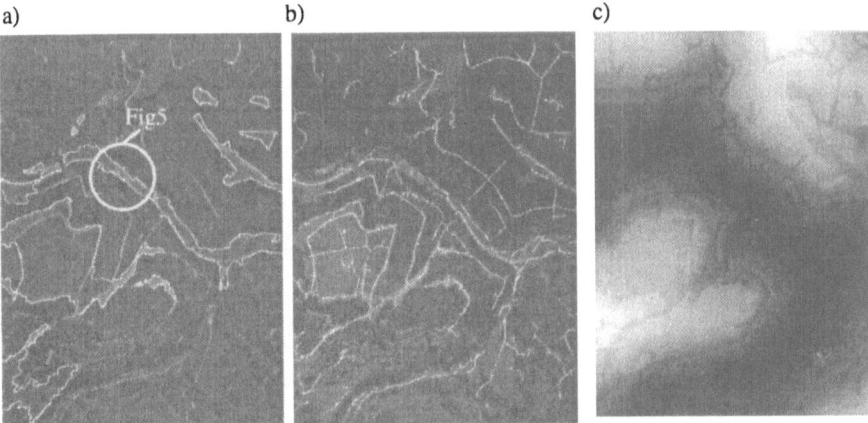

Figure 4:   Aerial image with (a) overlayed segmented woods, (b) roads and (c) height map with elevated woods

Knowledge is used both, for scene interpretation and model improvement. In the first case the knowledge indicates what objects are to be searched for and which are the eminent features for detection. In the second case knowledge is used to correct erroneous and complete missing signals. The landscape modelling employs knowledge about the photometric object features for object detection and geometric knowledge for model improvement. The height discontinuity of wood edges is missed by depth measurement due to image resolution. However, in aerial images woods can be segmented based on their texture [8]. Figure 4a shows the segmented woods represented by white contours. The segmented wood region is used as a mask to elevate the woods in the height map, where bright areas correspond to higher terrain (figure 4c). Further, to consider roads passing woods the road regions are detected (figure 4b) and not elevated.

For efficient visualization the model geometry is approximated by a polygon mesh. The polygon representation must consider height steps and breaklines. Continuous surfaces such as wood and roads are modelled by a separate polygon mesh.

In the aerial image the edges of woods are invisible. This lack of signal is overcome by a priori knowledge about wood models to photo texture the inserted wood edges.

Currently only a bottom–up analysis is implemented, allowing no iterating refinement. However, even integration of solely data driven image interpretation in the modelling process improves model realism significantly.

4.1   Results

Figure 5 shows a synthesized view of a landscape modelled from overlapping aerial images. Realism is improved by approximating wood and roads by a separate polygon mesh and inserting a height step at the edge of the forest.

The symbolic model description eases the postprocessing with computer graphics techniques. Thus the inserted edge of the forest is textured and the segmented but flat building is replaced by a CAD model.

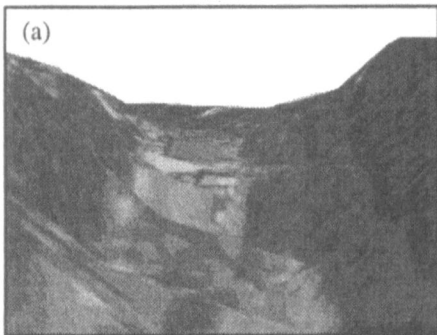

Figure 5:   Synthesized close up view of landscape section marked in figure 4 (a) without and (b) with usage of a priori knowledge by image interpretation.

5 Conclusions

The paper shows how a priori knowledge about scene objects in 3D modelling can be used to improve the realism of the visualized models. Knowledge based modelling focuses on model features that are sensitive for faults a human observer would detect.

The explicit formulated knowledge is used to derive geometric constraints, that lead to a better conditioning for the solution of the inverse projection and reduce the demand for independant depth measurements significantly. So the house model presented in section 3.1 could be modeled only from three camera views.

Further the knowledge base tackles the problem of incomplete objects due to lack of sensor signal as shown for the modelling of wood edges.

3D scene analysis results in an iconic 3D model and a symbolic scene description implemented as semantic net. The symbolic scene description offers the possibility to answer inquiries. For example the net can be asked for the number of houses with flat roofs in the scene. The query can also be extended with an action directive like: 'Set the color of roofs to red if the house has more than two floors'. The symbolic scene description establishes an interface between computer vision and computer graphic techniques.

6 References

[1]   Lemmens, M., "A survey on Stereo Matching Techniques", *ISPRS Conference*, Kyoto, Japan, 1988.

[2]   Koch, R., "Model–Based 3D Scene Analysis from Stereoscopic Image Sequences", *ISPRS Conference*, Washington, USA, Aug. 1992.

[3]   Tönjes, R., Grau, O., Koch, R.: "Analyse durch Synthese Modellierung von 3D Objekten in Stereobildfolgen", 1. Workshop visual computing, Darmstadt, 1994.

[4]   Winston, P.H., "Artificial Intelligence", Addison–Wesley Publ. Comp. 1992.

[5]   Niemann, H., "Pattern Analysis and Understanding", Springer Verlag, 1989.

[6]   Niemann, H., Sagerer, G., Schröder, S., Kummert, F., "ERNEST: A Semantic Network System for Pattern Understanding", *IEEE Trans. on Pattern Analysis and Machine Intelligence*, Vol. 12, No. 9, pp. 883–905, Sept. 1990.

[7]   Matsuyama, T., Hwang, V.S.–S., "SIGMA : A Knowledge–Based Aerial Image Understanding System", *Plenum Press*, New York 1990

[8]   Tönjes, R., "Realistic Landscape Modelling with High Level of Detail", IEEE International Conference on Image Processing, Austin, USA, Nov. 1994.

Real-time Collision Checking for 3D Object Positioning in Sparse Environments*

Jaume Jaume, Ricardo Galli, Ramon Mas and Miquel Mascaró-Oliver
Department of Mathematics and Computer Science, Universitat de les Illes Balears,
E-07071 Palma de Mallorca, Spain
(e-mail: gallir@anim.uib.es)

Abstract

This paper presents an implementation of real-time collision checking techniques included in a 3D scene generation system. These type of systems are designed to allow the user to define, create and modify a synthetic scene (environment) from isolated objects. When designers work on the environment, one of the most time-demanding tasks is the positioning of an object touching or lying on other objects or making sure that an object is collision-free. This collision checking for solid objects is expensive in terms of algorithm complexity and CPU use and some constraints should be imposed in its implementation in order to decrease the global complexity. We exploit the observation that the number of object collisions is small when defining a scene. Collisions mainly occur among the moving object and those who define supporting surfaces in the scene (floor-objects). As this reduction in scene complexity is not enough to achieve real-time collision detection, we use techniques which limit further the intersection domain complexity. Finally, we present some statistics of simulation results showing the performance characteristics of the method.

1. Introduction

In Computer Animation, 3D objects are usually represented by using geometric information about faces and vertices. We consider each face as a 2D polygon made of more than two coplanar vertices. Faces are grouped together to form an object. A set of objects will define a scene when the right position, scaling and orientation are properly defined. If the objects in a scene are considered to be solid, no collision among them must be allowed.

When no special attention is paid to object transformations, objects will sail through each other giving an undesirable visual effect. Many scene generation systems provide no collision checking methods, and require user action to visually check for objects collision. However, this approach increases the scene building time and does not guarantee consistent results. The inclusion of an automatic collision detection module in a scene generator increases reliability and performance

---

* Partially supported by Monalisa European Project.

([5], [8] and [9]) although it keeps being one of the most CPU consuming modules.

Within our geometric representation, we assume that two solids collide when one of the following conditions holds [6]:

- There is a face of the first object that intersects a face of the second object.

- One of the two objects fully contains the other one. Note that in this case there does not exist face intersection.

The main problems involved in collision checking include collision detection and collision response ([1], [5]). While in the first case an algorithm is used to decide whether a collision between objects has occurred, in the second case an action has to be defined when the collision has been detected. In scene generation, the corrective response might consist in finding a transformation which ensures that there is no object collision while being as close as possible to the user selected transformation.

In scene generation, the collision checking problem is posed in terms of a static environment. Only one of the objects is being transformed interactively at any time, while the other objects in the scene remain in their assigned position. This is what one calls Static Collision Checking (SCC). The objects are subject to linear transformations (translation, scaling or rotation) defined by user interaction and the aim of the SSC module is to check for collision each time the user transforms an object.

Collision detection algorithms vary mainly depending on three aspects:

(i) The Representation of the object: one can distinguish the Mathematical Representation and the Geometric Representation. In the first one, objects are defined as a set of mathematical equations and in order to find object collisions one has to solve the equations. In the second one, objects are defined as a set of faces, edges and vertices and the goal is to detect collisions between faces. In this case more sophisticated algorithms are required ([7]).

(ii) When the collision is detected (only for the geometric representation): The SCC problem can be solved before or after the object is transformed. In the first case, the goal is to determine which is the limit transformation of the object that originates a collision state. Then the system allows only for transformations within this limit ([6]). In the second case, collision is checked after the object has been transformed.

(iii) The convexity of polyhedra (only for the geometric representation): In the next section we present an algorithm that allows for non-convex polyhedra. As it is well known ([1], [5], [10]), non-convex objects require more sophisticated collision detection algorithms than convex ones.

2. Collision Checking Mechanism

In this section, a general collision checking mechanism allowing for non-convex polygons in a geometric representation is presented.

The algorithm consists of two steps. In the first one, the algorithm checks for intersection between faces. If no face intersection is found, then the second step checks for object containment ([6]).

Given objects A and B, made of a set of faces, $\{CA_i\}$ and $\{CB_j\}$ respectively, the algorithm :

1. Detect intersection between faces. For every CA_i of A, and every CB_j of B, the algorithm checks if CA_i intersects CB_j. (our Face Intersection Algorithm is described in more detail in the following section)

2. Detect if A is contained by B, or vice versa. To check if B contains A , a 3D generalization of the odd-parity ray-intersection test ([3]) is used. For a point $P1$ belonging to A , find a point $P2$ outside the bounding box of B. Determine the line r whose end-points are $P1$ and $P2$ and count the number of faces of B intersected by r. If r passes through any of the edges of B, then repeat this step with a new point $P2$ outside the box of B. Collision exists if the line segment intersects an odd number of faces.

If no collision has been detected during these two steps, there does not exist collision between A and B and the current transformation is valid.

2.1 The Face Intersection Algorithm

Due to the low probability for an object to be fully contained into another object without any face intersection, we concentrate mainly in the first step of the method proposed above. The outline of the algorithm for detecting intersections between pairs of faces would be:

> For each edge belonging to face A
>   if   it intersects the plane defined by the second face
>   and
>   the intersection point lies inside the second face
>   then
>   a face intersection is said to occur

The algorithm complexity is $O(m2)$, where m is the number of vertices per face. Let A be an object, CA a face of A and suppose that CA contains the set of vertices denoted by VCA_m. Similarly, let B be an object, CB a face of B and CB containing the set of vertices denoted by VCB_m The algorithm checks for intersection of CA against CB. The intersection of CB against CA is done analogously. Let PB be the plane defined by the vertices belonging to *CB* (Figure 1).

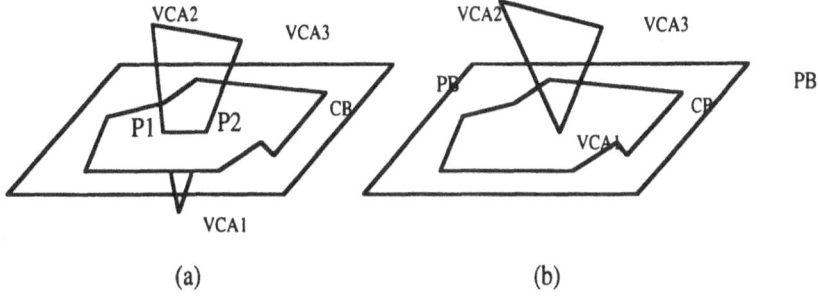

(a)   (b)

Figure 1: Face *CA* intersects face *CB*

For every VCA_m define D_m as follows ([6]):

$$D_m = (VCA_m - O) \bullet N$$

where O is a point of *CB* and N is the normal vector to *PB*. The sign of D_m is interpreted as the relative position of the point VCA_m with respect to *PB*:

1. If $D_m = 0$, then VCA_m lies on *PB* (see *VCA1* in Figure 1(b)).

2. If $D_m > 0$, then VCA_m lies on the positive side of *PB* (see *VCA2* in Figure 1(a)).

3. If $D_m < 0$, then VCA_m lies on the negative side of *PB* (see *VCA1* in Figure 1(a)).

If we calculate D_m for all the vertices VCA_m, then the next interpretation is valid:

1. If $D_m = 0$ and VCA_m lies inside *CB*, there is a collision at VCA_m (there is a collision at *VCA1* in Figure 1(b)).

2. If $D_k < 0$ and $D_{k+1} > 0$ (or $D_k < 0$ and $D_{k+1} > 0$), let P be the intersection point between *PB* and the line segment with end points VCA_k and VCA_{k+1}. If P lies inside *CB*, there is an intersection at P (there is a collision at *P1* in Figure 1(a)).

3. Implementation Aspects

The algorithm just described has been implemented in the Monalisa Scene Generation Module. The module interactively detects collisions while the user is transforming and locating an object in the scene. In this section we present the more important events occurred during the implementation and integration of the algorithm.

A scene is generally composed of many objects. Our aim is to detect a collision caused by a linear transformation (such as translation, rotation or scaling) among a selected object and all other objects in the scene. Exploiting the observation that users only require collision checking with few objects, namely those which usually define the "floors" of the scenes, such as floors, tables, chairs, etc., we construct a sparse scene from the original one. This sub-scene is in practice defined by a list of objects specified by the user. Therefore the program detects collision only among the selected object subject to transformations and objects of the user defined list of floor-objects.

When the user selects an object to move it and before any transformation occurs, quite a few values are calculated: the vertices' world coordinates, objects and faces' bounding boxes for each object. These computations are done in parallel using the same process configuration than the one described later.

For each transformation of the active object, our program computes the new world coordinates and bounding boxes of the object and then checks collision between the selected object and the sparse scene.

If a collision is detected, the program tries to find a legal transformation that avoids the object to collide but leaves it as close as possible to the other objects involved in the collision. The module takes the last transformation applied to the object and goes back using a binary search until no collision is detected while trying to leave the object close to the last transformation.

The algorithm was implemented using Inventor (an Object Oriented 3D Toolkit from Silicon Graphics) in C++. The linear transformations of the objects are controlled by some Inventor objects called Manipulators. The routines were implemented as callback routines attached to Manipulators and they are called whenever a change is detected in the transformation matrix of the selected object.

To speed up the collision checking process a parallel architecture is used. A main process is in charge of the interaction with the use, while other processes, which are synchronized by the former, perform actually the collision checking task. The goal of using different processes is to allow the operating system to assign different CPUs for collision checking.

The main process (agent) creates different slight processes (slaves) that are blocked themselves by semaphore operations. When collision must be checked, the agent stores the selected object and the list of objects belonging to the sparse scene in global variables and then signals to the slaves through the previously defined semaphores. The approach used is object-oriented, each process takes some objects from the list and checks collision against the selected object. The result from each process is stored in a global variable with a logical OR operation , the flag being 1 if any collision is detected. After all objects have been checked or any collision is found in any slave, the slaves return the control to the agent signaling other semaphores and blocking themselves again (see Figure 2). If no collision exists, the transformation is valid and no further action is taken by the agent. Otherwise, the agent interpolates the transformation matrix and signals the slaves repeatedly until no collision is found.

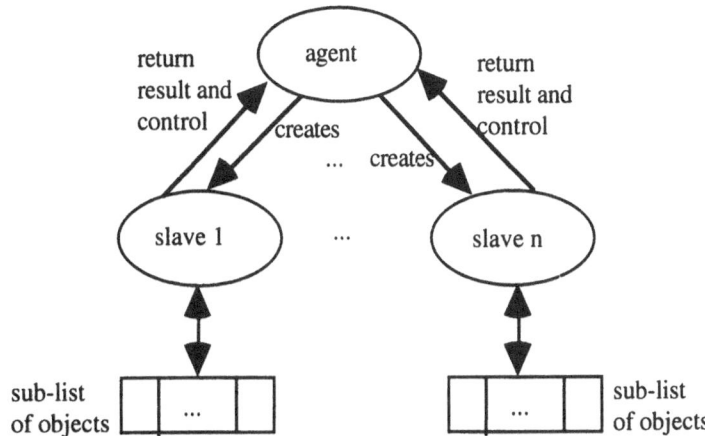

Fig 2: Parallel architecture

3.1   Speed-up Techniques

The complexity of the algorithm just described is $O(m^2 n^2)$ for m faces per object and n vertices per face. As this complexity is too high to be implemented directly in the Scene Generation Module, the scene is preprocessed using additional techniques to reduce the amount of faces m. The whole algorithm runs in 4 phases:

Phase 1.   Collision between the bounding boxes of the objects (OBB). A bounding box is a cube that contains the faces of an object and is defined by six points: the maximal and minimal of the set of vertices (Figure 3). If there is no collision between a pair of boxes and none is inside the otherone, no collision is feasible.

Phase 2.   Inclusion of the faces of one object in the bounding box (BB) of the other one. In this phase, the inclusion of the faces bounding boxes of one object in the bounding box of the other one is detected. If no intersection occurs, then no collision is feasible. Otherwise, only those faces BB intersecting with the other object BB are likely to collide.

Phase 3.   Intersection of the faces bounding boxes (FBB). In this phase, the collision between the bounding boxes of each pair of faces is checked. Only those pairs of faces that have their BB intersecting each other go over to the next phase.

Phase 4.   Face intersection algorithm. In this phase, the system checks face intersection between pairs of faces by running the Face Intersection Algorithm presented earlier in this paper.

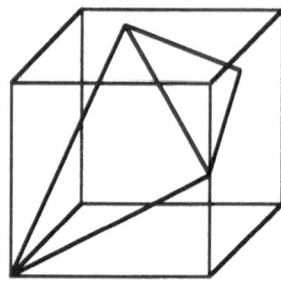

Fig 3: Bounding box of an object.

4.   Performance Results of the Speed up Techniques

A total of 12 objects, both convex and non-convex, were used to design interactively a sparse scene. We encouraged the user to look for collisions in different sessions. The number of pairs of faces for which intersection is computed at each phase of the algorithm was recorded. From a total of about 25000 transformations of the selected objects, only 3114 cases were stored, which came from phase 1 as the rough approximation by bounding boxes allowed for the possibility of collision.

We denoted by domain size the number of the pairs of faces for which collision is checked. This size is shown to decrease dramatically from each phase to the next one. We have taken as 100 the number of intersections checked in phase 2 and figures 4, 5 and 6 show how the domain reduces percentually in the different phases in different situations.

Figure 4 illustrates the mean reduction of faces checked in each phase. If we consider that phase 2 evaluates all the possibilities, then phase 3 will have to take into account only 31% of the faces and phase 4 only 1% of the initial amount.

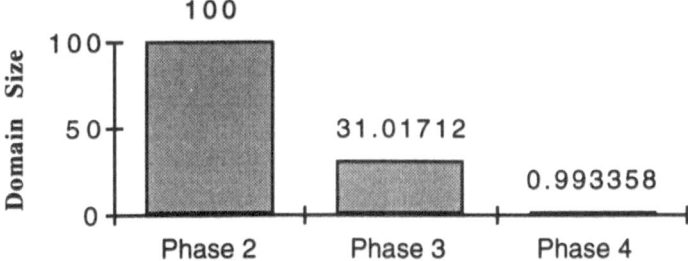

Figure 4: Average domain size of the sample

In figures 5 and 6 we show the rate of reduction of the faces checked when no collisions were detected among objects and when they were detected, respectively. In figure 5 we see that in phase 3 we got a 91% reduction and in phase 4 a 99.95%, while in figure 6, we see that the percentages show a lower reduction rate than when no collision is detected.

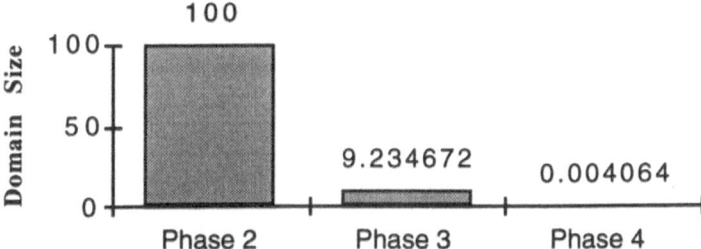

Figure 5: Domain size when no collision is detected

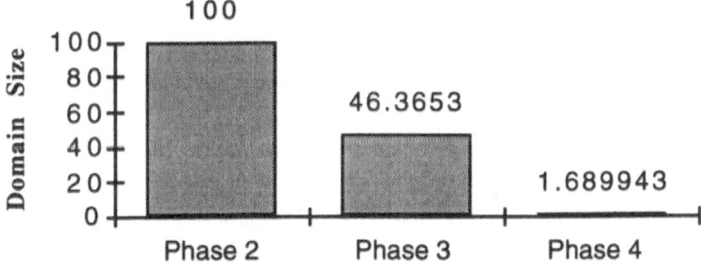

Figure 6: Domain size when collision is detected

We have thought interesting to show how the percentages of intersections computed in the phases 2 and 3 compare with the results of phase 4 - actual collisions -; the continuous line shows phase 2 while the dashed line phase 3. In figure 7 we see the results when we consider the whole sample while figure 8 shows when there is collision (% in phase 4 strictly positive).

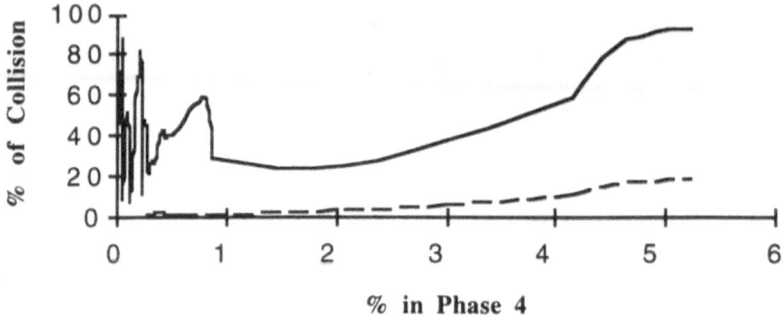

Figure 7: Comparison of intersections computed for the whole sample

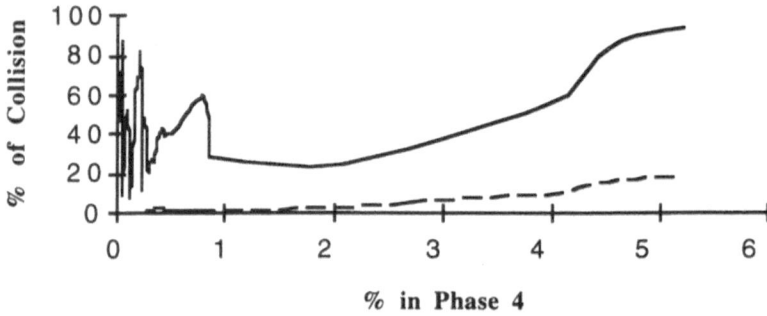

Figure 8: Comparison of intersections computed when collision is detected

5. Conclusion

One of the most serious problems in scene generation is to make sure that objects never collide with each other. We propose a real-time collision checking inside the Scene Generation module that can detect collision precisely among free-form (convex and non-convex) solids in a 3D-space when locating and transforming selected objects in a scene.

Although the high-complexity of the involved algorithms can make difficult to achieve real-time collision detection for complex scenes, some techniques can be used to lower such complexity. Exploiting the observation that users do not usually require to check collisions among all the objects in the scene, but only of the active object with the so-called floor-objects, we construct a sparse scene from the original one. This first step reduces enormously the domain of the computations. To allow the system to compute collision simultaneously with the floor-objects, a parallel implementation is used. Although the previous step reduces the processors load, the complexity is still too high to achieve real-time. To solve this we implemented and tested several techniques to reduce the amount of faces which must be checked. The final system consists of 4 phases, each one reducing the amount of faces to be processed by the next phase.

The results show that the domain of computing the expensive face intersection algorithm suffers a huge reduction in each phase, thus allowing for real-time collision checking to be achieved in the Monalisa system.

A possible improvement in the algorithm could be to replace checking the vertices faces bounding boxes by checking for faces vertices inclusion. At the lowest level of the system, a face-to-face algorithm verifies if face interference exists, this algorithm working for both convex and non-convex polygons. For convex polygons simpler algorithms can be used to reduce mathematical operations, for instance, algorithms derived from the two-dimensional Cyrus-Beck algorithm ([10]).

Acknowledgments: The authors would like to express their gratitude to the UIB - Computer Graphics Team members.

6. References

1. D. Baraff, Curved surfaces and coherence for non-penetrating rigid body simulation, *Computer Graphics*, **24**, N. 4, 1990.

2. J. Canny, Collision detection for moving polyhedra, *IEEE Transactions on Pattern Analysis and Machine Intelligence*, **8**, N. 2, 1984

3. Foley, vanDam, Feiner, Hughes, *Computer Graphics. Principles and Practice*, Addison Wesley , 1992.

4. J. Menna, *Geometría Analítica del Espacio: Enfoque Vectorial*, Limusa, 1981.

5. M. Moore, J. Wilhelms, Collision Detection and Response for Computer Animation, *Computer Graphics*, **22**, N. 4, 1988.

6. E. Podvin, Rapport de Stage Infographie: La Detection de Collision, BSCA report, preprint, 1989.

7. N. Magnenat - Thalman, D. Thalman (Eds.), *Computer Animation '91*, Springer-Verlag, 1991.

8. J. W. Boyse. "Interference Detection Among Solids and Surfaces", General Motors Research Laboratories, Technical Report, 1979.

9. T. Lozano-Perez, M. Wesley, An Algorithm for Planning Collision-Free Paths Among Polyhedral Obstacles, IBM Thomas J. Watson Research Center, Technical Report, 1979.

10. D. F. Rogers, *Procedural Elements for Computer Graphics*, McGraw-Hill, 1985.

Session 6: Synthesis 2

Depth Sensitive Image Compositing in a Multimedia System

D.E. Penna, P.A. Winser, J.G. Bellis, V. Seferidis, B. Gibson

Philips Research Laboratories

Redhill, United Kingdom

1. Introduction

This paper discusses the design of a mixer component for an interactive multimedia system which is designed to combine three video sources to form a final viewed scene. The aim was to achieve a flexible means of combining video material coming from an MPEG decoder with the outputs of two other graphics/image generation sources. Much of the graphics material was expected to comprise computer synthesised 3D graphics imagery.

Image mixing occurs in the computer graphics world and in the TV studio environment. In the computer graphics world there have been many techniques published. These include image opacity factor (alpha) processing as described by Porter and Duff [1,3]. Carpenter [2] describes the A-buffer for antialiasing in random depth order. The A buffer technique was too complex to apply here. A form of depth sort and alpha processing is used.

In the TV industry image compositing is common using such techniques as chroma key. In the computer games environment the use of natural video material is relatively new. Up to now most visuals have been formed from 2D sprites and graphics backdrops. There are often multiple backdrop planes with transparency and the sprites effectively have depth so that they can be arranged to be displayed between backdrop planes.

We are now arriving at the stage where consumer entertainment systems also include MPEG decoding capability for the display of high quality moving images. The mixer described here combines games graphics with an MPEG decoded video stream in a manner which allows considerable flexibility of use, including the division of the image material into regions at different distances from the viewer.

Each image source has a means to specify depth and opacity. This allows the mixer to perform a depth sort on he input images on a pixel by pixel basis. Once this has been done a final image can be produced taking the front to back order and the opacity values for the three planes into account. These depth and opacity values can vary for different regions in an image allowing the contribution from one source (say the MPEG source) to have regions at different depths in the scene.

There are two areas of interest. One is the operation of the mixer and the way in which it allows complex scenes to be built up. The other is the means by which MPEG sequences with regions of different depth and with opacity data for antialiasing are built up.

2. Why was this component required?

The task was to combine three video sources while providing the most flexible possible platform for multimedia entertainment software. The MPEG decoder in the system provides a single image plane of moving image material. The other two sources provide still photographic, moving cartoon and high performance texture mapped synthesised images. The requirement was to combine these together. For example, it would be desirable to construct a game scene where the background image was a moving picture (say a forest with interesting events going on there) and several other planes of action would carry on in front.

3. An example scenario

We can model this situation as a stage with several scenery flats and people, animals, cars and other objects moving about. The diagram below illustrates a possible game scenario.

Back

Backdrop, depth 63

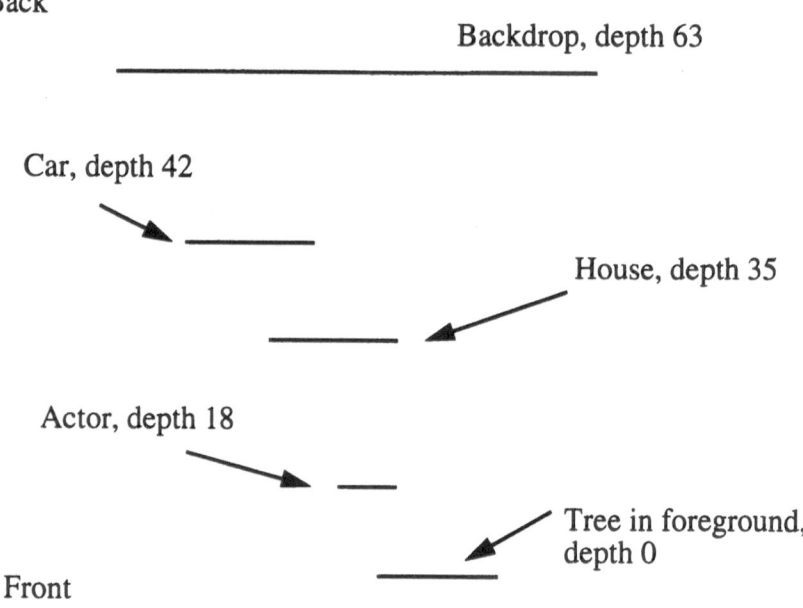

Car, depth 42

House, depth 35

Actor, depth 18

Tree in foreground, depth 0

Front

Here the backdrop, the foreground tree and the house in the mid-ground all come from the MPEG decoder. The actor and car come from the 3D graphics plane. The system is interactive so the user can ask the actor to walk around the scene. This means that he may be in front of or behind the house depending how the gameplay has gone. The arrival of the vehicle also depends on game events and will occur at different times in different runs of the game.

The actor has been generated by the graphics system along with a depth value of 18. Perhaps in another context the actor would have been generated at depth 50 in which case he would have been displayed as being behind both the house and the car.

The MPEG image has been decoded as a single full screen plane of moving data. It comes with some extra data which defines regions of the image as being of particular depth. The region containing the house is given depth 35 while the region containing the foreground tree has depth 0. The remainder of the image has depth 63.

On at least some edges there is opacity data which allows for blending of the foreground object with the background. It is also possible to specify opacity values for complete image planes to allow for translucent objects such as ghosts or the smoke from a bonfire.

In this scenario, the tree is always seen, the actor is seen except for that part of him hidden by the tree. The parts of the house which are not hidden by the actor and tree are visible. The car is partly obscured by the house. The background is only seen in those pixels where no other object is present.

4. The mixer

The mixer works one pixel at a time as the image is scanned out to the TV display.

It contains depth and opacity decoders for each input image stream. A set of comparators establishes which of the streams are in front, in the middle and behind for the current pixel. A contribution to the output pixel now comes from the colour value for the front stream. If the opacity of the front pixel (OF) is 100% then the output colour is identical to the colour from the front stream (CF). Otherwise there is a contribution of CF x OF from the front stream. A contribution of (1-OF) x OM x CM will come from the middle stream colour value. OM is the opacity value for the middle stream and CM is the colour for the middle stream. A contribution of (1-OF) x (1-OM) x CB will come from the back stream where CB is the background stream colour.

Various mechanisms are possible for determining depth and opacity. The simplest is to assign a constant value to all material coming from one stream.

Another possibility is to specify regions on the screen using colour keying or by specifying a rectangular window. One set of depth and opacity values would apply outside the selected region and a second set inside the region.

The most flexible arrangement occurs where an additional frame store can be used to specify depth and opacity for individual pixels. In the target system there was an option of using this technique when part of the video system was not in use so that the associated video bit planes were available.

The assignment of depth values to a variety of regions in a moving MPEG image stream proved the most problematic because the data required to specify these regions must share the same transmission or storage channel bandwidth as the MPEG coded image data. It must be compact so as not to reduce the MPEG image quality any more than is necessary.

The technique chosen was a form of 2D run length coding combined with huffman coding which traces the outlines of the regions. This is similar to that described in reference 4. Optionally, opacity values can be included to allow for edge anti-aliasing, although at the cost of increased data size.

The depth and opacity values arriving at the mixer are typically four bits wide to reduce the communication overhead. However they pass through lookup tables before being used in order to widen the depth values to six bits and the opacity values to eight bits.

The depth look up table (DLUT) allows 64 depth levels to be resolved in the system as a whole. Each of the image streams can use up to 16 of these at a time. Since there are three input streams then up to 48 levels can be occupied. By altering the DLUTs an object may be moved in the scene. this means that an MPEG actor can appear in front of or behind some other object depending on the progress of the game.

The opacity look up table (OLUT) allows objects to be smoothly faded in or out by manipulating OLUT entries. Without the OLUT the fade would have to take place in 15 discrete steps which would be very visible.

5. Creation of multilevel video sequences

The experiments which were done during the specification of this component used multidepth images made from components derived using a chroma key mixer. These components were then combined in software to produce the composite moving image which is one of the inputs to the depth sensitive mixer. This data might be part of a title distributed on a CD or might be delivered via an interactive Video on Demand system. The eight bit matte output from the mixer was used to provide edge opacity data. The processing of this colour and matte data caused a number of problems. Noise was particularly troublesome, although this problem was largely solved by improved edge detection techniques.

The final stage in the process was the encoding of the outline data which is to be distributed along with the MPEG encoded image data.

6. Anti-aliasing limitations

As described above, anti-aliasing was done by mixing foreground and background colours using an alpha (opacity) value. A problem arises where a plane, lets say the MPEG plane, has parts of its image at two depths. Along the join line between the depth regions each pixel has colour data for either the front part of the image or the part further away. No single pixel has both foreground and background colour information and so the mixer can perform no colour mixing along this edge.

It is of course possible to blend the colours in the pixels of the original image, so that a pixel which is half covered by the foreground object and half by the background object would contain a mixture of the two colours. However, in this case there will be a problem when some object from another plane is interspersed between the foreground and background image parts. In this case the edge pixels of the foreground object will have some past of the background part of that image plane mixed into them even although the background image is not visible.

The result is that, depending whether the MPEG plane image parts are antialiased with each other, the antialiasing will be correct when there is no intervening object (but not when there is) or correct when there is an intervening object (but not when there isn't).

7. Conclusion

This paper has described the goals and techniques of a project which specified a multimedia system mixer component. An important aim was to blend natural and computer generated imagery in a depth sensitive manner. This allowed each of the image planes to contribute to more than one depth in the scene. Edge anti-aliasing of MPEG coded natural image material was also provided to give a good blend with other material. Simulations of the results have shown results useful in entertainment Multimedia applications.

An important consideration for the MPEG stream was coding of outline data and edge opacity information for anti-aliasing. A huffman coded 2D run length coding scheme reduced this overhead to an acceptable amount for likely material.

8. References

1. Thomas Porter, Tom Duff. Compositing Digital Images. Computer Graphics, Vol. 18, No. 3, July 1984

2. Loren Carpenter. The A-buffer, an Antialiased Hidden Surface Method. Computer Graphics, Vol. 18, No. 3, July 1984.

3. Tom Duff. Compositing 3-D Rendered Images. Computer Graphics, Vol 19, No. 3, July 1985

4. Rafael C. Gozalez, Paul Wintz. Digital Image Processing. Addison Wesley, 1987, pp 289-292

Inverse Kinetics for Center of Mass Position Control and Posture Optimization

Ronan Boulic[1], Ramon Mas[2], Daniel Thalmann[1]

(1) Computer Graphics Laboratory, Swiss Federal Institute of Technology, DI-LIG, CH1015 Lausanne, Switzerland
(2) Department of Mathematics and Computer Science, Balearic Islands University, 07071-Palma de Mallorca, Spain

Abstract

The range of Inverse Kinematics has been extended by integrating the mass distribution information to embody the control of the position of the center of gravity of any articulated figure in single support (open tree structure). The underlying control architecture of main and secondary behaviors (or tasks) is used to associate the position control of the center of gravity with other behaviors. The combined quality of providing realistic postures in real-time improves significantly the potential interaction with human model in virtual reality applications and more generally for real-time video productions.

1   Introduction

In this paper we focus on interactive design of realistic postures in the sense of static analysis. Our approach only requires the topological, geometrical, and mass distribution information of the articulated figure. The range of Inverse Kinematics has been extended by integrating the mass distribution information to embody the control of the position of the center of gravity of any articulated figure in single support (open tree structure). The framework of Direct and Inverse Kinematics is still valid in this new context because it expresses the resulting combination of kinematics and mass distribution; we therefore refer to it as *Direct and Inverse Kinetics* . The underlying control architecture of main and secondary tasks (or behaviors) is used to associate the position control of the center of gravity with other optimization behaviors. We have focused on realistic balance behaviors while ensuring fast response thus allowing integration in virtual reality applications and more generally for real-time video productions.

First, we analyze the state of the art in the balance control of an articulated figure and stress the incomplete use of the mass distribution information. Then, we recall the basic concepts of inverse kinematic control, its strengths and weaknesses. The next section introduces how we can use the mass distribution information to evaluate the kinetic influence of any joint of the articulated figure. Our kinetic control is then combined with optimization behaviors regarding the balance of an articulated figure. The next section present the cascaded control scheme, which allows the hierarchical combination of various behaviors. The paper ends with various 2D examples and one 3D illustration with an emphasis on posture optimizations.

2   Background

2.1   Review

In [1] [2] and [3], the human balance control is one aspect of the design and analysis of body posture by mean of kinematic constraints and behavioral functions. Their approach to control the position of the center of mass is completely described in [2]. For these authors, the center of mass is considered as an end effector attached to the lower torso region. It is controlled by inverse kinematics with the ankle, knee, and hip joints of the dominant leg (the one supporting most of the weight) as the constraint variables. This approach has proven to be effective in managing the position of the center of mass but some aspects make its use rather limited and its background kinetically unrealistic. First, it is very specific to the human standing posture, which means that we cannot generalize it for any arbitrary articulated figure and even for a human structure with a different support or attach (hanging by the hands, sitting or else). Second, the kinetic influence of the joint variables is not evaluated with respect to the mass distribution in the whole body.

Although not directly focusing on the position control of the center of mass, the work of Lee [4] belongs to the same research stream as it tries to identify a comfort model integrating the human strength information in order to realistically perform some reaching task. As such, it should be able to improve the understanding of posture control for general reach tasks. Unfortunately, due to a lack of strength data for other joints, the model is limited to the upper body and especially the arm chain, from the shoulder to the hand[4]. The validation is limited to a comparison of the path obtained by the simulation with the measurements obtained from NASA experiments for three reach tasks without loads. It is difficult to assess the validity of this approach only from geometric data ; one would have expected the values of the joint torques over time, at least from the simulation. Other approaches [5], [6], [7] have also considered the control of the center of mass. The system presented in [6], dedicated to bipedal walking, is mostly kinematic but also includes some dynamic rules so as to maintain the center of mass within the support polygon. A similar approach [5] has defined kinematic and dynamic rules so as to partially control the balance via the position of the center of mass, and to minimize the effort developed by the muscles. The approach is applied to optimize various motions such as walking, sitting on a chair and climbing stairs. Despite the fact that this author can successfully manage the balance in the case of sitting (and especially, getting up from a seat), the control of the center of mass is actuated only with the bending of the torso, which limits its range of application.

Dynamic control of articulated figures has been proposed to produce physically realistic postures and animation [8] [9]. A recent approach [8] provides a control algorithm to generate realistic running and jumping motions. Such motions present a ballistic phase and at most a single support phase. As the authors themselves state, the control of double support phases, as in walking, is still very difficult to handle [10]. This is due to the requirement to manage the ground reaction force in order to perform a realistic motion. On the other hand, the results presented in [9] concentrate on statically stable multi-legged walking. There are always more than two legs supporting the articulated character so that the center of gravity generally lies in the sustentation polygon. In such a context the balance control is a less important issue than the coordination of the legs. Optimal control is a promising approach for natural postures and animation design [11] [12] [13] but it still faces severe limitations in terms of calculation cost.

2.2   Discussion

Physically realistic approaches, as dynamic or optimal control are not yet suited for interactive design of human postures due to the difficult handling of their associated parameter space (torque, muscle activation) or the additional parameter added by the control approach (energy storage, management of the ground reaction force). They are not intuitive and easy to handle for an animator as stated in [8]. Moreover, a higher level approach based on a human comfort model still faces severe lack of data for realistic strengths[4]. Finally, regarding optimal control, its major limitation comes from the high dimension of the human figure (*e.g.* 88 degrees of freedom in [2]) preventing real-time interaction on current workstations.

Conversely, Inverse Kinematics lacks physically based guarantees which limits its application either to interactive postural design and optimization or to motions with negligible dynamics (slow speed with minimal frictional and inertial effects [2]). This approach is rather successful within this context and especially by means of behavioral control [3], but we have quoted serious problems related to the control of the center of gravity which can reduce the validity of postures resulting from balance behaviors. Although the strength-based approach of Lee is very stimulating it does not address the position control of the center of gravity ; moreover it has not yet been validated. An equally important shortcoming of inverse kinematics, especially for redundant mechanisms, is its intrinsic property of providing a local solution without any means of knowing whether other solutions exist [14]. The optimization of a secondary criteria has been widely used in robotics to improve that aspect [15],[16],[17] but still there is no guarantee of avoiding local minima. Moreover, the analyzis of the unrealistic demands on mechanism performance induced by the use of the secondary task is clearly developed in [17].

For these reasons, we propose an extension of Inverse Kinematics which takes into account the mass distribution of the whole body, resulting in a new control metaphor we call Inverse Kinetics. Our approach is completed with optimization behaviors which allow a coherent and kinetically realistic management of postures with single support in the sense of static analysis. An important remark regarding joint strengths is the fact that we are mainly concerned by the optimization of postures while maintaining the balance of the articulated model and without carrying additional payload. In that context, we assume that the joint torques remain in the range of their allowable strength.

3   Inverse Kinematics

As stated before, Inverse Kinematics is a technique mostly used to control or constraint strategic parts of the articulated figure, whose location depends on a set of parameters, usually joints values. The associated control scheme is based on a linearization of this problem at the current state of the system. Consequently, its validity is limited to the neighborhood of the current state and, as such, any desired motion has to comply with the hypothesis of small movements. The discrete form of the general solution provided by inverse kinematics is:

$$\Delta\theta = J^+\Delta x + (I - J^+J)\Delta z \qquad (1)$$

where

$\Delta\theta$ is the unknown vector in the joint variation space, of dimension **n**.

Δx describes the so-called *main behavior* as a variation of one or more end effector(s) position and/or orientation in Cartesian space. Its dimension, noted **m**, is usually less than or equal to **n**, to be of interest for inverse kinematic control.

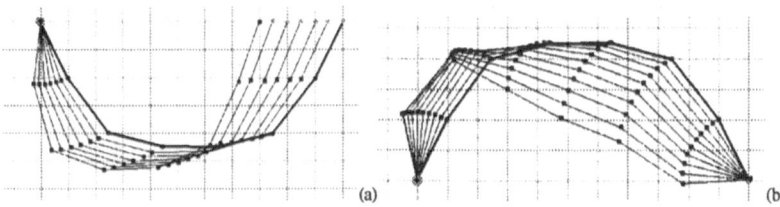

Figure 1 : Inverse kinematic control : (a) minimal norm solution for a desired translation (b) solution belonging to the kernel of the joint variation space

J is the Jacobian matrix of the linear transformation representing the differential behavior of the controlled system over the dimensions specified by the *main behavior* (figure 2).

J^+ is the unique pseudo-inverse of **J** providing the minimum norm solution which achieves the *main behavior* (figure 1a & 2).

I is the identity matrix of the joint variation space (**n** x **n**)

$(I-J^+J)$ is a projection operator on the *null space* of the linear transformation **J**. Any element belonging to this joint variation sub-space is mapped by **J** into the null vector in the Cartesian variation space (figure 1b & 2).

Δz describes a *secondary behavior* in the joint variation space. It is partially realized by the projection on the *null space*. The second part the of equation does not modify the achievement of the main behavior for any value of Δz.

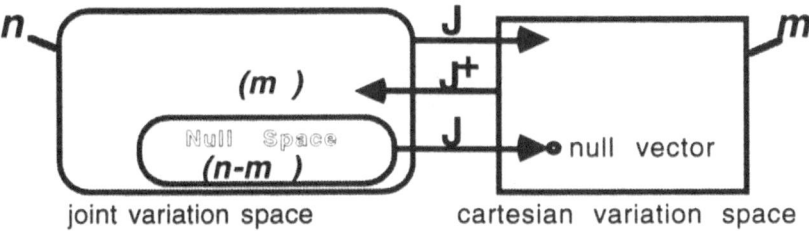

Figure 2 : Illustration of the joint variation space partitioning with Inverse Kinematics

238

Three characteristics of Inverse Kinematics are fundamental for the understanding of our approach. First, this methods provides a local solution [14]. For example, given a goal to reach with an end effector, the final posture of the articulated figure depends on the initial configuration. Other solutions, if they exist, cannot be evaluated ; they can only be guessed from the dimension of the null space. Second, the secondary behavior should express the minimization of a cost function. If the main behavior belongs to the image space of J then the null space is $(n-m)$ dimensional in the joint variation space. From this information we can deduce to what extent the secondary behavior may be fulfilled, or rather, may not be fulfilled. In the context of our study, we are interested in optimizing the posture with respect to balance and partially to effort cost. Based on these guidelines, we will use the mass distribution of the articulated figure to evaluate associated pertinent cost functions. Third, the configuration may become singular. This situation is due to an alignment of the segments constituting the articulated figure leading to a loss of mobility of the effector(s) in that direction. The Jacobian has a loss of rank or, even worse, a very small singular value along that Cartesian dimension inducing by inversion a solution norm growing to infinity when a behavior is required in that direction. We use an elegant solution to this problem called the damped least square and described in [18] where the norm of the solution is limited near the singular cases.

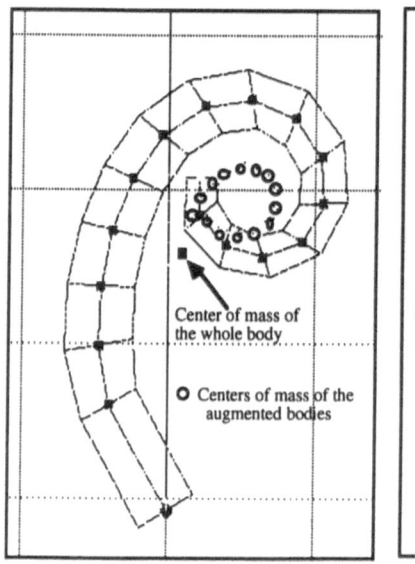 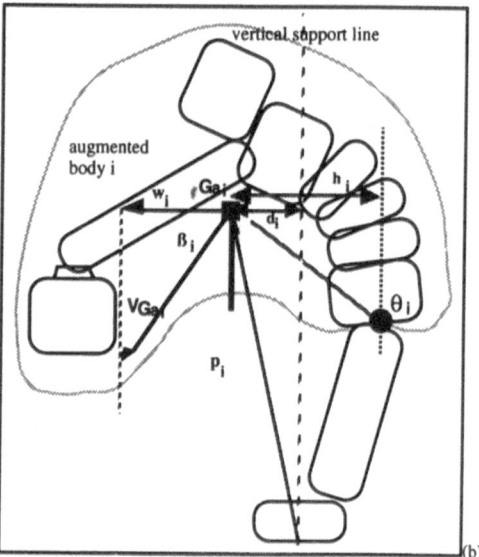

Figure 3: (a) centers of mass of the augmented bodies for one posture of a fern crozier
(b) concepts and variables used in Inverse Kinetics and balance optimization

4   Direct and Inverse Kinetics

Section 2 has reviewed different approaches related to the control of the center of mass and we have stressed a real need for a general and consistent method suited for such control. The basic principle of our approach is to evaluate the kinetic influence of the joints based on the fraction of the total body mass they support, *i.e.* their augmented body. More precisely, the augmented body associated with a joint is the imaginary rigid body which is supported by this joint at the current state of the system. Figure 3a shows the center of mass of all the augmented bodies of a fern crozier while figure 3b illustrates the augmented body associated with one joint.

Our method consists first in evaluating the kinetic influence of the joints by relating instantaneous joints variations with the corresponding instantaneous translation of the total center of mass (Direct Kinetics). In a second stage the matrix of the resulting linear transformation is inverted in a process similar to Inverse Kinematics. However, since it integrates the mass distribution information, we call it Inverse Kinetics.

Let θ be the parameter vector of an open articulated chain made of n elementary bodies. Each elementary body i has a mass m_i, a local origin O_i and a local center of gravity G_i. For the sake of clarity, the origin O_1 is located on the origin of the reference frame S_0. The position of the center of gravity G of the whole chain, with a total mass m, is given by the following formula:

$$O_1 G = \frac{1}{m} \sum_{i=1}^{n} m_i O_1 G_i \qquad (2)$$

We now introduce the intermediate links between O_1 and the G_i :

$$O_1 G = \frac{1}{m} \sum_{i=1}^{n} m_i (\sum_{k=1}^{i-1} (O_k O_{k+1}) + O_i G_i) \qquad (3)$$

By differentiating with respect to time, we get the instantaneous translation vector of the center of gravity V_G expressed in frame S_0 :

$$V_G = \frac{1}{m} \sum_{i=1}^{n} m_i (\sum_{k=1}^{i-1} \left(\left[\frac{dO_k O_{k+1}}{dt} \right]_{S_o} \right) + \left[\frac{dO_i G_i}{dt} \right]_{S_o})$$

Each vector first derivative with respect to time can be expressed as a function of the instantaneous rotation vector ω_j due to the variation of parameter θ_j, noted θ'_j, along the normalized vector r_j : $\qquad \omega_j = \theta'_j r_j \qquad (4)$

$$V_G = \frac{1}{m} \sum_{j=1}^{n} \omega_j \times (\sum_{i=j}^{n} m_i O_j G_i)) \qquad (5)$$

We can now introduce the position of the center of gravity G_{aj} of the augmented body (of mass m_{aj}) associated with the parameter θ_j. The augmented body is the instantaneous rigid body composed of all the elementary bodies supported by the joint j. Again we have :

$$O_j G_{aj} = \frac{1}{m_{aj}} (\sum_{i=j}^{n} m_i O_j G_i) \qquad (6)$$

So, using (4) and (6), (5) becomes :

$$V_G = \sum_{j=1}^{n}\left[\frac{m_{aj}}{m}\left(r_j \times O_j G_{aj}\right)\right]\theta_j' \tag{7}$$

and finally: $\qquad V_G = [J_G]\theta' \tag{8}$

where $[J_G]$ is the Jacobian matrix weighted by the mass ratio of the augmented bodies to the total body, relating instantaneous translation of the center of mass to the instantaneous variations on the parameters. Conversely, the pseudo-inverse of this Jacobian matrix can be evaluated, allowing to provide an instantaneous variation of the parameters related to a desired instantaneous translation of the center of mass. In that sense it is correct to propose terms of Direct and Inverse Kinetics because it extends significantly the range of Direct and Inverse Kinematics for the control of articulated structures. We can also apply the principle of conservation of momentum on the augmented bodies center of gravity to demonstrate the direct kinetics fundamental relationship [19].

5   Posture Optimization Behaviors

We present here two methods of posture optimization. The first one focuses on the minimization of moments with respect to the center of support (support torques) while the second tries to identify and minimize the torques exerted in the standing rest posture. Both use information related to the center of mass of the augmented bodies. As we are able to express their minimization in the joint variation space, they are suited as secondary behaviors in Inverse Kinematics or Inverse Kinetics.

The support torques tend to rotate the whole body around the center of support under the influence of gravity. We minimize the following cost function C_S expressing that every independent support torque T_i , should be geared to zero rather than their algebraic sum alone:

$$C_S = \sum_{i=1}^{n} \|T_i\|^2 \tag{9}$$

The relation between cost function C_S and the joints must be established in order to express its gradient vector in term of joint variations. Figure 3b illustrates the different elements entering this relationship for the augmented body associated with joint i. First, its support moment comes from the action of the weight p_i and is directly proportional to the distance d_i between G_{ai} and the vertical support line. Minimizing M_i is equivalent to minimize d_i . Now, the influence of a joint variation on d_i can be deduced from its influence V_{Gai} on point G_{ai} projected on the axis supporting distance d_i (noted W_i). The resulting term of the gradient vector is proportional to :

$$\Delta Z_{S_i} = -2 \cdot m_{ai} \cdot d_i \cdot \|W_i\| \tag{10}$$

The global minimum of this cost function is the configuration sub-space where the centers of gravity of all the augmented bodies lye on the vertical line of support.

The rest posture is a useful concept for the posture optimization of complex mechanisms presenting an active behavior (here for animals and human models). We consider it as the global minimum among standing postures regarding muscular cost (see [19] for justification). For this reason, we now propose a cost function converging to the rest posture and based on kinetic information. Although the minimization of the configuration interval to the rest posture clearly leads to the rest posture θ_r, it does not convey kinetic information and therefore has a low validity to express an effort cost. For this reason, a second factor representing such effort scales this cost function. We have retained the torque exerted by the augmented body weight with respect to the origin O_i of the joint rotation axis. Figure 3b illustrates the quantity h_i directly influencing the effort torque for joint i. Finally, the gradient term retained for the effort minimization is proportional to :

$$\Delta Z_{E_i} = -2 \cdot m_{ai} \cdot h_i \cdot (\theta_i - \theta_{ri}) \qquad (11)$$

Some gradient terms can be locally null whenever their effort torque vanishes due to the vertical alignment of the G_{ai} and O_i. By construction, they all vanish only for the rest posture.

Combining the two previous optimization behaviors is possible and even desirable to obtain the best compromise over the null space resulting from inverse kinematic or inverse kinetic control. Next section even introduces a third approach of posture optimization which can also be combined with the two presented here.

6   Integrated Kinetic and Kinematic Control

Kinetic and Kinematic control schemes share one common space, i.e. the joint variation space, hence allowing their integration into more sophisticated architecture as developed below. The control architecture presented now were paradoxically designed to overcome the optimal nature of the support moment minimization presented in section 5. This optimization minimizes each support moment independently which is not always desirable. For example, if we want to reach a distant target with the hand without moving the feet, it is necessary to allow lower augmented bodies to lean backward so as to counter-balance the forward leaning of upper augmented bodies containing the hand. Such a case is equivalent to ensure the algebraic sum of support moment to be null, *i.e.* to maintain the total center of mass on the vertical line of support. This sub-optimal approach has been identified in [2] but not treated kinetically. This is the purpose of this section.

We have shown in section 4 how to control the position of the center of gravity. It is now straightforward to integrate it as a secondary behavior of a classic kinematic control. In discrete form, we get the following cascaded architecture :

$$\Delta\theta = J_e^+\Delta x_e + (I - J_e^+J_e)(J_G^+\Delta x_G + (I - J_G^+J_G)\Delta z_o) \qquad (12)$$

Where J_e is the Jacobian of the kinematic transformation describing the effector control (for example a reach behavior), J_G is the Jacobian of the kinetic transformation describing the center of gravity control (balance behavior). Here the optimization behavior Δz_0 is integrated through a second partitioning level of the joint variation space. It could also directly share the kinematic null space with the kinetic control. Moreover, the underlying hierarchy of expression (12) can be inverted to favor the center of mass control over the reach behavior :

$$\Delta\theta = J_G^+\Delta x_G + (I - J_G^+J_G)(J_e^+\Delta x_e + (I - J_e^+J_e)\Delta z_o) \qquad (13)$$

7 Simulation Results

Our approach is better illustrated with 2D models in order to visualize unambiguously the position control of the center of gravity. However, our method can be used for general tree-structured 3D articulated chains in single support as we show in the last example. Our goal is to show that we can achieve realistic results only with a mass distribution of the model. Such data can be derived as a first approximation from a volume distribution or identified roughly from multiple views. Conversely, it is very difficult to find data on more elaborate quantities as strengths and general joint modeling as required by other approaches. Whenever possible the simulation results are compared with real postures obtained from images.

The 2D representation of the articulated structures reflects the mass distribution in the following way: a segment S_i is defined between joint i and joint i+1. It has a length L_i and a mass m_i ; its width l_i is only displayed at the end-effector side of the segment and its value is proportional to (m_i / L_i). In such a way the final display shows a continuous envelop if all the joint angles belong to the interval plus or minus $\pi/2$. Otherwise the sides of the envelop switch as can be noticed at the shoulder of the 2D human model (Figure 8).

7.1 The Fern Crozier

The fern crozier simulations highlight two points: first the interest of minimizing the support moments and second the precise position control of inverse kinetics on the center of mass. Although there is no explicit specification to unroll the fern crozier, this motion implicitly derives from the support moment minimization (Figure 4). Here, the center of gravity is pushed upward from the combined opening and closing variations of the augmented bodies in order to align their center of gravity on the vertical line of support. One can also notice that is slightly swaying along the vertical line of support. This characteristics also appear on the evolution of the support and the "joint" torques while globally decreasing to zero [19].

On the other hand, the Inverse Kinetics algorithm directly acts on the position of the center of gravity in Cartesian space. In Figure 5, it is interactively moved upward along the vertical line of support. As such the resulting postures strictly express the balance of the two parts of the fern between the two sides of the vertical line of support. The unrolling derives from the upward variation of position of the center of gravity by definition of Inverse Kinetics. The postures bear much less similarity with natural specimen. However, the simulation duration is much smaller (around 10%) than the one required for the minimization process to achieve the same decrease of torque amplitude (75% of the initial envelope amplitude) [19].

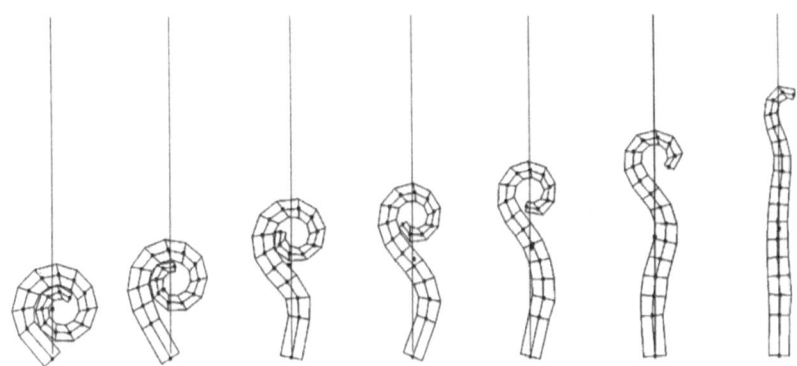

Figure 4 : Unrolling of a fern crozier with a minimization of the support moments

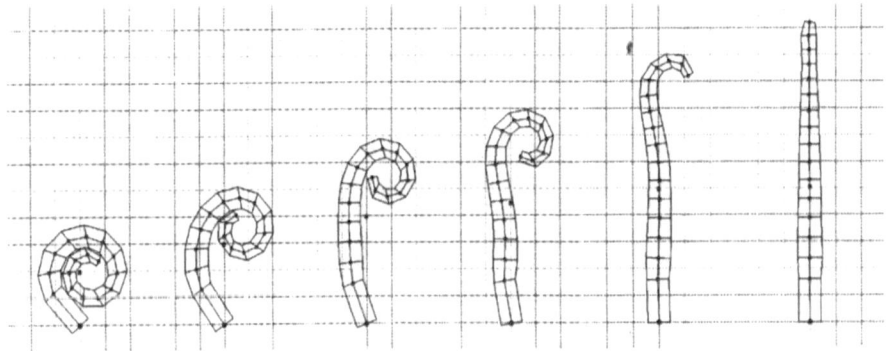

Figure 5 : Interactively unrolling a fern crozier with inverse kinetics

With this example we could also identify the center of gravity's reachable area in a straightforward manner. By construction Inverse Kinetics controls the position of the center of mass, so it just requires to span the Cartesian space and to draw the outer limit of the center of mass's excursion. As we know, the final configuration of the chain depends on the initial configuration. So the center of gravity's reachable area can be different depending on the initial configuration and the joint limits. It is important to associate independent reachable areas with their configuration sub-space

244

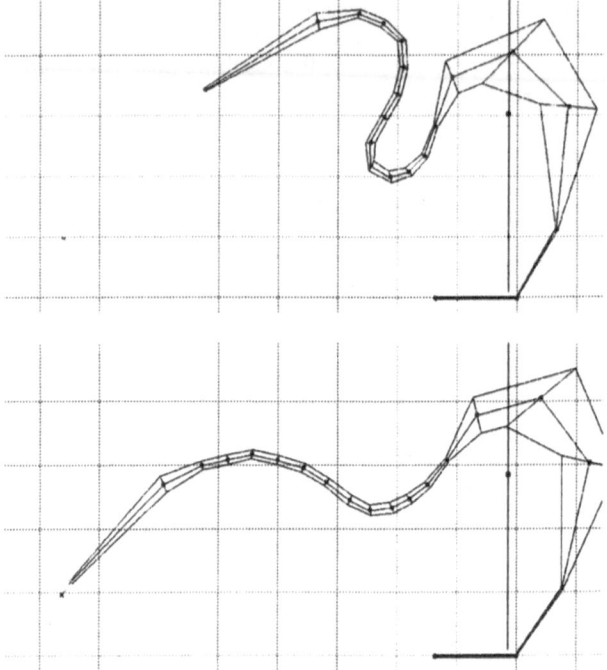

Figure 7 : initial and final stages of the Mallard bird maintaining its balance while reaching a water bowl (the top posture is considered as the rest posture of the subject)

7.2   The Mallard Bird

The bird example is of great interest due to some radiographs (see p 79 in [20]) which have been used to identify the initial rest posture of the bird and to validate the posture predicted with cascaded control. Three of the body segments are rigidly connected for this reach simulation. Their purpose is to adjust the mass distribution so that the center of mass projection lies just in front of the "palm" joint in the rest posture .

The cascaded control of inverse kinematics with inverse kinetics is used to ensure a reaching and orienting task of the beak as main behavior while maintaining the balance of the subject as secondary behavior. Figure 7 shows the initial and final stages of the reach behavior simulation. Some other tests have even adjusted the mass distribution of the final posture to match the additional water distribution in the lower neck and the algorithm still stabilized close to the real posture. In the context of the present case-study the major differences with other control architecture is either the realism of the final posture or a much faster convergence of the cascaded control (around 10% duration, see [19]).

7.3   Human Posture Optimization

The human skeleton chain includes eight degrees of freedom. We can recognize, from floor level to hand, the toe, ankle, knee, hip, lumbar and thoracic spine, shoulder and

elbow joints. In order to ease the correspondence with the 3D human skeleton, the lower limb segments have a double mass (foot, shank and thigh segments) and higher body segments integrate the mass of other body parts :
      - the thorax segment includes the head and one arm mass
      - the forearm segment includes the hand mass .

The projected center of gravity should be in the so-called *support polygon* made by the foot (or feet) between the ankle and toe joints. It should always remain in that space to maintain the balance of the whole body. When the toe joint is fixed the so-called *vertical line of support* is passing through the center of support located a few centimeters in front of the ankle joint. The first simulation consists in rising up from a squat posture with pure Inverse Kinetics.

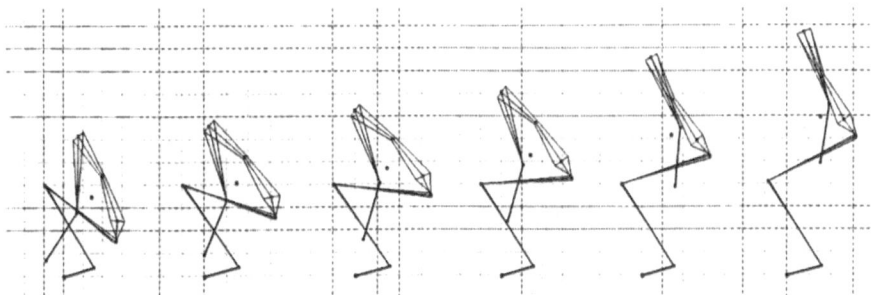

Figure 8 : partial sequence of a rising behavior from a squat posture (fixed toe joint)

For Figure 8, the toe joint is maintained fixed thus ensuring a constant support polygon. The evolution of the simulation is easier to read as the vertical line of support is constant. The center of mass is interactively controlled by inverse kinetics to move upward along the line of support. Figure 8 focuses on the first half of the motion. The overall minimization of the support and joint torques is ensured during the motion (see [19]). Such result validates the full erect posture as the best candidate for the standing rest posture among all the semi-erect postures.

The toe joint is allowed to vary in Figure 9. This new context raises the question of the support center location as a function of the toe flexion angle. Now, the support polygon is changing and the center of support is migrating from its rest location to the toe location as a function of the toe flexion angle. A dedicated function has been defined to model that phenomenon.

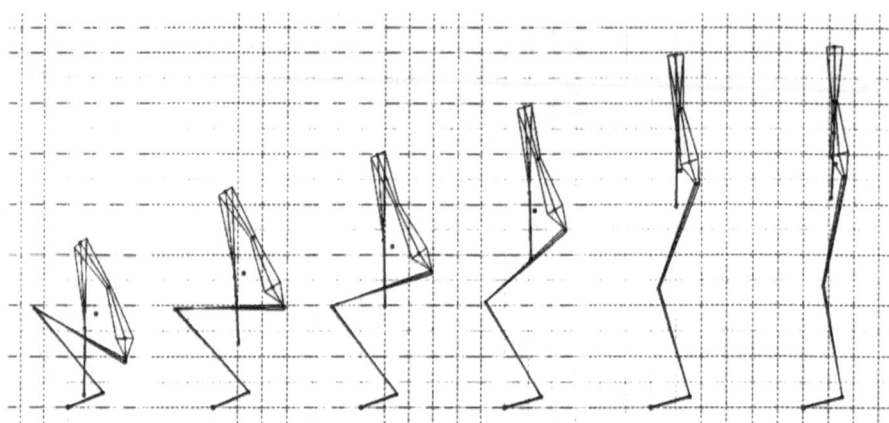

Figure 9 : partial sequence of a rising behavior from a squat posture (free toe joint)

The leftmost posture of Figure 9 has been obtained with a reach behavior to a floor location for the wrist (starting from the standing posture). One can notice the characteristic raising of the heel. The cascaded control equation is used with Inverse kinematics to guide the wrist position as the main behavior while maintaining the balance with Inverse Kinetics as the secondary behavior.

Figure 10 illustrate the use of Inverse Kinetics in a 3D context. The general tree structured human model is rooted at the right foot. The final posture shown here is also obtained by cascaded control with the reach behavior as the main task and the balance behavior as the secondary task. One can observe a significant bending of the lumbar vertebrae. We plan to evaluate more precisely the strain of the lower back due to this kind of posture.

8   Conclusion

In this paper we have intentionally focused on the presentation of the technical and fundamental aspects of inverse Kinetics to provide a broad view of its potentialities. Such technique has two important application fields :

First, Computer Animation for interactive control of articulated figure. Its purpose is to help the design of kinetically realistic postures in the sense of static analysis.

Second, Analysis of real images to enhance the identification and tracking of articulated figure postures. Our approach should improve the convergence of posture recognition by making some assumption on the position of the center of gravity (under the hypothesis of negligible dynamics).

Two major arguments advocate for the use of our approach for real and synthetic image processing. First, the mass distribution is a very intuitive set of parameters; it does not add the cognitive burden of the additional parameter space appearing in Dynamics for example. Once the mass distribution is set, the control is as intuitive as Inverse Kinematics. Our approach fits into existing high level interface of behavioral control of human figure; it brings the necessary realism for static positioning according to the mass distribution of the figure. Second, the calculation cost is comparable with Inverse Kinematics, hence allowing true interactive design of postures. One step further, it allows more convincing interaction of any articulated models with real subjects in the context of Virtual reality.

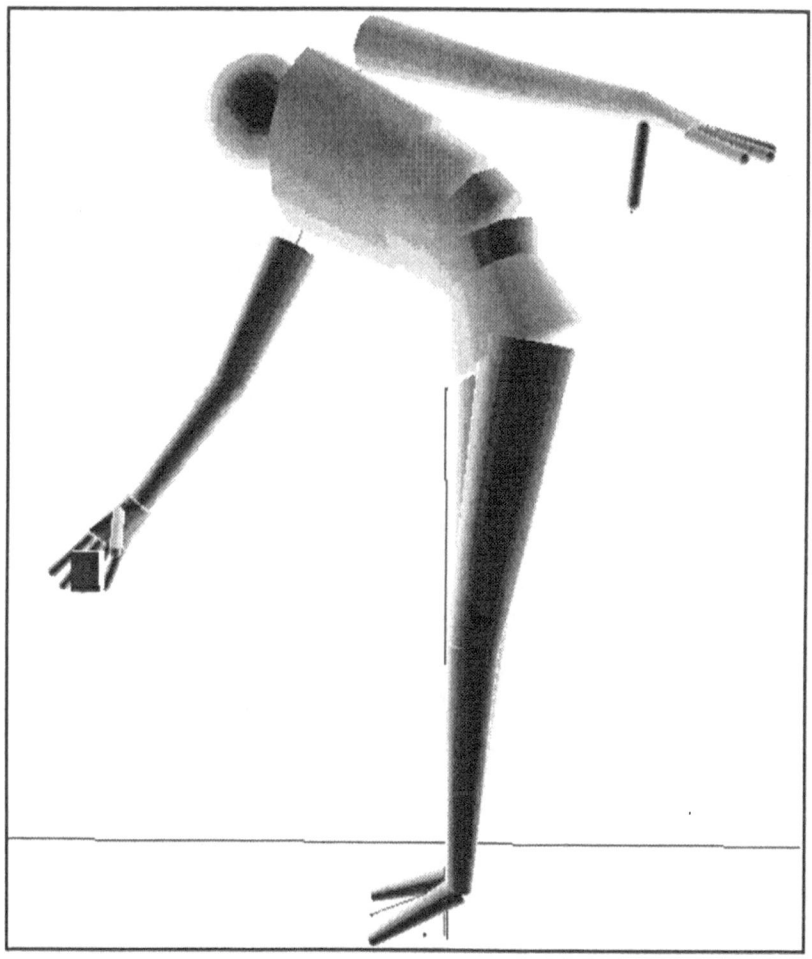

Figure 10 : 3D human model posture optimization (in single support)

9   Acknowledgments

We are grateful to our colleagues and friends who read this document. We also wish to thank Walter Maurel for fruitful discussions on mechanics. The research was partly supported by the Swiss National Research Foundation and OFES and is part of the ESPRIT Project "HUMANOID".

10 References

1   Philips C.B., Zhao J., Badler N.I. "Interactive Real-Time Articulated Figure Manipulation Using Multiple Kinematic Constraints", Computer Graphics 24 (2),pp 245-250, 1990

2   Phillips C.B., Badler N. " Interactive Behaviors for Bipedal Articulated Figures" Computer Graphics 25 (4), pp 359-362, July 1991

3   Badler N.I., Phillips C.B., Webber B.L., "Simulating Human, Computer Graphics Animation and Control", Chapter 4 "Behavioral Control", Oxford University Press 1993.

4   Lee P.L.Y. "Modeling Articulated Figure Motion with Physically- and Physiologically-based Constraints", PhD Dissertation in Mechanical Engineering and Applied Mechanics, University of Pennsylvania, 1993.

5   Maiocchi R "A Knowledge based approach to the Synthesis of human motion", IFIP TC5/WG5.10 "Modeling in Computer Graphics", Tokyo April 1991.

6   Girard M., Maciejewski A.A. " Computational Modeling for the Computer Animation of Legged Figures". Computer Graphics 19 (3),1985, pp263-270

7   Zeltzer D., Sims K. "A Figure Editor and Gait Controller to Task Level Animation", SIGGRAPH 88 Tutorial Notes on Synthetic Actors : The impact of A.I. and Robotics on Animation, (1988).

8   Raibert M.H., Hodgins J.K., "Animation of Dynamic Legged Locomotion", Computer Graphics 25 (4), pp 349-358, 1992

9   McKenna M., Zeltzer D., "Dynamic Simulation of Autonomous Legged Locomotion", Computer Graphics 24 (4), pp 29-38, 1990

10 Hodgins J.K., Raibert M. "Adjusting Step Length for Rough Terrain Locomotion", IEEE Trans. on Robotics and Automation, 7(3), pp 289-298, June 1991

11 Witkin Kass "Spacetime constraints", Computer Graphics 22 (4),1988, pp159-168

12 Girard M "Constrained optimization of Articulated Animal Movement in Computer Animation" in "Making Them Move: Mechanics, Control, and Animation of Articulated Figures", Badler, Barsky & Zeltzer Editor, Morgan Kaufmann, 1991, pp209-232

13 Park J., Fussel D., Pandy M., Browne J.C. "Realistic Animation using Musculotendon Skeletal Dynamics and Suboptimal Control", Third Eurographics Workshop on Animation and Simulation, EG92 AW, Eurographics Technical Report Series ISSN 1017-4656, 1992.

14 Klein C.A., Huang C.H. "Review of Pseudo-Inverse Control for use with Kinematically Redundant Manipulators", IEEE Trans. on SMC 13(3), 1983 .

15 Espiau B., Boulic R. "Collision Avoidance for Redundant Robots with Proximity Sensors", 3rd Int. Symposium on Robotics Research, Gouvieux, France, 1985.

16 Boulic R. "Conception Assistee par Ordinateur de Boucle de Commande Referencee Capteurs en Robotique et en Teleoperation", These de Docteur-Ingenieur, IRISA-Universite de Rennes I, Novembre 1986.

17 Maciejewski A.A. "Kinetic Limitations on the Use of Redundancy in Robotics Manipulators", Proc. of IEEE Conf. on Robotics and Automation, pp 113-118,1989.

18 Maciejewski A.A. "Dealing with Ill-Conditioned Equations of Motion for Articulated Figures", IEEE CGA 10,3, pp 63-71 (1990)

19 Boulic R. and Mas R. "Inverse Kinetics for Center of Mass Position Control and Posture Optimization", Technical Report 94/68, Computer Sciences Department, EPFL, DI-LIG, Switzerland, September 1994

20 Mac Lelland J.,"Form and Function in Birds" vol 4, p79, King & Mac Lelland Editors, Academic press Publisher, London, 1989.

Real-Time Walkthrough with Specular Effects

Andrzej Wojdala, Marek Gruszewski
Arconex Research & Development
Szczecin, Poland

1. Introduction

Recently, a lot of efforts have been directed towards interactive, realistic visualization of complex models. The problem is that realistic image synthesis algorithms have always been time-consuming, and their complexity is still raising with the introduction of new methods, covering broad range of real world phenomena. Design disciplines, such as architectural, interior and lighting design or industrial design demand images to be more realistic, and generated faster. In broadcast and video production the demands are even higher, ending up with real-time manipulation. The times when the efficiency of the algorithms could have been dramatically improved by pure software techniques seem to be over. It is therefore inevitable, that developed techniques require hardware that is not only number-crunching, but provides efficient implementation of the graphics algorithms. One of possible directions is utilization of the dedicated hardware. However, because in practice such hardware is never updated fast enough to fulfill the increasing demands, relying on graphics workstations seems to be the safer solution.

Recent years have established a typical set of graphics capabilities offered in hardware by the graphics workstations, such as z-buffer or Gouraud shading. Lately, designers have extended the capabilities of their workstations with texture mapping [1], a feature indispensable for images' realism. This paper describes how to take advantage of those features in order to improve the realism of walkthrough by adding specular reflection.

2. Simulation of specular reflection

Today's realistic image synthesis is dominated by multipass global illumination methods, in which we can distinguish two main phases:
- View-independent lighting simulation for diffuse component, e.g. with radiosity or ray tracing from light sources. Mature methods resolve also specular-to-diffuse energy transfer during this phase [2]. The result of this phase is radiosity mesh, which represents the distribution of luminance on the surfaces of the model.
- The second phase is reconstruction and rendering. In this phase, the raster image is generated based on the results of view-independent simulation. Interactive viewing of the scene (walkthrough), requires hardware-supported z-buffer and

Gouraud shading to be used for the reconstruction of the results of view-independent lighting simulation.

Being observer independent, radiosity phase does not consider specular reflection, inherently observer-dependent. Usual method of adding specular reflection to radiosity solution is ray tracing pass during reconstruction phase, naturally implemented in software. Unfortunately, while radiosity mesh can be frequently displayed in interactive time, software ray tracing of each frame would make walkthrough impractical, which is why walkthroughs do not consider specular reflections.

A technique intended as a step in the direction of walkthroughs with specular effects has been proposed in [3]; it is based on the assumption, that most real scenes have few specularly reflecting (or refracting) objects. In that technique, hardware-supported ray tracing is applied only for those pixels, through which such objects are seen. Computation time reduction allowed in some cases to reach interactive response time, but was usually far from frame rates acceptable for walkthrough.

The solutions proposed below employ "image method" [2] to simulate specular reflection with the hardware support.

In the first solution, for each mirror (i.e. specularly reflecting object) an "image" of the actual camera is created (fig.1). "Camera image" is a camera, that is symmetrical in location to actual camera in respect to the mirror plane, but looks in the direction of the mirror (so, it is usually asymmetric perspective). The scene is displayed (in backbuffer) with "camera image" viewing parameters, with front clipping located on the mirror plane. This way, all objects between the camera and the mirror (including it) are clipped out, while the rest of the scene is displayed in the viewport limited by the contour of the mirror (e.g. using stenciling mechanism, supported by the hardware). An image displayed this way is retrieved from the screen, and a texture is created of it; then the scene is displayed with normal, actual camera, with texture mapped on the mirror plane.

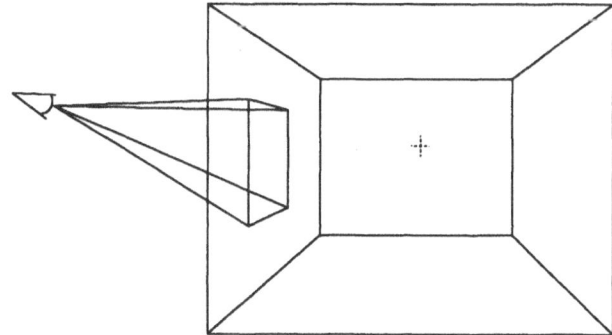

fig.1. Camera Image

Of course, mirror reflection is usually attenuated when rendered properly. To simulate this effect, mirror should not be clipped out when the scene is displayed with "camera image"; it should be transparent instead (transparency is also supported by the hardware). More accurate attenuation can be achieved by modification of the texture according to the z-value of particular pixels. To obtain reflection in color mirror (i.e. the effect of color filtering), transparent mirror should be additionally assigned the desired color (photo 2).

Described method can be used to simulate glass windows, which are both reflecting and transparent. When a texture image is created for reflection, it should be made partially transparent and mapped onto the glass with alpha blending, which is also supported by the hardware.

The solution presented above naturally requires, that new texture image is generated for each changed camera location. The disadvantage is that generation itself and loading the texture for each frame can slow down walkthrough. To avoid this, an alternative solution is possible.

First, the scene is displayed without concern for specular reflection. Then the mirror reflection (in respect to the mirror plane) of the scene is displayed in the viewport limited by the contour of the mirror (using stencil), with front clipping defined by the mirror plane (fig.2). To introduce attenuation, the same mechanism as described above can be used.

This solution does not use textures to implement mirror reflections; instead of creating "camera image", "geometry image" is created on the fly, and discarded right after display.

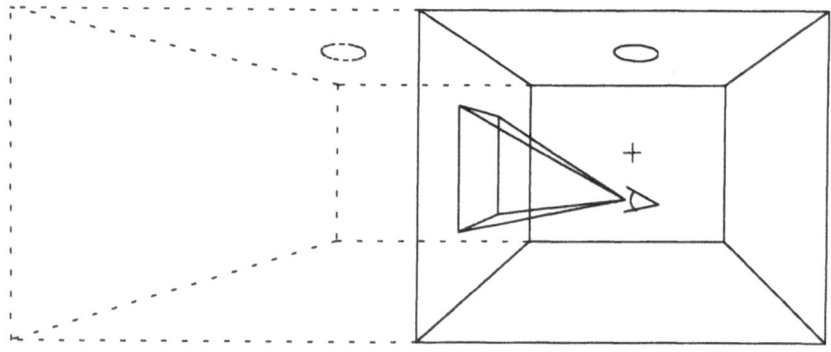

fig.2. Geometry Image

Both solutions presented above require multiple displays of the same scene: for each mirror, display of the whole scene is repeated, what inevitably affects walkthrough performance. To avoid this, for each mirror a list of objects that can be potentially reflected in it can be maintained. Such list can be created either by user specification, or in preprocessing phase. It should be noted, that multiple reflections are also possible; the order in which reflections are processed should be defined as well as the tree depth (maximum level of reflections).

3. Simulation of reflected light spots

Another specular effect that can be simulated with texturing hardware support is highlight spot caused by the light reflected from the mirror. This observer-independent effect involves specular-to-diffuse energy transfer, and as such is not handled by conventional radiosity or ray tracing. Mature image synthesis methods allow generation of radiosity meshes with reflected light spots [4, 5, 6]; for those that do not, a simulation of this effect is possible.

Employed technique is again image method, this time used for light sources. "Light image" is a light, that is created by mirroring original light in respect to the mirror plane (fig.3). "Light image" is used to create projective texture yielding a spot of the shape defined by the mirror (photo 1). The technique of projective textures was described in [7]; it was modified to eliminate first display pass (in last pass additive blending function was used instead of multiplicative).

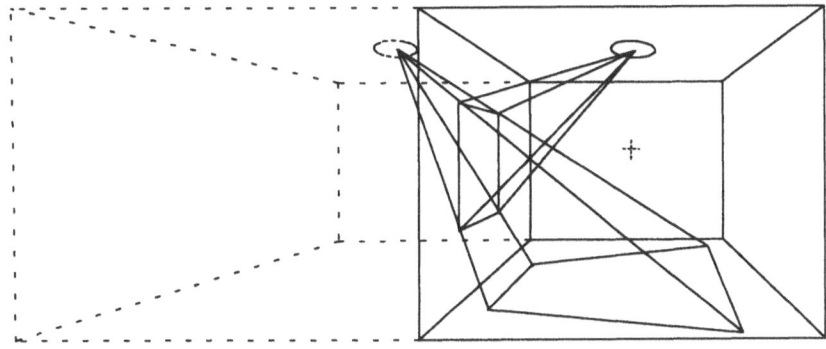

fig.3. Light Image

4. Results

Scenes presented on the photos, with radiosity meshes converted into textures [8, 9], were used for walkthrough with simulation of specular reflection. Walkthroughs were performed on Silicon Graphics' Onyx with four 150MHz R4400 processors and Reality Engine 2 graphics (four Raster Managers RM5). In PAL resolution (720x576), the speed for the scene without specular effects was 50 frames per second. Photos 1 and 2 show scenes, displayed using "geometry image" technique. A mirror on the wall reflects paintings and the door, added in order to make reflection easier to perceive. On photo 1 two levels of reflections are shown. Photo 2 shows the light spot on the floor, reflected from the mirror. Specular reflections introduce performance degradation, because each mirror needs additional display of the scene. Fortunately, they usually require only a fraction of the time necessary to display the whole scene, due to smaller viewport and preprocessing. For the presented scenes, as well as for several other tested scenes, the speed was kept on the level of 50 antialiased frames per second (the same as for the scene without the mirror).

photo 1. Two-level reflections

photo 2. Light spot on the floor

Reflected light spots, implemented as projective textures, require several display passes, and therefore are more time consuming. One additional display pass is needed for each spot, but certain inaccuracies of the graphics hardware caused second display pass necessary. For one spot it makes three display passes, and theoretical slow down by 67%. In practice, slow down was lower due to the slack caused by 50Hz display frame rate, and for scene on photo 2 (one spot) the speed was 25 frames per second.

5. Conclusions

This paper describes how walkthrough can be enhanced with such effects as specular reflection. Presented algorithms have certain limitations and drawbacks. Usually, only limited number of mirrors is reasonable, and all they should be planar. For curved surfaces approximated by polygons, better results can be obtained using environment mapping, specific form of texturing, supported in hardware on Silicon Graphic workstations. Multiple reflections require additional display passes and more complex logic. Being simulations, the effects are not physically justified. Reflected light spots normally should be considered in radiosity solution, because they influence the illumination of the other objects. On the other hand, light spots created in described way have certain advantage over those generated by radiosity: they allow light sources to be animated during walkthrough, what normally requires recalculation of radiosity solution. Of course, such animation has nothing in common with true lighting simulation. It should be pointed out however, that despite limitations, presented techniques visibly improve the realism of displayed scenes usually keeping the performance within frame rates acceptable for walkthrough, and as such are potentially very attractive for many disciplines, including broadcasting and video production. Combined with transparency already implemented in hardware, and shadows realized with hardware support as projective textures [7], described techniques make it possible to create quite realistic images in interactive time.

Acknowledgments.

Walkthroughs were performed with software ELSET/WALK, a product of VAP Video Art Production, Germany, developed by Arconex Research & Development, Poland. ELSET (TM) is a Registered Trademark of VAP Video Art Production.
Silicon Graphics equipment was provided by VAP Video Art Production.

References

1. Akeley K. RealityEngine Graphics. ACM Comput Graph (SIGGRAPH Proceedings) 1990; 24(4):109-116
2. Wallace J, Cohen M, Greenberg D. A two-pass solution to the rendering equation: a synthesis of ray tracing and radiosity methods. ACM Comput Graph (SIGGRAPH Proceedings) 1987; 21(4):311-320
3. Wojdala A, Myszkowski K, Rej P. Hardware support for realistic image synthesis. Machine Graphics & Vision 1992; 1(1-2):236-246 (in polish)
4. Sillion F, Puech C. A general two-pass method integrating specular and diffuse reflection. ACM Comput Graph (SIGGRAPH Proceedings) 1989; 23(3):335-344
5. Aupperle L, Hanrahan P. A hierarchical illumination algorithm for surfaces with glossy reflection. ACM Comput Graph (SIGGRAPH Proceedings) 1993; 155-162
6. Myszkowski K, Wicyński K, Khodulev A. Simulation of ideal specular light path by ray tracing. Machine Graphics & Vision 1994; 3(1-2):123-137
7. Segal M, Korobkin C, van Widenfelt R, et al. Fast shadows and lighting effects using texture mapping. ACM Comput Graph (SIGGRAPH Proceedings) 1992; 26(2): 249-252
8. Wojdala A, Gruszewski M, Dudkiewicz K. Using hardware texture mapping for efficient image synthesis and walkthrough with specular effects. Machine Graphics & Vision 1994; 3(1-2):139-151
9. Myszkowski K, Kunii T. Texture Mapping as an alternative for meshing during walkthrough animation. Proceedings of 5th Eurographics Workshop on Rendering, Darmstadt, Germany; 375-388

Real-Time Depth of Field Algorithm

Krzysztof Dudkiewicz
Arconex Research & Development
Szczecin, Poland

1 Introduction

There are many ways of creating depth of field effect during synthetic image creation. However, only few of them are applicable to hardware rendering. One commonly known method suggested first by Haeberli and Akeley [1] is using accumulation buffer and may produce real or near-real time results on Silicon Graphics workstations which support accumulation buffer in hardware. This method requires multiple rendering of the whole scene for every frame (each time with a viewpoint pseudo-randomly displaced on a surface of a hypothetical lens) and accumulating the results. The performance of this algorithm drops down with the increasing complexity of the scene and increasing blur required (because more samples are necessary). In fact linear increase of the diameter of the circle of confusion causes squared increase of the number of samples (and therefore the number of rendering passes).

Potmesil and Chakravarty [2] describe image postprocessing algorithm to simulate depth of field effect. It produces good results, but implemented in software does not allow interactive performance.

Rokita [3] proposed simplification of this algorithm. Such modified algorithm can be implemented in hardware.

In this paper a modification of Rokita's algorithm is presented. It does not have drawbacks of the mentioned accumulation buffer solution; in particular, there is no direct correspondence between complexity of the scene and processing time, also the linear increase of the size of the circle of confusion requires only linear increase of the number of processing passes. While it inherits drawbacks of Rokita's algorithm, it is able to generate same results in real or near real time on Silicon Graphics workstations with RealityEngine2 graphics.

2 Description of the algorithm

Potmesil and Chakravarty processed raster images with z-component (depth). For every input pixel their algorithm uses depth value to calculate the circle of confusion, and blends RGB components of input pixel onto a circle of output pixels.

Rokita modified this algorithm, by using convolution of input pixels with the matrix corresponding to depth value. As convolution operation is available in hardware, the algorithm is potentially very fast. Because of limited kernel size in available implementations (e.g. 3x3 kernel), convolution is performed several

258

times, what is equivalent to single convolution with greater size kernel. The author suggested construction of dedicated hardware, based on DSP equipped with convolution (e.g. HARRIS HSP48908) and did not present the results of performance tests.

This paper presents modified version of Rokita's algorithm, using capabilities of SGI RealityEngine graphics (3x3, 5x5 and 7x7 kernels). The process is optimized to perform as few convolutions as possible. Also, the shape of the convolution filter was modified.

Shape of the filter kernel is very important. If one convolution per pixel is used kernel should be as close to the circle as possible, but applying such a filter a few times would cause the effective kernel shape to change dramatically (for instance, applying box filter 3x3 twice is equivalent to a single pass of 5x5 filter, see fig. 1). There are functions, which do not change the shape during multiple convolutions, such as Gaussian normal distibution.

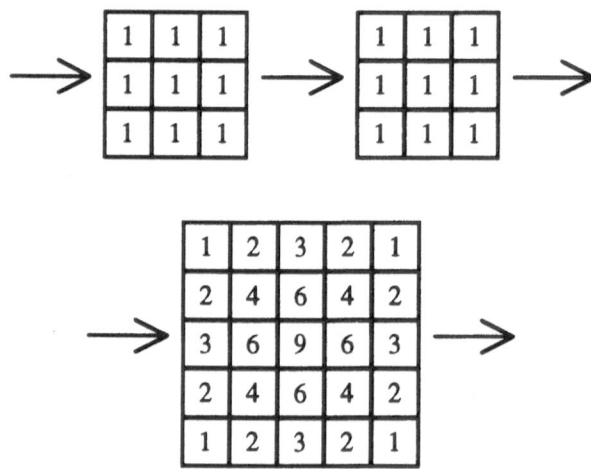

fig. 1.

The processing can be divided into five main stages:

Stage 1.
The scene is displayed using z-buffer, Gouraud shading, texture mapping, etc. RGB planes are read from frame-buffer to a temporary buffer.

Stage 2.
Z (depth) values are used to calculate circles of confusion. The circles (floating point values) are classified into a few ranges (for instance diameters [0, 1], (1, 3], (3, 5] etc.). Then an integer value is assigned to each such range and for every pixel this value is stored into stencil planes of the framebuffer.

Current settings of lens parameters (ie. focal length, aperture, etc.) are used to create the table containing the diameter ranges, their corresponding stencil planes values and depth ranges. The depth ranges are obtained from diameter ranges by using the following formula (which is in fact the inverse of Potesil's formula for diameter of a circle of confusion):

$$depth_{near}(diameter) = F * \frac{V_{u_{near}}}{V_{u_{near}} - F}$$

$$depth_{far}(diameter) = F * \frac{V_{u_{far}}}{V_{u_{far}} - F} \text{ exists only when } (V_{u_{far}} - F) > 0$$

$$V_{u_{near}} = \frac{F^2 * V_p}{F - diameter * n}$$

$$V_{u_{far}} = \frac{F^2 * V_p}{F + diameter * n}$$

$$V_p = \frac{P}{P - F}$$

$$n = \frac{F^2 * (far - P)}{far * (P - F)}$$

$$P = \frac{2}{\frac{1}{near} + \frac{1}{far}}$$

where:
near, far - boundaries of depth range which is rendered in sharp focus (no convolution is performed),
F - focal length of the lens,
n - aperture of the lens,
P - depth upon which the lens is focused.

An example below explains processing in stage 2. Let scene have depth values ranging from 5 to 20. Lens parameters are so that depth of field range is 7 to 8.

260

depth range min	depth range max	diameter required	kernel size	stencil value
min depth (5)	5.0909	(7,9]	9	5
5.0909	5.6	(5,7]	7	3
5.6	6.2222	(3,5]	5	2
6.2222	7	(1,3]	3	1
7	8	[0,1]	none	0
8	9.3333	(1,3]	3	1
9.3333	11.2	(3,5]	5	2
11.2	14	(5,7]	7	3
14	18.6666	(7,9]	9	5
18.6666	max depth (20)	(9,11]	11	6

Table 1.

It is worth noting that not all stencil values are used (4, 8, 12, ... are omitted, ie. values with null two least significant bits); this will become clear later.

The following processing is performed in stage 2: Stencil planes are appropriately filled by rendering a series of rectangles perpendicular to the viewing axis and covering the whole screen. In the above example rectangles distanced at 8, 9.3333, 11.2, 14, 18.66666 are drawn with the z test configured to pass (i.e. enable drawing) only when incoming pixels are nearer than those already in z-buffer. Drawing the first rectangle will fill stencil planes with value 1 for all pixels which are further than 8; drawing the second one will fill pixels further than 9.3333 with value 2 and so on. Then rectangles distanced at 7, 6.22222, 5.6, 5.0909 are rendered but the z test is configured to pass only when the incoming pixels are further than those already in z-buffer.

As a result pixels are classified according to depth range they lie in, and this clasification is represented in stencil planes.

Stage 3.

Before description of this stage another table will be explained. It shows kinds of convolution(s) which pixels falling into different depth ranges (with different stencil values) are subject to (stencil values in parenthesis are binary equivalents). This table is always the same regardless of scene or focus parameters.

diameter range	stencil value	convolution(s)	effective kernel size
[0,1]	0 (0000)	none	-
(1,3]	1 (0001)	3	3
(3,5]	2 (0010)	5	5
(5,7]	3 (0011)	7	7
(7,9]	5 (0101)	3, 7	9
(9,11]	6 (0110)	5, 7	11
(11,13]	7 (0111)	7, 7	13
(13,15]	9 (1001)	3, 7, 7	15
(15,17]	10 (1010)	5, 7, 7	17
and so on	....	....	....

Table 2.

During this stage the image that was read into the temporary buffer in stage 1 is written to RGB planes (z testing is disabled). At most three consecutive writes with convolutions: 3x3, 5x5 and 7x7 are performed, but every single pixel is convolved no more than once. The stencil test is configured to enable writing only the pixels for which two least significant bits of stencil planes are 01 (kernel 3x3), 10 (5x5) or 11 (7x7). For example convolution with kernel 3x3 is performed for pixels with stencil values 1, 5, 9, ... (see table 2).

The next two stages are repeated as many times as necessary to achieve required effective kernel size.

Stage 4.
RGB planes (partially filtered already) are read into temporary buffer.

Stage 5.
This stage convolves pixels, which require circle of confusion greater than 7. Stencil testing is configured to ignore two least significant bits of stencil planes and to pass (therefore allowing convolution) if stencil value is greater than or equal to a certain threshold. During first repetition of stage 5 this threshold equals 4 and pixels with stencil values 5, 6, 7, 9, 10, ... are processed, during second repetition threshold equals to 8, convolved are 9, 10, 11, 13, 14, ... and so on.

3 Results

In order to measure performance of the proposed algorithm a trivial scene was build. It consists of two rectangles parallel to the image plane, which fill the whole area of the screen (fig. 2). The distance between the observer and the rectangles is different and equals 5 meters for the left one and 10 meters for the right. The percentage of the screen area covered by both rectangles (A to B ratio) can be changed, but the two always cover the whole window space.

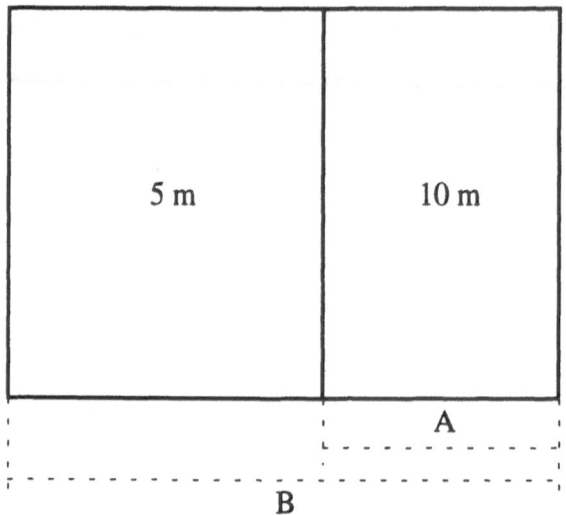

fig. 2.

The algorithm was repeatedly applied to the above scene. Six sets of depth of field parameters were used, each of them rendered left rectangle in sharp focus and defocused right one. The defocus ranged from 1 to 6 convolutions, and therefore used different processing time. Also the ratio of coverage of surfaces (A to B) was changed from 0% (only the left rectangle) to 100% (only the right rectangle). This changed the screen area actually being defocused. Tests were performed on a Silicon Graphics ONYX with RealityEngine2 graphics with four Raster Managers (RM5). The resolution of the window was 720 by 576 pixels (PAL). The results of tests are summarised in the below table and chart:

	0 %	50 %	100 %
0	0.033	0.033	0.033
1	0.104	0.104	0.104
2	0.250	0.250	0.251
3	0.525	0.525	0.526
4	0.800	0.801	0.803
5	1.079	1.082	1.083
6	1.359	1.363	1.366

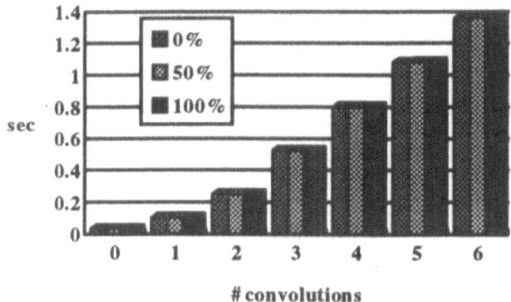

convolutions

Rows of the table show times in seconds of a processing of a frame for a given number of convolutions. Columns contain times of processing for a given screen coverage. Row corresponding to the number of convolutions 0 is an attempt to estimate overhead.

The results show almost linear dependence of processing time on the number of performed convolutions. The increase of the time depends on the size of kernel of additional convolutions (the addition of second convolution with 5x5 kernel increases the processing time by about 150 ms, while addition of third and next ones with 7x7 kernel increases by about 290 ms). On the other hand, the processing time depends very little on the actual area being convoluted, and therefore is almost independent of the scene contents.

A quality comparison between the images created by Potmesil's and presented algorithms has been made. For most real scenes the differences are hardly noticeable (photos 1, 2 and 3). Photo 2 is defocused by software implementation of Potmesil's algorithm, photo 3 is processed with the same settings by proposed hardware solution. Software processing took about 30 seconds, whereas hardware processing took about 1.4 seconds.

Photo 4 presents scene deliberately chosen to reveal the differences between both algorithms. It consists of three overlapping squares distanced at 5, 10 and 15 meters. Lens parameters are chosen to maintain middle square in sharp focus and blur near and far ones. The defocus on this picture is deliberately big. Photo 5 shows result of software processing.

Photo 6 is the result of hardware processing with same settings. The defocus is smaller than required. The reason is that effective kernel shape is far from circle. This effect may be minimised by applying filtering with effective kernel size deliberately increased. However, it increases also the postprocessing time.

Photo 7 shows the result of such approach. The effective kernel sizes were deliberately increased for all defocused pixels. Nevertheless, some artifacts remain, in particular overlapping edges are not processed correctly, which is the result of the fact, that convolution is the simplification of Potmesil's algorithm. Fortunately for many real scenes this drawback is insignificant. Another artifact visible on the same photo is incorrect rendering of borders of picture. This is caused by the fact, that some number of border pixels is lost during convolution. Problem can be easily overcome by rendering original picture bigger than required.

4 Conclusions

Most significant advantages of the algorithm are:
1. It allows real time postprocessing unlike one suggested by Potmesil .
2. It runs on comercially available graphics workstation and does not require dedicated hardware like Rokita's one.

Main disadvantages of the algorithm are:
1. The defocus achieved, particularly for more blur, is less than presumed. Fortunately, as already mentioned this problem can be overcome by artificially increasing effective kernel size.
2. The image after the convolution is smaller than original by number of pixels proportional to effective kernel size. As mentioned, this can be solved by rendering picture bigger than required.
3. Overlapping edges are not processed correctly (this concerns also Rokita's solution).

Acknowledgements
Silicon Graphics equipment was provided by VAP Video Art Production GmbH.

References
1. Haeberli P., Akeley K. The Accumulation Buffer: Hardware Support for High-Quality Rendering. Computer Graphics 1990; 24:309-318.
2. Potmesil M., Chakravarty I. A Lens and Aperture Camera Model for Synthetic Image Generation. Computer Graphics 1981; 15:297-306.
3. Rokita P. Fast generation of depth of field effects in computer graphics. C & G 1993; 17:593-595.

Photo 1

Photo 2

Photo 3

Photo 4

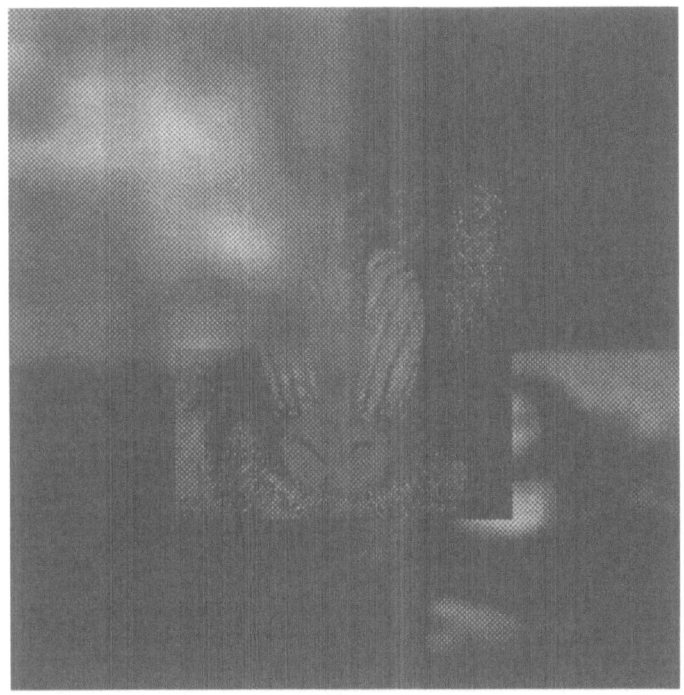

Photo 5

Photo 6

Photo 7

Session 7: Synthesis 3

Combining Method of Generation Realistic Images of Clouds

Jacek Raczkowski and Piotr Kamiński
Institute of Computer Science, Warsaw University of Technology,
Warsaw, Poland

Abstract

Modelling of clouds is a difficult problem in computer graphics. Shapes of clouds cannot be defined using traditional modelling techniques. Several authors presented their approaches to clouds modelling. They have applied complex mathematical models or used rough simplifications.

This paper presents a simple method that is used to model various types of clouds. The described technique involves fractals and sine functions to obtain realistic results. Part of the work relating to light scattering in clouds is based on the work of N. Max.

1 Introduction

Modelling of natural phenomena is a complex problem in computer graphics. On the one hand the physical description of such phenomena is very complicated and difficult to simulate. On the other hand frequently used simplifications give artificial visual effects.

Over the last few years many researchers proposed different models for visualization of clouds. Previously introduced models can be classified into two groups. One contains models which aspired to yield a picture of a cloud as fast as possible with little loss of accuracy. Fishmann and Schachter [1] constructed the layer of clouds with several randomly placed ellipsoids. Gardner [2] extended this idea and put texture on the three dimensional solid (ellipsoid). Max [3] developed a model of a cloud's geometry based on height fields. He used polynomials modified by sine functions to create the shape of clouds. Another group of models applied physical simulation. Voss [4] used fractal techniques to obtain a function of a clouds density. A few more efficient fractal algorithms for modelling cloud density were described by Sakas [5]. Kajiya and Von Herzen [6] evaluated the distribution of vapour density taking into account the accurate physical model. Ebert and Parent [7] used a random function of turbulence to describe the process of changing the cloud density. All these models involved fairly rigorous mathematics and produced large computational costs.

Several researchers have developed models for light attenuation in clouds. Blinn [8] applied the simplified model for light reflection from cloud surfaces. Kajiya and Von Herzen [6] used ray tracing of volume densities. Similar propositions were described by Max [3] and by Sakas [5].

This work presents the method of modelling which is convenient for different types of clouds. This concept uses a composition of wave functions and a randomly generated fractal.

2 Geometry of Cloud

The algorithm is divided into three basic steps. The first one creates a fractal using the midpoint displacement method [9]. Next, the wave function is defined by setting its parameters. The third step is required for the composition of fractal and wave function and setting the reference plane.

2.1 Fractal

The fractal used in the algorithm is evaluated via the recursive subdivision process. The base of fractal is the table $M \times N$ reals denoting the height of points. First we need to determine the heights in the corners of table (elements G_{11}, G_{1N}, G_{M1}, G_{MN}). We use the Gaussian random value generator where the average value equals zero. The standard deviation σ is the input parameter of the fractal generation process. This parameter has an influence on the range of fractal changes. Values G_{11}, G_{1N}, G_{M1}, G_{MN} are calculated using the formula:

$$G_{ij} = \Delta_0 \, Gauss(0,\sigma)$$

where Δ_0 is the range of fractal changes in the first step of the algorithm. We assume that Δ_0 is equal the standard deviation σ. $Gauss(0,\sigma)$ is the random value determined by random generator.

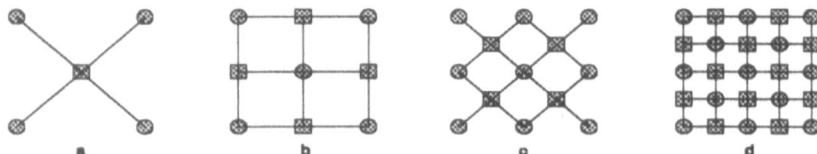

Figure 1. Creating the fractal - steps of the algorithm (points being calculated are marked with squares).

We can calculate the midpoint value by averaging the values in the corners and adding a random displacement value (fig.1a). The displacement value P_1 is also evaluated using the random generator and equals:

$$P_1 = \Delta_1 \, Gauss(0,\sigma)$$

where Δ_1 is the range of fractal changes for this step of algorithm.

Next, calculated points are joined using the mesh with edges parallel to the edges of the fractal (fig.1b). Heights of midpoints are calculated in the same way like in previous steps but with displacement P_2. Points laying on the edges are calculated by averaging three neighbour values and random modification. In the next step the mesh with slope 45 degrees is used again (fig.1c). The procedure is continued until the fractal is completed (fig.1d).

The range of changes of calculated values in the succeeding steps of algorithm, should depend on the level of details. The following formula is considered useful for representing the range of changes [10]:

$$\Delta_i^2 = \frac{1 - 2^{2H-2}}{(2^i)^{2H}} \sigma^2 \qquad i = 1, ..., n$$

Parameter H is in the range $0 < H < 1$ and the fractal dimension is $D = 3 - H$. According to the value of parameter H, the surface of fractal is either flat or jagged [9], [10].

2.2 Wave Function

Some formations of clouds have regular shapes. The modelling of them using only a fractal cannot assure the regularity. Therefore it is important to use a function with wave properties. Such a function can be obtained using several components of the Fourier series [2]:

$$F(x,y) = k \sum_{i=1}^{n} [c_i \sin(\omega_{x_i} x)] \sum_{i=1}^{n} [c_i \sin(\omega_{y_i} y)]$$

Parameters for subsequent components can be chosen by the relationships:

$$c_{i+1} = 0.707 \; c_i$$
$$\omega_{x_{i+1}} = 2 \; \omega_{x_i}$$
$$\omega_{y_{i+1}} = 2 \; \omega_{y_i}$$

The properties of such a function can be modified easily. Alteration of frequencies in one or in two dimensions can cause stretching or shrinking. The height of a cloud can be controlled by changing the amplitude. Because we need to obtain a regular surface without details we can only use up to the five first components of the function $F(x,y)$.

2.3 Composition of the Fractal and Wave Function

Basic parameters for fractal generation and wave function can be fixed according to the type of modelled cloud. Fractal values are added to the values of the wave function calculated for all points in the table. After this the table contains the

274

heights of the points. Next we need to establish the spatial shape of cloud.

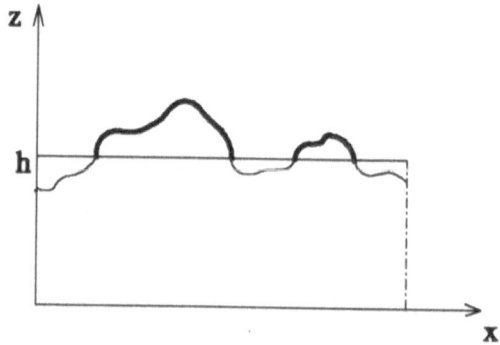

Figure 2. Creating of cloud geometry using reference plane (projection in the XZ plane)

We choose the reference plane laying on height h which is smaller than the maximum value [3]. This plane is parallel to the XY plane. The height h is chosen according to the assumed type and dimension of the cloud. Small cloudlets are modelled using the h value near the maximum. Thick and dense clouds need a smaller h value. The reference plane crosses the height field thus eliminating points with height less then h. The remaining points construct the upper surface of cloud (fig.2). This surface can be modified by involution (emphasizes local extrema) or by extraction of the root (gives effect of flatness). The lower surface of cloud is a scaled and mirrored reflection of the upper one. Both surfaces are joined on the reference plane. On the tangent plane of the junction some discontinuities of the first derivative may occur. Hence operations of flatting are done [3].

3 Light Scattering in Clouds

In order to visualize clouds authors used the light scattering model described by Max [3]. This model assumes that light beam energy after one reflection from a cloud particle is so small that the analysis of next reflections can be negligible. Therefore only single reflections are taken into account. Additionally the optical density of cloud is constant.

A viewing ray from the eye pierces the cloud surface at points Q and R. We will consider the point P as a representative scattering point along the ray QR. The ray from the sun to the point P meets the cloud surface in S (fig.3). The sunlight is attenuated along the ray SP, scattered by a particle in the point P toward the eye and attenuated along the ray PQ. Taking into account a small part of ray QR we can calculate the total energy reaching the eye by integration along the ray QR.

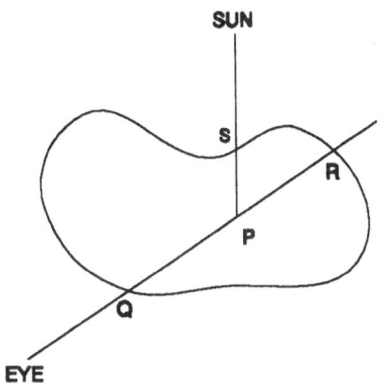

Figure 3. Rays traversing the cloud

4 Results

The described algorithm of cloud modelling was used on different types of clouds. Colour plates show obtained results.

Figure 4 shows the image of a stratus cloud from the long distance. The main influence on it's shape is the surface of the fractal with rather small dimension (about 2.1). The model of cumulonimbus is demonstrated on figure 5. The shape of this cloud is described by the fractal with dimension 2.5. The cloud altocumulus composed with the fractal and wave function is shown on figure 6. The regularity of surface is obtained by intensifying the influence of sine functions. The shape of the altocumulus is dependent on the wave movement of air masses. Single cumulus clouds are shown on figure 7. The shape of the cumulus is strongly dependent on the wave function. Single clouds are extracted by decreasing the basic frequency of the wave function.

Approximate values of parameters used in the generation of the model are collected in the table. Values of the amplitudes and frequencies should be interpreted as scale factors in relation to the unit values of these parameters.

Fig	Fractal dimension	Amplitude of the fractal	Number of Fourier serie components	Amplitude of the first component	Frequency for X direction	Frequency for Y direction
4	2.1	5	N/A	N/A	N/A	N/A
5	2.5	5	N/A	N/A	N/A	N/A
6	2.5	1	1	1	2	4
7	2.3	1	2	3	1	1

Figures 8 and 9 shows the possibility of composing different types of clouds in one image. The cumulonimbus (lower layer) and altocumulus are shown on figure 8. On figure 9 cumuluses are viewed over the layer of stratus.

5 Conclusions

In the paper the algorithm for modelling clouds using fractals and wave functions is presented. The main advantage of the algorithm is the elastic way of modelling different types of clouds. The two components of model (fractal and wave function) allow us to generate both regular and irregular clouds. According to the needs the thickness of the cloud layer can be modified by choosing the height of the reference plane. The proposed method allows us to obtain realistic models of cloud geometry.

References

1. Fishmann B., Schachter B., Computer Display of Height Fields, Computers & Graphics 1980, 5:53-60
2. Gardner G.Y., Visual Simulation of Clouds, Computer Graphics 1985, 3:297-303
3. Max N., Light Diffusion through Clouds and Haze, Computer Vision Graphics and Image Processing 1986, 33:280-292
4. Voss R., Fourier Synthesis of Gaussian Fractals: 1/f noises, landscapes and flakes, In: SIGGRAPH 83, Tutorial on State of the Art Image Synthesis 1983
5. Sakas G., Cloud modeling for visual simulators, In: Von Bally G., Bjelkhagen H.J. (eds) Optics for protection of man and environment against natural and technological disasters, Elsevier Science Publishers B.V. 1993 pp 323-333
6. Kajiya J.T., Von Herzen B.P., Ray Tracing Volume Densities, Computer Graphics 1984, 3:165-174
7. Ebert D.S., Parent R.E., Rendering and Animation of Gaseous Phenomena by Combining Fast Volume and Scanline A-buffer Techniques, Computer Graphics 1990, 4:357-366
8. Blinn J.F., Light Reflections Functions for Simulation of Clouds and Dusty Surfaces, Computer Graphics 1982, 3:21-29
9. Fournier A., Fussell D., Carpenter L., Computer Rendering of Stochastic Models, Communication of the ACM 1982, 25:371-384
10. Peitgen H.O., Saupe D. (eds), The Science of Fractal Images, Springer-Verlag, Berlin 1988

Figure 4. Stratus

Figure 5. Cumulonimbus

Figure 6. Altocumulus

Figure 7. Cumuluses

Figure 8. Cumulonimbus and altocumulus

Figure 9. Cumulus over the layer of stratus

Methods for Volume Metamorphosis

M. Chen, M.W. Jones and P. Townsend

Department of Computer Science, University of Wales Swansea,
Singleton Park, Swansea SA2 8PP, United Kingdom
E-mail: {m.chen, m.w.jones, p.townsend}@swansea.ac.uk

Abstract

The problem of creating a sequence of inbetween volumes smoothly transforming from one given volume to another is referred to as volume metamorphosis or volume morphing. Several methods that provide the solution to the problem are described and compared in this paper. Tests have shown that some of these methods are capable of produce good quality metamorphosis within an acceptable time.

1 Introduction

Volume data, which is used widely in scientific computation and medical imaging to represent 3D scalar fields, provides a uniform way of modelling 3D objects. As voxel calculations are much simpler than polygon calculations, most algorithms for manipulating and rendering volume data are suitable to be embedded into special hardware [1, 2]. For modelling 2D objects in video production, perhaps there is no doubt that image representations have significant advantages compared with vector representations. When it comes to the synthesis of 3D models for creating images sequences, volume-based techniques cannot be overlooked.

Image metamorphosis [3, 4], more commonly called image morphing, is a computer animation technique for creating an image sequence smoothly transforming from one given image to another. The technique has recently received much attention, especially from the film and television industry. Also relatively more recently, graphics tools have become widely available for visualising volume datasets [5], and such tools have the potential to be developed into methods for volume metamorphosis. In addition to the synthesis of 3D models in video production, the application areas of such methods include computer animation, scientific visualisation, medical imaging and many aspects of natural science.

In this paper, several methods for volume metamorphosis are presented, most of which are developed based on the 2D methods widely used for image metamorphosis. A classification of morphing algorithms is given, and a set of volume distortion techniques, many of which have not yet been documented in the literature, are described. In addition to the static analysis of the complexity and usability of these methods, some graphical results and data of their run-time performance are presented.

2 The Process of Volume Metamorphosis

A general volume is collection of scattered voxels, each of which is associated with a set of values (of size S), that is

$$V = \left\{ (x_i, v_i) \mid x_i \in R^3, v_i \in R^S, i = 1, 2, ..., n \right\}. \tag{1}$$

One of the most commonly used volume representations is one where voxels are organised in the form of a 3D regular grid and each voxel is associated with a value. We will use the general volume representation in the following discussions, with the assumption that all volumes are of the same size and there is a one-to-one correspondence between voxels in any two volumes.

Given a starting volume V_a and a finishing volume V_b, the metamorphosis between them is a process which generates a sequence of inbetween volumes, V_1, V_2, ..., V_L, obtained using an interpolation function

$$V_k \leftarrow F_{intp}\left(V_a, V_b, \frac{k}{L+1} \right), \quad [k = 1, 2, ... L]. \tag{2}$$

This sequence of volumes represents a smooth transformation from V_a to V_b, and may then be rendered to give an illusion of continuous metamorphosis. Perhaps it is arguable that such an illusion could also be obtained by morphing between two images resulted from rendering V_a and V_b, or by interpolating the isosurfaces [6] of V_a and V_b. However, it would be extremely difficult for the image-based morphing to accommodate 3D geometric changes between two volumes, while the isosurface interpolation would require the establishment of a complex correspondence between two surfaces. Neither of the methods would be able to retain complete volumetric information in the inbetween sequence.

The morphing process is usually controlled by two control datasets, C_a and C_b, which specify the key features in V_a and V_b and their correspondence. Prior to the interpolation, V_a and V_b are deformed according to C_a and C_b so that every pair of corresponding key features have the same location. This leads to the problem of volume distortion that can be formulated with a distortion function

$$V_a' \leftarrow F_{dist}\left(V_a, C_a, C_k \right), \quad V_b' \leftarrow F_{dist}\left(V_b, C_b, C_k \right); \tag{3}$$

where C_k is obtained in the same manner as V_k in (2). In some applications, volume distortion may be used beyond the context of volume metamorphosis.

3 Volume Morphing Methods

According to the use of control datasets, approaches to volume metamorphosis can be classified into three categories, namely
- *cross dissolving* — which requires no control datasets;
- *field morphing* — where control datasets are used to specify coordinate mappings; and
- *mesh warping* — where control datasets define volume subdivisions as well as coordinate mappings.

3.1 Cross Dissolving

Cross dissolving is a process of metamorphosis that involves the interpolation but not the distortion of volumes. The following pseudo-code outlines this process

```
Procedure:      VolumeMetamorphosis-CrossDissolving;
Input:          Va, Vb: Volume; L: Integer;
Output:         Vout[1], Vout[2], …, Vout[L]: Volume;

for k:=1 to L do
    t = k / (L + 1.0);
    Vout[k] := InterpolateVolume(Va, Vb, t);
end for;
```

The simplest cross dissolving method is a linear interpolation between $\mathbf{V}_a$ and $\mathbf{V}_b$, which often yields unsatisfactory results. To enhance the smoothness of the inbetween volumes, Fourier transformation may be used to schedule the interpolation non-linearly by favouring voxels whose values are close to the threshold of an interested isosurface [7]. Although they are easy to use and fast to run, both methods have difficulty in producing high quality results in most cases, especially when the transformations between two volumes involve scaling or rotation.

3.2 Field morphing

Given a pair of volumes, $\mathbf{V}_a$ and $\mathbf{V}_b$, and their associated control datasets, $\mathbf{C}_a$ and $\mathbf{C}_b$, the following pseudo-code outlines the general process of field morphing.

```
Procedure:      VolumeMetamorphosis-FieldMorphing;
Input:          Va, Vb: Volume; Ca, Cb: Control; L: Integer;
Output:         Vout[1], Vout[2], …, Vout[L]: Volume;

for k:=1 to L do
    t = k / (L + 1.0);
    Ck := InterpolateControlData(Ca, Cb, t);
    Va := DistortVolume(Va, Ca, Ck);
    Vb := DistortVolume(Vb, Cb, Ck);
    Vout[k] := InterpolateVolume(Va, Vb, t);
end for;
```

The key features of each volume are defined using a set of control fields. For the kth inbetween volume, a set of inbetween control fields Ck is first obtained, and is then used to distort $\mathbf{V}_a$ and $\mathbf{V}_b$.

The volume distortion operates as an inverse mapping [3] from a *destination* volume $\mathbf{V}_d$ back to a *source* volume $\mathbf{V}_s$ that may be $\mathbf{V}_a$ or $\mathbf{V}_b$ in this case. Given two corresponding sets of control fields, each pair of fields, $c_{d,j} \in \mathbf{C}_d$ and $c_{s,j} \in \mathbf{C}_{s,j}, [j = 1, 2, ..., m]$, determines a coordinate mapping

$$p_{i,j} \leftarrow f_j(x_{d,i}, c_{d,j}, c_{s,j}), [i = 1, 2, ..., n], [j = 1, 2, ..., m] \qquad (4)$$

from each voxel $(x_{d,i}, v_{d,i}) \in \mathbf{V}_d$ to a point $p_{i,j}$ relative to $\mathbf{V}_s$. Associated with each coordinate mapping is a weight $\omega_j(x_{i,j})$ that is normally computed according to the distance between $x_{i,j}$ and $c_{d,j}$. For each voxel $(x_{d,i}, v_{d,i})$ a point p_i is obtained as

$$p_i \leftarrow \sum_{j=1}^{m} \omega_j(x_{i,j}) \cdot p_{i,j}, \text{ with}$$

$$\sum_{j=1}^{m} \omega_j(x_{i,j}) = 1, [i = 1, 2, ..., n], \qquad (5)$$

and a voxel in $\mathbf{V}_s$ nearest p_i is then identified and its values are assigned to $v_{d,i}$. When volumes are represented by 3D regular grids, it is usually more accurate to identify the corner voxels of the cube containing p_i and tri-linearly interpolate their values.

3.2.1 Point Fields

Two types of fields, namely *point* [8] and *line* [4], are often employed in 2D image distortion. A volume morphing method can be easily derived from the image morphing method using point fields. Let each control field be simply the coordinates of a 3D point. A simple mapping function

$$p_{i,j} \leftarrow f_j(x_{d,i}, c_{d,j}, c_{s,j}) = c_{s,j} + x_{d,i} - c_{d,j} \qquad (6)$$

defines a geometric translation from $x_{i,j}$ to $p_{i,j}$. A weighting function, with a slight modification to the one proposed in [8], can be written as

$$\omega_j(x_{i,j}) = \frac{\sigma(x_{i,j}, c_j)}{\sum_{k=1}^{m} \sigma(x_{i,k}, c_k)}, \text{ with}$$

$$\sigma(x_{i,j}, c_j) = \left[\frac{1}{a + b \cdot \|x_{i,j} - c_j\|} \right]^d, \qquad (7)$$

where a, b and d are three user-defined constants whose values are in the ranges of $(0, \infty)$, $[0, \infty)$, and $[0, \infty)$ respectively. The main use of the constant a is to keep the denominator from becoming zero. When b is equal to or barely greater than zero, the weight of a point field at different voxels is hardly differentiated by the distances from the field to these voxels. The greater the value of b, the more differentiation between different distances. The constant d is used to control the relative influence which each point field has upon a voxel. When d is of a large value, the voxel is likely to be affected only by the strong and nearby fields.

Inevitably this method inherits from its 2D progenitor the inability to control any transformation other than simple translation. The results produced by simple point field morphing are generally no better than those by cross-dissolving methods. In order to perform more complex distortion, Ruprecht et al [9] introduced a 3×3 transformation matrix $\mathbf{T}_j$ into (6), resulting in

$$p_{i,j} \leftarrow f_j\left(x_{d,i}, c_{d,j}, c_{s,j}\right) = c_{s,j} + \mathbf{T}_j \cdot \left(x_{d,i} - c_{d,j}\right). \tag{8}$$

The elements of $\mathbf{T}_j$ are determined by solving a set of error functions. An alternative method which was also described in [9] is to construct the interpolant as a linear combination of basis functions whose coefficients are determined using control points.

3.2.2 Line Fields

The extension of 2D line fields to three dimensions is slightly less straightforward, as a coordinate mapping from a voxel in $\mathbf{V}_d$ to one in $\mathbf{V}_s$ cannot be consistently defined by a pair of line segments. The problem can be solved by using a supplementary vector in each line field.

A 3D line field consists of two end-points c_1 and c_2 of a line segment, and a supplementary vector N. With the field, a Euclidean coordinate system can be established, which is centred at $\dfrac{c_1 + c_2}{2}$ with an orthonormal basis (U, V, W) defined as

$$U = \frac{N}{\|N\|}, \quad V = \frac{N \times (c_2 - c_1)}{\|N \times (c_2 - c_1)\|}, \quad W = U \times V. \tag{9}$$

Given a pair of line fields, $\mathbf{L}_{s,j}$ and $\mathbf{L}_{d,j}$, a voxel located at $x_{d,i}$ in $\mathbf{V}_d$ can be mapped onto a point $p_{i,j}$ relative to $\mathbf{V}_s$ as follows

$$
\begin{aligned}
dp_{i,j} &\leftarrow f_{coord}\left(x, \mathcal{E}(\mathbf{V}_d), \mathcal{E}(\mathbf{L}_{d,j})\right), \\
sp_{i,j} &\leftarrow dp_{i,j}\frac{\|c_{s,2} - c_{s,1}\|}{\|c_{d,2} - c_{d,1}\|}, \qquad [i = 1,2,\ldots,n], [j = 1,2,\ldots,m], \tag{10} \\
p_{i,j} &\leftarrow f_{coord}\left(sp_{i,j}, \mathcal{E}(\mathbf{L}_{s,j}), \mathcal{E}(\mathbf{V}_s)\right),
\end{aligned}
$$

where $\mathcal{E}(\mathbf{X})$ represents the Euclidean coordinate system associated to $\mathbf{X}$ that may be either a volume or a line field, and the function $f_{coord}\left(x, \mathcal{E}_a, \mathcal{E}_b\right)$ transforms a point from one coordinate system to another. The weight of each mapping may be calculated using the following weighting functions

$$\omega_j\left(x_{i,j}\right) = \frac{\sigma\left(x_{i,j}, \mathbf{L}_j\right)}{\sum_{k=1}^{m}\sigma\left(x_{i,k}, \mathbf{L}_k\right)}, \text{ with}$$

$$\sigma\left(x_{i,j}, \mathbf{L}_j\right) = \left[\frac{\left\|c_{j,2}-c_{j,1}\right\|^c}{a+b\cdot\delta\left(x_{i,j},c_{j,1},c_{j,2}\right)}\right]^d, \tag{11}$$

where used-defined constants a, b and d have the same meaning as with a point field. The constant c, usually in the range of $[0, 1]$, is used to moderates the strength of line fields which is proportional to the length of the line segments. When c is zero, all fields have the same strength regardless of their length. Let $u = \frac{(x-c_1)\bullet(c_2-c_1)}{\|c_2-c_1\|^2}$. The function $\delta(x,c_1,c_2)$ computes the distance from a point to a line segment as follows

$$\delta(x,c_1,c_2) = \begin{cases} \|x-c_2\|\dfrac{\left|(x-c_1)\bullet(c_2-c_1)\right|}{\|x-c_1\|\cdot\|c_2-c_1\|} & \text{if } 0 < u < 1; \\ \|x-c_1\| & \text{if } u \leq 0; \\ \|x-c_2\| & \text{if } u \geq 1. \end{cases} \tag{12}$$

The conditions where a line segment is degenerated to a point or it is parallel to N may be dealt with by introducing a second supplementary vector or simply disallowing such a condition.

3.2.3 Disk Fields

Alternatively, a *disk* field can be established with a centre point c, a normal vector N and a radial vector R, and it gives more control over three dimensional transformations in comparison with a line field. Any arbitrary point may thereby be represented in cylindrical coordinates $[\zeta, \rho, \varphi]$ with respect to the disk field $\mathbf{D}=[c, N, R]$. Each pair of corresponding disk fields, $\mathbf{D}_{s,j}$ and $\mathbf{D}_{d,j}$ defines a coordinate mapping that can be used to control the distortion from $\mathbf{V}_s$ to $\mathbf{V}_d$ as

$$\left[\zeta_{i,j}, \rho_{i,j}, \varphi_{i,j}\right] \leftarrow f_{eu\_to\_cy}\left(x_{d,i}, \mathcal{E}(\mathbf{V}_d), \mathcal{C}(\mathbf{D}_{d,j})\right),$$

$$\zeta'_{i,j} \leftarrow \zeta_{i,j}\frac{\|N_s\|}{\|N_d\|}, \quad \rho'_{i,j} \leftarrow \rho_{i,j}\frac{\|R_s\|}{\|R_d\|}, \quad \varphi'_{i,j} \leftarrow \varphi_{i,j},$$

$$\rho_{i,j} \leftarrow f_{cy\_to\_eu}\left(\left[\zeta'_{i,j}, \rho'_{i,j}, \varphi'_{i,j}\right], \mathcal{C}(\mathbf{D}_{s,j}), \mathcal{E}(\mathbf{V}_s)\right), \tag{12}$$

$$[i = 1, 2, \ldots, n], [j = 1, 2, \ldots, m].$$

In (12), $\mathcal{C}(\mathbf{D})$ gives a cylindrical coordinate system defined by a disk field, and $f_{eu\_to\_cy}$ and $f_{cy\_to\_eu}$ facilitate the transformations of a point between a Euclidean system and a cylindrical system. A weighting function similar to (11) may be used for disk field. A detail description of this method can be found in [10].

Other types of fields may also be constructed by varying the primary shapes and their influence upon voxels. Using a combination of different fields is also feasible, and some interesting work has been reported recently [11]. The results of morphing with line and disk fields are generally of satisfactory quality, but the extra degree of freedom introduces difficulties into the process of specifying a volume morphing. Without a good user interface, defining a reasonable number of fields is likely to require some arduous work.

3.3 Mesh Warping

Mesh warping [3] is the most popular method used for image metamorphosis. The control dataset associated with each image specifies a planar subdivision over the image, typically a parametric grid or a triangular mesh. Extrapolating from the method to a three dimensional analogue, a volume warping method can be derived. Volumes V_a and V_b are first partitioned respectively by two spatial subdivisions that are of an equal number of elements. Deformed subdivisions are then obtained for inbetween volumes by interpolation. A voxel in an inbetween volume is mapped onto a voxel in each of V_a and V_b. Similar to field morphing, the values of voxels in the inbetween volume are determined by linearly interpolating those of the corresponding voxels in V_a and V_b.

It is the distortion algorithms employed by mesh warping distinguish it from field morphing. The elements of a subdivision, mostly the vertices, are used to define coordinate mappings. In addition to this, some elements, mostly the polyhedra, are also used to restrict the control of each coordinate mapping to a very small set of elements. A variety of image warping algorithms [3] have been developed and most are often designed specifically for particular type of meshes. The 3D extensions of two widely used image warping algorithms [12-14] are described below.

3.3.1 Parametric Grid

Consider a given source volume V_s, a destination volume V_d to be constructed, and two subdivisions G_s and G_d which are defined by two 3D parametric grids. Each grid consists of m vertices, and partitions a volume into a contiguous set of eight-cornered bricks. The bricks may be fitted with either linear or curved edges and surfaces. With such grids, a 3-pass warping algorithm can be used to map all voxels in V_d to those in V_s with two intermediate volumes V_{i1} and V_{i2}. The 3 passes of the algorithms are

- first pass — where an intermediate grid G_{i1} is constructed such that

$$G_{i1} = \left\{ v_j = \left[x_{d,j}, y_{s,j}, z_{s,j} \right] \middle| \begin{array}{l} \left[x_{s,j}, y_{s,j}, z_{s,j} \right] \in G_s, \\ \left[x_{d,j}, y_{d,j}, z_{d,j} \right] \in G_d, \\ \left[j = 1, 2, \ldots, m \right] \end{array} \right\}. \tag{13}$$

With respect to G_s, each of the eight-cornered bricks in G_{i1} can be deformed only in the x direction. The intermediate volume V_{i1} is then obtained by interpolating its voxels along scan-lines parallel to the x-axis using $\mathbf{G}_s$ and $\mathbf{G}_{i1}$.

* second pass — where $\mathbf{G}_{i2}$ is obtained with $v_j = \left[x_{d,j}, y_{d,j}, z_{s,j} \right]$ and $\mathbf{V}_{i2}$ is constructed from $\mathbf{V}_{i1}$ along scan-lines parallel to the y-axis under the control of $\mathbf{G}_{i1}$ and $\mathbf{G}_{i2}$.

* third pass — where $\mathbf{V}_d$ is constructed from $\mathbf{V}_{i2}$ along scan-lines parallel to the z-axis under the control of $\mathbf{G}_{i2}$ and $\mathbf{G}_d$.

3.3.2 Tetrahedral Mesh

Given a set of points, a tetrahedral mesh may be constructed using a 3D triangulation algorithm. To construct a destination volume $\mathbf{V}_d$ from a given source volume $\mathbf{V}_s$ and two corresponding meshes $\mathbf{T}_s$ and $\mathbf{T}_d$, each voxel in $\mathbf{V}_d$ is first mapped to a set of bary-centric coordinates $\left[\beta^1, \beta^2, \beta^3, \beta^4 \right]$ with respect to the tetrahedron $t_{d,j} \in \mathbf{T}_d, [j = 1, 2, \ldots, m]$ containing the voxel as follows

$$\beta_{i,j}^k \leftarrow \frac{\Delta\left(\ldots, t_{d,j}^{k-1}, x_{d,i}, t_{d,j}^{k+1}, \ldots\right)}{\Delta\left(t_{d,j}^1, t_{d,j}^2, t_{d,j}^3, t_{d,j}^4\right)}, [k = 1, 2, 3, 4], \text{ with}$$

$$\Delta\left(v^1, v^2, v^3, v^4\right) = \det \begin{bmatrix} v_x^1 & v_y^1 & v_z^1 & 1 \\ v_x^2 & v_y^2 & v_z^2 & 1 \\ v_x^3 & v_y^3 & v_z^3 & 1 \\ v_x^4 & v_y^4 & v_z^4 & 1 \end{bmatrix}, \tag{14}$$

where $t_{d,j}^k$ is the kth vertex of $t_{d,j}$. The bary-centric coordinates are then transformed back to Euclidean coordinates as

$$p_{i,j} \leftarrow \sum_{k=1}^{4} \beta_{i,j}^k \cdot t_{s,j}^k. \tag{15}$$

With both methods, it is however necessary to make sure that there is no element whose corresponding element has a "fold-over" structure. With the warping approach, distortion is constrained by individual element, and it is therefore relatively easier to achieve desired transformation without causing "ghost shadows". In most cases, they require much more control elements than field morphing methods.

4 Comparison

For each of the methods discussed above, Table 1 summarises the worst-case time complexity, allowed operations, usability and the general quality of its results,

Table 1. Comparison of volume morphing methods.

Method	Complexity	Operations	Results	Usage
Linear Interpolation	$O(n)$	C	poor	very easy
Fourier Interpolation	$O(n \cdot \log n)$	C	mostly poor	fairly easy
Simple Point Field	$O(n \cdot m)$	C,D,T	poor	easy
Point Field with T	$O(n \cdot m + m^2)$	C,D,T,S,R	average	average
Vector Field	$O(n \cdot m)$	C,D,T,S,R	average	difficult
Disk Field	$O(n \cdot m)$	C,D,T,S,R	good	difficult
Grid Warping	$O(n+m)$	C,D,T,S,R	good	difficult
Tetra-Mesh Warping	$O(n+m)$	C,D,T,S,R	average	average

In the above we assume the volume size is n, and the size of control datasets is m. Operations considered are cross-dissolving (C), one-way distortion (D), translation (T), scaling (S) and rotation (R).

A subset of these algorithms, including cross-dissolving with linear interpolation, simple point field morphing, disk field morphing and tetrahedral mesh warping, have been implemented in C on a DEC Alpha workstation. Results were rendered using the Advanced Visualisation System (AVS).

One of the tests is the metamorphosis from a volume containing a cube as shown in Figure 1(a) and one containing a sphere in Figure 1(b). Both volumes represent continuous functions from high voxel values at the volume centre to low values around the boundary. Four sets of inbetween volumes generated with different methods are given in Figure 2, 3, 4 and 5 respectively. Both cross dissolving and simple point field morphing produced reasonable results in this case. However, the results would have been of a much poorer quality had the given volumes contained discrete solid objects. With tetrahedral mesh warping, some undesirable visual artifacts are obvious as the mesh does not seem fine enough though 96 tetrahedra were used to produce this sequence. The most satisfactory results were produced using disk field morphing.

Another test carried out is to transform a sphere volume to a volume containing a CT (Computed Tomography) scan of a head, as shown in Figure 6. Because the head was not placed at the centre of the volume, the metamorphosis involves translation as well as deformation of the volumes. As shown in Figure 7, the cross-dissolving method was incapable of accomplishing such a task. On the other hand, with 12 control fields, disk morphing produced some satisfactory results.

Some of the execution times obtained during testing are listed in Table 2, where the number of fields or tetrahedra is fixed at 10 for all methods except for cross-dissolving with linear interpolation.

Table 2. the run-times (1/60 sec.) of volume morphing algorithms.

Method	16^3	32^3	64^3	128^3
Linear Interpolation	<1	<1	12	106
Simple Point Field	43	343	2782	22184
Disk Field	140	1120	8979	71953
Tetra-Mesh Warping	20	146	1125	8860

5. Conclusions

Several volume morphing methods have been described in this paper. The tests of these methods has shown that some of them are able to produce with good quality morphing results, even with relatively simple control datasets. Like image-based metamorphosis, the volume morphing technique can be found useful in a variety of applications, especially in the synthesis of 3D models for creating images sequences in video production. Future work in this area undoubtedly includes the development of methods that are fast to run, easy to use, and able to produce smooth and consistent morphing results. There is also a need to establish a set of benchmark problems and define a set of quantifiable attributes in order to carry out a more accurate comparison. With volume data, it is beneficial, sometimes necessary, to use a volume morphing method rather than morphing individual slices of the volumes or interpolates the isosurfaces of the volumes. Therefore, the most important task perhaps is to make sophisticated tools for volume morphing available to users as soon as possible.

References

1. Kaufman A, Bakalash R. Memory and processing architecture for 3D voxel-based imagery. IEEE Computer Graphics and Applications 1988; 8(6):10-23
2. Meagher D. Applying solids processing to medical planning. In: Proc. NCGA'85, Dallas, 1985, pp 101-109
3. Woldberg G. Digital image warping. IEEE Computer Society Press, 1990
4. Beier T, Neely S. Feature-based image metramorphosis. SIGGRAPH Computer Graphics 1992; 26(2):35-42
5. Elvins TT. A survey of algorithms for volume visualisation. SIGGRAPH Computer Graphics 1992; 26(3):194-200
6. Herman GT, Liu HK. Three dimensional display of human organs from computed tomograms. Computer Graphics and Image Processing 1979; 9(1):1-21
7. Hughes JF. Scheduled Fourier volume morphing. SIGGRAPH Computer Graphics 1992; 26(2):43-45
8. Shepard, D. A two-dimensional interpolation function for irregularly spaced data. In: Proc. 23rd National Conference of ACM, 1968, pp 517-524
9. Ruprecht D, Nagel R, Müller H. Spatial free form deformation with scattered data interpolation methods. Research Report: 539, Department of Computer Science, University of Dortmund, Germany, 1994

290

10. Chen M, Jones MW, Townsend P. Volume morphing using disk field. Research Report: CSR 28-94, Department of Computer Science, University of Wales Swansea, UK, 1994
11. Lerios A. 3D volume morphing. World Wide Web page, Stanford University, USA (hhcp://www-graphics.stanford.edu/~tolis/morph.html), 1994
12. Smythe DB. A two-pass mesh warping algorithm for object transformation and image interpolation. ILM technical Memo: #1030, Computer Graphics Department, Lucasfilm Ltd., 1990
13. Goshtasby A. Piecewise linear mapping functions for image registration. Pattern Recognition 1986; 19(6):459-466
14. Goshtasby A. Piecewise cubic mapping functions for image registration. Pattern Recognition 1987; 20(5):525-533

 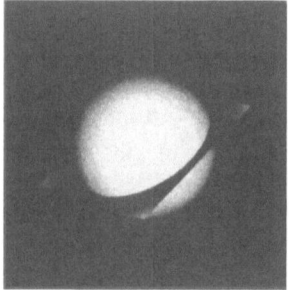

Figure 1. (a) A volume representing a cube function, and
(b) a volume representing a sphere function.

  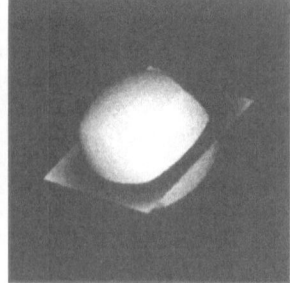

Figure 2. Three inbetween volumes generated using the cross-
dissolving method with linear interpolation.

Figure 3. Three inbetween volumes generated using the simple
point field morphing method.

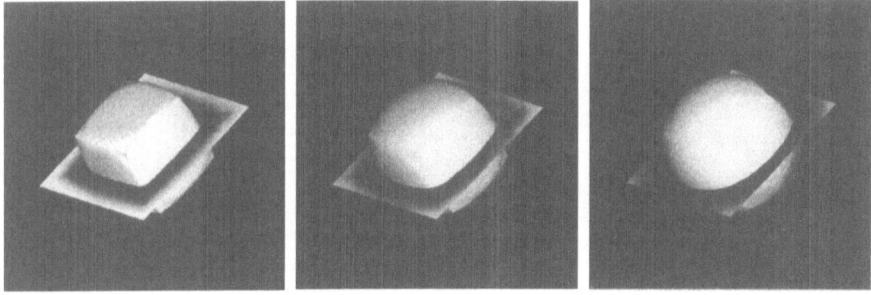

Figure 4. Three inbetween volumes generated using the disk field
morphing method.

Figure 5. Three inbetween volumes generated using the tetrahedral
mesh warping method.

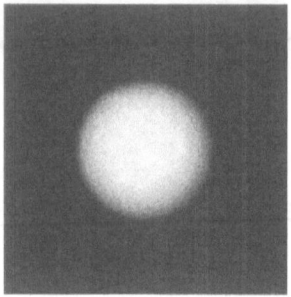 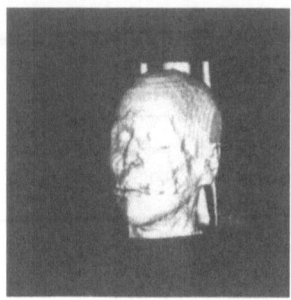

Figure 6. (a) A volume representing a sphere function, and (b) a CT scan of head.

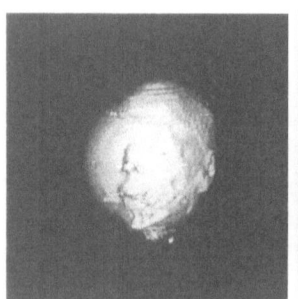 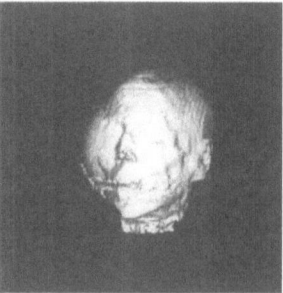 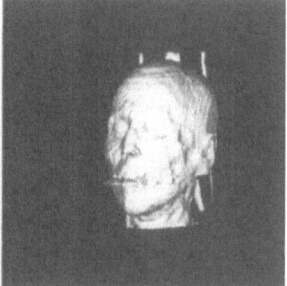

Figure 7. Cross-dissolving from the sphere to the head.

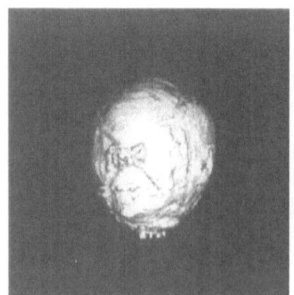 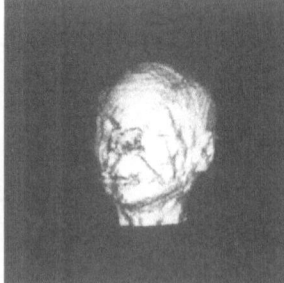 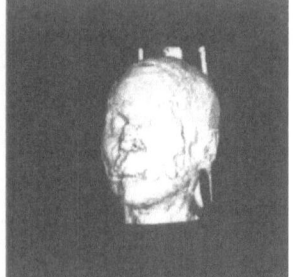

Figure 8. Disk field morphing from the sphere to the head.

Author Index

Z User Workshop, York 1991, Proceedings of the Sixth Annual Z User Meeting, York, 16–17 December 1991
J.E. Nicholls (Ed.)

Formal Aspects of Measurement
Proceedings of the BCS-FACS Workshop on Formal Aspects of Measurement, South Bank University, London, 5 May 1991
Tim Denvir, Ros Herman and R.W. Whitty (Eds)

AI and Cognitive Science '91 University College, Cork, 19–20 September 1991
Humphrey Sorensen (Ed.)

5th Refinement Workshop, Proceedings of the 5th Refinement Workshop, organised by BCS-FACS, London, 8–10 January 1992
Cliff B. Jones, Roger C. Shaw and Tim Denvir (Eds)

Algebraic Methodology and Software Technology (AMAST'91)
Proceedings of the Second International Conference on Algebraic Methodology and Software Technology, Iowa City, USA, 22–25 May 1991
M. Nivat, C. Rattray, T. Rus and G. Scollo (Eds)

ALPUK92, Proceedings of the 4th UK Conference on Logic Programming, London, 30 March – 1 April 1992
Krysia Broda (Ed.)

Logic Program Synthesis and Transformation
Proceedings of LOPSTR 92, International Workshop on Logic Program Synthesis and Transformation, University of Manchester, 2–3 July 1992
Kung-Kiu Lau and Tim Clement (Eds)

NAPAW 92, Proceedings of the First North American Process Algebra Workshop, Stony Brook, New York, USA, 28 August 1992
S. Purushothaman and Amy Zwarico (Eds)

First International Workshop on Larch
Proceedings of the First International Workshop on Larch, Dedham, Massachusetts, USA, 13–15 July 1992
Ursula Martin and Jeannette M. Wing (Eds)

Persistent Object Systems
Proceedings of the Fifth International Workshop on Persistent Object Systems, San Miniato (Pisa), Italy, 1–4 September 1992
Antonio Albano and Ron Morrison (Eds)

Formal Methods in Databases and Software Engineering, Proceedings of the Workshop on Formal Methods in Databases and Software Engineering, Montreal, Canada, 15–16 May 1992
V.S. Alagar, Laks V.S. Lakshmanan and F. Sadri (Eds)

Modelling Database Dynamics
Selected Papers from the Fourth International Workshop on Foundations of Models and Languages for Data and Objects, Volkse, Germany, 19–22 October 1992
Udo W. Lipeck and Bernhard Thalheim (Eds)

14th Information Retrieval Colloquium
Proceedings of the BCS 14th Information Retrieval Colloquium, University of Lancaster, 13–14 April 1992
Tony McEnery and Chris Paice (Eds)

Functional Programming, Glasgow 1992
Proceedings of the 1992 Glasgow Workshop on Functional Programming, Ayr, Scotland, 6–8 July 1992
John Launchbury and Patrick Sansom (Eds)

Z User Workshop, London 1992
Proceedings of the Seventh Annual Z User Meeting, London, 14–15 December 1992
J.P. Bowen and J.E. Nicholls (Eds)

Interfaces to Database Systems (IDS92)
Proceedings of the First International Workshop on Interfaces to Database Systems, Glasgow, 1–3 July 1992
Richard Cooper (Ed.)

AI and Cognitive Science '92
University of Limerick, 10–11 September 1992
Kevin Ryan and Richard F.E. Sutcliffe (Eds)

Theory and Formal Methods 1993
Proceedings of the First Imperial College Department of Computing Workshop on Theory and Formal Methods, Isle of Thorns Conference Centre, Chelwood Gate, Sussex, UK, 29–31 March 1993
Geoffrey Burn, Simon Gay and Mark Ryan (Eds)

Algebraic Methodology and Software Technology (AMAST'93)
Proceedings of the Third International Conference on Algebraic Methodology and Software Technology, University of Twente, Enschede, The Netherlands, 21–25 June 1993
M. Nivat, C. Rattray, T. Rus and G. Scollo (Eds)

Logic Program Synthesis and Transformation
Proceedings of LOPSTR 93, International Workshop on Logic Program Synthesis and Transformation, Louvain-la-Neuve, Belgium, 7–9 July 1993
Yves Deville (Ed.)

Database Programming Languages (DBPL-4)
Proceedings of the Fourth International Workshop on Database Programming Languages – Object Models and Languages, Manhattan, New York City, USA, 30 August–1 September 1993
Catriel Beeri, Atsushi Ohori and Dennis E. Shasha (Eds)